Modernity and the Millennium

•

Modernity and the Millennium

The Genesis of the Baha'i Faith in the
Nineteenth-Century Middle East

•

Juan R. I. Cole

Columbia University Press
New York

Columbia University Press
Publishers Since 1873
New York   Chichester, West Sussex
Copyright © 1998 Columbia University Press
All rights reserved

Library of Congress Cataloging-in-Publication Data
Cole Juan Ricardo.
Modernity and the millennium; the genesis of the Baha'i faith
in the nineteenth-century Middle East / Juan R. I. Cole.
p.   cm.
Includes bibliographical references and index.
ISBN 0-231-11080--4. — ISBN 0-231–11081–2 (pbk.)
1. Bahai Faith—History—19th century. Middle East—Religion—19th century. I. Title.
BP530.C64 1998
297.9'3'09034—dc21   97–45661
                                                                          CIP

Casebound editions of Columbia University Press books are printed on
permanent and durable acid-free paper.

Printed in the United States of America

c 10 9 8 7 6 5 4 3 2 1

Contents

Maps and Illustrations

Acknowledgments

This book could not have been written without the help of many kind friends who either supplied me with rare primary sources or read drafts or both. Professor Amin Banani commented on a conference presentation of what are now chapters two and three and has since 1979 been a key mentor. In my youth Firuz Kazemzadeh and Soheil Bushrui encouraged me in the academic study of the Baha'i religion, for which I remain grateful. A great supporter, morally and bibliographically, has been my dear friend John Walbridge of Indiana University, who favored me with many rare books and manuscripts and with sage advice and comments. I am deeply in debt to Moojan Momen and indirectly to the National Spiritual Assembly of the Baha'is of the United Kingdom for facilitating my access to books and manuscripts of the late H. M. Balyuzi held in the Afnan Library, which was open at Esslemont House in Uckfield in the early 1990s. Dr. Momen was also among those who early on and consistently urged me to write this book. Stephen Lambden of Newcastle-upon-Tyne offered me his hospitality and gems from his magnificent library as well as an opportunity to circulate working papers through his *Baha'i Studies Bulletin*. Dr. Ahang Rabbani likewise was selfless in sharing rare manuscripts and printed books from Iran. Dr. Vahid Rafati, director of the Research Department at the Baha'i World Centre, Haifa, Israel, kindly provided me with invaluable materials. Richard Hollinger and R. Jackson Armstrong-Ingram shared with me archival material from their researches in the National Baha'i Archives in Wilmette, Illinois. I must express my gratitude for providing access to research materials, as well, to Manuchehr Derakhshani, director of the Per-

sian Affairs office at the National Baha'i Center, Wilmette, Illinois, to
Dariush Lamie, to Habib Riazati, to Sholeh Quinn of the Ohio University,
Athens, to Franklin Lewis of Emory University, and to Christopher Buck.
Many of these same individuals kindly read and commented on drafts of
chapters, some of which I presented first on panels at the Middle East
Studies Association of North America or at Persia Religiosa meetings held
in connection with MESA. Part of chapter 3 was delivered at the Association
for Baha'i Studies, Religion Section, in San Francisco in October of 1995,
and I am grateful to the chair of the session, Robert Stockman (director of
the Research Office, Baha'i National Center, Wilmette, Illinois), for solic-
iting the paper and for commenting on this and other presentations of the
material over the years. In addition, I am grateful for their comments to
Abbas Amanat, Mehrdad Amanat, Terry Culhane, Khazeh Fananapazir,
Seena Fazel, Bill Garlington, B. Todd Lawson, Anthony Lee, Denis
MacEoin, Sen McGlinn, Susan Stiles Maneck, Afsaneh Najmabadi, Daniel
Orey, Steven Scholl, and Linda Walbridge. Flaws that remain are, of course,
my own responsibility. Jonathan Rodgers, Middle East bibliographer at the
University of Michigan's Hatcher Research Library, has offered invaluable
help in acquiring microfilms of rare materials over the years, as has the
interlibrary loan division of the library.

Attesting to the issue of globalization, taken up below, some of this
book was actually written on a series of electronic mail networks. I began
a fairly intense e-mail correspondence with John Walbridge about my dis-
coveries of Baha'i contacts with the Young Ottomans in 1988. These discussions continued on a small e-mail group called, playfully, Majnun, in
the early 1990s, that included some of the scholars thanked above. But
the bulk of the book was written interactively on a later series of larger,
more public e-mail forums called: Talisman@indiana.edu (1994–1996,
now defunct), Talisman@umich.edu (still operating in fall 1997), Irfan@-
umich.edu, and, finally, a list that forms part of the H-Net consor-
tium (http://h-net.msu.edu/) at Michigan State University: H-Bahai@
h-net.msu.edu (subscriptions through listserv@h-net.msu.edu). I presented paragraphs, or arguments, and received interactive comments from
prospective readers throughout the world! I also received comments
from drafts and translations posted at Web sites, http://www-person-
al.umich.edu/~jrcole/bahai.htm and http://h-net2.msu.edu/~bahai/. I am
deeply grateful to my many interlocutors on these Internet lists and on
the World Wide Web and hope that I have repaid their interrogations of
my work with increased clarity and cogency.

I am grateful to the University of Michigan's Office of the Vice President for Research and its College of Arts and Sciences Faculty Research Fund for directly subventing research trips to the United Kingdom and France in connection with this book. Parts of chapters 2 and 3 appeared in a different form as "Iranian Millenarianism and Democratic Thought in the Nineteenth Century," *International Journal of Middle East Studies* 24 (1992): 1–26, and are used here by permission of Cambridge University Press.

For the convenience of nonspecialists I have omitted many diacriticals, except for 'ayn and hamzah. The transliteration system employed for Ottoman Turkish is that of the *International Journal of Middle East Studies;* in ambiguous cases I have preferred an orthography that retains the visual connection to Arabic words and so have not shown the hardened final dental (Abdülhamid, not Abdülhamit). Arabic and Persian have been transliterated according to the official Baha'i system (with only a few minor modifications, such as dropping most diacritics and putting the dash directly after the *tā' marbūṭah* when showing the Persian construct state), so as not to confuse that audience.

Modernity and the Millennium

•

Introduction

Modernity, like a prize fighter, has its proponents and detractors, observers who bet on it and against it. Some intellectuals, mired in dreams of old empires and authentic peasant ethnicity, have been nostalgic for premodern times. Others have declared modernity over with and insist that the world has entered a postmodern phase. Some have staunchly defended it as an ongoing progressive process. Modernity's admirers have given it an impressive résumé. French thinkers in particular tend to put modernity under the sign of reason. A prominent French sociologist sees the three central processes characteristic of modernity as the organization of a society governed by the rule of law, an individualism seeking self-interest and freedom from constraints, and, finally, more efficient production via science, technology, and administration. "What," he asks, "could provide a basis for this correspondence between a scientific culture, an ordered society, and free individuals, if not the triumph of *reason*?"[1] Modernity, which is generally held to date to the eighteenth century, is contrasted to what went before, which many authors describe as "feudalism," or "absolutism."

Premodern society in this view was characterized by divine-right monarchy and absolutist rule in the political sphere. The economic system was structured around special perquisites for certain estates that one could only enter by being born into them (such as the nobility) or through a long apprenticeship and conformity to group rules (guilds, the clergy of the state-backed Established Church). Free inquiry was curbed or impeded by a regime of censorship and by the sway of scholastic religion. The American and then French Revolutions were seen by proponents of modernity to have liberated human beings from royal despotism by establishing representative governments. The expansion of the market and the advent of the Industrial Revolution, they said, led to a more dynamic economic system in which the corporate privileges of the nobility, clergy, and guilds were abolished and individual merit was rewarded. The complex of the eighteenth-century political revolutions and the Industrial Revolution (1760–1840) has been referred to as the "dual revolution."[2] The separation of religion and state and the promulgation of religious liberty and freedom of conscience in the U.S. Bill of Rights and the French Declaration of the Rights of Man removed the tyranny of religion over minds and opened the way for wide-ranging scientific and social inquiry. Formal state censorship was abolished and a relatively free civil society emerged, a public sphere outside the state, consisting of newspapers, stage plays, salons, and coffeehouses, where public opinion could be formed.[3] With the decline of royal authority, which had held together polyglot empires and principalities, a new form of political organization was imagined into being, the nation-state, based upon territory and upon the positing of a "people" with a set of common characteristics (such as language, "race," or religion). Expanding labor markets and universal education raised the question of women's rights in society. Essential to the project of modernity, though little discussed by its celebrators, was the modern bureaucracy that could administer the newly created nation (as Weber recognized).

This narrative of the liberation of humankind from the clutches of absolutism has not gone unchallenged. Some have concentrated upon the manner in which modernity bestowed upon the state and other large social institutions new powers to monitor, discipline, and shape human beings, through the penitentiary, the hospital, the laboratory, the sanitarium.[4] It has been argued that Reason of State in the early modern period was identical to the notion of policing society, and that reason was identified with state coercion and control.[5] The awesome violence by which the modern nation-state is constituted, the regimentation of the individual by the modern bureaucracy and military, the establishment of colonialism, the exploitation of the worker in industrial capitalism, the subversion of democracy by big money, and the disenchantment of the world brought on by secularization have all figured in critiques of the phenomenon. Some of these themes were struck in the nineteenth century by Marx, others early in the twentieth century by the pessimistic German sociologist Max Weber.

Surely there have been many modernities rather than a single unified phenomenon. Still, *modernities* is an awkward word, and these various strands must be related in order for us to speak of them meaningfully under the same rubric, so why not employ a singular, overarching noun? What we recognize better now than ever before is how complex have been the processes associated with modernity or modernities, how developments in one sector, such as the economy, deeply affected developments elsewhere, such as in religion or politics, and vice versa. This book treats the interaction of religion and modernity, and underlines this reflexivity, since religion has often been crucially important to modern societies and has both been shaped by and helped shape modernity itself. Rather than attempt a global definition or evaluation of modernity, I wish in this book to come at the subject peripherally. I will argue from a set of case studies on the ground, in one corner of the world, rather than from a central, overarching ideal. My treatment is peripheral in the sense that my evidence comes not only from Europe but also from the nineteenth-century Middle East, a relatively much less studied region. I treat modernity in the context of the rise of a millenarian movement in Iran, the Baha'i faith (*Ā'īn-i Bahā'ī*), a story little enough known yet profoundly implicated in the advent of modernity that it may enable us to look upon the phenomenon with new eyes.

I concentrate here upon five themes that are both central to modernity and central to the Middle Eastern religious response to it. The first is the struggle over the relationship of religion to the state. The American and French revolutions, templates for the great political upheavals of modern times, both involved a repudiation of the idea of a state-imposed religion. The number of modern nation-states that continue to mandate a state religion is vanishingly small, though religion plays an important role in some forms of nationalism (e.g., the Irish, Polish, Bolivian, Swedish, and Egyptian). The disentanglement of religion and state has seldom been complete, and should be seen on a spectrum, rather than as an absolute value. Given the inescapable religious diversity of any human society, only a neutral stance toward religion allows the government to treat all citizens equally, something recognized by Luther, Machiavelli, Hobbes, Locke, and Rousseau alike.[6] For

> Machiavelli, the important thing is to free the state from the dominance of the Church. . . . This triumph of Reason of State . . . leads . . . from the theocracy of Geneva to the idea of popular sovereignty, to the modern conviction . . . that the rationalism of the state is the precondition for the freedom of citizens, and that individuals will flourish only if they take part in

public life. On the other hand it can—and always does—lead to the absolute authority of a State.[7]

Obviously, whereas Hobbes and Locke thought of reason and revelation as coexisting principles, other modern thinkers such as Jefferson and Marx held reason in itself to be a sufficient basis for society and government.

Opposition to this key element of modernity, visible in many Vatican encyclicals and Muslim fatwas, must also be acknowledged, as must the justice of some religious critiques of the republican state as easily falling into authoritarianism, amorality, and the purely instrumental use of reason characteristic of capitalism and bureaucracy. As German sociologist Max Weber so clearly saw, "Rationalization makes the world orderly and reliable, but it cannot make the world meaningful."[8] Weber referred to the way in which modern science and rational politics and economics led to a disenchantment of the world, which was no longer understood as a mysterious stage for magical correspondences or divine interventions but as a machine, the workings of which are amenable to rational understanding.

Still, anyone who contrasts the sort of religion-state relations that prevailed in the majority of countries in 1600 with those that exist today will easily discern that a sea change has occurred. The prospect of Japan persecuting Christians or of Germany waging a cultural struggle against Catholicism now seems remote. The disentanglement of state from religion is not the same as secularization, as both Poland and the United States demonstrate. Indeed, it has been argued by observers and social scientists since de Tocqueville that the end of a state monopoly on religion actually creates spaces for greater citizen participation in religious affairs. In eighteenth-century British North America, where there was an Established Church in each colony, only 17 percent of the population belonged to a church, in contrast with 68 percent in a United States with separation of religion and state at the end of the twentieth century.[9]

The second grand theme of modernity that concerns me here has been a move away from political absolutism toward some form of democratic or representative government, a shift in the basis for the polity from divine-right monarchy to the sovereignty of the people. "The call for modernity is defined not so much by its opposition to traditional society as by its struggle against the absolute monarchy."[10] For the British and North American political traditions such a shift further involves a displacement of power from the exercise of royal prerogative to the operation of a new sort of *reason* among the public.[11] The good decision is not good because of its source (in the divinely constituted monarchy) but because of the process whereby it is arrived at, in the parliamentary reasoned debate of the people and their representatives. Whereas almost all polities in 1600 throughout the world were absolute monarchies of some sort, at the end of the twentieth century this form of rule is virtually extinct and what monarchies survive are almost entirely constitutional in nature. States based on reason tend to mix an emphasis on public contract (Rousseau, Marx) with an emphasis on private contract (Locke), but in practice one or the other emphasis often wins out, producing authoritarian states aiming at egalitarian community in the first case or states that support individualism (with all its attendant inequalities) on the other.[12]

The demand for representative government was not unrelated to the decisive demise of elements of the old feudal economic system that had survived into the age of early modern absolutism. The transition from economies largely based on agriculture and on mercantile capitalism to an industrial world order (with its own divisions of labor) created new social classes impatient with the symbolic power of unproductive kings, nobles, and clergy. Although the Middle East did not industrialize in any significant way in the nineteenth century, despite episodes such as the munitions factories of Cairo, the silk factories of Beirut, and the soap factories of Nablus, European industrialization did affect the region by creating a demand for cash crops such as cotton. Taxes on these commodities flowed into state coffers, rendering the government more powerful than before. The local landowning and mercantile elites, as well as artisans and elements of the peasantry, began to have powerful economic interests directly affected by the state, over the policies of which they increasingly wished to exert some control or at least influence. A population consisting largely of subsistence farmers or producers of a slight agricultural surplus might have been able to afford the luxury of absolutist rule, but the industrial world economy created a new situation, especially in Middle Eastern societies where the government tended to intervene heavily in the economy. In this region movements of economic protest, such as that mounted in 1892 by Iranian farmers and merchants against the state's licensing to a British investor of a monopoly on the marketing of Iranian tobacco, tended to be directed at the state and to overlap with movements for more democracy (see chapter 3 of this volume). British sociologist Anthony Giddens has located continuing movements for free speech and democratic politics in reactions against the growing power of the modern state, whatever its form. He argues that major developments in modernity (such as the rise of nation-states, of capitalism, of industrialized warfare, and of industry) tend to interact with society and with one another, producing what he calls a "reflexivity" or a tendency for their effects to ricochet at increasing velocity. He terms populist responses to these developments forms of "utopian realism," into which category he places movements for democracy.[13]

The third aspect of modernity is the rise of an international system of nation-states that are constituted by violence both within their borders and with their neighbors. A major concomitant of this national sovereignty is the world military order, based on the modern armed forces and their military technology.[14] While warfare has been a constant of human existence, the industrialization of war during the past two centuries has lent it a destructive potential, in terms of absolute numbers, that is new in history. The modern period saw the unprecedented conscription of hundreds of thousands of peasant civilians into the French army under Napoleon, the introduction of increasingly destructive artillery and ever more accurate handheld weapons, and the development of new forms of drills, military organization, and tactics. The advent of total war in the twentieth century led to the deaths of unprecedented millions of human beings in scores of deadly conflicts, some of them global in scope, and to the ultimate atrocities of Dachau on the one hand and of Hiroshima on the other. As noted above, peace movements may be seen as utopian idealist responses to this phenomenon of global state violence.[15]

I employ the hyphenated term *nation-state.* If the modern state is entangled with international violence on a vast scale, it is often underpinned by the phenomenon of nationalism, my fourth topic within modernity. The nation and the state are different phenomena. The state is the bureaucracy and the politicians who preside over it, and Weber saw clearly their increasing resort to instrumental rationality in dealing with the populace. On the other hand, the nation over which the state rules was imagined (in Benedict Anderson's now famous phrase) into being in the late eighteenth century, first of all in Latin America, then in Europe, and finally in postcolonial societies. The illusion of national homogeneity and relatedness was fostered not only by state elites, in his view, but also by the printing press, by the novel, and by the newspaper, media that allowed individuals to identify with others on the basis of their invented "nation."[16] Other theorists have protested the way in which Anderson tied the fashioning of modern nations to the literate middle and upper classes, but he clearly feels that it was a bourgeois project that gradually brought in the rest of the population. Alternative theories have attributed the formation of the nation to peasant struggles, to the transition from agrarian to industrial society, and to the policies of state actors themselves. Most theorists, however, agree that nationalism is a modern phenomenon, unlike, in its complete outline, the more limited forms of ethnic and cultural identity that preceded it.

Any nation can be rather easily deconstructed. French citizens speak Breton, Basque, German, and Arabic as well as French; the country has a Huguenot Protestant heritage as well as a Catholic one and is now 5 percent Muslim; citizens of many ethnic origins now come under the rubric "French," including hundreds of thousands of Poles who immigrated as guest workers in the early twentieth century; substantial regional variations exist in economies and styles of life. The propensity of nationalist historians to create a "France" through history, threading together Charlemagne (who ruled over much of Western Europe and did not speak anything we could now recognize as "French") with Joan of Arc and Napoleon (a Corsican!) is a simple parlor trick, a sleight of hand of identity politics writ large. All modern nations engage in this duplicity, with often amusing results, as Anderson points out. Thus, the Norman William the Conqueror ends up being a "British" ruler! The fashioning of nations depends not only upon the perception of similarities among the persons living on a particular territory and under a specific state but also upon a stress on the alienness of those who do not. Nationalism involves, in other words, the creation of an "Other," and when nationalism becomes psychopathic the Other is demonized. Nation as distinct from state must be given more prominence in our understanding of the making of modernity. Utopian realist responses to the darker side of nationalism have recently included multiculturalism and world federalism.

Finally, I wish to treat the impact of modernity on patriarchy and conceptions of gender roles. Women's movements and feminism are often overlooked in discussions of modernity, perhaps in part because they were not prominent in the genesis of Enlightenment rationality in the eighteenth century (though one should not forget the pioneering work of Mary Wollstonecraft in that era). Early modern absolutist societies were wedded to a thoroughgoing patriarchy, and if modernity is the attempt to supersede the legacy of absolutism, then the "woman movement" of the nineteenth century in places such as the United States is part and parcel of modernity. Feminism might be seen as a reflexive response to the articulation of Enlightenment freedoms, which were largely framed by thinkers such as Thomas Jefferson with white males in mind. A wave of nineteenth-century social movements, including the women's movement, Abolitionism, and anticolonial parties, might best be characterized as inclusivist, as insisting that rights proffered the republic of white males by the Enlightenment be extended to all human beings, regardless of sex or race or national origin. Such currents might thus be thought of as modernity's second wave. In other respects some feminist thought might best be understood not as an essential component of modernity, which has after all been highly patriarchal for most of the past two centuries, but as a utopian realist response to the heightening of gender distinctions characteristic of modern thought. It has been suggested that a liberal feminist demand for equal rights, while facing obstacles, can at least win grudging acceptance by male proponents of modernity, whereas the cultural-feminist demand for recognition of women as a corporate group and basis for identity politics has faced more opposition.[17]

Islam, even more than Roman Catholicism or the religious civilizations of India and East and Southeast Asia, has become a symbol for North Atlantic thinkers of antimodernism. Beginning in the eighteenth century, European Orientalist discourse constructed the Middle East as an object of knowledge that consisted in a set of oppositions with the West. The Orient was despotic, the West free; the Orient was stagnant, the West dynamic; the Orient was sensual and self-indulgent, the West ascetic and virile.[18] Those who view the Middle East as especially resistant to modernity can cite some evidence for this position. Some countries in the Middle East, such as Saudi Arabia, Iran, and Afghanistan, have rejected the notion of disentangling the civil state from religion, asserting that no distinction can be drawn between the two. Multiparty parliamentary democracy has not been a characteristic form of government in the region, though it has been more important than is usually realized. Freedom of speech, the press, and religion have been absent or far more circumscribed than has been common in the North Atlantic countries. Because of a heritage of gender segregation and norms of male honor invested in preserving the chastity of female kin (norms shared by the most conservative forms of Orthodox Judaism, by southern European Catholics and Orthodox, and by conservative Hinduism even outside the Middle East), the Middle East is among the more patriarchal set of societies in the world with regard to the public sphere. In other respects the Middle East gets bad press for having too successfully adopted the modern nation-state system, with its power hierarchies determined by warfare and with its tendency toward the imposition of homogeneous national ethnicities. The image of the Middle East as a site of warfare during the past two centuries is not completely without foundation, insofar as wars have actually occurred, some of them major (e.g., the Ottoman-Egyptian struggles of the 1830s, the Iran-Iraq War of the 1980s). But a dispassionate review of these wars and their centrality to state making would reveal that they are typical of the modern state system, not exceptions. The image of the Middle East as especially prone to a virulent nationalism appears to me to be in part an artifact of twentieth-century national liberation movements against colonialism and neocolonialism, since Westerners have found themselves the object of Middle Eastern nationalist critiques and so these have loomed large in their consciousness. Still, there seems no doubt that vehicles of Arab nationalism such as the Baath Party in Iraq have committed racist acts against the non-Arab Kurdish minority that can only be called genocidal. Israel's Zionism is likewise intertwined with racial and religious hierarchies, insofar as it insists on a state for and by Jews, leaving the one-fifth of its population that is ethnically Arab and religiously Christian or Muslim in a quandary as to where it fits in. Turkey's nationalism, centered on Turkish chauvinism, has often repressed the Kurds, while Iran's emphasis on Persian under the Pahlevis served to oppress Turkic-speaking Azeris and other linguistic minorities.

Yet to posit the Middle East or Islamic culture as intrinsically antimodern is to commit two fallacies of essentialism, implying somehow that modernity is a unified phenomenon and that there is a single, civilizational Muslim or Middle Eastern response to it. Both propositions have been persuasively argued against.[19] Modernity, as shall be discussed below, is multidimensional and has a dark side. "The modern Middle East" is not a unified phenomenon with a single history; it has had many histories, only some of which have been told or represented by scholars. What really happened? Modernity came to the Middle East in the nineteenth century like a pent-up reservoir suddenly released. The intellectual, economic, and bureaucratic aspects of the phenomenon made the strongest impact at the beginning. In the space of decades intellectuals forsook Ptolemaic for Copernican astronomy and translated works of Voltaire and other Enlightenment figures, businessmen formed joint stock companies (not originally allowed in Islamic law), generals had their armies retrained in new drills and established munitions factories, regional patriotism intensified and prepared the way for nationalism, the population began growing exponentially under the impact of cash cropping and the new medicine, steamboats suddenly plied the Red Sea and the Persian Gulf, and agrarian capitalism and the advent of factories led to new kinds of class conflict. Great engineering works such as the Suez Canal and the Ottoman railroad lines linked the region internally and tied it more closely to the world economy. During the nineteenth century the external trade of Iran expanded twelvefold, of the Ottoman Empire twenty-five-fold, and of Egypt fifty-fold.

Modernity came in telescoped form, so that the moveable type printing press (developed in Europe 1430–1450) and the telegraph (invented in 1844) arrived virtually together. Vesalius and Darwin also entered the discourse of intellectuals at the same time.

With regard to the separation of religion and state, many developments came later. In 1856 the Ottoman Empire made Christian and Jewish subjects legally equal to Muslims. From the 1920s Turkey instituted a thoroughgoing, Jacobin, French-style secularization. In so doing it probably separated civil law from local, religiously influenced custom more rigorously than most European countries, though it recently has moderated its Jacobinism, accommodating an Islamic party in the same way that Germany accommodates Christian Democrats. In many other Middle Eastern states religious courts have been abolished or relegated to personal status matters, while most law has been rationalized and put in the hands of civil judges. Compared to the Ottoman practice, there actually has been a large degree of separation of religion and state in some Middle Eastern countries such as Iraq, Tunisia, Algeria, and the Yemen, while theocratic states (Iran, Saudi Arabia, Sudan) clearly form a small minority in the region. Within each of these countries a lively contest for power is being fought out between secularists and theocrats, among others, so that one cannot speak of an undifferentiated culture—a myth at which nationalists, ruling classes, and some scholars have connived.[20] The picture is mixed and ambiguous, and a comparison to the United States of the 1820s or the France of the 1830s, or even to twentieth-century England, Spain, and Italy (none of which can be excluded from modernity), might be more instructive than a comparison to contemporary practices in the United States. Nor are the significant movements toward increasing the entanglement of religion with the state in the Middle East without their parallels in the United States or in India.

In the last quarter of the nineteenth century one begins seeing significant movements for parliamentary governance and more freedom of conscience and inquiry. The first of these is the first Ottoman constitutional movement of 1876–1878, followed by Egypt's 'Urabi Revolution in 1881–1882. Both of these failed, and both failed in some degree because of foreign intervention (the Russians went to war against the Ottomans, the British invaded Egypt and stopped the constitutionalists). In 1905–1911 Iranians launched a constitutional revolution, with the goal of gaining parliamentary governance and placing constraints on royal absolutism, but it resulted in a weak government exploited by the imperial powers and its order was overthrown by the dictatorial Pahlevi dynasty from 1926. The second Ottoman constitutionalist movement, spearheaded by the Young Turks, succeeded in 1908, but was followed by military-bureaucratic dictatorship only a few years later, first instituted by the military wing of the Young Turks themselves, then by Ataturk. Egypt had a constitutional and parliamentary regime after independence from England, 1922–1952, but it was dominated by a small class of very large landlords. Other postcolonial Arab societies had similar "liberal" governments for a while, but in the 1950s these tended to be replaced with military-bureaucratic dictatorships. From the late 1940s Turkey and Pakistan turned toward multiparty democracy and, despite stretches of military rule, have consistently come back to that form of polity. Turkey and Pakistan are, along with Israel, the only approximations to genuine democracy in the Middle East in the 1990s, where the prime minister can actually lose an election. Because Turkey and Pakistan have a combined population as of this writing of about 190 million, however, and given the small populations of many Middle Eastern states, their experiences with parliamentary democracy have affected a large plurality of the region's inhabitants.

With regard to the nation-state system, the Middle East has been no different than any other region of the world. Although it has been the scene of numerous wars, many of these have been launched by European powers (Russia, Italy, Germany, and England) or, if entirely indigenous, have frequently been of short duration and characterized by relatively few casualties. The major exception here was the Iran-Iraq war of the 1980s. Certainly, European wars dwarf Middle Eastern ones in the number of human beings they have killed in the twentieth century. This greater European-led slaughter indicates not that Europeans are more bloodthirsty than Middle Easterners but that they industrialized warfare long before the latter did, making it a far more efficient system of mass killing. Southeast Asia has seen far more state-led violence in the twentieth century than has the Middle East, insofar as it was the scene of Japanese atrocities during World War II, of the genocide against a million and a half leftists in Indonesia in the mid-1960s, and of the Cambodian genocide against urbanites and intellectuals, which killed one million out of a population of six million. (The number of Iraqi Kurds killed can only be numbered in the thousands, and the Lebanese civil war killed only tens of thousands, not millions). Nor is Middle Eastern nationalism in its procedures or forms obviously different from that which exists anywhere else in the world.

As for gender issues, the common perception in the outside world of Muslim societies is one of a religiously inspired and thoroughgoing patriarchy unusual in world terms. It is true that Middle Easterners, like many others in the greater Mediterranean world, often subscribe to an ethos that makes family honor dependent on the ability of the males to ensure the chastity of kinswomen. It is also true that urban, literate, Muslim norms favor modest dress and even veiling for women, and some Muslim thinkers go so far as to call for secluding them in the house. But the picture is not as uncomplicated as an attention only to the "little tradition" of religious texts and norms might suggest. Deniz Kandiyoti has argued that Middle Eastern patriarchy is a subset of what she calls "Asian patriarchy," and that women's status in modern societies has been much more a function of individual state policy, and of women's ability to organize to influence it, than it has been a result of large, essentialist, civilizational influences such as Islam.[21]

When one has closely examined the myths, it must finally still be recognized that antimodernism has possessed, in world terms, an unusual political and intellectual saliency in the Middle East. But it must finally also be admitted that antimodernism is not always a damning epithet. The conventional journalistic language about Middle Eastern resistance to modernity seems not to acknowledge what the postmodernist movement of the late twentieth century vividly recognized: that the modern has a dark side, much of which could be usefully resisted. Total war, genocide, ultranationalism, class conflict and the impoverishment of some strata, religious fundamentalism, soulless positivism, and colonialism are basic constituents of modernity, not aberrations from a liberal march of progress. For Middle Easterners "modernity" often served as a cloak for European domination; France's armies killing North African villagers and pastoralists were said to be on a "civilizing mission" (*mission civilisatrice*). The expropriated subjects in their colonies might be forgiven for understanding themselves only to be oppressed by the foreigners, rather than having been much civilized by them. Some of the Middle East's antimodernism, then, is utopian rather than merely reactionary, and this point forms one central thesis of the present book.

The nineteenth century saw not the simple encounter of European-led "modernization" with a traditional Middle East but the selective and active appropriation by one dynamic culture of elements from another. (Nineteenth-century modernity was also experienced as alien by many in Europe itself and caused many dislocations there as well). The degree to which Europe was in its turn transformed by the encounter with the Orient has often been hidden in its somewhat nativist historiography, but some of this story has begun to be told.[22] Europe itself departs from any ideal construct of the modern. Germany, Italy, Spain, and Russia have all had highly ambiguous relationships with democracy, which has in some sense been imposed on them from the outside in the period since 1945. Sweden, Ireland, Great Britain, and Greece have continued to see strong state entanglement with an Established Church. Europe remains highly patriarchal.

Peter Berger, writing of Western Christianity, has seen only three major responses to modernity, those of rejection (fundamentalism or traditionalism), capitulation (liberalism), or a third way he advocates of employing modernity to reconstitute religion on its own fundament. But this simplistic typology, tied so strongly to the theological divide in the contemporary United States, hardly captures the richness of the interplay.[23] We can see the diversity of possible responses to modernity if we examine the modern Muslim world.[24] The reactionary option was, again, very popular in the nineteenth century (and after), with some important section of the Muslim clerics affirming the goodness of absolute monarchy (or at least of authoritarian government), of corporate social hierarchies, and of scholastic knowledge based on the textual authority of the ancients or of scripture against modern canons of critical inquiry. Ironically, this "normal" clerical conservatism of the nineteenth century has been very little studied.[25] It should also be remembered that some Muslim clergy also did play a progressive role, as with Ottoman reforms in the nineteenth century or the Iranian Constitutional Revolution.[26] A different approach, Muslim revivalism, attempted to reinvigorate existing religious institutions such as Sufi orders to resist Western dominance, as with 'Abdu'l-Qadir in Algeria, or Shamil in the Caucasus, or Ahmad Barelvi in North India, exhibiting, despite their conservatism, social activism and reformism in a way that the reactionary clergy did not.[27]

Another response was millenarianism, as with the Babi movement in the 1840s in Iran, its successor, the Baha'i faith from 1863, and, in a different setting, the Sudanese Mahdi later in the century.[28] Such movements threw up charismatic religious leaders who proclaimed that the end-time had arrived and that therefore great changes in Muslim social customs were necessary and appropriate. Millenarians were quite diverse in their approach to the key features of modernity, some remaining conservative and resembling the revivalists (as with the Sudanese Mahdi), and others becoming something close to modernists themselves (as I will argue happened in the instance of the early Baha'i faith).

Then there is Islamic modernism. Some Muslims, such as the Egyptian Muhammad 'Abduh (d. 1905), accepted the basic outlines of the modernist project. He struggled as a young man, during the 'Urabi Revolution of 1882, for the sake of parliamentary governance, and later in life he defended modern practices such as taking interest on loans, allowing greater liberty to women, and the pursuit of modern science and critical thought. Indeed, Leonard Binder has argued that Muslim modernism or liberalism has become the official ideology of the modern Egyptian state.[29] Finally, one sees from the early twentieth century the growth of what has come to be called Muslim fundamentalism, which accepts republicanism and a reformed state bureaucracy, but rejects democracy and free inquiry, and often adopts elements of a command economy.[30]

In this book I employ microhistory in order to help diversify our image of the region. I explore the thought of Mirza Husayn 'Ali Nuri (1817–1892), known as Baha'u'llah ("Glory of God"). An Iranian from the class of high government officials, in 1844 he embraced the chiliastic Babi movement centering on the messianic claims of Sayyid 'Ali Muhammad Shirazi (d. 1850). Exiled from Iran, he became an Ottoman subject in 1853 and spent the next forty years in Baghdad, Rumelia, and Palestine. Acclaimed by his adherents as a Manifestation of God (*mazhar-i ilāhī*) and bearer of divine revelation, he founded the world's youngest significant independent religion, the Baha'i faith. This book examines the responses of Baha'u'llah and his early followers to modernity, which, I will argue, are complex and ambiguous. What were Baha'u'llah's views of the relationship between religion and state? How did this scion of high Iranian courtiers feel about parliamentary democracy? What was his response to the rise of the modern nation-state, the system of industrialized warfare, and the spread of nationalist ideas? How did he feel about the region's changing gender roles and the implications of the Western woman movement for the Middle East? How may the Baha'i faith be categorized with regard to the five religious reactions to modernity just surveyed? How does this narrative enrich our understanding of the multiple and discontinuous responses to modernity in the Middle East? The answers to these questions, I would argue, shed light not only on the genesis of a new religion but on important aspects of Middle Eastern and especially Iranian social and cultural change in the nineteenth century.

The answers are now of even wider relevance. While the Middle East, and particularly Iran, continues to form the site of among the largest Baha'i communities (some three hundred thousand strong before the 1978–1979 Islamic Revolution), the religion Baha'u'llah founded has spread throughout the world and claims about five million adherents in the late 1990s.[31] (This number is probably somewhat exaggerated if one is counting only persons who consider their primary identity to be Baha'i, which, for example, would exclude many Hindus with Baha'i sympathies in India) It should be stressed, however, that I am here concerned mainly with the earliest three decades of the Baha'i movement, which underwent profound changes later on, in the twentieth century. This book, then, focuses on the intersection of nineteenth-century modernity—of what might be called modernity's first wave—with Iranian society and the *early* Baha'i faith. Although almost all Americans have heard of Imam Ruhu'llah Khomeini and of his authoritarian views on politics and religion, many fewer realize that modern Iran also produced a Baha'u'llah, who preached a rather different set of values. There has been little historical writing about the Baha'i religion.[32] Most of what adherents have written is theological in tone and intent, such that it has an internalist focus and often pays little attention to context. It is my hope that this book can, through the techniques of formal historical scholarship, restore to the saga some of the narratives that have dropped out as it has been told and simplified by generations of believers and other observers.

1 • Religious Liberty and Separation of Religion and State

Thomas Jefferson once supported a legal action brought against a corrupt Anglican clergyman who was maintained at the American taxpayers' expense and backed by the authorities in England. The incident led him, as the revolution was brewing in the early 1770s, to read widely in the history of church-state relations and to discover the full depths of the Virginia Anglican establishment's actions against members of dissenting churches such as the Quakers. Quakers, indeed, had been punished even for ritual matters, for example, not accepting baptism. Jefferson thereafter strove to separate church from state and to ensure religious liberty, drafting a Virginia Bill for Establishing Religious Freedom in 1777. Nor was he alone in these sentiments, which were shared even by most evangelical Baptists. Modernity as it developed in North Atlantic societies of the late eighteenth century involved a demand that the state treat all citizens alike in the law and renounce any right to coerce the white male citizen in matters of religion and private conscience. Many believed that these steps were crucial to the development of modern science, as well, since unfettered rational inquiry is difficult to accomplish under a system of religious censorship.[1] These aspects of modernity proved challenging to older conceptions of societal order rooted in the medieval period. Leo XIII, an archconservative pope (1878–1903), strove all his life to prevent Roman Catholic political collaboration with liberals, to see that the whole range of modern ideas was condemned, and to revive the authority of Thomas Aquinas as the bedrock of political and social thought. He proclaimed in his "Libertas Praestantissimum" ("On Human Liberty") of 1888 that "justice therefore forbids, and reason itself forbids, the State to be godless; or to adopt a line of action which would end in godlessness—namely, to treat the various religions (as they call them) alike."[2] Nineteenth-century Catholic authorities insisted that the state had a duty to enforce the one true religion. Most Muslim clerics held a similar view in premodern times, and even in the largely secular Iranian Constitutional Revolution of 1905–1911 the prominent Shi'ite leader Shaykh Fadlu'llah Nuri demanded the exclusion of non-Shi'ites from the newly established parliament and objected to provisions for freedom of opinion and for equality before the law of non-Muslims.[3] On the other hand, the modern state has often attempted to establish reason as superior to religion, actively interfering with religious liberty, as in the revolutionary tradition in France or in the Soviet policy of enforced atheism. How did the emergent Baha'i religion confront the issues of religious liberty, the separation of religion and state, and the militant secularism of some modern governments with positivist or scientistic ideologies?

Many rulers in medieval and early modern societies of the Greater Mediterranean had attempted to establish a single religion, adherence to which among the subjects was required. The disciplining of subjects' consciences by a religious absolutism was seen by many as a cornerstone of state power. In its most virulent forms this policy led to gory European tragedies such as the Crusades, the expulsions or forced conversions of Jews and Muslims after the Christian reconquest of Spain in 1492, the Inquisition and its Protestant equivalents, and the Wars of Religion (1562–1598). Of course, there were medieval proponents of toleration, such as Nicolas of Cusa, and medieval societies, being less regimented, sometimes allowed for pluralistic situations such as the fair degree of tolerance and communication that was sometimes achieved in Spain between Jews, Christians, and Muslims (though these moments were punctuated with rather darker ones). One result of the Reformation was the introduction of the principle at the Peace of Augsberg in 1555 that the adherence of the prince determined that of his subjects (*Cuius regio, eius religio*), so that potentates who declared for Lutheranism or for Roman Catholicism took their subjects with them, willy-nilly. Refusal of the individual to conform to the state religion resulted, at the least, in heavy sanctions and often in persecution and death. In the sixteenth-century Middle East a similar sentiment led to attacks on Shi'ite Muslims in the Sunni-ruled Ottoman Empire and to the attempt of the Shi'ite Safavid dynasty to wipe out Sunni Islam from Iran. The mixing of state making with religion making had its successes, of course, but these were seldom total. English Catholics, French Huguenots, Ottoman Shi'ites, and Iranian Sunnis continued to exist, along with a host of other sectarian movements, despite the best efforts of government officials to establish religious monopolies in their territory. The state could never truly dictate the consciences of human beings, succeeding only in imposing a broad umbrella of outward conformity (especially in the cities) and a fear of speaking one's mind that impeded the progress of rational thought and scientific discovery.

Even in late eighteenth-century northern Europe, where some forms of legislated toleration began to be established, active government bias toward those who upheld the state religion, and active discrimination against those seen as dissenters or heretics, was common. Although the beginnings of toleration of Roman Catholics and dissenters (non-Anglican Protestants) in England dates from the aftermath of the 1688 Glorious Revolution (with the decree of 1689), non-Anglicans continued to be barred from high government service and to suffer constraints on their speech. Indeed, the whole idea of toleration, as opposed to liberty, implied a system of first-class citizens who merely tolerated the second-class citizens.[4] John Locke, who wrote on religious tolerance in this period, argued that magistrates had no business interfering with the religious beliefs of individuals or with public worship. He wrote,

> Thus if solemn assemblies, observations of festivals, public worship be permitted to any one sort of professors, all these things ought to be permitted to the Presbyterians, Independents, Anabaptists, Arminians, Quakers, and others, with the same liberty. Nay, if we may openly speak the truth, and as becomes one man to another, neither pagan, nor Mahometan, nor Jew ought to be excluded from the civil rights of the commonwealth because of his religion.[5]

But Locke denies the rights of churches that taught doctrines undermining the foundation of society, that rejected the principle of toleration, or that required loyalty to a foreign ruler. Ominously, he gives with regard to his last exclusion the example of any Muslims who felt bound to support the Ottoman emperor out of religious loyalty, and in earlier drafts he had explicitly excluded Catholics with foreign sympathies as well.[6] The British tradition of religious tolerance, although subsequently widened, fell short of genuine religious liberty or equal treatment of all religions under the law, and no true separation of religion and state was ever effected. The monarch remained the head of the Anglican church and "defender of the Faith," and Anglicanism continued to enjoy many special privileges. All that England achieved was a broad religious tolerance that increasingly made a place for the dissident sects, Catholics, and even, in the twentieth century, for Asian religions. But the place made was often grudging and a bias toward the state religion remains palpable to this day.[7] In America Jefferson's bill for establishing religious freedom in Virginia (passed in 1785) and the First Amendment to the U.S. Constitution laid the groundwork for a more thoroughgoing religious liberty in that country, though there, too, inequities remained. Eighteenth-century France was extremely intolerant of the Calvinist church, which dwindled to insignificance, and Jews had to pay what was essentially a poll tax. But the Calvinists were finally granted toleration just before the revolution, and after the revolution religious liberty was proclaimed in the Declaration of the Rights of Man. In Russia Catherine the Great adopted Enlightenment ideals with regard to religious toleration, bestowing it on her subjects, including Muslims.

Explaining why the ideal of toleration should have emerged so strongly in the late 1700s in the North Atlantic would take us somewhat far afield from our subject. But several factors may be mentioned. The spread of the printing press in Western Europe from around 1450, and the subsequent increases in literacy (already to around 33 percent in early seventeenth-century England) made religious ideas more easily communicated and enabled unorthodoxy. The burgeoning urban middle classes of the mercantilist age sought more freedoms, but so did dissenting artisans and workers. In England the Civil War and weakness of the state in the mid-seventeenth century allowed religious dissent to flourish. The potential for more powerful bureaucratic states in the early modern period had been thwarted in some instances by religious factionalism, and some reformers thought the state would be strengthened by disentanglement from religion. Genuine concern for individual human dignity also played a significant part for most thinkers of this persuasion. In the thirteen colonies uneasiness about any Anglican monopoly formed part and parcel of the growing resentment more generally toward perceived British authoritarianism among the landed elite, urban workers, and yeomen farmers.

Many of these causes affected modern societies across the board, though not all at the same time. Modernity's imposition of reason as the referee of religious rivalry did not become salient in the Middle East until the mid-nineteenth century. Tellingly, at this time the impact of the printing press was finally being experienced on a large scale, international trade was greatly increasing and the urban middle classes expanding, imported manufactured goods threatened the livelihoods of artisans, peasants began turning to cash crops and engagement with the global market, and the state was developing a bureaucracy based on impersonal, instrumental rationality rather than on mere patronage. Modernity in West Asia met distinctive premodern traditions of religion-state interaction, which are little enough known among the English-speaking public that rehearsing them here is worthwhile as a means of laying the ground for my argument about the early Baha'i faith's commitment to separation of religion and state.

Religion and State in Islam

Although early Islam did not conceive of a separation of religion and state, it has been argued that in the medieval period a de facto distinction between the two came to exist.[8] The Prophet Muhammad (d. A.D. 632) had ruled a theocratic city-state in Medina, which gradually started expanding toward the end of his life. The first four caliphs (632–661) are honored in Sunni Islam both as rulers of the nascent, Islamic, Arab empire and as vicars of the Prophet, some of whose rulings continue to have force today. The dissident Shi'ites held that members of the House of the Prophet should have ruled instead of the first three caliphs, and should have combined in their persons temporal and spiritual sway over the empire (only 'Ali [d. 661], the cousin and son-in-law of the Prophet, managed actually to do so, becoming the first Shi'ite "imam" and simultaneously the fourth Sunni caliph). Thereafter the Umayyad dynasty came to power, though some of 'Ali's supporters believed that the rightful spiritual leader (imam) of the Muslim community after his death were his sons Hasan (624–679) and then Husayn (626–680). Husayn, in fact, launched a revolt against the ruling Umayyads in 680 but was defeated and killed with most of his family. He became a martyr in the eyes of the "faction of 'Ali" (*shī'at 'Alī*), or Shi'ites, and in subsequent centuries mourning for the doomed grandson of the prophet became central to Shi'ite ritual.[9] The dispute between the supporters of 'Ali and of the third caliph, 'Uthman, was not over the scope of the power of the Prophet's successor, only over who should have filled the post. The Umayyad and early 'Abbasid empires were likewise ruled by caliph-emperors. But later in the 'Abbasid period the caliphs became weak and were supplanted by civil princes who maintained the vicars of the Prophet only as symbolic figureheads.

Most Shi'ites believed that Husayn's son, 'Ali Zaynu'l-'Abidin, was his spiritual successor. One faction of the Shi'ites (the "Twelvers") continued to believe in each of the lineal descendents of 'Ali and his wife Fatimah (the Prophet's daughter) until the twelfth imam, Muhammad al-Mahdi, who was thought to have disappeared as a child around A.D. 880 (A.H. 260). Shi'ites came to believe that the Twelfth Imam had entered a mystical realm beneath the earth, Jabulsa or Jabulqa, and supernaturally would rule the world in Occultation (*ghaybah*) until his second advent sometime in the far future. This belief in the Hidden Imam's disappearance and future return resembles Christian doctrine about the ascension and parousia. The disappearance of the imam constituted a profound difficulty for the Shi'ite ethos. Shi'ites had been committed to the belief that there was always an appointed successor to the Prophet, on earth, deriving from his line, who possessed esoteric knowledge and should reign as theocrat. They thought that only this imam could lawfully collect Islamic taxes, appoint judges and mosque preachers, and distribute alms to the poor. Now the imam was invisible.

The Mongol invasions of the thirteenth century brought to the Muslim Middle East the East Asian steppe conception of the ruler as legislator by virtue of his tribal chieftaincy, and this idea was passed on to the post-Mongol states, such as the Ottomans, the Safavids, and the Mughals, which attained their zenith in the sixteenth and seventeenth centuries. In these later empires the ruler issued laws and regulations that governed the functioning of the state and bureaucracy. But other sorts of law, such as that governing personal status, inheritance, and commerce, remained the purview of Muslim clerical judges (qadis) on the state payroll. Here we have not a separation of religion and state at all but a differentiation within the state of civil and religious functions, insofar as religious officers were appointed and paid by the state and performed their duties on its behalf. That is, while it is true that Muslim states did not remain theocracies on the model of the caliphal empire, and civil norms of governance came to predominate in many areas of life, this situation cannot be called a separation of religion and state. Islamic law was in many areas the only law. Although Jews and Christians were largely tolerated, they suffered disabilities and were clearly second-class subjects (though note that Muslims were on the whole more generous even toward Christians with mixed loyalties than John Locke was toward his hypothetical English Muslim partisans of the sultan).

Despite the crisis of authority at the core of Twelver Shi'ism, because of the absent imam, it went on to flourish as a minority branch of Islam, at first mainly in old Arab centers of Islam, such as what are now Lebanon, Syria, Iraq, Bahrain, and Eastern Arabia. Especially in the sixteenth century it experienced an efflorescence. The Safavid dynasty (1501–1722), supported by Turkmen tribespeople, conquered Iran and imposed Shi'ism as the state religion, so that over the next two centuries traditionally Sunni-majority Iran became largely Shi'ite. Several Shi'ite dynasties emerged in India at this time as well, creating substantial communities following this branch of Islam there.

Within the hierocracy, or religious sphere, the crisis of authority inscribed in Twelver Shi'ism by the trauma of the occultation of the imam was resolved in a number of ways, none of them satisfactory to all believers. The Akhbari school adopted a legalist approach, saying that all Shi'ites, the laity as well as the learned men, should interpret for themselves and follow literally the sayings of the imams. The Usuli school preached that in the absence of an imam the laity should turn to professional clerics for religious and legal advice and should blindly emulate (*taqlīd*) these learned men (called ulama). The Safavids on the whole threw their authority behind the Usuli school, depending on these clerics to justify the Shi'ite-ruled state. In the eighteenth century the old Safavid-Usuli condominium collapsed when the capital of Isfahan was besieged and then reduced by rebel Afghan Sunni tribespeople.

After the Afghan invasions came the deluge, as the adventurer Nadir Shah (r. 1736–1747) built up a short-lived tribal military coalition that allowed him to conquer, for a time, Iran, Baghdad, Central Asia, Afghanistan, and North India, pillaging and looting everywhere his armies went. From 1785 the Qajar tribe and its allies succeeded in establishing a new dynasty in Iran that restored Shi'ite Islam as the state religion. The scholastic Usuli school became dominant but was challenged by a resurgent Shi'ite Sufism, or system of mystical brotherhoods, based upon the charisma, ethical insight, and miracle-working of the pir, or venerated elder. In the late eighteenth century another branch of Twelver Shi'ism came into being, the Shaykhi. It coalesced around the gnostic teachings of Shaykh Ahmad al-Ahsa'i (1753–1826), who derived from Eastern Arabia but emigrated to Iran in 1806, where he spent most of the rest of his life. Al-Ahsa'i taught that at all times a perfect Shi'ite existed on earth who had a direct intuition of the will of the imam, who Shaykhis, like many other Shi'ites, thought would return in the thirteenth Islamic century (nineteenth century A.D.). Subsequent leaders of the Shaykhi school such as Sayyid Kazim Rashti (d. 1844) and Muhammad Karim Khan Kirmani were presumably viewed by their followers as this perfect Shi'ite. Shaykhism greatly resembled the Shi'ite Sufi orders both in its emphasis on intuition and gnostic motifs and in its organization around a leader thought to possess esoteric knowledge. It differed from most Sufism in rejecting monist metaphysics, insisting on a strong division between the divine and the creation.[10] There was yet another possible path to resolving the crisis of the imam's disappearance, the messianic. That is, the imam might, as he was expected to,

Baha'u'llah's Exiles in Iran and the Ottoman Empire, 1853-1868

return. Shi'ites believed that at the end-time after the imam had restored the world to justice Christ (or Imam Husayn, or a figure called the Qayyum, or perhaps all these rolled into one) would also reappear. Messianic, or "mahdist," movements had been common in Islam, but most were put down and persecuted by the state and the urban ulama.

The urgency of finding a resolution to the long-term problem of authority in a Shi'ism lacking an imam was greatly increased in the nineteenth century by the impact of modernity. Qajar Iran in the early nineteenth century was quickly receding into the backwaters of the new industrial order centered in the capitalist core countries of the North Atlantic— Great Britain, France, Holland, and, increasingly, the United States and what was to become Germany. Whereas its silk industry had once made Iran a country with a respectable standard of living in world terms, that one commodity could no longer drive its economy. European manufactures flooded the Middle East after the end of the Napoleonic wars in 1815, driving many weavers and other artisans into poverty. Manufactured weaponry and reorganized drills gave European powers a decisive advantage on the battlefield. Shi'ite Iran was increasingly caught in the pincers of a British advance up from India and a Russian advance from the north. Under the Safavids the saying had come into being that "Isfahan is half the world." In the early nineteenth century Isfahan had been reduced to a small city of ninety thousand whose commerce was increasingly controlled by half the world. As if the European humiliations were not enough, Iran's Middle Eastern neighbor, the Ottoman Empire, inflicted more. In 1843 Ottoman troops brutally put down a rebellion in the Shi'ite shrine city of Karbala, in the Ottoman province of Baghdad, killing thousands, and provoking a war fever in Iran that the government barely resisted.[11] Shi'ites increasingly felt helpless, surrounded by powerful enemies and buffeted by rapid social change the roots of which they could only dimly comprehend.

The mainstream clerical tradition in Shi'ite Islam adopted a complex stance toward the Iranian state. Strict jurisprudence led the clerics to deny ultimate and true legitimacy to any ruler but the absent imam, for whose return they fervidly prayed. The Safavid shahs claimed descent from the Prophet Muhammad and possessed their own religious charisma, so that they attempted to project an aura of divinely appointed kingship. Some clergy rejected such pretensions, but on a pragmatic basis they had no choice but to recognize their dependence on the goodwill of the Safavid state, and most chose to see it as an ally. Muhammad Baqir Majlisi (d. 1699), shaykhu'l-Islam or chief religious dignitary of Isfahan, wrote that "the Kings of the Right Religion have many rights upon their subjects, as they protect them and repel the enemies of Religion from them. . . . Therefore [the subjects] must pray for the kings and recognize their rights."[12]

In nineteenth-century Qajar Iran some of the clergy developed a theory of the state as having two wings, that of civil governance and that of religious learning. The sovereign, in his own sphere of civil rulership and military action, and the clergy, in their sphere of interpreting and implementing the sacred law, each represented an aspect of authority that had once been conjoined in the imam. Thus the king was the special deputy of the imam with regard to the sword and the clergy were collectively the special deputy of the imam with respect to the Law. Only by cooperating through mutual consensus could each wing of the state hope to discharge its office.[13] In the Shi'ite-ruled kingdom of Awadh (Oudh), in nineteenth-century North India, the leading cleric appears to have considered his government a "common law" (*'urfī*) state rather than an Islamically sanctioned one, since only the imam could head up a truly Islamic government. But he nevertheless demanded that Shi'ites recognize and obey the authority of this civil state. The rulers conceived themselves as presiding over not a civil but a Shi'ite state (*dār ash-shi'ah*), and one Nawab of Awadh saw himself as the full deputy of the Twelfth Imam.[14] Nineteenth-century Shi'ite states looked to the clergy for some sort of legitimation and delegated to them authority over public religious ritual, large parts of the legal sphere, and most education.

Repression of Babism by the State and the Clergy

The profound entanglement of the state with religion characteristic of Qajar Iran led to the persecution of dissenters from the orthodoxies of Usuli Shi'ism. Some strict clerics gloried in putting Sufi mystics to death in the late eighteenth and early nineteenth centuries, so that one, Muhammad 'Ali Bihbahani of Kirmanshah, proudly wore the epithet "Sufi killer." The most significant episode of church-state collaboration in suppressing a dissenting religious group during the nineteenth century was the conflict with the Babis.

In 1844 a young merchant in Shiraz, who had earlier lived for a while in the shrine city of Karbala and associated with the Shaykhis there, declared himself to have a special relationship to the Twelfth Imam and gradually asserted that he was himself the return of that figure. Sayyid 'Ali Muhammad Shirazi (1819–1850) became known as the "Bab," (Arabic for "door"), a technical term in Shi'ism for someone with special access to the imam. His movement spread like wildfire through Iran, and by 1849 one European observer estimated that there were one hundred thousand Babis (in a population of about six million Iranians).[15] This estimate, however, is little more than a guess and may be exaggerated. The Bab had promised to turn the world upside down, to do away with the feudal, unscriptural oppressions of the Qajar aristocrats, to allow merchants legally to charge interest on loans, to allow more freedom of movement and social interaction to women, and to end the vast power of the Usuli clergy by banning their sermons, their pulpits, and their disquisitions on the minutiae of theology and metaphysics. He would restrict the freedom of movement of carpetbagging European merchants, whose trade in manufactured textiles had begun badly hurting Iranian artisans and merchants. The Bab predicted that after him another, greater figure would arise, "He whom God shall make manifest" (*man yuẓhiruhu Allāh*). The Bab was arrested for heresy in Shiraz, in 1845, but escaped the city in 1846 for Isfahan. He was thereafter again imprisoned, in 1847, and kept in fortresses in northwestern Iran. He was examined by the chief Shi'ite clerics of

Tabriz in 1848 and they pronounced him a heretic deserving of death. At this point, it should be noted, the Bab was a prisoner of conscience, having committed no crime save doctrinal noncomformity. On July 8, 1850, the Qajar government carried out the clergy's sentence in the wake of fighting that had broken out in Mazandaran, Zanjan, and Nayriz between Shi'ites who had accepted the Bab and those who had rejected him.

The Bab's martyrdom closed the first chapter of the encounter between religious absolutism and millennialism. It opened a second, however, insofar as it paved the way for a successor religion, the Baha'i faith, founded in 1863 by Mirza Husayn 'Ali Nuri (1817–1892). His father, Mirza 'Abbas "Buzurg" Nuri, had served the Qajar court as a high government official (minister to the prince in charge of the Qajar tribe, tax revenue officer for Burujird and Luristan, then governor of the same provinces), and he even, late in life, married into the royal family. The latter marriage ended up ruining him financially, and the new shah who acceded in 1834 became his enemy, so that he died a broken man in 1839. Five years later, in 1844, his son Mirza Husayn 'Ali Nuri adopted the Babi religion, in which he ultimately became known as Baha'u'llah (glory of God; Babis were encouraged by the Bab to take exalted nicknames). Baha'u'llah, an idealistic young magnate, preached the new faith in Tehran and in his ancestral province of Nur. He brought into the religion his younger half-brother, Mirza Yahya "Subh-i Azal," along with his full brother, Mirza Musa "Kalim," as well as many relatives and friends in Takur, the seat of the family estate.[16] He helped to finance the Babi gathering in Badasht in the summer of 1848, where leading disciples of the Bab declared Islamic law abrogated.[17] When, thereafter, fighting broke out at the shrine of Shaykh Tabarsi between Shi'ites and Babis, Baha'u'llah attempted to go to the area, apparently with the intention of using his family's high social standing as a platform for negotiating an end to the fighting. He and his party, however, were arrested before they could reach the site of the clashes, and Baha'u'llah was beaten on the soles of his feet till they bled.[18] Muhammad Shah issued a death warrant against Baha'u'llah (again, he had as yet committed only a thought crime in accepting the Bab), but it lapsed when the monarch died abruptly on September 4, 1848.

After the Bab's death a number of Babi leaders and sects grew up. Some were antinomian, declaring all laws and restraints on behavior abolished, whereas others looked to the Bab's holy book, the *Bayan*, for guidance. Some followed one or another prominent disciple of the Bab, though by 1852 most of these were dead.[19] In Tehran most Babis followed 'Ali " 'Azim" Turshizi.[20] During the last year of his life the Bab had also corresponded from the fortress of Chihriq with the Nuri brothers in Tehran. Because of Baha'u'llah's prominence, and because a death warrant had already been once issued against him, great care was taken to avoid putting him in the spotlight as leader of the Babis; even the letters of the Bab came addressed to his little brother, Mirza Yahya.[21] Baha'u'llah, one of the Bab's secretaries, and Mirza Yahya agreed that the younger Nuri would be put forward as a *mirror* and focus of Babi leadership, so as to protect Baha'u'llah from reprisals. The plan, however, went awry. Azal grew attached to his exoteric position, and the government discovered Baha'u'llah's importance anyway. 'Azim's group attempted to assassinate Nasiru'd-Din Shah in August 1852.[22] At around the same time Azal and other Babi radicals mounted a revolt in Nur against the government, which was brutally crushed.[23] Baha'u'llah, summering in Shemiran near Tehran with the brother of the prime minister, had opposed such militancy, but because of his fame as a Babi leader he was soon arrested and falsely charged. After months in the festering Siyah-Chal (black pit) dungeon, where he underwent a profound religious experience and determined to reform the Babi religion, he was found innocent of any involvement.[24] He was nevertheless exiled to Ottoman Baghdad in 1853, having still committed no crime save unorthodox belief. A vengeful shah pursued a vicious pogrom against real and suspected Babis inside Iran, with much public torture of those accused, resulting in several thousand deaths.[25] The truly gruesome aspect of church-state entanglement was demonstrated in the joint efforts of officials and clergy to invent ever more ingenious ways of inflicting pain on those branded heretics. The hierocracy decreed that, owing to their collective guilt, Babis be punctured and candles set in the wounds or that their feet be skinned and thrust in hot tar, then they be made to run.

Babism as a religion went underground. In the 1850s many Babis came to look upon Subh-i Azal, who had joined Baha'u'llah in Baghdad, as the leader of the movement. Beginning in the late 1850s, however, Baha'u'llah began circulating spiritual works of his own, invoking both the themes of Babi millenarianism and those of Sufi ethics and ecstatic worship, and he began building up an independent following among Babis back in Iran. He became so popular among Iranian pilgrims who visited Baghdad as part of their pilgrimage to the nearby Shi'ite shrine cities that the Iranian government put pressure on the Ottomans to remove him farther away. As a result, Sultan Abdülaziz issued a firman, or edict, early in 1863 calling Baha'u'llah to Istanbul. Before he left Baghdad Baha'u'llah in April of 1863 set up tents in the garden of Necip Pasha, which he called the Garden of Ridvan (paradise), and there he declared himself to a handful of relatives and close friends as the "He whom God shall make manifest" promised by the Bab.

Baha'u'llah refused to curry favor in Istanbul and in consequence was banished to the provincial city of Edirne (Adrianople), near Bulgaria. He lived in that city from December 12, 1863, until August 12, 1868, and it was from there that he made his public declaration as the promised one of the Bab and an independent prophet. His younger half brother, Azal, had come to believe in himself as the rightful vicar of the Bab, and he reacted angrily to Baha'u'llah's declaration. Ultimately, Azal attempted to have Baha'u'llah assassinated, but failed, and thereafter the two broke off relations. Back in Iran Babis began accepting Baha'u'llah in great numbers as their messiah, leaving Azal head of a tiny sect of only a few thousand Azali Babis. Baha'u'llah continued to enjoy far more freedom of movement and access to visitors than the Iranian government wanted, and it put further pressure on the Ottomans to banish Baha'u'llah once more. In the summer of 1868 Azal and his supporters were exiled to Cyprus, while Baha'u'llah was sent to the pestilential, decaying port of Akka on the coast of Ottoman Syria. For two years he and scores of companions endured harsh imprisonment in the city's fortress, until he was released to house arrest in Akka. Throughout the two decades from the death warrant of 1848 till his brutal incarceration, without adequate food or water, in the Akka fortress, Baha'u'llah had never committed any civil crime or been convicted of any infraction against the law in any judicial court. He was punished by fiat, at the whim of Muslim monarchs who saw themselves as defenders of the one true faith against a prominent heretic, a dangerous claimant to religious charisma.

Separation of Religion and State

During his last years in Baghdad, and then in Istanbul and Edirne, under the close supervision of the Ottoman sultan and ministers, Baha'u'llah began grappling with a new approach to relations between religion and state, different from that envisaged in Shi'ite Islam or in Babism. His Ridvan declaration would have implied, in traditional Islamic political theory, that Baha'u'llah himself now had a right to become a theocrat and to demand the acquiescence of the civil governments to his authority, on the model of the Prophet Muhammad or of Imam 'Ali. Baha'u'llah, however, eschewed any such claims. His ideas about sovereignty were probably influenced by the Sufi enthusiasms of his youth. Sufi traditions such as the Ni'matu'llahi saw authority as separated into the spiritual and the civil. The great mystics were often titled "shah," or king, to acknowledge their suzerainty over the world of mystical phenomena and spiritual progress. They on the whole were quite willing to acknowledge the power in this world of civil governments but held the view that the fortunes of the civil state depended in a supernatural manner upon how well the government treated the Sufi master. Thus, Ni'matu'llahis attributed Qajar political reverses to the lack of reverence of some shahs toward leaders of the order.[26]

In the same way Baha'u'llah viewed his station as implying spiritual sovereignty but not secular power. The Sufi theory is strained, however, when the state acts against the spiritual master. The first test of his relationship with the Ottoman state came when he was ordered by the sultan to leave for Edirne. Baha'u'llah wrote a defiant letter to the sultan and his ministers denouncing their tyranny, which, according to the Ottoman official (Şemsi Bey) who delivered it, caused Grand Vizier Âli Pasha's face to pale. Baha'u'llah himself admitted that, while the Ottoman treatment of him up till that point had been purely despotic (*zulm-i ṣirf*), "whatever action the ministers of the sultan took against us after having become acquainted with its contents, cannot be regarded as unjustifiable [*Anchih bar mā vārid tavānand, miyāvarand*; literally, "Let them do to us what they can"]."[27] Baha'u'llah was reported by Nabil-i Zarandi to have been extremely upset by the actions of the Iranian ambassador and the Ottoman ministers. He strode into the house's private chambers and said within hearing of his companions and of Şemsi Bey that he would turn the affairs of the twelve-man Ottoman cabinet upside down (*munqalib mīkunam*) and would go on to establish a divine sovereignty (*salṭanat-i ilāhiyyah*). He did not mean by this diction that he wanted an outward theocracy but rather that his spiritual sovereignty would cause civil authorities who mistreated him to suffer supernatural reverses and that in the long run his spiritual sovereignty would be recognized by the world's peoples.[28] He had taken the same view of the Bab, whose short life had ended in imprisonment, exile, and execution, despite Islamic prophecies that the Mahdi would establish his dominion on earth. The sovereignty of the Mahdi, he explained around 1862, the year before, "is not the sovereignty which the minds of men have falsely imagined. . . . By sovereignty is meant the all-encompassing, all-pervading power which is inherently exercised by the Qá'im whether or not He appear to the world clothed in the majesty of earthly dominion."[29] From Baha'u'llah's point of view, "Earthly sovereignty is of no worth, nor will it ever be, in the eyes of God and His chosen ones."[30] Baha'u'llah's next response was to formulate a plan of noncooperation against the Ottomans. He announced that he and those loyal to him would simply refuse to leave Istanbul, a stance that would either overturn the sultan's edict or force the Ottomans to martyr him, giving him a sort of victory either way. But such a plan required unanimity, and when Azal declined to go along it fell through.[31] Baha'u'llah was willing to cede temporal power to the civil state, retaining for himself and his religion only spiritual and ethical authority. But when the state encroached on his human rights, he also reserved the right to defy it.

In an unguarded moment in January of 1866 Âli Pasha (who had become Ottoman foreign minister) confessed to the Austrian ambassador that Baha'u'llah, then in exile in Edirne, was "a man of great distinction, exemplary conduct, great moderation, and a most dignified figure" and spoke of Babism as "a doctrine which is worthy of high esteem."[32] He said that he still found the religion politically unacceptable because it refused to recognize a separation of religious and temporal authority. Mehmed Emin Âli Pasha (1815–1871) and his colleague Keçecizade Fuad Pasha (1815–1869) had been at the forefront in promoting and implementing the 1856 Imperial Rescript, part of the reform laws (Tanzimat) of the Ottoman Empire, which made Jews and Christians equal to Muslims under the law and created the secular conception of "Ottomanism" as the basis for a political loyalty for all subjects of the sultan.[33] The rescript

> laid more stress on the full equality of the Sultan's non-Muslim subjects and abolished the civil power of the heads of the various Christian communities. Churches were henceforth to be governed by synods of the clergy in cooperation with national councils of the laity. Full liberty of conscience was guaranteed and all civil offices were declared open to all Ottoman subjects without distinction. Non-Muslims were made technically eligible for military service but were given the option of buying their exemption. Torture was prohibited and prison reform promised.[34]

These reforms dethroned Islam as the foundation of the Ottoman state, and from the reformers' point of view a messianic movement such as Babism, whatever its virtues, threatened such achievements by seeking to put all authority, religious and secular, back in the hands of a charismatic spiritual leader. Âli Pasha would have been briefed on the theocratic spirit with which Babism was imbued by his fellow cabinet minister and old Iran hand, Kemal Pasha, and may have gained the impression from Baha'u'llah's 1863 letter to the Sublime Porte that Baha'u'llah himself held theocratic sentiments. Although he may have been right about Babism, he misunderstood Baha'u'llah's own ideas, which were more compatible with the Tanzimat than he thought.

In fact, Baha'u'llah opposed the theocratic currents in Islam and the general Shi'ite denial of ideal legitimacy to civil governments not ruled by the divinely appointed imam. Throughout Islamic history rebels against the state had wrapped themselves in the banner of religion, claiming that civil authority had degenerated into little more than pharaonic rule, in need of being scourged by the staff of a Muslim revivalist Moses. The association between dissident religion and antistate feeling was strong in Babism, as well. Baha'u'llah attempted to rein in the theocratic assumptions of the Babis who had become Baha'is.

About a year after the Ottoman grand vizier made his remarks, Baha'u'llah addressed a general letter from Edirne to the reigning monarchs, which contained apostrophes to Ottoman cabinet officials and to Sultan Abdülaziz. The mahdist claims of the Babi-Baha'i religion would have implied to these cabinet ministers, as we have seen, that it was at core theocratic and posed a threat to civil governance. Baha'u'llah denies this impression, saying that he has not come in order to take from them their worldly possessions; rather, they should know that he does not oppose the sultan and is not in rebellion against him. Indeed, Baha'u'llah wants not a jot or tittle of what God has bestowed on the Ottoman ruler. He urges Abdülaziz to be grateful to God for having made him "sultan of the Muslims," and calls him the "shadow of God on earth."[35] In the "Tablet to the Kings," then, civil government ultimately derives its authority from God, and Baha'u'llah's own prophetic advent does not detract from the sovereignty of existing governments. His role is that of counselor and ethical preacher, and his diction implies that his religion has a similar role, outside the state.

In spring of 1868 Baha'u'llah addressed a comparable letter to Nasiru'd-Din Shah of Iran. In this *Lawh-i Sultan* Baha'u'llah again appeals to the "Mirrors for Princes" tradition of political thought in the Middle East, a secular and rationalist discourse that originated in the books of counsel for monarchs written by sages in Sasanian, Zoroastrian Iran before the advent of Islam—though the tradition was influenced, as well, by Aristotle. Zoroastrian tradition saw the monarch as sacred, a representative of cosmic order (Pahlevi *arta*), who enjoyed the halo (*khvarena, farr*) of divine approval. After the advent of Islam in Iran this genre was taken up and refined by Muslim courtiers, notables, and thinkers such as as the medieval official Nizamu'l-Mulk, and it remained a distinctive discourse differing from that of the Muslim clergy. Indeed, it was explicitly associated in Muslim texts with the Zoroastrian, Sasanian ruler Ardashir. These secular writers saw kingship and religion as twin sources of authority, each needing the support of the other but autonomous in its own realm.[36] As a leading authority has written in this regard,

> The attribution to the sultan, as the Shadow of God on Earth, of autonomous charisma as divine reflection upon the temporal world, and the emphasis on the exercise of substantive justice by him, minimized the effects of Islamic tenets on the patrimonial theories of temporal rule. The notion of justice that came to prevail in these theories was the unformalized substantive justice of Sasanian patrimonialism: protection of the weak from the strong, removal of oppression and administration of punishment for wrongdoings and for contraventions of customary norms of fairness.[37]

Standing in this Iranian tradition of Ardashir and Nizamu'l-Mulk, Baha'u'llah declares, "The just king is the shadow of God on earth."[38] Civil governments enjoy divinely bestowed legitimacy, in this view, and are not simply inadequate and temporary substitutes for the absent Twelfth Imam's political sovereignty (the latter being the farthest most Shi'ite clergy would go in legitimating the shah). Baha'u'llah, however, derives an unusual conclusion from this premise. "All," he says, "must take refuge in the shadow of his justice and find repose in the shade of his grace. This status [recipient of justice] is not something specialized or limited to some and not extended to others, for the shadow speaks of the one who casts it."[39] That is, the authority of the civil government to rule, which is conferred by God, depends on its justice. And its justice in turn depends upon its being equitable and evenhanded among all its subjects. Baha'u'llah has here merged the "covenant of Ardashir" with the ideals of the Ottoman Tanzimat reforms, implicitly advocating that the shah issue an imperial rescript similar to the 1856 Ottoman decree that made all subjects equal under the law regardless of religion. One author writing of Luther, Hobbes, Locke, and Rousseau says that a unifying theme runs through their thought: "the equality of all human beings under the sovereign," adding, "this notion I take to be one of the essential elements of early modern thought, a notion that has no antecedent in the ancient world."[40] Such equality was also foreign to classical Islamic jurisprudence, so that Baha'u'llah is as much an innovator in his tradition as were they in theirs.

Elsewhere in the same work Baha'u'llah calls upon God to aid the shah in manifesting divine justice and in judging the Baha'i community by the same criteria he judges others.[41] He adds,

Numerous denominations and diverse religious communities repose in the shadow of the king, and this people is one of them. Indeed, the shah's officials must with the highest determination and character . . . arrange matters so that all religions will come under the shadow of the king, and he shall rule among them with justice. Implementing the law of God simply consists in justice.[42]

Baha'u'llah is in these passages making an argument for religious liberty and equal rights for all citizens, based upon the normative foundations of Iranian monarchy, which requires that the king show fairness and impartiality to all subjects. This view of the civil government differs starkly from that of the Muslim clergy, who accepted the state as just only if it discriminated against non-Muslims and persecuted those they deemed heretics and apostates. In implicit reply to ulama who would insist that the shah uphold Islamic law, Baha'u'llah insists that even elements of the Qur'anic code such as *qiṣāṣ* (the law governing sanctions for causing loss of life) require retribution for homicide, regardless of the religion of the murder or manslaughter victim. (In fact, Shi'ite ulama denied this notion, insisting Muslims were not subject to retribution for killing non-Muslims.) At this point, in the late Edirne period, Baha'u'llah has not yet turned decisively away from divine right monarchy, as he would do later in 1868 after his exile to Akka. But the outlines of his argument thereafter remain the same, since he also sees parliamentary governance to rest upon a foundation of justice and of divine bestowal. As we shall see, these ideas were elaborated by Baha'u'llah's eldest son, 'Abdu'l-Baha.

Once he reached Akka Baha'u'llah on numerous occasions made it quite clear that he and his religion accepted the separation of religion and state. In a letter to his follower, Dhabih, he wrote, "The One true God . . . hath bestowed outward sovereignty (*mamlakat-i ẓāhirih*) upon the kings. No one is permitted to commit [*irtikāb*] an act that would run contrary to the judgment of the leaders of the country [*ra'i-yi ru'asā-yi mamlakat*]. That which He [God] hath desired for Himself are the cities of the hearts of his servants."[43] I see this passage not as a command to political quietism but as a relinquishing of any theocratic claim by the Baha'i religion. Baha'u'llah forbids his followers, to be sure, from committing crimes against the state. But he was in other writings of this period calling for principles such as parliamentary rule, which were fiercely opposed by the Ottoman and Qajar monarchs (see the next two chapters). The point was not a withdrawal from politics but the avoidance of religious crime and violence and the granting of legitimacy to the civil state.

In another passage Baha'u'llah vigorously denies the accusations launched against him by enemies, that he had theocratic designs for his religion:

> Most imagine that this Servant hath the intention of establishing a full-blown government (*ḥukūmat-i kulliyyih*) on earth—even though, in all the tablets, He hath forbidden the servants to accept such a rank [of rulership]. For it yieldeth naught but trials and tribulations, save if a soul should accept this matter as a means of aiding the cause of God. Kings are the manifestations of divine power, and our intent is only that they should be just. If they keep their gaze upon justice, they are reckoned as of God.[44]

Baha'u'llah is pointing out that it would be inconsistent of him to decree the end of absolutist rule (as he does in other tablets) and then to turn around and attempt to establish a Baha'i state.

As we shall see in more detail below, Baha'u'llah created democratic governing institutions for his community, called "houses of justice," which were to operate through group discussion. The head of the religion after Baha'u'llah's death would eventually be the elected universal house of justice. In the eighth paragraph of his "Splendors" (*Ishrāqāt*) Baha'u'llah spelled out the authority of the house of justice as being over the affairs of the Baha'i religious community (*umūr-i millat*) rather than being universal.[45] In the "Tablet of the World," written during Iran's Tobacco Revolt in 1891, Baha'u'llah makes explicit that he sees society divided into a legitimate sphere of secular governmental authority and a separate religious sphere, with its own authority and responsibilities in civil society: "All affairs are committed to the care of just kings and presidents (*salāṭīn va ru'asā*) and of the trustees of the house of justice."[46] In his *Epistle to the Son of the Wolf* Baha'u'llah cited in support of his position Mk 12:17, "Render to Caesar the things that are Caesar's, and to God the things that are God's." He says that Caesar could not have come to the throne against God's will in any case. He supports this verse with Qur'an (4:59), "Obey God and obey the Apostle, and those among you invested with authority," which he says refers first of all to the imams and then to secular rulers. On this theme Baha'u'llah also quotes the apostle Paul's Epistle to the Romans (13:1–2), "Let every soul be subject to the higher powers."[47] John Locke had employed such verses to argue against the possibility of a Christian state and for the state's need to be religiously evenhanded. Classical Shi'ite doctrine, on the contrary, had held that all power, civil and religious, should be concentrated in the hands of an infallible imam, and even the compromises of Shi'ite political theory in the nineteenth century had not recognized a true separation of religion and state. Baha'u'llah, claiming to be the promised one of Islam, would have been justified in the terms of this tradition in claiming the prerogative of rule. But he refused to do so, either for himself or for his religion. He repudiated the entire notion of an absolutist state, and of a theocratic one.

In his will Baha'u'llah reaffirmed the principle of the legitimacy of the civil state and the end of theocracy, writing

> O ye the loved ones and the trustees of God! Kings are the manifestation of the power, and the daysprings of the might and riches, of God. Pray ye on their behalf. He hath invested them with the rulership of the earth and hath singled out the hearts of men as His Own domain. Conflict and contention are categorically forbidden in His Book. This is a decree of God in this Most Great Revelation. It is divinely preserved from annulment.[48]

Again, the real point here is not that kings cannot be contradicted or their power curbed. "Kings" by this time is Baha'u'llah's shorthand for "civil, constitutional monarchies." (To spell this out in every tablet would have made them dangerous for couriers to carry in the Ottoman and Qajar realms.) The key statement is that God has bestowed rule (*ḥukūmat*) on these civil authorities and wants only the hearts of men for Himself. The Baha'i religion, in short, has renounced any claim on temporal governance. Historian Mangol Bayat has cannily pointed out that Baha'u'llah's policy in this regard "embraced what no Muslim sect, no Muslim school of thought ever succeeded in or dared to try: the doctrinal acceptance of the de facto secularization of politics which had occurred in the Muslim world centuries earlier."[49] Baha'u'llah's attitudes, in accepting the equality of all religious communities under the state, were thus not so far removed from those of the Tanzimat reformers of Istanbul after all.

The most wide-ranging statement on freedom of conscience and religious liberty in the nineteenth-century Baha'i texts comes toward the end of *A Traveller's Narrative*, a chronicle of the Babi and Baha'i movements written in 1888 by Baha'u'llah's eldest son, 'Abdu'l-Baha. The latter moves away from basing his demands for justice on Iranian political thought about monarchy and draws instead on the North Atlantic tradition of Locke and Jefferson. He begins this section by describing Qajar Iran's persecution of the Babis and Baha'is for crimes of conscience, decrying the savagery displayed.[50]

> Yet nought has been effected and no advantage has been gained; no remedy has been discovered for this ill, nor any easy salve for this wound. [To ensure] freedom of conscience (*āzādīg-yi vujdān*) and tranquillity of heart and soul is one of the duties and functions of government (*vaẓā'if va savāl-*

iḥ-i ḥukūmat), and is in all ages the cause of progress in development and ascendency over other lands.

This passage emphasizes that to ensure freedom of conscience is a duty of the state. It is a duty, moreover, that if fulfilled leads a country to progress and to become so powerful as to be able to dominate its neighbors. In the context freedom of conscience can only be understood as the right to publish whatever religious views one wishes, even if they strike the majority as heretical. This seems to me the beginning of an argument against the establishment of religion, that is, against the enforcement of a monopolistic state religion. I see it, in turn, as a sentiment very similar to that expressed in the First Amendment of the U.S. Constitution. It implies a separation of church and state in the sense that 'Abdu'l-Baha refuses to recognize the legitimacy of any coercive measures that would interfere with freedom of conscience. There is a plausible conduit for 'Abdu'l-Baha's awareness of U.S. First Amendment ideals in the form of John William Draper, a professor at the University of New York who published *A History of the Intellectual Development of Europe* in 1863. A French translation came out in 1868, and, because of the author's high opinion of Muslim contributions to European civilization, this Paris edition was quickly translated into one of the Middle Eastern languages and circulated (at the very least in manuscript). 'Abdu'l-Baha read a translation before 1875. Draper, an American liberal rationalist, saw a close connection between the separation of religion and state (which followed, in his view, upon the Reformation) and the achievement of religious liberty. And he attributed to this development the flourishing state of religion in the United States.[51]

Equality under the law and evenhanded treatment of all citizens by the state are prerequisites, in 'Abdu'l-Baha's view, to ending sectarian strife of a sort which he sees as a prime cause for the weakness of Middle Eastern states in the nineteenth century. He continues, "All are one people, one nation, one species, one kind. The common interest is complete equality (*maslaḥat-i 'āmmih musāvat-i tāmmih ast*); justice and equality amongst mankind are amongst the chief promoters of [world rehabilitation] (*jihānbānī*)." He demands, in short, that all citizens be dealt with "according to one standard" by the state, which should ensure "complete equality." Such values clearly rule out any sort of theocracy or purely religious state, since such a state would inevitably create disenfranchised or less privileged religious minorities. These provisions involve a complete repudiation of classical Muslim jurisprudence concerning infidels, which prescribes making war on the belligerant ones, demanding conversion of the polytheistic ones, and reducing Christians and Jews to "protected minority" status. In fact, the complete absence of any such provisions in Baha'u'llah's *Most Holy Book* is quite striking. The Baha'i faith is a religion that seeks the civil and political equality of non-Baha'is with Baha'is.

'Abdu'l-Baha admits that the state has a right to punish sedition and rebellion against its authority. But he maintains that the Baha'i religion is not seditious.[52] He insists that modernity authorizes a change in the monopolistic religious practices of the past (the "need and fashion of the world are changed"), adding, "Inteference with creed and faith in every country causes manifest detriment, while justice and equal dealing towards all peoples on the face of the earth are the means whereby progress is effected." He admits that some political factions and "materialists" that pose a threat to the state might properly inspire fear, probably here referring to nihilists and anarchists. The date of composition is the late 1880s, and such radical groups were by then notorious and often mentioned in the press. Such groups as practice "hypocrisy" (*nifāq*, probably with the sense of "sedition") toward the state may suffer sanctions. 'Abdu'l-Baha may be recalling such incidents as the assassination of the tsar, which would put a group beyond the pale. His point, however, is that Baha'is are not nihilists or assassins but adherents of a religion like Christianity or Judaism or Zoroastrianism and that members of all religions should be treated equally in civil law.

Having again condemned religious persecution of Baha'is, 'Abdu'l-Baha points to the example of Europe:

> In other countries when they perceived severity and persecution in such instances to be identical with . . . incitement, and saw that paying no attention was more effectual, they abated the fire of revolution. Therefore did they universally proclaim the equal rights of all denominations, and sounded the liberty of all groups (*lihādhā bi kullī i'lān-i musāvat-i ḥuqūq-i aḥzāb namūdand va āzādigī-yi 'umūm-i ṭavā'if gūsh zad sharq va gharb*).[53]

The argument here is a practical and historical one. For the state to attempt to suppress a religious group only incites it to radicalism and violence, whereas the withdrawal of the state from matters of faith and the granting of all members of the polity equal rights regardless of confession tends to depoliticize religion. Here as elsewhere, his argument echoes that of Locke, who noted that religious rebellion against state restrictions was a natural human reaction to persecution.[54] In advocating total equality among members of various religions, 'Abdu'l-Baha is going further, however, than Locke had gone, and further even than most European states of the late nineteenth century had gone.

'Abdu'l-Baha contrasts two historical periods in Iran, that of the ancient Achaemenids and that of the Safavid dynasty and its successors, with regard to religious policy. The Achaemenids were famed for religious tolerance, he argues. It is certainly the case that Achaemenid rulers based in southwestern Iran (550–330 B.C.) extended their empire to Egypt in the west and the Indus Valley in the east, encompassing within their domain a large number of beliefs—Zoroastrianism, Hinduism, Buddhism, Judaism, and the pagan faiths of Iraq, Egypt, and Greece. Cyrus the Great's freeing of the Jews from their Babylonian exile is only the most famous instance of the Achaemenid policy of religious tolerance, and this empire achieved a geographical extent and cultural richness unrivaled in subsequent Iranian history. 'Abdu'l-Baha contrasts this ancient polity unfavorably with Iran's governments from about 1690 till 1888. The late Safavid period, he says, saw an increased influence over state affairs by the Shi'ite clergy, who urged the persecution of Sunni Muslims as well as members of other religions. He puts the blame on this shortsighted monopolistic policy with regard to religion for the revolt of the Sunni Afghan and Baluchi tribes of the early 1700s, which led to the fall of the Safavids in 1722 and to decades of political turmoil in Iran. "But when the custom of interference with the creeds of all sects arose, and the principle of enquiring into men's thoughts became the fashion and practice, the extensive dominions of the empire of Persia diminished."

The Qajar tribe that came to power in the late eighteenth century had revived the Safavid policy of alliance with the Shi'ite clergy, which 'Abdu'l-Baha sees as both unwise and as detracting from Iran's social cohesion and political strength. He points out that enforcement of strict Usuli Shi'ite orthodoxy would lead to the imprisonment of perhaps a majority of the population, given that outside the urban literate classes many Iranians were Sufis, Nusayris, and Shaykhis (and one could add Ismailis, Sunnis, Ahl-i Haqq, Armenian Christians, Jews, or peasants steeped in unorthodox folk belief). He concludes, "Under these circumstances what need that the government should persecute this one or that one, or disturb itself about the ideas and consciences of its subjects and people?"[55]

Remarkably, 'Abdu'l-Baha argues for freedom of conscience for members of all religions, even for groups like the Nusayris, who had from an urban literate point of view quite unorthodox views. Here he goes beyond a "millet" system as in the nineteenth-century Ottoman Empire, where a few recognized religious groups are granted toleration (Jews, Eastern

Orthodox Christians, Catholics). He is avoiding categorizing religious groups at all, advising the state to withdraw completely from interference in anyone's religious beliefs. As we saw earlier, this removal of the government from the realm of faith entails the granting of precisely equal rights to all citizens regardless of religious background. In order to illustrate the pragmatic benefits of liberty, he contrasts the religious policy of Shi'ite Iran, which was weak and losing territory in the nineteenth century, with that of the British Empire. British administrators, building on a century of thought and law concerning toleration, on the whole developed a policy of impartiality across religious groups.[56] The British, he says, implemented equality and "uniform political rights" for diverse religious groups. Finally, 'Abdu'l-Baha affirms that such a policy of allowing equality among the adherents of various religions is not areligious and can be pursued by state officials who are themselves pious believers, just as the British bureaucrats who foreswore a Christian assault on India were themselves Christians. He seeks to deny any necessary link between freedom of conscience and irreligion or atheism.

The East India Company conquered Bengal province away from the Mughal Empire in 1757–1764, but the company gave no assistance to missionary work there. As the EIC established ever greater control over other parts of India, it formalized a policy of noninterference in religious matters and in 1793 issued regulations that pledged to the Indian people to "preserve to them the laws of the Shaster [Shastra] and the Koran in matters to which they have been invariably applied, to protect them in the free exercise of their religion."[57] This broadminded policy derived in part from the company's military and economic considerations as a garrison state, for to interfere in local religion would surely risk, at the very least, a diversion of energies from commerce and, much more seriously, might provoke rebellion against the British. Yet this choice of conduct cannot be dismissed as only self-interested cynicism, for some eighteenth-century company officials were freebooters, romantics, or Lockeans who disdained what they saw as the narrow-mindedness of the evangelicals and had formed a favorable opinion of Indian culture. They simply did not believe that Hindus or Muslims were damned to hell for not being Christians. Despite the subsequent protest in Parliament launched by evangelicals, the noninterference policy and ban on missionary provocations was maintained until 1813, and even then Christian missionary work was restrained for another decade and a half. Younger East India Company officials in the 1830s–1850s had more sympathies with evangelicalism and gave missionaries greater freedom of movement. Indians' own resistance to proselytization, however, and the company's caution about alienating its own Indian troops and subjects, prevented any large numbers of conversions from occurring.[58] In the Great Rebellion of 1857–1858 Muslims and Hindus rose up against British rule partially because they feared a conspiracy to make them lose their caste and convert to Christianity.[59] While evangelicals managed to find a way of blaming the uprising on the neutral religious policy followed by the East India Company, many British public figures denounced missionary work as having contributed to the upheaval. As Powell points out, Benjamin Disraeli gave "our tampering with the religion of the people" as a cause of Indian "general discontent" in a speech in the House of Commons in 1857.[60] When the rebellion was put down in 1858, the British Government of India superseded the East India Company as ruler of the subcontinent, and Queen Victoria made a proclamation of religious "toleration" in India that constrained missionary audacity. Herbert Edwardes, a Punjab civil servant, was censured in 1858 for advocating open evangelization, including the introduction of the Bible into government schools, and apparently even other evangelicals in the Punjab agreed that he had been unwise.[61] 'Abdu'l-Baha was well-informed about the Indian scene, in part through his correspondence with Baha'is in Bombay and elsewhere, and he makes the pragmatic point that the British Empire certainly could not have grown so large and powerful had the British insisted on launching a new wave of crusades. (Although he approves of this one policy, elsewhere, as we shall see, both 'Abdu'l-Baha and Baha'u'llah are severely critical of European imperialism and militarism).

Returning to his theme, 'Abdu'l-Baha deplores the sway that clerics had over society in the Middle Ages, which he says led to sanguinary religious conflicts, persecution, the weakening of central state authority, and civilizational decline. He surely has in mind incidents such as the Crusades (waged in principle against Muslims but in practice also against Byzantine Christians and against European Christians branded heretics), which we know he read about in Draper's *History of the Intellectual Development of Europe*.[62] He contrasts medieval intolerance with the Enlightenment reforms of the eighteenth century:

> But when they removed these differences, persecutions, and bigotries out of their midst, and proclaimed the equal rights of all subjects and the liberty of men's consciences, the lights of glory and power arose and shone from the horizons of that kingdom in such wise that those countries made progress in every direction. . . . These are effectual and sufficient proofs that the conscience of man is sacred and to be respected; and that liberty thereof produces widening of ideas, amendment of morals, improvement of con-

duct, disclosure of the secrets of creation, and manifestation of the hidden verities of the contingent world.

Up until this point 'Abdu'l-Baha had been arguing to Iran's rulers and notables that a policy of religious freedom has the effect of strengthening the state. He now points to other benefits of religious liberty and equal rights for all citizens, including improved morality and conduct. He does not say so explicitly here, but he implies that religious liberty allows believers actively to choose their adherence and so contributes to personal morality, whereas an imposed religious monopoly detracts from it. Sociologists of religion find confirmation of this proposition, and one study shows a correlation between high rates of religious participation and the lack of a state-supported religious monopoly.[63] The benefits also involve "disclosure of the secrets of creation," that is to say, modern science, which could not really flourish until the Enlightenment reforms freed latter-day Galileos from the interference of popes. The Shi'ite clergy would have said that freedom of conscience and religious liberty destroys public morals, leads to widespread ignorance, and weakens the foundations of the state.[64] 'Abdu'l-Baha is in Middle Eastern terms making a counterintuitive argument. In fact, he says, these reforms would have the opposite of the expected effect, all along the way. Although 'Abdu'l-Baha does not name the Enlightenment, that is clearly the period in which religious liberty was established as a principle, in the French Rights of Man and the First Amendment of the U.S. Constitution. He makes one further argument about freedom of conscience, that belief and private morals are matters of personal choice, not the state's prerogatives. "Moreover, if interrogation of conscience, which is one of the private possessions of the heart and soul, take place in this world, what further recompense remains for man in the court of divine justice at the day of general resurrection? Convictions and ideas are within the scope of the comprehension of the King of kings, not of kings." 'Abdu'l-Baha concludes by observing that if all the energy that had gone into suppressing Babi belief had instead been invested in strengthening the state and in making the country prosperous, Iran would have achieved "splendor."[65]

In later years 'Abdu'l-Baha continued to maintain these ideals not only with regard to the civil state but even in respect to the Baha'i institutions themselves. Noting that early Christianity's history had been marred by schisms and persecutions of heretics over theological issues, he said that such strife in his religion had been made impossible by Baha'u'llah, because he had "appointed an interpreter (*mubayyin*) of Scripture and had established the general (*'umūmī*) House of Justice," and "had commanded that there be no interference with beliefs (*'aqā'id*) and conscience (*vuj-dān*)."[66] That is, in theory the Baha'i institutions themselves were to have no power to intervene in the expression of individual conscience with regard to religious doctrine.

In respect to the civil state 'Abdu'l-Baha argued for the irrelevance of beliefs to civil status, a stance quite different from the schema of classical Islamic jurisprudence, which ascribed status and rights in society based on religious adherence. He greatly appreciated the American Constitution. At the Central Congregational Church in Brooklyn on June 16, 1912, he said:

> Just as in the world of politics there is need for free thought, likewise in the world of religion there should be the right of unrestricted individual belief. Consider what a vast difference exists between modern democracy and the old forms of despotism. Under an autocratic government the opinions of men are not free, and development is stifled, whereas in a democracy, because thought and speech are not restricted, the greatest progress is witnessed. It is likewise true in the world of religion. When freedom of conscience, liberty of thought and right of speech prevail—that is to say, when every man according to his own idealization may give expression to his beliefs—development and growth are inevitable.[67]

At the Universalist Church Washington, D.C. on November 6, 1912, he said: "Praise be to God! The standard of liberty is held aloft in this land. You enjoy political liberty; you enjoy liberty of thought and speech, religious liberty, racial and personal liberty."[68] Shoghi Effendi, 'Abdu'l-Baha's grandson and the guardian and interpreter of the Baha'i faith, 1921–1957, wrote of Baha'i institutions that they were not to "allow the machinery of their administration to supersede the government of their respective countries."[69]

The final argument in *A Traveller's Narrative* echoes Locke, who wrote, "The care of souls cannot belong to the civil magistrate because his power consists only in outward force; but true and saving religion consists in the inward persuasion of mind, without which nothing can be acceptable to God."[70] Locke contrasted the tendency toward theocracy in Old Testament Judaism with the new dispensation of Christ, wherein power and reason are separated so that the former must not constrain the latter. This stance yields the paradox that Christian universalism is not incompatible with tolerance for diverse beliefs.[71] 'Abdu'l-Baha presents a similar picture of the Baha'i faith, as a universal religion that nevertheless eschews power and the coercion of conscience in favor of allowing personal decisions about the truth, decisions that are judged by

God alone rather than by officials of the state. This new ideal contrasts with Islamic theocracy, a contrast that parallels Locke's distinction between ancient Judaism and Christianity.

The Critique of Hegemonic Secularism

Separation of religion and state in the positive sense of providing religious liberty has been twinned in modern history with a darker phenomenon, the establishment of the tyranny of reason over religion. In revolutionary France an outright antireligious policy was adopted, in accordance with Voltaire's dictum on any form of intolerant religion, "Crush the infamous thing!" Herein the secular state usurped the place of the Church in, and strictly barred religious organizations from, many areas of life. As late as the Third Republic, in the early twentieth century, churchgoers were barred from serving in the French cabinet.

Such state hostility toward the corporate autonomy of the religious sphere in civil society also characterized Bismarck's much later drive against Roman Catholicism during the Kulturkampf, or culture wars, of 1872–1887. The German state then expelled the Jesuits, restricted citizenship rights of German Jesuits, dissolved monasteries, sought state control over the training and appointment of priests, and denied funding to bishoprics that resisted these measures.[72] Protestant observers noted the difference between Imperial Germany and the United States, with one German historian of that time writing that "for us the state is not, as it is for the Americans, a power to be contained so that the will of the individual may remain uninhibited, but rather a cultural power." Another argued that the "most essential tasks in the struggle against the clerical system could be mastered only through the positive influence of state power."[73] The policy of cultural struggle was widely and effectively resisted by lay Catholics and their institutions, and ultimately most of the repressive laws were revoked. Partially in reaction to the French and German state onslaughts, the nineteenth-century popes portrayed secular liberalism as a religious sect in its own right that was attempting to gain for itself a monopoly over state power. At its most extreme militant positivism eventuated in such policies as Atatürk's forced secularization of Turkey and Stalin's campaigns in the Soviet Union for official atheism, which led to the punishment of individuals for studying Scripture. Science and a metaphysic of materialism is here installed as the state ideology, displacing religion.

Baha'u'llah and his eldest son were strongly opposed to the militant secularism characteristic of the Jacobin French version of modernity. Baha'u'llah laments, "The vitality of men's belief in God is dying out in every
land; nothing short of His wholesome medicine can ever restore it. The
corrosion of ungodliness is eating into the vitals of human society; what
else but the Elixir of His potent Revelation can cleanse and revive it?"[74] In
his *Secret of Divine Civilization* 'Abdu'l-Baha argued for the blindness and
foolishness of modern atheism, attacking Voltaire in particular (apparently considering him more or less an atheist, though in fact he was a deist).
The arguments atheists made against religion, he says, ignored its essential
ability to unite human beings across all sorts of cleavages into a single spiritual and civilizational enterprise. The Voltairean critique focused on the
behavior of a few popes while ignoring the power of Christ; it failed to recognize that any good institution can be misused.[75] Elsewhere in the same
book 'Abdu'l-Baha explicitly refers to the Kulturkampf, condemning the
"hatreds and hostilities between Catholic religious leaders and the German government," along with the excesses of the Franco-Prussian War, the
Paris Commune, and conflict in Spain between republicans and Carlists,
as signs that Europe was "morally uncivilized."[76]

Whereas Voltairean modernity envisaged a state-backed domination of
reason over other cultural forms, exercised through the state, Baha'u'llah
foresaw reason and revelation, state and religious institution, coexisting
peaceably. In this perspective he resembled Locke and Kant more than the
French philosophes, and, indeed, anticipated in some ways the postmodernist revolt against hegemonic reason. Modern science was justified, in
Baha'u'llah's view, because it rested ultimately on the metaphysical foundations established in the ancient world by prophetic monotheism (through
the influence of the Zoroastrian and Judaic traditions), but it must not become a tool of atheism.[77] Indeed, for Baha'u'llah, revelation itself was a
manifestation of the Neoplatonic Universal Intellect. The human need for
the irruption into the world every millennium or so of the Universal Intellect via a prophetic advent derives from the finite and limited character of
human reason.[78]

Baha'u'llah approved of much in modernity. "This modernity (*in 'ahd-
i jadīd*),' he wrote, "is itself a powerful army whereby We have ordained
that the cities of the hearts be conquered in Our Name, the Mighty, the
Beloved. Our hope is that through these modern and wondrous means,
the foundation of the divine Cause will become firm and unassailable."[79]
Still, Baha'u'llah recognized that modernity has a dark side and held that
religion serves to moderate the excesses of which reason, ironically, is capa-

ble. "Consider for instance such things as liberty, civilization and the like," he says, "[even though they have gained the acceptance of the people of knowledge], they will, if carried to excess, exercise a pernicious influence upon men."[80] Elsewhere, he reaffirms this sentiment: "If carried to excess, civilization will prove as prolific a source of evil as it had been of goodness when kept within the restraints of moderation. . . . The day is approaching when its flame will devour the cities."[81] Enough in the way of silk, soap, and other industries may have been established in his neighborhood in Palestine by this time for Baha'u'llah to notice the unpleasant by-products of industrialism, but more probably he is referring to modern warfare.

'Abdu'l-Baha, like his father, sees science and technology as either beneficial or destructive, depending upon whether they are used under the guide of religious ethics or are unleashed in the service of destructive nationalisms. He justifies science and technology on pragmatic grounds, as fruits of human endeavor whereby the material condition of the world is improved. He attempts to refute nineteenth-century Muslim divines who denounced modern science as un-Islamic and forbade its adoption in the Middle East.[82] We have seen that he saw the separation of religion and state as a prerequisite for free scientific inquiry, which he praised. Ultimately, he was to put forth the principle that where religion contradicted science in scientific matters it was mere superstition, while true science could not be incompatible with reasoned religion.[83]

The experience of horrific persecutions at the hands of the Qajar state and the Shi'ite clergy (which acted in concert) contributed to Baha'u'llah's and 'Abdu'l-Baha's embrace of the principle of the separation of religion and state in the last third of the nineteenth century. They surely were among the first major religious figures in the region to do so, and to this day this position is controversial among Middle Easterners. The Baha'is' situation resembled that of the American Baptists, who also, despite their evangelicalism, strongly supported the principles enshrined in the U.S. First Amendment.

Baha'u'llah's and 'Abdu'l-Baha's views on this matter changed greatly over time. Baha'u'llah, having been close to the Qajar court and enjoying good relations with the first minister of the 1850s, Aqa Khan Nuri, probably never embraced a theocratic vision of Babism with the same fervor that some other Babis did. Still, his appeal in the 1860s to Nasiru'd-Din Shah to treat all religious communities equally, despite being phrased in the language of the "Mirrors for Princes" literature, comes as a departure from classical Muslim political thought. Earlier authors had called the shah the "shadow of God on earth" to emphasize the ruler's unrestrained sovereignty. Baha'u'llah argued that the phrase implied an impartial meting out of justice to all, regardless of their religion, so that it imposed limits on the shah's arbitrariness and his preferential treatment of Muslims. He thus turns the phrase into a constitutional slogan! In addition to the travails the Babis faced from the Muslim state, other developments probably led Baha'u'llah to adopt the principle of equality among adherents of various religions, most notably the impact of the 1856 Ottoman Reform Decree.

One witnesses a shift in the rhetorical grounding of Baha'i thought on freedom of conscience, from Baha'u'llah's earlier appeal to old Iranian ideals of universal monarchy to an increasing rapprochement with the civil rights philosophy of Western modernity. Many of 'Abdu'l-Baha's arguments in *A Traveller's Narrative* are very similar to those of Locke. It is likely that, insofar as he was a well-read Middle Eastern intellectual living at a time when there were many Ottoman, Arabic, and Persian newspapers and printed translations, 'Abdu'l-Baha knew something serious about the idea of civil rights and adopted it wholeheartedly into the Baha'i religion. The contrast between his ideals and those of conservative jurists in classical Islam was stark. In place of the descending hierarchy of true believer, protected minority, heretic and apostate, 'Abdu'l-Baha substituted "complete equality." His advocacy of freedom of religion and of conscience is far more thoroughgoing than that of either Locke or of the Ottoman Tanzimat reformers and comes closest to the ideals of the U.S. Bill of Rights.

Baha'u'llah and 'Abdu'l-Baha favored modern science in the service of social development as well, in contrast to many among the Muslim clergy who rejected these advances as heretical innovations. Nevertheless, neither Baha'u'llah nor 'Abdu'l-Baha wished to give in to modernist secularism in a wholesale manner. They continued to conduct a vigorous critique, of Enlightenment deism and disparagement of organized religion, of state repression of religion, and of science and reason gone wild, which they feared would lead to weapons of mass destruction and to environmental disaster. This simultaneous advocacy and critique of modernity was made possible by Baha'u'llah's utopian realism. The same principle is evident in his championing of constitutional monarchy in absolutist Iran and the Ottoman Empire, to which we shall now turn.

2 • Baha'u'llah and Ottoman Constitutionalism

Modernity has proven lethal to absolutist monarchies, which have seen their legitimacy undermined, their power destroyed, their symbols mocked, and occasionally their incumbents beheaded in revolution after revolution since the late eighteenth century. These changes in the rhetorical bases of political power had compelling social as well as intellectual roots. The language of divine or hereditary power and privilege increasingly contrasted with the rhetoric of achievement and reason favored by the rising industrialists and the new middle and working classes of the nineteenth century. The moral economy of premodern times broke down, to be replaced by a regime of rights (as in the U.S. Bill of Rights or the French Declaration of the Rights of Man), demanded not only by the bourgeoisie but also by intellectuals and workers, though each emphasized the priority of some rights over others.[1]

Two cautions are in order here. First, the shift from absolutist to more democratic forms of governance characteristic of modernity did not usually weaken the state. Indeed, in the United States democracy required a decennial census, which is to say, a closer surveillance of the people in some respects. The ability of the state to reconnoiter and to discipline its citizens has on the whole increased, leading to a constant reflexive interplay between government officials seeking to establish a national security state and grassroots organizations of citizens seeking greater freedoms and more democracy.[2] Still, the ideological and rhetorical foundations of absolute monarchy have in all but a few instances decisively crumbled, and few would now argue that it makes no difference whether one is judged by the whim of an unelected monarch or receives due process from a popularly elected and representative state. Second, it should be kept in mind that parliamentary forms of government remained relatively rare in the eastern hemisphere until the past century and a half. In 1850 China, Japan, Siam, Russia, Spain, Austria, Morocco, Hyderabad (India), Bukhara, Iran, and the Ottoman Empire, for instance, were absolute monarchies. Although Imperial France and Germany had elected legislatures, these were often weak in the face of powerful monarchs. Of course, Great Britain and Holland were constitutional monarchies, but even the British and Dutch Empires (including vast swaths of Asia and Africa) were largely ruled by the fiat of viceroys and colonial bureaucrats, and only in the metropole were parliamentary liberties enjoyed, mainly by propertied white males.

In the region with which we are most directly concerned, the Middle East, signs of change began to emerge in the mid-nineteenth century. The growth of stronger states in the southern and eastern Mediterranean during the nineteenth century, bolstered by increased tax revenues from the spread of cash cropping, by the influx of foreign capital, and by better communications and transportation technology, contributed to the rise of movements demanding representative government. As the state proved able to affect the population in a much more direct way than had earlier been the case, the groups thus affected mobilized against absolutism. Moreover, the rhetoric of popular sovereignty that developed in France and the United States was available, through translations and modern schools, to Middle Easterners for appropriation to their own purposes. The Young Ottomans in Istanbul in the 1860s and 1870s and the 'Urabi movement in the Ottoman vassal state of Egypt in 1881–1882 both demanded popular representation.

As suggested above, it is not only the modern logic of reason that impelled these movements but rather an increasing desire among individuals and local groupings to have a say in their government. It was not a general will they wanted to exercise but a specific local one. Seldom were demands for parliamentarism in the Middle East rooted very strongly in the Enlightenment. Popular sentiment and the writings of intellectuals alike sought a basis for consultative government in Islam, and the demand for radical change was often clothed in utopian rhetoric. Despite the tendency of French intellectuals to subsume parliamentarism under the sign of reason, historians have in fact noted a frequent link between millenarianism and democratic or populist thought. They have recognized the importance of chiliastic ideas in the English Revolution of the seventeenth century and spoken of a "civil millennialism" that tinged the republicanism of American dissidents and revolutionaries. Millenarian thinkers such as the English preacher Joseph Priestly and the French prophetess Suzette Labrousse saw an apocalyptic significance even in a largely secular upheaval like the French Revolution.[3] The demand for parliamentary governance, a requirement of reason for some, more resembled a utopian and apocalyptic project for the little people, for its ideals involved a seemingly miraculous reversal of the social order in which not the lineages of kings but the votes of the commoner decided the contest for political power.

I want to explore the circumstances under which Baha'u'llah developed a commitment to representative government and to discover whether his social teachings and his religious ones are related in some way. Can we link his precocious championing of democracy and his millenarian ideas?[4] He saw himself, after all, as a universal messiah, as the promised one of the Jews, the symbolic return of Christ for Christians and Muslims, the Shah-Bahram of the Zoroastrians.[5] His advent would surely turn the world upside down. Was the coming of a more egalitarian society one manner in which the prevailing order would be upset? For democracy would represent a massive change for so hierachical a society as the nineteenth-century Middle East.

I will present evidence of a convergence between the ideas of the democratic Young Ottomanist movement in Istanbul and those of the Baha'i movement. Some research on the link between millenarianism and nationalism in Iran has been devoted to the tiny Azali sect of Babism, which produced some prominent radical intellectuals in the late nineteenth and early twentieth century.[6] Yet Browne estimated that by 1909 for every hundred Baha'is there were only three or four Azalis (yielding two to four thousand if our estimates for Baha'is above are in the correct range); moreover, Azali intellectuals who embraced modern ideas beginning in the 1890s on had often left their faith and become secularists.[7] The Baha'is were therefore demographically much more significant, and, as I will show, more united at a much earlier time on this issue.

Sometimes Western scholars have misconstrued Baha'i attitudes in the period 1866–1892. For instance, the Hungarian Orientalist Ignaz Goldziher, in an otherwise penetrating discussion, concluded from the criticism made by Baha'u'llah of aspects of liberty (*ḥurriyyah*) that Baha'is were not in the liberal camp.[8] Goldziher made the correct observation that the Baha'i scriptures contain a moral critique of modern liberty but failed to see the simultaneous affirmation of political liberty. If by "liberals" Goldziher meant persons opposed to absolutism, it should be pointed out that Baha'u'llah advocated representative government and freedom of conscience, and that he did so at some risk, since in the absolutist nineteenth-century Middle East, as in many parts of Europe, this advocacy was a punishable offence under the law. In order to understand Baha'u'llah's views of liberalism and absolutism, I would suggest that we need a more nuanced and contextualized understanding of what he meant by ḥurriyyah.[9]

The "Tablet to the Kings" and Constitutionalism

The Middle East was undergoing great changes in the 1860s, as the Baha'i faith began. In 1861 the Ottoman vassal state of Tunisia put a sort of constitution in place—the first of its kind in the Muslim realms, and the Ottoman province of Egypt instituted a chamber of deputies (*Majlis Shūrā an-Nuwwāb*) for the first time in 1866, forming a representative body that would in the succeeding decade and a half attempt to become a full-blown parliament. In Middle Eastern salons and the press intellectuals and officials debated the merits of constitutionalism. Many observers attributed the immense power of Great Britain, a constitutional monarchy that had defeated Napoleon early in the century and then Russia in the Crimean War of 1854–1856, to its liberal political institutions. The Ottomans had instituted a strong cabinet that somewhat offset the power of the sultan. The reforms implemented in the vassal states of Tunisia and Egypt raised the question of whether Istanbul itself should not move even further away from absolute monarchy. These pressing and ubiquitous questions arose in Baha'u'llah's milieu of officials, intellectuals, and other dissident exiles in Edirne and then Akka.

With regard to the question of whether governments rule by divine fiat or by the consent of the ruled, Baha'u'llah's views were complex and changed a good deal over time. His participation in the Babi movement of the 1840s indicates that he then believed there were times when it was legitimate to stand up to the government, and he was clearly willing to fight at Fort Shaykh Tabarsi in 1848. There were times, even later, when he refused to obey government orders. In fall of 1863 Baha'u'llah had been received by high Ottoman officials in Istanbul but declined to curry their favor. In response, the Ottomans bowed to Iranian pressure by exiling Baha'u'llah to the backwater of Rumelia in Turkish-speaking Europe (he may as well have been sent to Bulgaria). Baha'u'llah at first refused to leave Istanbul and wanted to make a stand against the Ottomans, seeking either to overturn the sultan's edict or to attain martyrdom when troops came to arrest the Babis. But such a plan required unanimity, and when Azal de-

clined to go along it fell through.[10] The episode suggests that, despite his later attempt to move the Babis into the political mainstream, even after his declaration he recognized that there were times when the governed had to defy the state. In part this conviction derived from Baha'u'llah's Babi background and his reversal of society's normal hierarchies. In the Surah of God (*Sūratu'llāh*, circa spring 1866), Baha'u'llah writes that a subject is better than a thousand rulers, a subordinate is more exalted than a myriad of superiors, and one oppressed is more excellent than a city full of tyrants.[11] This inchoate Babi defiance, however, soon became channeled into a more structured belief in consultative governance.

As we saw in the last chapter, in fall-winter 1867 Baha'u'llah produced a wide-ranging statement, entitled "Surat al-Muluk" ("Tablet to the Kings"), addressing in a general way the political and religious leaders of the time but including apostrophes to Sultan Abdülaziz.[12] In his "Tablet to the Kings" Baha'u'llah declared that he had not come to wreak corruption in the Ottoman lands but to elevate the cause of the sultan by giving him good counsel. Baha'u'llah here made public his complete break with the proactive violence promoted by radical Babis such as 'Azim Turshizi and Subh-i Azal. Still, he did not offer to give way on any matters of principle and continued to advocate reforms at variance with state policy. He desired, by recognizing the legitimacy of the civil state, to achieve the position of spiritual counselor for it. He complained that the sultan's ministers and courtiers had spurned his counsel, and he urged Abdülaziz to retain some autonomy from them.[13] Baha'u'llah advised the Ottoman sultan not to pay his ministers and aides so well that they would be enabled to "lay up riches for themselves" or to be "numbered with the extravagant." He attacked the vast extremes of wealth he witnessed in the Ottoman imperial capital, where destitute rural immigrants lived near rich landlords, tax farmers, and import-export merchants. In his words, "We observed upon Our arrival in the City" (Constantinople or Istanbul) that some of its inhabitants "were possessed of an affluent fortune and lived in the midst of excessive riches, while others were in dire want and abject poverty. This ill beseemeth thy sovereignty, and is unworthy of thy rank."[14] The huge wealth inequalities visible in a Mediterranean city like Istanbul during the incipient Age of Capital shocked and dismayed Baha'u'llah.[15] He correctly saw that government officials were among the chief exploiters of the people, amassing private fortunes from their public service, and warned the sultan not to "aggrandize thy ministers at the expense of thy subjects. Fear the sighs of the poor and of the upright in heart who, at every break of day, bewail their plight, and be unto them a benignant sovereign." He calls the poor the ruler's "treasures on the earth" and urges him to safeguard them from those who wish to rob and expropriate them. "Inquire into their affairs, and ascertain, every year, nay every month, their condition, and be not of them that are careless of their duty."[16] Not only do the rich owe an absolute responsibility to the poor, but so does the government. The state is charged with intervening against extremes of wealth and poverty and continually monitoring the welfare of the subjects. In the context of these remarks it seems likely that Baha'u'llah meant for the sultan to take the counsel of more than just a few ministers, that he already had in mind a somewhat populist project.

Among the offending ministers was, prominently, Mehmed Emin Âli Pasha, who had become first minister for the fifth time in February 1867. Davison says of this politician,

He was of a high natural intelligence; though shy and reserved, he was notably witty; he acquired a mastery of French; and from the date of the [1856] Paris peace conference he enjoyed a European reputation as an outstanding diplomatist of perfect manners and rare integrity. Among his countrymen he became unpopular. He was in fact secretive, solemn, and overbearing, and was regarded as vindictive. During his final Grand Vizierate 'Abd al-'Aziz would have been glad to get rid of him, but recognized Âli's standing in Europe to be such that he could not afford to; and Âli profited by this security to insist on his correct treatment by the sultan, on his right to have all governmental matters of importance to be referred to him, and on the immunity of ministers and officials from banishment (in the bad old way) except after due trial.[17]

In the "Tablet to the Kings" Baha'u'llah still speaks of the need for the monarch to take an active role in ruling, but only after consulting able ministers. Perhaps he feared the reports emanating from Istanbul, that Âli Pasha was making himself a sort of dictator and shunting the monarch aside altogether.

In the same work Baha'u'llah for the first time invokes the need for consultation in government, as opposed to unadorned absolutism, advising the sultan to gather together his ablest ministers and consult with them (the verb is *shāwara*) on affairs.[18] Baha'u'llah's advocacy of a powerful role for ministers in high-level decision making probably had its ultimate roots in the reformist ideas of the early nineteenth-century Iranian prime minister Qa'im-Maqam, to whom his father had been close.[19] "Consultation," as an ideal, of course, was innocuous enough. It occurs in the Qur'an, where even the Prophet is instructed, with regard to the believers, "Take counsel (*shāwirhum*) with them in the affair" (Q. 3:153/159). And taking counsel among the believers is considered a virtue along with forgiveness and prayer: "Their affair being counsel (*shūrā*) among them" (Q. 42:36). The more secular "Mirrors for Princes," or guidebooks on how to govern, also invoke the term. The medieval *Qabusnamih* advises the king to consult with his grand vizier, who serves as his rational faculty.[20] Yet the word took on new connotations with the advent of modernity. The Iranian intellectual Mirza Salih Shirazi in his famed travelogue and description of Europe referred to the French parliament as *mashvirat-khānih*, or house of consultation.[21] Practical meanings were ascribed to "consultation" in the nineteenth-century Ottoman Empire, of limitations on the monarch's absolute power, at first through appointed councils (*meclis, meclis-i şura*) and later through an increasing emphasis on cabinet government, wherein the majority view was to win out. During the Reform, or Tanzimat, period a

Supreme Council of Judicial Ordinances was among the more powerful such consultative bodies. In 1868 the latter was transformed into the State Consultation Council (Şura-i Devlet); the Turkish phrase contains a word from the same root as the verb *shāwar*a, which Baha'u'llah used.[22] Thus, Baha'u'llah's use of the word *counsel* at this point (late 1867) seems largely compatible with the Tanzimat reforms as they were then being practiced. Nevertheless, his stated conviction that a subject is better than a thousand rulers and one oppressed is better than a thousand tyrants suggests that he had a much more democratic outlook than the top-down, bureaucratically organized Tanzimat reformers.

It is not clear whether a copy of the letter was actually delivered to the Sublime Porte. If so, Sultan Abdülaziz and his courtiers decisively rebuffed Baha'u'llah's approach only a few months later when, in reaction to Azali complaints and the importuning of the Iranian ambassador, they ordered him and his companions exiled from Edirne to Akka. Inevitably, the first minister, Âli Pasha, and the foreign minister, Fuad Pasha, were intimately involved in this decision, which affected the Ottoman Empire's relations with Iran and potentially (because of the issues of freedom of conscience it raised) with the European powers. Fuad and Âli, both committed to a powerful reorganization of the empire from the top down, had in common with the reactionary and superstitious Sultan Abdülaziz only an autocratic temperament. Although their motives may have been different from his, lying in modernist worries about a politically vigorous mahdist movement rather than in concern about heresy, their decision was the same. In his firman to the governor of Akka the sultan wrote:

> Mirza Husayn 'Ali and a group of his companions have been sentenced to life imprisonment in the fortress of Akka. When they have arrived at that fortress and been delivered into your custody, incarcerate them within the fortress for the rest of their lives. Institute complete surveillance over them, to ensure that they mix socially with no one. Your officials must inspect them with great care, such that they not be allowed to move from place to place. They must remain always under close supervision.[23]

The Ottoman state had clearly decided to silence Baha'u'llah for all time, in the most rigorous fashion possible short of actual execution.

The governor of Edirne 1866–1869 was Mehmed Hurşid Pasha, a progressive official close to reformers such as Midhat Pasha, who later served as undersecretary to the prime minister (essentially, as the interior minister) during the First Constitutional Period, 1876–1878.[24] The governor, who had come to admire Baha'u'llah, tried to intervene on his behalf, according

to eyewitness Aqa Husayn Ashchi. When that failed, Hurşid Pasha, embarrassed at the injustice being done, absented himself from Edirne on vaca-
tion, leaving affairs in the hands of a colonel (*miralay*).[25]

Baha'u'llah was understandably furious over the Ottoman government's
decree. Initially he was to be sent to Akka virtually alone, but he insisted
that his household and companions be allowed to accompany him. His
request was at first refused by the sultan. When the major (*binbaşi*) with
whom he was dealing reported back to him that this negative response was
the "decree of the sultan," Baha'u'llah replied with words to this effect:
"What is the royal decree? The decree is my decree; now go and send a
telegram."[26] This time the request was granted, but the defiant tone
adopted by the Persian prophet demonstrates once again that there continued to be circumstances in which he refused obedience to what he saw
as an unjust state.

Baha'u'llah speaks of how on August 12, 1868, he and his companions,
men, women, and children, were abruptly surrounded by soldiers, who
kept them under tight surveillance as they began the journey into yet another exile. In a letter (*Sūrat ar-Ra'is*) written at way stations on the road
to Gallipoli, Baha'u'llah apostrophizes the first minister, Âli Pasha, adopting the stern voice of an Old Testament prophet and pronouncing dire
jeremiads concerning the future of the Ottoman Empire:

> The day is approaching when the Land of Mystery [Edirne and Rumelia],
> and what is beside it shall be changed, and shall pass out of the hands of the
> king, and commotion shall appear, and the voice of lamentation shall be
> raised, and the evidences of mischief shall be revealed on all sides, and con-
> fusion shall spread by reason of that which hath befallen these captives at the
> hands of the hosts of oppression. The course of things shall be altered, and
> conditions shall wax so grievous, that the very sands on the desolate hills will
> moan, and the trees on the mountain will weep, and blood will flow out of
> all things. Then wilt thou behold the people in sore distress.[27]

Soon after his arrival in Akka Baha'u'llah wrote another letter to Âli
Pasha, this one more dismissive than apocalyptic, in which he compares
all the pomp and circumstance of the Sublime Porte to the fleeting illusion created by a puppet show: all the finery in the end is unceremoni-
ously tossed in a trunk and exits the stage. I think it significant of Baha'u'llah's commitment to the rule of law and to more democratic procedures that he complains in this missive about being the victim of an absolutist fiat. "It was incumbent," he wrote, "that an assembly (*majlis*) be con-
vened wherein this youth might have been gathered together with the

learned men of the age, and it could have become clear what these servants' crime was."[28] Only an entire assemblage of learned individuals could have come to a fair decision, and then only by means of a thorough inquiry into the truth.

In his "Lawh-i Fu'ad" ("Tablet of Fuad," spring 1869) Baha'u'llah branded Sultan Abdülaziz a tyrant and predicted that social unrest and divisions would soon overtake the empire. Of Fuad Davison writes that

> he was a convinced westernizer. He worked on many of the reforms of the later Tanzimat period. He may have favoured representative government, though he was in no hurry to achieve it. His main objective was preservation of the Ottoman Empire through diplomacy and reform. He loved high office, but was not so jealous and grudging as 'Ali, and rather bolder in innovation. His honesty has been impugned, especially as regards gifts from Isma'il [Pasha of Egypt].[29]

Fuad Pasha, one of those responsible for the exile, died in Nice of heart trouble on February 12, 1869. In response to the minister's death Baha'u'llah wrote, "Soon will We dismiss the one [Âli Pasha] who was like unto him, and will lay hold on their Chief [the sultan] who ruleth the land."[30] He boasted that this tablet had shaken the foundations of the sultan, whom he referred to as al-'Uzza, the name of a pagan Arab goddess condemned in the Qur'an (this is a pun on the element 'Azīz, "Mighty," in the sultan's name, which is from the same consonantal root).[31]

Baha'u'llah was not alone in being outraged at Fuad's autocracy, or even in being exiled because he was seen as a threat to it. Mardin notes that among the early Young Ottomans of 1868 "Sarıyerli Hoca Sadık Effendi . . . incurred the disfavor of the Porte [Ottoman Sultan] because he mentioned the evils of oppression in his sermons. Because of these sermons Sadık Effendi was accused of favoring the Young Ottomans and was exiled to [Akka,] Syria." Mardin goes on to paint a fascinating miniature portrait of the political and cultural scene in Istanbul in late 1868 and early 1869:

> A contemporary French periodical made the following comment on this banishment: 'It is not only among the Christian populations that there reigns at this moment a lively and deep-seated agitation. This is much more prevalent among the Moslem populations. . . . The discontent of the Moslems is mostly evidenced by the daring shown in religious publications against the governments of Âli and Fuad Paşa. . . . Ulamas who were delivering sermons on the Ramazan . . . in the presence of the sultan have dared state to his face that he would lose his empire and his people.' After having described the saintliness of Sadik Effendi, the author of the article added:

'Such is the man that the government of Âli Paşa has just arrested and interned at the fortress of St. John of Acre. For he preached in Istanbul [the merits of] democracy, liberty, equality, brotherhood between all men, be they Christian or Moslem, Greek or Ottoman.[32]

This episode obviously provides further context to Baha'u'llah's "Tablet of Fuad." It suggests, for one thing, that predictions of the sultan's downfall, such as Baha'u'llah made in that tablet, were not unusual but rather were commonplaces of the religious discourse of the time. It shows how a mosque preacher at the time might get enough Western education to be considered a member of the effendi (Westernized secretary) class, and how such men were mixing an Islamic critique of what they saw as Fuad and Âli's extreme Westernization with an Enlightenment critique of their top-down, highly authoritarian approach to government. The French periodical describing Sadık Effendi's exile to the fortress of Akka is dated February 28, 1869. It seems to me almost certain that he interacted with the Baha'is also imprisoned in the fortress, and while Baha'u'llah had his own reasons to condemn Fuad Pasha, his dialogue with Young Ottoman thought of the time is part of the picture. Baha'u'llah later explained further concerning the "Tablet of Fuad":

> This tablet was revealed when Fuad Pasha was the foreign minister of the Ottoman Empire. He had (earlier) returned to his home base, and became the cause of the recent crisis and of our own exile from Rumelia to Acre. Two individuals were, after the sultan, supreme chief (*ra'īs-i kull*): One was Fuad Pasha and the other was Âli Pasha. Sometimes the one was first minister, and the other foreign minister, and sometimes the other way around. In that tablet (God), may his majesty be glorified, says: "We shall depose the one who was like him and seize their prince, who rules the lands; and I am the glorious, the mighty."[33]

In letters written in the early Akka period Baha'u'llah describes in stark terms the horrible experience of being confined with about seventy other Baha'is in the Ottoman barracks at the fortress, speaking of the poor food and tainted water, the way the prisoners' health declined and they became skin and bones, the lack of water for bathing, and the forced isolation from Iranian Baha'is who attempted to visit the town, which Baha'u'llah decried as the "most desolate of cities."[34] We know that most of the prisoners became ill of malaria or dysentery and that three of them perished from the unhealthy conditions of their prison.[35]

Baha'u'llah recognized his virtual solitary confinement at the fortress in Akka as a deliberate attempt on the part of the Ottoman and Iranian states to destroy him and his religion, and he thought it abetted by the indifference of the entire Crimean system of European powers. He says defiantly, "When we arrived in the Prison, we desired to send to the monarchs the epistles of their Lord, the master of men, that they might know that tribulations have not deprived God of His sovereignty."[36] After his arrival in Akka he continued to write individual letters to the rulers of the world—including Napoleon III, Queen Victoria, the tsar of Russia, and the pope, in which he announced himself as the promised one of all religions and set forth the needed global and national reforms he foresaw.[37] Despite the sultan's instructions, the Baha'is managed to find ways of getting letters out of the fortress, sometimes inside the hat of a friendly visiting physician. As we have discovered, a major theme of the epistles to the Muslim rulers was the acceptance in the new Baha'i religion of a separation of religion and state, the legitimacy of the secular state, and the abstention of Baha'is from violent sedition. Although these epistles do not betray the wrath evident in the "Tablet of Fuad," they are characterized by a novel emphasis on the need for the monarch to withdraw from active rule in favor of competent ministers and parliamentarians. Perhaps this new concern derived from his unfortunate experience with the modified absolutism of the Tanzimat type, which he believed had committed a great wrong in regard to him and his religion. Whatever the reasons, his social message took an increasingly radical-reformist turn, and the new program placed the Baha'is somewhat in the same camp as progressive Ottoman dissidents for whom the Tanzimat reforms had not gone far enough.

Soon after his arrival in Akka Baha'u'llah wrote two letters bearing on monarchy. In one he says that it is a great shame (*bisyār ḥayf*) for the like of these persons (kings) to be burdened by weighty affairs and they would be gaining for themselves more leisure and repose if they gave over the reins of government into the hands of trustworthy, wise ('āqilih) souls.[38] This advice is couched in the court etiquette of the traditional "Mirrors for Princes" literature, but no amount of politeness could disguise its implication of constitutional monarchy, which would have been anathema to both Sultan Abdülaziz and Nasiru'd-Din Shah, not to mention Napoleon III and the kaiser. At around the same time, in a tablet to Shaykh Salman, a follower in Iran, Baha'u'llah said, "Among the signs of the maturity of the world is that no one will agree to bear the burdens of autocratic rule. Sovereignty will remain with no one volunteering to bear it alone. Those will be the days when Reason [*'aql*] will become manifest among humankind. Only in order to proclaim the cause of God and to promulgate his religion will any soul shoulder this crushing burden."[39] This passage shows that Baha'u'llah now unequivocally thought absolutist monarchy would completely die out, and he here gave only two conditions for the survival of monarchy in any form. The first was that the monarch share the burden of governing with others rather than attempting it all alone (*wāḥdahu*); the other was that the sovereign become a Baha'i and employ his or her prominence to spread the new religion. This passage assumes that the only good monarchy is a constitutional one, and that such authoritarian despotism will be replaced by the reign of human reason. Elsewhere, he wrote, "From two ranks amongst men power hath been seized: kings and ecclesiastics."[40]

In the Edirne period Baha'u'llah had already stated that a good king ruled consultatively, a sentiment in accord with his lifelong dislike for arbitrary government, deriving both from his background in the Iranian bureaucratic class and his own family's experiences. Early in the Akka period he widened his political horizons to include parliamentary government as the specific form of consultation that he favored. Iranian travelers had described the British parliament to their readers back home for over a century, so well-read Iranians knew something about representative government.[41] The Baha'i turn in this direction converged with several other dissident movements of the time. A group of intellectuals, mainly translators and journalists, began a secret society called the Patriotic Alliance in Istanbul in 1865 that criticized Âli Pasha and Fuad Pasha for subservience to the European powers and for ruling autocratically. A high official from the viceregal family of Egypt, Mustafa Fazil Pasha, then out of power, published an open letter to the sultan in 1866, denouncing corruption and pleading for political liberalization. As noted above, in the same year his brother, Isma'il Pasha, governor of Egypt, created a Chamber of Deputies in that Ottoman vassal state. In 1867 Mustafa Fazil met with the young intellectuals to form the Young Ottoman Society, which decided to publish its newspaper, the *Muhbir*, from London to avoid censorship. From August 31, 1867, the editor, Ali Suavi, openly advocated the establishment of a national representative body, the exclusion of foreign influence from the Ottoman Empire, and reform along Islamic and Ottoman lines.[42]

About a year later, in June of 1868, another expatriate liberal journal was begun by Namık Kemal, also a Young Ottoman. These newspapers, smuggled back into the Ottoman Empire, apparently enjoyed a wide circulation. Significantly, Namık Kemal challenged the notion that the high state councils favored by the Tanzimat bureaucrats could legitimately be referred to as consultative (şura), insisting that only a national assembly or parliament could fulfill that role and establish general liberty.[43] Of this linguistic shift Lewis notes,

> The most important of the organisational progeny of the Ottoman *medjlis-i shūrā* [Council of Consultation] was the Ottoman parliament. The link to the earlier councils appears both in the Ottoman name for the parliament, *medjlis-i 'umūmī* [General Assembly] and in the adoption . . . of the concepts of *shūrā* and *meshweret* [consultation] to refer to parliamentary government.[44]

The Young Ottoman movement exercised a general influence on Iranian thinkers resident in Istanbul, including Iranian ambassador Mirza Husayn Khan Mushiru'd-Dawlih himself.[45]

One reform-minded Iranian expatriate in Istanbul, Mirza Malkum Khan (1833–1908), was in contact with the Young Ottomans and wrote for the London-based newspapers. Malkum, an Armenian convert to Islam, had studied in Paris, 1843–1852. He then returned to Tehran work for four years as a translator for the Iranian government. In 1858–1859 he began giving serious thought to Iranian reform and wrote a tract called the "Unseen Pamphlet," which called for a move away from absolutism toward councils and other forms of consultation. In 1860 he founded a reformist organization loosely based on Western freemasonry, which he called the House of Forgetfulness (*Faramūshkhānih*), but only a year later Nasiru'd-Din Shah angrily disbanded it and exiled Malkum to Baghdad. Malkum Khan had once sought refuge with Baha'u'llah in Baghdad from the wrath of the shah and probably knew Baha'is in Istanbul.[46]

Baha'u'llah's stance differed from that of the Young Ottomans not only in his lack of faith in clerical jurisprudence as the solution to all ills but also in his millenarianism. For the Young Ottomans constitutionalism resolved the problem of legitimating Muslim governance in the absence of the Prophet. For Baha'u'llah parliamentary rule was the sign and instrument of a new prophetic advent. He repeatedly linked chiliastic concerns with democratic themes, showing the way in which he saw his appearance as a world messiah to have turned the world upside down. He melded four themes together in his epistles to the rulers. First, he announced himself as the fulfillment of the millenarian hopes of all the world religions. Second, he expressed his advocacy of political democracy both directly and through apocalyptic imagery. Third, he insisted on the duty of the state to care for the poor and to provide them with essential services. He linked this principle to his fourth, the need for international cooperation. He believed that there would be much smaller military budgets and reduced taxes on the poor if the world's major states would implement the principle of collective security.

Baha'u'llah's letter to Queen Victoria, written sometime during his first year of banishment to Akka, stands out in combining all four of these themes in one letter. He began by proclaiming himself, in essence, the return of Christ: "All that hath been mentioned in the Gospel hath been fulfilled. The land of Syria hath been honoured by the footsteps of its Lord."[47] What are the social consequences, in his view, of this advent? We may surmise them from his concentration on social reforms of an egalitarian nature. He singled out Queen Victoria for praise on two counts. He first commended her for abolishing the slave trade, saying that slavery was also forbidden in his religion. (It was still practiced in most of the Middle East.) Second, he congratulated her on having "entrusted the reins of counsel into the hands of the people [*awda'ti zimāma al-mushāwarati bi ayādī al-jumhūr*]."[48] He added, "Thou, indeed, hast done well, for thereby the foundations of the edifice of thine affairs will be strengthened, and the hearts of all that are beneath thy shadow, whether high or low, will be tranquillized."

Although Baha'u'llah spoke only of the "counsel" offered to the queen by the people, he clearly was using the word in the new sense of representative government. But what had Queen Victoria done to warrant this praise? She hardly initiated the British parliamentary system. The reference must have been to the Reform Act of 1867, which greatly extended the franchise, so that it now included even some urban union workers. In the new postadvent world, he was saying, the voice of the ordinary folk would be heard in the halls of state. Although *jumhūr* could be used in several ways in Arabic in the 1860s, the word had connotations of what we would now call democracy. A writer of the time could use it as an abstract noun to denote "democracy" or "republicanism" but also could employ it to refer to a concrete republic or democratic country. Such words remained fluid in the nineteenth century. Baha'u'llah seems to have used the word *jumhūr* here in its older sense of "the populace," making it clear that he was not speaking of oligarchy. That he intended by the word *mushāwarah*, or consultation, a parliamentary form of government is made even clearer by his subsequent discussion of the duties of members of parliament (which he refers to by the terms *al-majma'* and *al-majlis*).[49]

Baha'u'llah's attitude to other Western forms of government differed starkly from his stance toward Britain's. He disapproved of Napoleon III (r. 1852–1870), partially because this ruler had neglected to have his consuls respond to his letter announcing himself as the world messiah and asking the French to put pressure on the Ottomans to stop their persecution of the Baha'is. The French Empire was deeply involved in Middle Eastern affairs because of its North African colonies and had in the 1860s intervened in what is now Lebanon and Syria to protect the interests of the minority Christian population. Baha'u'llah instructed the emperor to have his priests cease ringing the church bells in anticipation of Christ's second coming and urged the monks to issue from their cloisters, since Baha'u'llah was himself that advent. He taunted Napoleon III for having boasted of his compassion toward the oppressed when he joined Great Britain and Austria in the Crimean War (1854–1856) against the Russians, who had invaded Ottoman territory (it was common knowledge that the French emperor had little use for the Ottomans or other Muslims and was half-hearted about defending them). Napoleon's indifference to the plight of the Baha'is, Baha'u'llah said, showed decisively the falsity of that boast. He added, "For what thou has done, thy kingdom shall be thrown into confusion, and thine empire shall pass from thy hands, as a punishment for what thou hast wrought."[50] This letter was smuggled out of the Akka prison and delivered to Cesar Catafagu, son of the French consul in Akka, who translated it into French and sent it on to Paris. Of course, Napoleon III went down to defeat before the Prussians at Sedan only a year later (September 1870), an event that much added to Baha'u'llah's prophetic charisma among Iranians who had read the widely circulated 1869 letter to the emperor. Catafagu himself became a Baha'i on seeing the prophecy of Napoleon III's fall fulfilled.[51]

Later, around 1873, Baha'u'llah apostrophized Kaiser Wilhelm I (r. 1861–1888) in his *Most Holy Book* (*al-Kitab al-aqdas*), warning that the same fate that he inflicted on Napoleon could befall him. He added, "O banks of the Rhine! We have seen you covered with gore, inasmuch as the swords of retribution were drawn against you; and you shall have another turn. And We hear the lamentations of Berlin, though she be today in conspicuous glory."[52] The kaiser offended Baha'u'llah not through hostility or indifference toward the Baha'i faith, as "Napoleon the Little" had done, but on account of his militaristic pride.

Also in the *Most Holy Book* Baha'u'llah denounces the absolutist rule of Sultan Abdülaziz in no uncertain terms. Apostrophizing Istanbul, Baha'u'llah declares, "The throne of tyranny hath, verily, been established upon thee," and he complains that "we behold in thee the foolish ruling over the wise, and darkness vaunting itself against the light." He says that he hears from the capital the hooting of the owl, a symbol of desolation, and prophesies that "thy daughters and thy widows and all the kindreds that dwell within thee shall lament."[53] Had this book fallen into the wrong hands early on, Baha'u'llah could easily have been executed for his open denunciation of Sultan Abdülaziz as a tyrant. Such statements were quite illegal and even capital offenses.

In the same work Baha'u'llah addressed "Tehran" (i.e., Iran), predicting that "affairs within you will undergo a revolution, and you will be ruled by a democracy of the people" (*sawfa tanqalibu fiki al-umūru wa yaḥkumu 'alayki jumhūrun min an-nās*).[54] In his letter four or five years earlier to Queen Victoria Baha'u'llah had commended the parliamentary form of government, but here he went even further and spoke of popular sovereignty. The word he used for "the people," *an-nās*, indicates the ordinary people and suggests that he had a genuine democracy in mind, not a parliamentary oligarchy. Ayalon has shown that *jumhūr* by this time could bear the meaning of "a democracy" or "a republic," and it seems redundant in the above sentence for it to mean only "the masses," since "the people (*an-nās*)" are mentioned in their own right as the agent of rule. The statement likely indicates a vision of Iran as a democracy, governed by the people themselves.

Baha'u'llah, then, saved his dire predictions and apocalyptic imagery for undemocratic states (as noted above, Napoleon III and Bismarck handily outmaneuvered their generally weak legislatures).[55] On the whole, these states also showed the least interest in protecting freedom of conscience for Baha'is in the Middle East. Although he apostrophized the presidents of the republics in America in his *Most Holy Book*, he simply advised them to "bind ye the broken with the hands of justice, and crush the oppressor who flourisheth with the rod of the commandments of your Lord, the Ordainer, the All-Wise."[56] As with Britain, Baha'u'llah made no sanguinary predictions about the American republics and simply hoped that they would prove just toward the oppressed. His letter to Tsar Alexander II (d. 1881) is not as warm as one might expect, given that the Russians extended some help to Baha'u'llah when he was imprisoned in 1852 (his brother-in-law was employed in the Russian legation in Tehran). The Russians had, however, taken territory away from Iran in 1811–1813 and in 1826–1828, had launched a war of naked aggression against the Ottoman Balkans, and only been restrained from further incursions on Muslim lands by the 1856 Treaty of Paris that ended the Crimean War. Moreover, the tsar ruled as an absolute monarch. While expressing his gratitude for the help he had received from the Russians in 1852, Baha'u'llah warned the tsar, "Beware lest ye barter away this sublime station."[57]

In general, Baha'u'llah singled out for praise constitutional monarchies and republics and foresaw toppled thrones, revolutions, or rivers of blood in Bonapartist France and the absolutist states of Prussia, the Ottoman Empire, and Iran. These changes, in his view, were intimately connected with his own messianic advent. He wrote in 1873, "The world order has been upset through the influence of this most great Order [an-nazm al-a'zam]. A change has been introduced into its organization [or constitution] through this novelty—the like of which mortal eyes have never witnessed."[58] I take this passage to suggest that the messianic advent not only turns the world upside down spiritually, but politically as well. The Arabic word at-tartib could also bear the meaning of "constitution" in the nineteenth century, so that readers may have read this passage to say that an alteration had been introduced into the organic laws governing society.[59]

For Baha'u'llah the term hurriyyah could be deconstructed into two warring significations: political freedom, which was good, and moral license, which was bad. The word thus carried the additional connotations of antinomianism, abandonment or persecution of religion, and, perhaps, political nihilism. Middle Eastern authors often attributed precisely these attributes to 1789. A typical Ottoman report on the French Revolution said,

> When the revolution became more intense, none took offence at the closing of churches, the killing and expulsion of monks, and the abolition of religion and doctrine: they set their hearts on equality and freedom, through which they hoped to attain perfect bliss in this world, in accordance with the lying teachings disseminated among the common people by this pernicious crew.[60]

Many authors writing in Persian, whether in British-influenced India or in Iran itself, took a similarly dim view of the French Revolution.[61] Since Middle Eastern writers of the nineteenth century frequently portrayed both liberty and the French Revolution in this manner, Baha'u'llah naturally had apprehensions about the full implementation of such hurriyyah.

Thus, Baha'u'llah in the *Most Holy Book* criticized liberty/license for leading to sedition, or public turmoil (fitnah), and immorality. On the other hand, he did not reject the positive aspects of liberty, writing, "We approve of liberty in certain circumstances and refuse to sanction it in others."[62] He concluded by averring that perfect liberty lay in following the commandments revealed through him. Clearly, Baha'u'llah approved of political liberty as manifested in democratic institutions, but not of antireligious libertinism (the other connotation of hurriyyah in nineteenth-century Arabic).

Some idea of how the word was used by its proponents can be gathered from the Young Ottoman, Namık Kemal, who wrote:

> Every book, in explaining the subject of "political rights," takes a different approach to categorizing them. Even so, among authors a great deal of agreement has been achieved on such articles, drawn from universal principles, as: popular sovereignty, separation of governmental powers, answerability of officials, personal liberty (*hurriyyat*), equality, freedom of thought, freedom of the press, freedom to assemble, the right to dispose of one's own property (*hakk-i tasarruf*), and the inviolability of one's home. Popular sovereignty means that the powers of the state are derived from the people, and in Islamic Law is referred to as the right of giving fealty (*bay'at*).[63]

Since Baha'u'llah called for constitutional monarchy and parliamentary governance, for justice and equality for all subjects regardless of religion, and for a rule of law, it is easy to see why he should "approve of liberty under certain circumstances." As for his insistence on tying the idea to obedience to the Law, this was a common idea among liberal thinkers. Other Middle Eastern reformers linked liberty with the fulfillment of duties. The Syrian Christian journalist Adib Ishaq, as Ayalon has written, "defined liberty as 'the right to fulfil the known duty (*haqq al-qiyām bil-wājib al-ma'lūm*).' "[64] (This is also essentially Montesquieu's definition.) Ishaq, a freemason, courageously and indefatigably advocated representative government in Egypt in the late 1870s and early 1880s, showing that even someone who was obviously a liberal in Middle Eastern terms could still hold a conception of liberty as the fulfillment of duty. Goldziher erred in attempting to use the French Revolution as a universal template for measuring the left and the right, in which religionists were generally on the right. After all, the Young Ottomans, revolutionaries demanding a constitution and parliament, were also committed believers. So, too, were the American Baptists who supported the American Revolution.

Baha'u'llah's reservations about liberty/license did not, as Goldziher apparently suspected, derive from a belief in political absolutism or in the monopoly of a church over opinion. Elsewhere Baha'u'llah explicitly uses the term *liberty* in its positive sense. He wrote approvingly to the Afnan clan of Shiraz and Bombay in the late 1880s that "in reality, liberty (*hurriyyat*) and civilization (*madaniyyat*) and their prerequisites are increasing day by day."[65] In 1889 he wrote a letter in which he characterized his policy of allowing Baha'is to consort peacefully with members of other religions, read their Scripture, and wear Western clothing as the bestowal upon them of liberty (*hurriyyah*).[66] We have seen that his son 'Abdu'l-

Baha, who in this period published nothing without his father's concurrence, extensively argued for liberty of religion and conscience, for equality, and individual rights in *A Traveller's Narrative* as well as in his 1875 *Secret of Divine Civilization* (to be discussed in the next chapter). Only two years after *al-Kitab al-Aqdas* was completed, 'Abdu'l-Baha was arguing to Iranian conservatives that "this liberty (ḥurriyyat) in the universal rights of individuals (ḥuqūq-i 'umūmiyyih-' i afrād) " is not "contrary to prosperity and success."[67]

Although he framed his views in an apocalyptic style, Baha'u'llah's writings of the late 1860s and early 1870s brought the nascent Baha'i movement into the mainstream of modernist thought in the Middle East. On each essential social question—restrictions on monarchy, representative government, and the abolition of slavery—his position was similar to that of reformers such as the Young Ottomans and Midhat Pasha, though he lacked the Young Ottomans' faith in traditional Islam as a bulwark against tyranny. In Ottoman terms, in the late 1860s and early 1870s, Baha'u'llah stood on the far left with Namık Kemal. In the late 1860s and early 1870s these Baha'i stances constituted a radical critique of the existing royal-absolutist regimes. This opposition to absolutism and embrace of elements of modernity was tempered by a utopian realism in which the libertinism and exaggerated secularism of European modernity are also strongly criticized.

The Baha'is and the Young Ottomans

Clearer connections can be drawn in the 1870s between Baha'is and Middle Eastern reform movements, whether the Young Ottomans or the administrative innovators in Iran. These relationships took the form of actual meetings as well as Baha'i writings that respond to this decade of change. Baha'i leaders now made more explicit the sort of society they wished to see in the Middle East, moving from apocalyptic vision to rational exposition. I am not so much interested here in demonstrating an influence of one movement on another as in pointing to the intertextuality of reformist thought in this period, of the ways in which some ideas were "in the air."

We have already seen that in 1869 Baha'u'llah was incarcerated in Akka with Young Ottoman Sadık Effendi. In the early 1870s the Young Ottoman expatriates in Europe came home from exile, after the death in 1871 of First Minister Âli Pasha, their chief nemesis. In 1873, however, the sultan banished several Young Ottomans to provincial prisons, partially because of their close links with the impatient heir apparent, Murad Pasha. The state exiled Namık Kemal to Cyprus, Ebüzziya Tevfik to Rhodes, and Nuri Bey and Hakki Effendi to Akka. During their exile they certainly came into contact, and interacted intellectually, with the Baha'is. Ebüzziya mentioned the earlier banishment of the Baha'is, to whom he referred as Babis, from Istanbul to Akka via Rhodes (his own place of exile). He took their side, seeing their imprisonment in the fortress as a result of foreign (Iranian) interference in internal Ottoman affairs, of which he took a dim view. He defended the Baha'is from the Ottoman charge of proselytizing within the empire, and although he accepted "Babism" as a "religious belief," he mistakenly thought the core of the movement a political doctrine clothed in religious garb. It was, he said, "interested in revolutionary activity solely in Iran." He ended by noting that the first news to reach him from Akka about his fellow Young Ottomans, Nuri Bey and Ismail Hakki Effendi, came through the "demonstrated humanity of an individual . . . called Bahaeddin Effendi" who was himself a "Babi."[68] He was certainly referring to Baha'u'llah, whose name outsiders often confused with the more common "Baha'u'd-Din." That Baha'u'llah was in correspondence, in 1873, with exiled Young Ottoman leaders such as Ebüzziya Tevfik makes it even more plausible that he was aware of their political ideas. Perhaps he had been in contact with sympathizers in Edirne even before he met Sadık Effendi in Akka.

Namık Kemal, sent to Cyprus, had more contact with Azalis than with Baha'is, though he developed a friendship with the Baha'i Mishkin Qalam, whom the Ottomans had sent to the island with the Azalis. One of his closest companions in exile was Shaykh Ahmed Effendi, a participant in the reactionary 1858 Kuleli uprising, who was rumored to have adopted Babism or the Baha'i faith in his Cyprus exile. By 1876, the year of his release, Namık Kemal was constrained to deny rumors circulating in Istanbul that he himself had become a "Babi."[69] Namık Kemal corresponded extensively with 'Abdu'l-Baha, Baha'u'llah's son, though the Baha'i leader later burned the letters for fear of government searches.[70] The relationship between the Baha'is and the Young Ottomans Nuri Bey and Hakki Effendi in Akka was clearly very warm, and Hakki Effendi paints a vivid picture of the Baha'is as cosmopolitan intellectuals who had their children tutored in European languages and took a keen interest in the international press.[71]

Since the Young Ottomans and the Baha'is had the same enemies high in the Ottoman state, and since they shared many ideals, they naturally viewed one another sympathetically. When the reformer Midhat Pasha (a sometime patron of the Young Ottomans and framer of the first Ottoman

constitution) became governor of Syria in 1878–1880, he called
Baha'u'llah's eldest son 'Abdu'l-Baha to Beirut for a meeting.[72] Baha'i contacts with Ottoman dissidents continued even after the government's turn
to reaction in the 1880s. Abdullah Cevdet, one of the five founding members of the later Young Turk movement, at some point became a Baha'i.
He praised the religion in his journal, *Ictihat* (Reasoned Judgment), during the teens and twenties and he was tried for heresy in this connection
in the early 1920s.[73]

Throughout the late 1860s and early 1870s the Young Ottoman thinkers had spread ideas of modern representative government. They might
have had little practical success, however, save that they attracted the support of some very high-ranking officials, who for their own reasons wanted to reduce the sultan's power. Among these was Midhat Pasha (1822–
1884). After bureaucratic service at the Sublime Porte in 1869–1872 he
served as governor of Baghdad, into which province he introduced a large
number of ambitious reforms during his short tenure. In May of 1872 he
angrily resigned over disputes with the then first minister, Mahmud
Nedim Pasha, especially over the way the revenues of his province were to
be used. In June the first minister had him appointed governor of Edirne,
to keep him away from the capital and the ear of the sultan. But Midhat
succeeded in seeing Abdülaziz, and by the end of July 1872 he was appointed first minister of the Ottoman empire. Midhat Pasha only served
for eighty days in this capacity at that point, making powerful enemies.
He refused Egypt the right to contract European loans independently but
was overruled by the sultan, who took a bribe to allow Khedive Isma'il to
seek greater debt. He blew the whistle on the financial scandals of the
palace and at one point caracoled, mounted on his steed, right into the
third court of the palace, a prerogative, Davison tells us, heretofore exercised only by the sultan. By October 1872 he was out of power and was
given only brief desultory appointments for the next four years. In 1873
he fell into disfavor when it was revealed that he and the then first minister had consulted at length about the necessity of implementing a constitution and parliament. Among the impetuses for such drastic action was
the Ottoman Empire's increasing debt to foreign banks and nations,
fueled in part by the sultan's own borrowing, the corruption of tax farm-
ing in the provinces, and non-Muslim unrest in the Balkans.[74]

The empire's ailing finances were among the discontents that led to
widespread public protests in 1876. Seminarians demonstrated during
that May, possibly at Midhat's instigation. As a result, the reformist Mütercim Mehmed Rüşdü Pasha became first minister and Midhat returned

to government as minister. Midhat, with the minister of war and others, plotted the deposition of Sultan Abdülaziz, which they carried out on May 30, 1876. The distraught and despondent former monarch committed suicide, alone in his baths, on June 4. War broke out in Serbia. The heir apparent, Murad V, grew mentally unbalanced, perhaps because of the stress of these dramatic events, and had to be relieved of his scepter. The next in line for the throne, Abdülhamid, having told Midhat he would accept a constitution, mounted the throne on August 31 as Abdülhamid II.

By December 23, 1876, the new constitution had been hammered out and approved, though Abdülhamid stood firm against the introduction of a full prime ministerial system and retained some broad powers, including the right to exile persons he considered threats to the state. Midhat Pasha became first minister again in December. The first Ottoman parliament was elected and met in 1877.[75] The Istanbul-based Syro-Lebanese journalist Ahmad Faris ash-Shidyaq supported the new parliament in his Arabic-language weekly, *al-Jawa'ib*, which was probably among the main channels for information about the constitution to Arab provinces such as Akka. He wrote of the superiority of a parliament to simple cabinet government:

> The intent of the phrase "assemblies of consultation" is those assemblies that the delegates of the community attend, having been legally elected. The phrase does not refer to cabinets attended by the ministers and agents of the country's ruler, for this regime cannot dispense with a parliament, insofar as the members of the aforementioned cabinet will compete with one another to please the ruler so as to avoid losing their posts.[76]

The journalist defended the right of members of parliament to criticize the government and to counterbalance the power of the sultan.

In a chain reaction this movement helped provoke a similar but slightly later struggle for parliamentary government in the Ottoman vassal state of Egypt, where the khedive Isma'il had shunted aside his Chamber of Delegates. The events in Istanbul were watched and interpreted by Iranians as well. Some seventeen thousand Iranians were resident in the Ottoman capital, largely Azeri merchants and their families. The Persian-language, Istanbul-based newspaper *Akhtar* (Star) commented extensively on the parliamentary elections and deliberations, and on the new Ottoman constitution, saying that these developments were auspicious for the entire Orient. *Akhtar* also discussed the controversy over the sultan's dismissal and exile of Midhat Pasha in February 1877, which did not, however, prevent parliament from continuing to deliberate and legislate in the ensuing year. The newspaper argued that a parliamentary regime required equality (*musāvat*) among all Ottoman subjects, regardless of religion and ethnicity, and the paper supported the ideals of justice (*'adālat*), liberty (*ḥurriyyat*), and humanity (*insāniyyat*).[77]

Baha'u'llah clearly felt vindicated by the overthrow and suicide of Sultan Abdülaziz and the establishment of parliamentary governance in the Ottoman Empire. In an undated letter presumably penned soon after these events, he wrote to a correspondent in Iran,

> We have seized them all by means of our own sovereignty: thus was it revealed in the "Tablet of Fuad." Blessed are those endued with insight. We seized the first [Âli Pasha, d. 1871] as we had avowed in the Book. And we seized the second [Sultan Abdülaziz, d. 1876] along with his courtiers, with a wrath at which the hearts of the profligate trembled. They awoke, and nothing could be heard in their palaces save an empty echo and the croaking of the raven.[78]

As we saw above, Baha'u'llah blamed the autocratic rule of Tanzimat reformers such as Fuad Pasha for the revolution.[79] Elsewhere he explained that divine judgment took Sultan Abdülaziz relatively quickly, because the Ottoman ruling house had shown Baha'u'llah enmity and condemned him to solitary confinement for no reason and without any provocation, whereas Nasiru'd-Din Shah had been fired on by ignorant Babis in 1852 and so his persecution of the Babis and Baha'is could at least be understood.[80] Baha'u'llah rhetorically presents himself as the apocalyptic incarnation of a vengeful democratic order, a raging torrent that Abdülaziz had attempted to dam up in order to preserve his absolutist regime and that ultimately swept the hapless sultan away. The officials of the constitutional government allowed Baha'u'llah in 1877 to move out of the town of Akka, to a house in the nearby countryside where he could enjoy the greenery he so missed (he was, after all, from the lush province of Mazandaran along the Caspian). Now he was, as an Ottoman subject, even represented by a delegate in parliament.

That the Ottoman Empire became, in 1876–1878, a constitutional monarchy along the lines Baha'u'llah had been advocating put it in stark contrast with despotic Iran, where the shah had turned against even cabinet government. In a letter written in the late 1870s Baha'u'llah went so far as to say that he did not think it desirable for his correspondent to reside in the lands ruled from Tehran, adding that the command had been revealed that a parliamentary regime be established (*ḥukm-i shūrā nāzil*) and it must be implemented.[81] The juxtaposition of these two statements suggests that Baha'u'llah at that point saw a cloud over Iran because it was

still an absolute monarchy, and this completely unreformed despotism led
him to urge some of his followers to emigrate to the then more democratic Ottoman lands. In a letter to one of his followers, Ibn-i Asdaq, Baha'u'llah complains of the kings:

> Among them is he who declares that he desires autocratic power (*as-
> salṭanah*). Say: Woe unto you, O heedless one who is distant [from God].
> We have commanded the monarchs to toss it behind them, and to advance
> instead toward God, the Almighty, the Beauteous. We affirm (*nuṣaddiq*) the
> appearance of Reason (*al-ʿaql*) among all human beings. Therefore, you
> will see absolutism (*as-sulṭah al-muṭlaqah*) discarded upon the dust, nor will
> any approach it. Thus was the matter decreed in a manifest tablet. Say: It
> [despotism] is the most degraded of stations in my view, though you might
> see it as the most exalted station.[82]

More forthrightly than in any other piece of writing, Baha'u'llah here
unreservedly condemns absolute monarchy and despotism of any sort and
explicitly links its demise to the advent of reason among all (making
explicit what remained implicit in his 1868 "Tablet to Salman," quoted
above). We have seen that he prophesied the advent of popular sovereignty in Iran in his *Most Holy Book.* Here he bestows a rationale on popular
sovereignty, grounding it in universal reason. This privileging of rationality might seem strange coming from a prophet, except if we remember
that Baha'u'llah had renounced claims for his religion upon civil governance, where he expected instead a communicative rationality he called
"consultation" to be the mode of operation. And here he grounds democratic consultation in human reason. He felt that his revelation had mainly ethical and spiritual import.[83] It thus did not constrain the workings of
reason in the political and public spheres but rather encouraged it.

Some more radical Middle Eastern thinkers, including Babis and Baha'is, appear to have dreamed of going even further and instituting a full-
blown republic (possibly inspired by the success of the republicans in
France in 1871). In a tablet that may have been penned during the First
Ottoman Constitutional period or soon thereafter, the *Bishārāt* (Glad Tidings), Baha'u'llah discouraged his followers from pursuing this even more
radical goal, expressing a personal preference for constitutional monarchy.
He wrote, "Although a republican form of government (*jumhūriyyat*) prof-
iteth all the peoples of the world, yet the majesty of kingship is one of the
signs of God. We do not wish that the countries of the world should remain deprived thereof. If the sagacious combine the two forms into one,
great will be their reward in the presence of God."[84] Note that Baha'u'llah

did not reject republicanism outright but praised it. He did say that it lacks the unifying symbol provided by a constitutional monarch. The form of his statement resembles the categories of Islamic law, in which things are ranked forbidden, disapproved, neutral, approved, and required. Approved actions are said to be rewarded, if performed, but not punished if neglected. He seems imply, then, that constitutional monarchy is approved rather than required, and republicanism not forbidden. As noted above, he is generous in his remarks about the republics of the New World, which he appears to accept as they are. Since no organized movement for republicanism existed in the nineteenth-century Middle East, Baha'u'llah's stance accords, again, with that of the most liberal Ottoman thinkers such as the Young Ottomans, who did not seek a pure republic. The journalist ash-Shidyaq, who, as we have seen, supported the Ottoman constitutional movement in 1876–1878, also favored a constitutional monarchy, which he said was not much different from a republic.[85] Constitutional monarchy was itself a radical ideology at this point in the Middle East, to which sovereigns such as Nasiru'd-Din Shah and, eventually, Sultan Abdülhamid II were violently opposed.

The Baha'i leaders also watched developments in Egypt, where constitutionalist intellectuals and notables had begun a nativist movement. 'Abdu'l-Baha followed the Egyptian constitutionalist press, such as the newspaper *Misr* (Egypt), and penned a letter to one of its contributors, the expatriate Iranian Sayyid Jamalu'd-Din Asadabadi "al-Afghani." He wrote, "I read your splendid article printed in the newspaper *Misr*, which refuted some English newspapers. I found your replies in accord with prevailing reality and your eloquence aided by brilliant proof. Then I came across a treatise by Midhat Pasha, the contents of which support your correct and magnificent article. So, I wanted to send it along to you."[86] 'Abdu'l-Baha here comes across as a widely read intellectual with a brief against Western imperialism, who attempted to establish connections among reformists like Sayyid Jamalu'd-Din and Midhat Pasha and, implicitly, among them and the Baha'is. Sayyid Jamalu'd-Din (d. 1897) was from a village in northwestern Iran and was probably devoted to the Shaykhi school of Shi'ism, but in the Sunni world he gave it out that he was a Sunni Afghan. He attempted to rise high in politics in a number of places, including Afghanistan in the 1860s and then in Istanbul, from which he was exiled for heresy in 1871. In Egypt 1871–1879 he gathered around himself a number of young intellectuals and reformist notables, using freemasonry and the local press as vehicles for his anti-imperialist and reformist ideas. He was exiled from Egypt in 1879 for having, after some delay, publicly advocated constitutionalism in that vassal state of the Ottoman empire. Sayyid Jamalu'd-Din appears in the late 1870s to have on occasion expressed a positive view of Babism, and under his influence the Lebanese journalist Adib Ishaq classed the Babi movement with the French Revolution, European socialism, and the Ottoman Constitutional Revolution of 1876 as an exemplar of the struggle for liberty.[87] Sayyid Jamalu'd-Din was also capable, however, of writing a scurrilous and wholly inaccurate description of the movement for Butrus Bustani's Beirut encyclopedia, and the Baha'i leaders felt betrayed by him when it appeared.

In January of 1877, in the midst of the constitutionalist experiment in Istanbul, war broke out between the Russians and the Ottomans over the Balkans. The Ottoman empire's Christian subjects in the Balkans, such as Bulgars, Serbs, and Romanians, were increasingly affected by currents of nationalism and desire for independence. Russia's Tsar Alexander II, after some hesitation, took their side, and the Russians advanced through the Balkans, slowly and bloodily. By January 1878 they had taken Rumelia and were approaching the capital, Istanbul. The desperate Ottomans agreed to talks and were in the end forced, at the Congress of Berlin in June 1878, to grant independence to Romania, Serbia, and Montenegro. Rumelia was divided into three regions: western Rumelia, eastern Rumelia, and the Edirne province, and western Rumelia was detached from the empire and incorporated into an independent Bulgaria. Baha'u'llah commented on these events from Akka. He urged the recipient of his letter to contemplate the straits that Sultan Abdülhamid II (*ra'īs*) found himself in during the war, estimating that it left five hundred thousand dead and pointing out that it led to the Russian occupation of Edirne and dyed Ottoman soil red with blood. He said that he had prophesied these calamities in his 1868 "Sūrat ar-Ra'īs" ("Tablet to the Premier") for Âli Pasha, but that even so Ottoman officialdom remained oblivious to the truth of his cause.[88] Although by far the worst effects were felt in Rumelia and Anatolia, the Baha'is in Akka were also adversely affected by the war. Baha'u'llah's secretary reports that during the war years Akka suffered from hyperinflation and the Ottomans cut to one-third the stipends they had been giving the Baha'i prisoners, as a war economy measure, causing distress among the some three hundred Baha'is resident there.[89]

The disastrous course of the war gave the young Sultan Abdülhamid II a pretext for ending the constitutionalist experiment, on the grounds that it had weakened the Ottomans in the face of efficient Russian absolutism, and he therefore disbanded the parliament. In 1908 a second constitutional revolution shook Istanbul, led by the Young Turks (and leading to

the freeing of 'Abdu'l-Baha from captivity). But this constitutional movement, too, soon deteriorated into dictatorship. Only from the 1950s was
Turkey finally able to begin achieving with some consistency some of the
ideals of Baha'u'llah, Namık Kemal, and Abdullah Cevdet Bey, regarding
parliamentary governance.

Baha'u'llah gradually moved away from the Hobbesian position, expressed
in the tablet to Nasiru'd-Din Shah of spring 1868, that kings were the
shadows of God on earth and ruled by divine right. Although this view fit
with his turn away from Babi theocratic ideals toward a rapprochement
with the state, in an unnuanced form it was incompatible with his conviction that government should be consultative and that it was necessary to
oppose the state when it acted arbitrarily. By the second half of 1868 or the
first half of 1869, he had, in tandem with the Young Ottomans and other
reformers, moved to a profound appreciation for British constitutional
monarchy, parliamentary rule, and consultative government, urging sovereigns to relinquish actual rule in favor of cabinet ministers and the elected
representatives of the people. The monarchies that refused to bend before
the new wind, he proclaimed, would find themselves consigned to the
dustheap of history, as with Napoleon III—or the rivers of their realms
would run red with blood, as he prophesied to the kaiser—or the despot
would face public turmoil and deposition, as with Sultan Abdülaziz. By
1873, in his *Most Holy Book*, he had gone even further and begun speaking of popular sovereignty, predicting that the people would rule over Iran.
Elsewhere he gave as the rationale for the abolition of absolute monarchy
the advent of universal reason among humankind. These various strands of
thinking were reconciled in the Glad Tidings of the late 1870s or the
1880s, wherein he preferred constitutional monarchy, which preserves the
democratic principle that government derives its legitimacy from the consent of the governed, while yet retaining the monarch as a symbol of divine
sanction for the state. Baha'u'llah's views were not expressed in reasoned
treatises but in prophetic utterances and apocalyptic visions of a millenarian character. He thereby did, however, create a space for the operation of
individual human reason, for liberal rights and democracy.

Goldziher's confusion about whether the early Baha'i faith stood in the
liberal or the absolutist camp can now be resolved. In predicting and advocating government by the people, Baha'u'llah sounds more like Joseph
Priestley than like Hobbes. In explicitly seeking to replace absolutism with
a reign of reason, Baha'u'llah sounds more like Rousseau and Voltaire than
like Joseph de Maistre. In urging religious toleration, the Baha'i leaders

resemble John Stuart Mill more than Pope Leo XIII. In championing the poor against the feudal classes, in seeking to promote modern science and industry, in looking toward the establishment of a single global government, Baha'u'llah sounds remarkably like Saint-Simon, a point to which I will return later. Combining messianism, an option for the poor, and a firm belief in representative government, the Baha'is upheld what was in a Middle Eastern context a progressive program of social reform, though their mix of cultural motifs has made it difficult for Western scholars clearly to fix them on the European political spectrum. Although the Baha'i movement differed from the Young Ottoman society and from the 'Urabist revolutionaries in Egypt in being a new religion, its political ideas were formed at the same time and in response to many of the same circumstances as were the other early constitutionalist forces. Even in regard to religion there were some convergences. Young Ottoman activists like Namık Kemal experimented with mysticism and the 'Urabi Revolution had millenarian overtones.

The Babis, as they became Baha'is, traded militancy for peace advocacy, anti-intellectualism for a commitment to modern science and technology, conspiracies for community discussions of reform and representative government. Close and cordial relations developed between the Baha'i leaders in Akka and Ottoman reformers, and Baha'i authors responded seriously to moves toward reform in Iran itself, helping communicate modern ideas to that more isolated country. Baha'u'llah's new message was spread by traveling apostles, many of them highly learned men, by notable families of Sayyid merchants, physicians, and landowners, by women with their own networks, by artisans such as goldsmiths and tailors, and by scribes who conscientiously copied out and circulated hundreds of manuscripts of his tablets and letters. His major works were printed in Bombay and circulated in the Middle East. His supporters, impeded by governmental and clerical persecution, nevertheless attracted thousands of adherents. Let us turn, then, to Baha'u'llah's primary audience and community in this period, that of Iran.

FIGURE 1 Midhat Pasha

FIGURE 2 Mehmed Emin Âli Pasha

FIGURE 3 Fuad Pasha

در دیارِ خطِ شهِ صاحبِ عَلَم
بنده باب بها مشکین قلم

FIGURE 4 (LEFT PAGE) Mishkin Qalam

FIGURE 5 (ABOVE LEFT) Sayyid Javad Karbala'i

FIGURE 6 (ABOVE RIGHT) Front row (right to left): Sayyid Muhammad
Isfahani, Mirza Musa Kalim (Baha'u'llah's brother), Mirza 'Ali Sirri; back row:
Aqa Jan Kashani (Khadimu'llah), Sayyah

FIGURE 7 Sayyid jamalu'd-Din "Afghani"

FIGURE 8 Nasiru'd-Din Shah

محمد نامق كمال ـ ١٢٥٦ ـ ١٣٠٦

FIGURE 8.5 Namık Kemal

FIGURE 9 Sultan Abd-ul-Aziz

FIGURE 10 'Abdu'l-Baha

FIGURE 11 Bahiyyih Khanum
(Baha'u'llah's daughter).

FIGURE 12 Women of the Holy Household

FIGURE 13 (RIGHT PAGE, TOP) Group of Baha'is at Akka, February 1909

FIGURE 14 (RIGHT PAGE, BOTTOM) Akka

FIGURE 15 Akka Fortress, where Baha'u'llah was imprisoned

FIGURE 16 House of 'Abbud, Akka, where Baha'u'llah lived in the 1870s

3 • "Ere Long Will the Reins of Power Fall Into the Hands of the People": Reform in Iran

Between 1905 and 1911 Iranians engaged in a protracted struggle over whether a constitutionalist regime would replace royal absolutism.[1] Since this period also witnessed the rise of Iranian socialist groups and feminist thinkers, an underlying issue in modernity for Iran appears to have been the possibility of greater egalitarianism. Little in that country's political culture before 1905 had hinted that this conflict was building, and for the past thirty years historians have been seeking an intellectual genealogy for it. Most have searched among the papers of officials and diplomats, often examining unpublished or posthumously published manuscripts with little or no contemporary circulation, at least before the revolution.[2] Despite the tracts written by reformers calling for innovations such as cabinet government, and despite the revolt in 1890–1892 against a tobacco concession granted by the shah to a British company, traditional historiography does not report a popular movement for representative government in Iran until 1905.[3] But it should be clear from what I have written above that Iran was not in fact isolated from the constitutionalist movements of the 1870s and 1880s in the Ottoman realm. I have been arguing that we might get closer to the real context of Iranian reform by looking at what was going on outside the governmental elite. In the last chapter I explored the growth of belief in representative government within the Baha'i faith in the last third of the nineteenth century, as an example of how the new ideas that led to the conflict circulated.

We saw in the last chapter some Baha'i interactions with Ottoman constitutionalists, but of course the vast majority of nineteenth-century Baha'is lived in Iran.[4] What were the Baha'is' relations with other Iranian reformers? Were they really the quietists the secondary literature would lead us to expect in the period 1866–1892, or did they form part of the "dissident milieu" in the Middle East? In what way did Baha'u'llah's message manage to hold together this diverse Baha'i community back in Iran, with its impatient artisans, its visionary intellectuals, its activist women, its staid import-export merchants?

Governmental Reform

Baha'u'llah from about 1869 called for the kind of limits on the shah's absolute power that went far beyond the program of reformers who merely advocated cabinet government. Among the few other writers in Persian at that time who championed parliamentary government was Fath-'Ali Akhundzadih (1812–1878), who resided in tsarist Tiflis. Akhundzadih's father was Azerbaijani and became a merchant in the tsarist-ruled Caucasus. Fath-'Ali was an official interpreter for the Russian government, and from about 1850 he began writing satirical plays and reformist tracts. His "Letters of Kamalu'd-Dawlih" of the mid-1860s advocated the power of the people and an end to despotism, though the argument was couched in an anti-Arab racism and a hatred of Islam and of religion in general that was very far from Baha'u'llah's own stance.[5] For Akhundzadih, as for many other Qajar intellectuals, the example of parliamentary regimes in the West was influential. Even conservative travelers such as Mirza Fattah Garmrudi were capable of praising parliamentary decision making:

> Individually the people of Farangistan [the West] are not very wise or mature nor are they endowed with much eloquence or intelligence; but the parliament and house of consultation that they have established apparently conceal these shortcomings. When the interests of the government and the country are at issue, a number of selected wise men (*'uqala*) and governmental trustees (*umana*), through consulting and advising each other, reach the depth of an issue and evaluate the good and bad of a claim and, finally, from the views of the wise men, a thoroughly considered position is adopted and used. Accordingly, it is clear that mistakes and errors are reduced and affairs are based on an expedient conscience.[6]

The realization that group decision making of a parliamentary sort, which Muslim thinkers tended to gloss as "consultation," might offer concrete advantages to those in government made adoption of this process tempting for Qajar reformers. The shahs tended to be less impressed with its potentialities.

Among the promoters of consultative power sharing, at least between the shah and his ministers, was Mirza Husayn Khan Mushiru'd-Dawlih (1828–1881). He had studied briefly in Paris as a young man and was posted to Bombay, becoming consul in 1851, then was consul in Tiflis (Tblisi) 1855–1858. He was minister and then ambassador in Istanbul 1858–1870, where, as we have seen, he was a prime mover in Baha'u'llah's exiles. In 1870 Mirza Husayn Khan was recalled to Iran as minister, first of justice and then of war. In September 1871 he became first minister (*sadr-i a'zam*) in Tehran. Influenced by Ottoman reforms, he attempted to work out a system of cabinet government with Nasiru'd-Din Shah, and a body was set up in imitation of the Tanzimat, called the Great Consultative Council (*Majlis-i Shūrā-yi Kubrā*), though this was an appointive institution subservient to the shah rather than a representative one. Mirza Husayn Khan made the mistake of seeking to develop Iran's economy and resources by granting a huge concession to Baron Julius de Reuter, a British subject. This unwise policy aroused the opposition of merchants, intellectuals, some ulama, and of the Russians, and the whole scheme had to be canceled. The fiasco, along with Nasiru'd-Din's ultimate unwillingness to share any power with his cabinet, led to Mirza Husayn Khan's demotion to foreign minister in 1873.[7] The experiment in cabinet government failed, and Iran reverted to absolute monarchy. This event convinced Akhundzadih that Iranians could not implement French-style constitutionalism until the masses were educated.[8]

Although as Iranian ambassador to Istanbul Mirza Husayn Khan showed great enmity to the Baha'is up to 1870, he later changed his mind about them and once let a Baha'i courier caught at Aleppo go free. Indeed, one of his close relatives, Mirza Muhammad 'Ali Kadkhuda, became a Baha'i, which may have moderated the minister's views of the movement. By the mid-1870s he was reportedly praising it and is said to have upbraided one of Baha'u'llah's Muslim brothers for being embarrassed about the relationship.[9] The thaw in relations was mutual. In the early 1870s Baha'u'llah quizzed one visitor to Akka from Iran about the behavior of Mirza Husayn Khan, and in return described the reformer as "wiser than the rest" (*a'qal az sā'irīn*) of Iranian politicians.[10] Elsewhere Baha'u'llah notes with approval that toward the end of his life Mirza Husayn Khan ceased speaking badly of the Baha'is and shows a willingness to forgive him for his enormities.[11]

'Abdu'l-Baha, Baha'u'llah's eldest son, responded much more hopefully to the Iranian reformism of the 1870s than did Akhundzadih, writing a

Persian book in Palestine in 1875 known in English as *The Secret of Divine Civilization*, which he published in Bombay in 1882.[12] Baha'u'llah had asked him to write a book on the "science of politics" (*'ilm-i siyāsat*) to demonstrate that not only prominent reformist intellectuals could speak on such matters but those inspired by God as well.[13]

'Abdu'l-Baha begins his *Secret of Divine Civilization* by praising reason or intellect (*'aql*), drawing for support upon Qur'an verses and the rhetoric of medieval Islamic philosophy. In both the Qur'an and in Greco-Islamic philosophy knowledge and the intellect are prized. Philosophy had long flourished in Iran, and in the sixteenth and seventeenth centuries had its center in the School of Isfahan; the Illuminationist current (really a form of Neoplatonism) was also influential. The Shaykhi school, out of which the Babi and Baha'i religions developed, was more or less Illuminationist in orientation and, despite its kabbalistic esotericism, prized the intellect. Into this humanist rationalism of the urbane Islamic tradition, the tradition of Avicenna, Suhrawardi, and Mulla Sadra, 'Abdu'l-Baha infuses the nineteenth-century notion of civilizational progress. He presents early Islam itself as a civilizing force for the tribes of the Arabian peninsula. He explains that he is impelled to write by the shah's own announcement of his determination to reform Iran (probably referring to the reformist period of 1871–1873).[14]

He recalls for his audience the greatness of pre-Islamic Iran, the cultural achievements and imperial greatness of the Zoroastrian Achaemenid empire of Cyrus the Great, contrasting this glorious past with the sad state of nineteenth-century Iran, especially in comparison with Europe and the Americas. He uses history to relativize and to refute racist arguments of inherent Iranian inferiority and European superiority, recalling Europe's own dark ages and the progress it made from the fifteenth century on, saying it was mainly a result of the encouragement given to learning and the learned. He denounces Iranian conservatives and reactionaries among the clergy and the notables who reject the new knowledge and technologies of nineteenth-century Europe on the grounds that they are foreign to Iran and derive from infidels, who ought not be emulated.[15] Both of these themes, of Iranian pre-Islamic greatness and the attack on resistance to modernity as foreign, had been sounded more than a decade earlier by Akhundzadih as well.[16]

He argues for the benefits of extending education, developing useful arts and sciences, enacting just legislation, preserving liberty (*ḥurriyyat*) and the general rights of individuals, and promoting trade, manufactures, mining, and commerce. He criticizes the lack of statecraft and of binding treaties with neighbors and condemns the arbitrary power of provincial and district governors, arguing for a greater role for state councils (*majālis*) in passing judgment on those charged. He urges an anticorruption campaign to combat bribery and reforms in the pay, training, and equipment of the military forces.[17]

'Abdu'l-Baha says, however, that all problems cannot be resolved solely by moving away from the fiat of individual autocratic rulers and establishing councils and parliaments (*maḥafil-i mashvirat*). He points to the occasional failures of such parliamentary movements in Europe (he may be thinking of the Great Terror after the French Revolution or the bloodshed in Paris during the transition from empire to republic in 1870–1871). Rather, he urges that representatives serving in state councils and parliaments be persons of high moral character, be well-educated in both religious and civil law, and know something about the prerequisites for economic development.[18] The emphasis on moral qualifications for office resembles the classical Islamic insistence that leaders be morally upright and is not a concern one would find in the technical rationalism of the Enlightenment. Sa'idi has argued that this stress on moral and spiritual qualities differentiates 'Abdu'l-Baha's thinking from Western parliamentarism. This reading, however, ignores the diversity of Western liberalism, which includes an individualist "procedural liberalism" as well as "formative republicanism," committed to community and virtue, that resembles the ideas of the Baha'i thinker.[19] 'Abdu'l-Baha's critique aims not at excluding persons from the popular classes from serving as representatives (some artisans were both pious and literate) but rather at critiquing the patrimonial practice at the Qajar court of promoting individuals to high rank merely on the basis of their relationship to the shah or their intimacy with him or with one of the princes. This custom had resulted in persons of limited experience and little or no education becoming powerful officials, a result criticized by other reformers, such as Akhundzadih, as well.[20] Clearly, the goal of employing large numbers of well-trained public servants could only be achieved through universal public education.

'Abdu'l-Baha presses on the shah the same democratic program that Baha'u'llah had been advocating, in tandem with the Young Ottomans in the Ottoman empire. Noting that the shah had moved to devolve some of his absolute power on appointed state councils, 'Abdu'l-Baha writes,

> In the present writer's view it would be preferable if the election [*intikhāb*] of nonpermanent members of consultative assemblies [*majālis*] in Iran [*mamālik-i maḥrūsih*] should be dependent on the good-pleasure and election of the people [*manūṭ bi riḍāʾiyyat va intikhāb-i jumhūr*]. For elected

representatives will on this account be somewhat inclined to exercise justice, lest their reputation suffer and they fall into disfavor with the public.[21]

Later in the book he again defends parliamentary governance as an ideal, citing in support of it the Qur'an verses "and whose affairs are guided by mutual counsel" (42:36) and "and consult them in the affair" (3:153), verses that had already been appealed to for this purpose by Mirza Yusuf Khan in Iran and Namık Kemal, among others, in the Ottoman Empire. 'Abdu'l-Baha concludes, "In view of this, how can the question of mutual consultation be in conflict with the religious law? The great advantages of consultation can be established by logical arguments as well."[22]

This suggestion is probably the most radical idea put forward in the book. It was still revolutionary in the Ottoman Empire in 1875, when it was written, and when it was published in Bombay in 1882 it was again radical, in the wake of the defeat by absolutism and imperialism of both the Ottoman constitutionalist movement and of the 'Urabi Revolution in Egypt. 'Abdu'l-Baha suggests politely and in reformist language what Baha'u'llah had thundered at Tehran in apocalyptic visionary terms in the *Most Holy Book* two years earlier: "Affairs within you will undergo a revolution, and you will be ruled by a democracy (*jumhūr*) of the people (*annās*)."[23] Popular sovereignty was being put forward as an ideal in Persian in this period only by Akhundzadih, from tsarist Russia, and was not again taken up by a major reformist figure until Malkum Khan began advocating it from London in his journal, *Qanun*, in the 1890s. Within Iran itself such statements would have been considered seditious by Nasiru'd-Din Shah and severely punished.

'Abdu'l-Baha urges a separation of powers, including an executive, a legislature, and a judiciary, though he sees the first two as primary. The regime (*ḥukūmat*) is in charge of the executive, but the learned and scientists (*danāyān-i hushmand*) should be in charge of the legislature. In view of the scarcity of well-educated individuals at that time, he advocates that as a stopgap measure a council of science (*hay'at-i 'ilmiyyih*) be established, to which experts in various fields of the sciences and the arts would be appointed and that should be charged with equitably resolving Iran's problems.[24] This passage seems to me to coincide with the ideas of the Saint-Simonians, a utopian socialist movement in early nineteenth-century France, which will be discussed at greater length in the next chapter.

'Abdu'l-Baha demonstrates a special commitment to the poor and to social justice, in accordance with Baha'u'llah's earlier statements in the "Tablet to the Kings." He writes,

Wealth is most commendable, provided the entire population is wealthy. If, however, a few have inordinate riches while the rest are impoverished, and no fruit or benefit accrues from that wealth, then it is only a liability to its possessor. If, on the other hand, it is expended for the promotion of knowledge, the founding of elementary and other schools, the encouragement of art and industry, the training of orphans and the poor—in brief, if it is dedicated to the welfare of society—its possessor will stand out before God and man as the most excellent of all who live on earth and will be accounted as one of the people of paradise.[25]

He therefore stigmatizes the class stratification inherent in the Qajar system of tribal feudalism, which produced vast numbers of impoverished subjects and only a small number of wealthy indolent nobles. Again, this "utopian socialist" element in his thought rather resembles that of the Saint-Simonians.

He calls for a reform of the curriculum of Iran's schools and seminaries, so that more practical subjects would be stressed in the place of theology and metaphysics. Universal education should be provided; intellectuals should be free to publish books and articles that contain suggestions for improving the public welfare. An educated public opinion should be encouraged.[26] He concludes by arguing against reactionaries who reject all progress and European importations:

If the country were built up, the roads repaired, the lot of the helpless improved by various means, the poor rehabilitated, the masses set on the path to progress, the avenues of public wealth increased, the scope of education widened, the government properly organized, and the free exercise of the individual's rights, and the security of his person and property, his dignity and good name, assured—would all this be at odds with the character of the Persian people?[27]

The argument is made on pragmatic grounds here, but elsewhere in the book the tradition of Persian Neoplatonic rationalism is appealed to, and still elsewhere Islamic precedents for modernism are put forward. Although *Secret of Divine Civilization* often appears a thoroughgoing defense of and plea for the adoption of key elements of modernity, a sort of manifesto for Weberian rationalization, it should be remembered that the book is extremely critical of other aspects of the phenomenon.[28] It condemns Voltairean atheism, European militarism, moral laxness, nationalism, and the exaltation of Self over Other, state persecution of religion as in Germany's Kulturkampf, and the violence associated with the Paris Commune and the Carlist uprising in Spain. As already noted, 'Abdu'l-Baha's critique in some important respects resembles that of Saint-Simonianism, which similarly condemned nationalism and war and refused to abandon the spiritual dimension of life, arguing for a "New Christianity."

'Abdu'l-Baha's book has something in common with those of a handful of Iranian reformers such as Akhundzadih and ministers such as Muhammad Khan Majdu'l-Mulk and Mirza Muhammad Husayn Khan Dabiru'l-Mulk, who were writing in the same period (but whose works circulated only in manuscript until much later).[29] Mirza Yusuf Khan Mustasharu'd-Dawlih (d. circa 1895) did actually publish his reformist tract, in Tehran in 1870, and it was probably read by 'Abdu'l-Baha. While posted as an Iranian diplomat in Paris in the late 1860s, Mirza Yusuf Khan wrote the manuscript of *Yik Kalimih,* or "One Word" (that is, Law or *qānūn*), which attempted to find Islamic textual support for the ideals of the French Declaration of the Rights of Man.[30] Yusuf Khan points out that not only law but most affairs of the state (*umūr-i dīvānī*) in France are implemented with the acceptance of both the people and the state, and no one can act in an absolutist fashion, outside the rule of law. He locates the crux of modernity and progress in this one factor, the establishment of a rule of law, and calls for a gathering of men learned in both Islamic law and in European law codes who could produce a modern, codified Iranian legal system.[31] He lists twenty-one basic rights and legal principles he finds to underlie the progress of France, mostly articles of the Declaration of the Rights of Man, and then attempts to find Islamic texts to support each. The first is that the law should be no respecter of persons, applying equally to high and low. He argues that this is an Islamic value, as well, insofar as ordinary Muslims asked for blood money even from the Prophet Muhammad and a Jew was said to have brought the caliph Harun ar-Rashid to an Islamic court.[32] He goes on to discuss the French ideals concerning such rights as security of wealth and person, freedom of the press, freedom of assembly, popular sovereignty, the accountability of government officials, and so forth. He embellishes each with quotations from the Qur'an and from the hadith, or sayings and doings of the Prophet and the imams, though in some instances his quotes do not actually seem very apropos. Because of his published book, he was favored by reformers such as Mirza Husayn Khan Mushiru'd-Dawlih, and he went on to advise a number of cabinet officers in the 1870s and early 1880s. Sometime after 1881 he was dismissed from government service and imprisoned for complaining in a reformist article published in the Istanbul-based newspaper, *Akhtar,* about injustices committed by cabinet bureaucracies. He was soon rehabilitated and around 1883 sent as a consular official to the Iranian embassy in

Bombay. Later he was given a post in Tabriz. Around 1890 he was dismissed again, for his links to Mirza Malkum Khan, who had become a dissident and a fierce critic of Nasiru'd-Din Shah. He was sent in chains to Qazvin, where his eyesight was weakened by the beatings he received. He was soon thereafter freed, and died five years later. The story is told that his Qazvin prison guards beat him with copies of *Yik Kalimih*.

Majdu'l-Mulk (1809–1873) was a member of the cabinet in the 1860s and 1870s. Writing in 1870, he also complained about the lack of codification or uniformity in Iranian law and about the arbitrary despotism of provincial officials. He urged an active role by newspapers in creating an informed public opinion. He wanted greater implementation of the principle of the rule of law and of the separation of powers.[33] As a member of the short-lived House of Forgetfulness (quasi-freemasonry) movement of the late 1850s and early 1860s he had subscribed to the manifesto put forward by Mirza Malkum Khan and others that the state should guarantee the preservation of life and property, and the freedom of conscience and expression, of all Iranians, and these ideals underpin his essay.[34] Whatever he believed, however, his book is somewhat cautious, mainly attacking two or three Qajar officials he thought especially corrupt and oppressive rather than putting forward many general reform principles. His book was not published until the twentieth century.

In his treatise on "Leadership" (*siyāsat*), Dabiru'l-Mulk Farahani, another high official, defended the rational reorganization of the armed forces (*nizām*) from the charges by reactionaries that a modern, drilled, standing army is a heretical innovation unlawfully borrowed from the infidel Europeans. He points to England's rule of law and organized military as secrets of that empire's growth over the previous two centuries, while Iran's territory inexorably shrank as it lost control of Afghanistan, western Kurdistan, and Turkic Central Asian territories.[35] He said that reform depended on four pillars of state policy. The first was putting the government on a firm financial footing, through revised taxation and accounting procedures. The second was the establishment of a drilled standing army (something Iran never did, in fact, attain under the Qajars). The third was increasing the prosperity of the subjects, which, he said, was necessary for the first two pillars in any case. The fourth was foreign policy (*pūlītīk-i dawlat*). At present, he said, Iran had formed no alliances with any foreign powers, such as the Ottoman alignment with the British, which had protected them from the Russians.[36]

This reformism of the officials, however, focused on restraining government officials from running down the country with their rapaciousness, on strengthening the central state, and on ensuring the security and property of individuals. It was a reformism for the elite of great property. A different point of view can be seen in a work written after 1868 by Muhammad Shafi' Qazvini, a hatmaker and shopkeeper in Qazvin. Qazvini is also concerned about corruption and arbitrariness among high government officials, and also wants a rule of law. But he shows more interest than the government reformers in building up the country's infrastructure, in promoting trade and commerce, in addressing Iran's currency drought, and in protecting artisans from competition with shoddy imports from Europe. He also complains about the misery of the poor and of the state's inadequate response to the Great Famine of 1868–1871. (He knew what modern economists only recently demonstrated, which is that people die in famines not because there is no food but because they cannot afford what food there is, and therefore their deaths are the result of inadequate government intervention).[37] Like the works of the officials, Qazvini's book remained unpublished and circulated, if at all, only clandestinely in manuscript.

'Abdu'l-Baha's treatise brought together the concerns of the three sorts of reformist tract then being produced in Persian. The first was the argument for an end to despotism and for popular sovereignty made by Akhundzadih from Tiflis. The second was the stress on the rule of law, ministerial responsibility, and cabinet government found in Mirza Husayn Khan, Majdu'l-Mulk, Dabiru'l-Mulk, and others. The third was the reformism of the middle and artisanal classes, who worried about poverty, famine, impoverishment through European competition, lack of infrastructure, and the arbitrariness of the high government appointees. 'Abdu'l-Baha argued comprehensively for a limitation on the absolute power of government appointees, the establishment of representative, elected governmental institutions, the relieving of the poverty of the masses, the improvement of the country's infrastructure, the setting up of a modern school system, and the systematization of Iran's secular and religious laws. His program was egalitarian in the sense that he thought the masses should be able to elect their governmental representatives directly and that positions in the government and in the professions should be open to educated talent. It is a very different vision of society than that held by the more conservative Qajar nobles, with their hereditary privileges, their overtaxation of the people, their frequent lack of a modern education (or much of any education at all), their arbitrary and autocratic rule. It also differs radically from the view of most of the Shi'ite clergy of the time, who had a similarly hierarchical view of society, though they, too, were critical of the high nobles. Finally, the non-Iranian intellectual context of

the book should not be forgotten. The program 'Abdu'l-Baha laid out con-
curs at many points with the ideas of the Saint-Simonians and the Young
Ottomans—some of the latter were, after all, in exile too in Akka while he
was writing this book. The works of Majdu'l-Mulk and of Qazvini, different as they are, resembled one another in their Iranian nativism and their
criticism of foreigners. 'Abdu'l-Baha's view, while vaguely patriotic, is far
more internationalist, a point to which I will return in the next chapter.
He was, after Mirza Yusuf Khan, only the second Iranian author of a treatise in the new reformist genre to publish it in book form and to see it circulate in Iran.

How were the egalitarian ideals in the Baha'i writings received by Baha'is
back in Iran? Nineteenth-century sources make it clear that the reformist
and constitutionalist ideas of Baha'u'llah's tablets to the monarchs circulated widely among Baha'is during the 1870s and after. A Christian minister
in Isfahan referred in 1874 to a collected volume he had read of Baha'u'llah's
letters to the monarchs as "the latest *Bible* of the Baabis" and added that "the
sect of Baabis which is now increasing in Persia is that called Baha'i."[38]
Some of Baha'u'llah's letters to the rulers were thus bound together and circulated in manuscript from 1869, being collectively known as the Book of
the Temple (*Kitab al-Haykal*). In 1890 they were published in Bombay, and
a copy of this book was purchased for Browne in Hamadan in 1896.[39] In
1875 a brilliant young seminary teacher named Mirza Abu'l-Fadl Gulpaygani (1844–1914) was investigating various religions in Tehran. At a Baha'i
meeting he saw a copy of the "Lawh-i Fuad," discussed in the last chapter,
which said God would "take hold of" Sultan Abdülaziz for his treatment of
Baha'u'llah. The constitutionalist coup of 1876, followed by the sultan's suicide, in appearing to fulfill the prophecy, helped convince Mirza Abu'l-Fadl
to become a Baha'i.[40] We do not know whether these events so moved him
only because they seemed a prophetic confirmation of a millenarian turmoil
abroad in the world or whether he already had some political sympathies
with constitutionalism of the Young Ottoman sort as well (he certainly did
later on). The story of his conversion, in fact, suggests the inseparability of
the two motifs within Baha'i culture at this point.

The promise of reform offered by the 1870s in the Ottoman Empire
and Iran proved false, or at least highly premature. As noted above, in 1878
Sultan Abdulhamid, in the wake of military losses to Russia, prorogued
parliament and reverted to absolutism (though with an important role for
the cabinet and bureaucracy) until the 1908 Young Turk Revolution.[41] By
the mid-1870s Iran's Nasiru'd-Din Shah had also turned against the idea of
any administrative reform that would limit his power, and had in any case

never contemplated calling a parliament.[42] Iranians from the class of high officials who traveled to Istanbul in the 1880s, such as Mirza Muhammad Husayn Farahani, condemned the bureaucratic-reform government of the Tanzimat as an odd mixture of republicanism and monarchy, with too much power invested in the bureaucracies instead of in the king, where it belonged: "thus millions of people may fear one ruler and accept his commands."[43] Even the despotic regime of Abdülhamid was too "liberal" for Tehran in this period! The reactionary minister of publications (and Iran's chief censor), I'timadu's-Saltanih, defended absolutism in Hobbesian terms as necessary to prevent a war of all against all. He criticized the Babis and Sayyid Jamalu'd-Din "al-Afghani" as "foolish persons who demanded liberty (āzādī)." He dismissed Mushiru'd-Dawlih's reform attempts of the 1870s as incompetent attempts to emulate the Ottoman Tanzimat innovations of Âli Pasha and Fuad Pasha, whom he depicts as "traitors" to their monarch. He calls Malkum Khan a "charlatan" and lauds Nasiru'd-Din Shah's move away from cabinet government, saying "Nasiru'd-Din Shah restored the inviolable sovereignty of the monarchy."[44]

Royal absolutism and cultural conservatism dominated high politics in the 1880s and 1890s, though officials contemplated or implemented some infrastructural improvements (more in the Ottoman Empire than in Iran). Both the Ottoman and the Iranian rulers even grew suspicious of modern Western-style education. Sultan Abdülhamid's censors forbade mention of names such as Namık Kemal, Rousseau, and Voltaire, and banned words like *liberty, strike, constitution, revolution,* and *socialism.* Nasiru'd-Din's censors had similar instructions, at least from 1883 when Muhammad Hasan Khan became minister of publications. Nasiru'd-Din Shah and his officials had offending publications, or those that had not been vetted, burned and had their authors beaten, bastinadoed, and even imprisoned.[45] The new tradition of government officials writing reformist tracts continued, but now it caused increasing trouble. As we saw above, even Justice Minister Mirza Yusuf Khan Mustasharu'd-Dawlih was jailed in 1881 for a reformist article and again around 1890 for his connections with Mirza Malkum Khan.

In this increasingly conservative environment Baha'u'llah's writings praising representative government looked more seditious than ever, though the sedition possessed a more peaceful character than that of the earlier Babis, to be sure. Not only Baha'u'llah's more important writings but 'Abdu'l-Baha's treatise on civilization as well contained ideas, such as limits on the power of state officials and parliamentary government, that were explicitly proscribed by the shah and the sultan. These, moreover, had a potentially wide audience because of the increasing use of the printing press. E. G. Browne noted after his visit to Iran of 1887–1888 that the Bombay printed editions of the *Secret of Divine Civilization* and of Baha'u'llah's doctrinal opus, *The Book of Certitude*, were widely circulated.[46] Like many other printed materials, the Baha'i tracts most often evaded the vigilant but overworked censors.

Consultative Community Organizations

Baha'u'llah devoted the last nineteen years of his life to imbuing the Baha'i community in Iran with an ethos and set of rituals and religious laws that differed substantially both from those of Islam and from the Babi regulations of the *Bayan*. Consultative forms of community self-government formed a cornerstone of Baha'u'llah's vision, as he sought to avoid the Usuli Shi'ite system of dominance by clerics, and these local ideals tied in nicely with his pro-democracy views on national government. Was the turn to community building partially a consequence of the political reaction in Istanbul and Tehran from the late 1870s into the next century? After all, reform programs at the national level—such as that set out by 'Abdu'l-Baha in 1875—were now out of fashion among the Middle Eastern monarchs and their high officials, and there seemed little point in working to influence things at that level.

Starting in the late 1870s, manuscripts of Baha'u'llah's new (1873) book of laws, the *Most Holy Book*, began to reach Iranian Baha'i communities. Much later, in 1890, this central text was printed in Bombay by the Afnan merchants based there. The new religion emphasized community participation and collective leadership, which harmonized well with the political doctrines of representative government. The *Most Holy Book* stipulates that in every city the Baha'is should set up a local governing body called a "house of justice" (*bayt al-'adl*) composed of at least nine members. Baha'u'llah told these local assemblies that "it is incumbent to take counsel together and to have regard for the interests of the servants of God" and to implement Baha'i laws.[47] The word used for taking counsel together is a verbal form of the *mushawarah* we saw employed above to refer to parliamentary government.

Clearly Baha'u'llah saw these houses of justice as consultative steering committees for local Baha'i communities, and the centrality he gave them worked against any substantial power for the Baha'i class of seminary-educated learned men. A Shi'ite community, in contrast, would have

been led by an individual Muslim jurisprudent, to whose rulings laymen
owed blind obedience (*taqlīd*). The idea of reducing the absolute power
of the clerical hierarchy over the religious community and putting more
authority in the hands of lay councils was common among religious
minorities in the nineteenth-century Middle East. The notion formed an
element of the Tanzimat reforms in the Ottoman Empire. The 1856
Reform Decree stated, "The temporal administration of the Christian
and other non-Muslim communities shall . . . be placed under the safeguard of an assembly to be chosen from among the members, both ecclesiastics and laymen, of these communities."[48] To some extent this decree
only recognized changes already occurring in the minority religious communities. In 1838–1841 the Armenian moneylenders, artisans, and merchants of Istanbul challenged the priestly hierarchy and gained an imperial decree that put civil affairs of the *millet* under the control of an elected council of laymen; by 1847 the patriarch had been forced to accept a
separate lay council. Similar conflicts occurred between businessmen and
Orthodox rabbis among the Jewish community.[49] Even in Iran lay councils called *anjumāns* were growing up in the late nineteenth century
among the Zoroastrian and other minority communities, challenging the
prerogatives of the clergy. Baha'u'llah's demotion of the "learned," or clergy, in the Baha'i faith from positions of institutional authority in favor of
elected councils has its context in this move toward a religious civil society among the millets.

   Once the *Most Holy Book* began openly circulating among Baha'is back
in Iran from the late 1870s, they began to put into effect some of its provisions. Baha'i notables set up a secret house of justice, or assembly of consultation, in Tehran in 1878, and from there in the 1880s the institution
spread to towns in the provinces of Khurasan, Mazandaran, Fars, and
Kashan.[50] At one point the assembly members were Mirza Asadu'llah
Isfahani, Ibn-i Asdaq, Mirza Haydar 'Ali Isfahani, Akhund Mulla 'Ali Akbar,
Aqa Mirza 'Ali Naqi, Aqa Sayyid Abu Talib, Aqa Muhammad Kazim Isfahani, and Aqa Muhammad Karim " 'Attar," the seller of broadcloth. These
persons for the most part came from among the Baha'is with a Muslim seminary training (ulama), and Baha'i government officials, who otherwise
played a prominent role in the Tehran community, are not represented. The
great merchants, another important group, provided only one member. Nor
were any from a Jewish or Zoroastrian background—though it is true that
significant conversions from these communities to the Baha'i faith probably
began only later, in the 1880s.[51] Aqa Jamal Burujirdi, descended from a distinguished family of mujtahids (jurisprudents), and himself at this time one

of the major Baha'i ulama, was then in the capital. The Tehran house of justice offered to have him join them, but he made his acceptance contingent on his becoming chairman of the body. The members replied that there was no chairman and none had been prescribed in the *Most Holy Book*. Aqa Jamal was finally kept off the assembly because of his demand for leadership and his conviction that his knowledge made his judgment superior to that of laymen (he said that one vote of his should equal six of anyone else's). In response, he began to put it about that it was not yet time to establish such consultative assemblies. Both parties at length asked Baha'u'llah to resolve the controversy. He responded by sending Aqa Jamal Burujirdi to Mosul to preach the faith. Then he assured the consultative assembly that he was pleased with their work. That is, he decided the case against Aqa Jamal but tried to avoid embarrassing him.[52]

Baha'u'llah actively encouraged the development of consultative assemblies. He wrote to the Afnan clan of Shiraz late in 1883 and again early in 1884 urging them to set up a consultative assembly and to abide by its rulings. He said that the local Baha'i community was obliged to make its decisions democratically (by *mashvirat*, or consultation, which as we saw in the letter to Queen Victoria had for Baha'u'llah connotations of parliamentary procedure). He assured the Afnan family that divine inspiration (*ilhām*) would descend upon "the hearts of those souls who gather for the sake of God in a parliamentary meeting (*maḥall-i shūrā*)."[53] Those Middle Eastern political activists who demanded a parliamentary regime frequently referred to it as a *shūrā*, a consultative body, and it is remarkable that Baha'u'llah employs precisely the same terminology for the Baha'i consultative assemblies being set up in Iran. It is further astonishing that even while he was living, and despite his immense charisma and authority among Baha'is as their messenger of God, Baha'u'llah devolved a great deal of decision making on the early consultative assemblies scattered throughout Iran, bestowing upon them his cachet as "inspired" organizations. In reply to a Baha'i who wrote concerning how to divide up property, Baha'u'llah replied, "With regard to the property and other issues that you have mentioned, in the divine Book such matters have been made dependent upon parliamentary consultation (*mashvirat*). Deliberate democratically (*mashvirat kunīd*) and cling to that (decision)."[54] Baha'u'llah sacralized communicative rationality within both the polity and the Baha'i community, giving it the sanction both of reason and of revelation.

The houses of justice were responsible for the welfare of the poor, as well, and were ultimately to collect the poor tax or *zakāt*, a form of alms originating in Islam (*Most Holy Book*, para. 146). In contemporary Muslim countries such as Pakistan zakāt is formally assessed as a 2.5 percent annual levy on liquid wealth (principally bank accounts), and the funds are distributed in poor neighborhoods. Another way the houses of justice were to help the poor was through the larger Baha'i one-time tax of 19 percent on profits or accumulated wealth called the Right of God (*ḥuqū-qu'llāh*).[55] In his own lifetime Baha'u'llah supervised the distribution of the Right of God to indigent Baha'is. One community asked him if they should support the impoverished with these funds, and he replied that this should only be done with his permission—he wanted an accounting of Right of God contributions and the particulars of its possible recipients among the poor. He feared that giving blanket authority for such measures to the new Baha'i communities in Iran might prove a cause of dissension.[56] (Some who thought themselves deserving might blame the local believers in charge of the funds if they were excluded, whereas no one would argue with Baha'u'llah). Baha'u'llah paid personal attention to the needs of impoverished Baha'is.[57] In a letter to a prominent believer in Shiraz probably written around 1879–1880, Baha'u'llah instructs that half the Right of God collected in that city be given to the poor. He adds that the community should strive, however, to see that all are provided with gainful employment, since being reduced to dependence on charity is inappropriate to the station of a human being.[58]

Membership in the consultative assemblies at first resembled induction into a cell of a secret society, but the invitation no doubt arose from a community consensus on the most qualified elders. At that time only men served on the assemblies, though in Iran's gender-segregated society women developed their own committees, classes, and informal networks. As will be discussed at greater length in a later chapter, Baha'u'llah himself wrote that "today the handmaidens of God are regarded as men (*rijāl*)," but the Iranian community appears to have implemented this principle in private spheres (such as educating girls) rather than in public ones.[59] The houses of justice functioned in a consultative and collective manner and differed from the sort of leadership offered in Qajar society by individual hereditary nobles or clerical jurisconsults who demanded absolute obedience from ordinary folk. Some of the assemblies, such as that in Tehran, put in place ambitious plans for the expansion of the religion and for financing community activities. The Tehran body's institution of morning group prayers, and its establishment of an investment fund to increase the value of believers' contributions, were reported to Baha'u'llah by Sayyid Mihdi Dahaji, Baha'u'llah replying that these steps were "most acceptable."[60] The progress of these bodies in Baha'u'llah's lifetime was impeded by governmental persecution, and in 1882 the members of the Tehran Baha'i consultative assembly were arrested, with about a dozen other prominent Baha'i intellectuals and preachers, and kept in prison for over a year while they were interrogated and the government assured itself that they were not a center of political conspiracy. They were at length released, but it seems that for the rest of Baha'u'llah's lifetime Baha'is were cautious about setting up such formal bodies, which could easily be targeted by the Qajar state.⁶¹

The language Baha'u'llah uses with regard to the consultative assemblies in Arabic and Persian is indistinguishable from the way he speaks about civil parliamentary bodies. He refers to both with such terms as *shūrā, shawr, mashvirat,* and *mushāwarah,* all deriving from the root of an Arabic verb meaning to "consult." It seems likely, then, that he intended all along for Baha'i assemblies to be democratically elected. Such a procedure was impossible to implement in Nasiru'd-Din Shah's Iran, however, since to hold elections for any body might imply a commitment to a national parliament. When Baha'i institutions spread outside Iran to places where such elections were possible, membership in them soon came to be based on election. Thus, in Ashkhabad, Turkmenistan, then under Russian rule, the substantial expatriate Baha'i community elected a Spiritual Board of Counsel in 1895 or 1896.⁶² When Baha'u'llah's son and successor, 'Abdu'l-Baha, instructed the American Baha'is to hold elections in the opening years of the twentieth century, he wrote, "The rules for election are those that are customary in that country."⁶³

Baha'u'llah saw a need to organize his religion on more than a local level. In his later supplements to his *Most Holy Book* Baha'u'llah said that a universal house of justice would be established in the future for the entire Baha'i world. In the "Splendors" (*Ishrāqāt*), he wrote, in the eighth ishraq,

This passage is now being written by the pen of the most high and is reckoned to be of the *Most Holy Book.* The affairs of the community (*millat*) are dependent upon the men of the divine house of justice. They are trustees of God among his servants and dawning points of the cause in his lands. O party of God: That which rears the world is justice, which possesses two pillars: rewards and punishments. These two pillars are two eyes for the life of the people of the world. For every day there is a new matter and every moment a wisdom is required. Therefore, affairs are referred to the house of justice, so that they may implement that which they understand to be beneficial at that time. Souls that arise to serve the cause for the sake of God are inspired with unseen, divine inspirations. From all, obedience is required. Matters having to do with leadership [or "the imposition of sanctions, *umūr-i siyāsiyyih*] are all under the house of justice. But matters of ritual and worship (*'ibādāt*) must be carried out as revealed by God in the Book.[64]

Here Baha'u'llah gave the house of justice specific duties. It is to oversee the affairs of the Baha'i community (*umūr-i millat*). The current official Baha'i translation of this text from the "Splendors" misrepresents the underlying Persian by saying that the "affairs of the people" had been given into the hands of the house of justice. The word *millat*, however, referred to a bounded religious community, and here can only mean the Baha'i millet.

Baha'u'llah intended the religious institutions he set up to have authority only over his followers, not over everyone. He also gave the divine house of justice the authority to legislate and to repeal new laws enacted to meet specific situations but not to abrogate any of his own revealed laws and principles. Among the spheres of authority Baha'u'llah devolved on the house of justice was *umūr-i siyāsiyyih*, an ambiguous phrase here. *Siyāsat* derives from an Arabic word having to do with controlling horses. In classical Islamic law it had the denotation of "setting punishments."[65] This may well be the sense in which Baha'u'llah employed it with regard to the house of justice. In Islamic philosophy *siyāsat* had to do with leadership of various sorts. Baha'u'llah's meaning has been obscured because the modern European conception of politics, which had no indigenous equivalent, was translated in Persian by *siyāsat* in the twentieth century. However, in the late nineteenth century the word still had not taken on that connotation for the most part, and contemporaries of Baha'u'llah who wished to refer to "politics" most often simply transliterated from the French, using *pūlītīk*. The current offical Baha'i translation of this passage renders *siyāsat* as "matters of state," which is certainly a major error if the goal is to understand what Baha'u'llah meant by the term, which was either "matters of leadership (of the Baha'i community)" or "matters involving the application of sanctions." Baha'u'llah spoke of the house of justice as "inspired" (*mulham*), but, as we have seen above, he connected inspiration with parliamentary deliberation; that is, it is the democratic character of these religious institutions, and their embodiment of public reason, that guaranteed their inspiration. Baha'u'llah never used the word *ma'sūm*, or sinless, or infallible to describe these institutions and appears to have seen them more as instruments of spiritual republicanism than as inerrant centers of unchallengeable theocratic dicta.

Baha'u'llah also instructed that the house of justice was to promote peace and lobby against burdensome military budgets, should help choose a world language, safeguard and exalt the place of religion in human affairs, and fix interest rates (Baha'u'llah allowed the taking of fair interest on a loan from anyone, contrary to the principles—but seldom the practice—of Islamic law).[66] On the other hand, as we saw in chapter 1, he clearly envisioned the Baha'i houses of justice as coexisting alongside secular parliaments and rulers, since he urged the retention of monarchy and praised the British parliamentary system.

That the Baha'i religion held no place for a formal clergy required the creation of new collective forms of leadership, such as the assemblies of consultation or houses of justice on which prominent believers served. The concentration on collective decision making and community consultation in Baha'u'llah's writings accorded well with his democratic political program. The new institutions were in principle egalitarian, though in practice they tended to be dominated in the first generation by males with seminary training and by great merchants—though consultation at the nineteen-day feasts, where Baha'is gathered regularly for worship, community business, and hospitality, was open to all. The openness would have been even more inclusive in poorer villages with Baha'i populations.

The Tobacco Revolt

Despite the arrest of a large number of prominent Baha'is in Tehran in 1882, the Baha'i religion continued to attract adherents, sometimes from the upper ranks of society. Baha'u'llah, unlike his much later successors, did not forbid Baha'is to enter into politics, and by the late 1880s and early 1890s a number of Baha'is held high positions, including the governorate of Bushire, the mayoralty of Tabas, and high provincial positions in Tabriz and Shiraz. Among the more prominent secret Baha'is was Muhammad Rida Mu'taminu's-Saltanih, the chief treasury official and chief minister for many years in Khurasan. Around 1885 Mu'taminu's-Saltanih even emerged as a candidate for the open post of prime minister, and he went to Tehran to pursue the candidacy, but his enemies let it be known that he and his brother were Baha'is, damaging his reputation with Nasiru'd-Din Shah. Two years later Ruknu'd-Dawlih and Mu'taminu's-Saltanih were reinstated as governor and chief minister, respectively, of Khurasan.[67]

Despite Baha'u'llah's attempts at a rapprochement with the Qajar state and the increasing possibilities for significant government contacts made possible by such high-ranking converts, he refused to alter the challenging parliamentary principles to which he was committed and to which

Nasiru'd-Din Shah was adamantly opposed. The democratic and egalitarian message evident in the tablets to Queen Victoria and the *Most Holy Book* continues to appear in the major writings of Baha'u'llah in the last twenty years of his life, as Iran's politics became more contentious, leading to the Tobacco Revolt of 1890–1892. He made it clear again in the 1880s, for instance, that he disapproved of absolute monarchy. In Words of Paradise ("Kalimat-i firdawsiyyih"), written in 1889, Baha'u'llah condemned the tyranny of Muhammad Shah (r. 1834–1848). He said, "His Majesty Muhammad Shah, despite the excellence of his rank, committed two heinous deeds. One was the order to banish the . . . Primal Point [the Bab]; the other, the murder of the Prince of the city of statesmanship and literary accomplishment [Qa'im-Maqam]."[68] Qa'im-Maqam served Fath-'Ali Shah as first minister 1821–1834 but was in 1835 put to death by the newly installed Muhammad Shah, and Baha'u'llah's own father was dismissed from his governorship at the same time. This passage combines the two major indigenous sources of Baha'u'llah's constitutionalism. The first derived from the threat of arbitrary dismissal, mulcting, or even execution faced by government officials in an absolutist system. Baha'u'llah, of course, came from the Persian bureaucratic (*dabīr* or *nawkar*) class that suffered most from this administrative form of arbitrariness. The second source was the monarch's role in upholding the state religion, Shi'ite orthodoxy, which had led to state collusion in the persecution of the Bab and his followers. Only constitutional and parliamentary restraints on the ruler, Baha'u'llah was convinced, could ensure security of life and property and freedom of conscience.

At the very end of Baha'u'llah's life a glimmer of political change in Iran appeared in the Tobacco Revolt of 1890–1892. Arguably the first popular rebellion with a nationwide impact since that of the Babis in mid-century, this revolt protested the granting of a concession in the marketing of Iranian tobacco to a British speculator.[69] The shah and his officials stood to profit from kickbacks in the deal and hoped foreign expertise would increase revenues from this commodity. But the move endangered the profits of Iranian brokers, merchants, and growers. It also raised the specter of stronger British imperial influence in Iran, angering the Shi'ite clergy and many intellectuals. The concession provoked a series of demonstrations that eventually made the shah rescind it.

In May 1891 a sayyid, or descendant of the Prophet, in the southern tobacco-marketing city of Shiraz led protests against the foreign monopoly and was arrested and exiled from the city. That a scion of Islam's own Prophet should be so roughly handled for the sake of a foreign tobacco concern provoked riots, and fighting broke out between the people and Qajar troops. The British alleged that the local notable Qavamu'l-Mulk was behind the protests. In the northwestern commercial city of Tabriz there were petitions that summer to the government, as well as mosque sermons, protesting the monopoly. The danger of a general uprising, and actions against the European expatriates resident there, were said to be growing. In fall of 1891 agitation broke out in the eastern city of Mashhad, center of the shrine to the eighth Shi'ite imam, Rida. Tobacco sellers, protesting, took refuge in the shrine. In November in Isfahan the leading Shi'ite authorities, including Aqa Najafi, declared tobacco unclean, and their seminary students went about breaking water pipes. Many Iranians ceased smoking and boycotted tobacco products, acting on a fatwa, or religious ruling, falsely attributed to the leading Shi'ite cleric of that age, Mirza Hasan Shirazi of Samarra' in Iraq (but note that he did not deny authorship). Another riot broke out in Qazvin. Even the women in the shah's own harem are said to have ceased smoking, to the annoyance and frustration of the helpless monarch. By January of 1892 Nasiru'd-Din Shah felt he had no choice but to cancel the tobacco concession he had granted to Major Talbot. Historian Nikki Keddie says that the latter in the meantime had set up a fraudulent dummy corporation to which he alleged he had sold the concession, and this paper corporation then demanded reimbursement from the shah for its supposed expenses and was backed in this demand by the British government. The Iranian government not only had to buy back the tobacco corporation's assets in Iran, which was fair enough, but had to pay several hundred thousands of pounds sterling in compensation—the justice of which is questionable.

The tobacco concession typifies the sort of changes occurring during the nineteenth century that may have made acquiring some control over government policy increasingly appealing to Iran's growing middle classes and to the peasants and artisans. The volume of Iran's external trade increased twelve times 1800–1900. The country was further incorporated into the world market as a supplier of raw materials, and although disease devastated the silk industry from the 1860s, farmers supplemented it with tobacco, opium, cotton, and rice. The population doubled over the century and became more sedentary and slightly more urban. Although Anglo-Russian rivalry prevented the building of a railroad, the expanding telegraph network aided national integration.[70] The constant temptation the poverty-ridden agrarian state faced of attempting to farm out the country's resources to foreigners for development increasingly brought it into conflict with a growing middle class and with guildsmen and peasant farmers.

In July of 1891 Baha'u'llah addressed some of the cultural and political themes in the air in his "Tablet of the World" ("Lawh-i Dunya"). In a passage that demonstrates a strong Iranian patriotism, despite his internationalist sentiments, he lamented the loss of Iran's ancient position as a world center of knowledge and polite culture and its descent into a self-destructive fractiousness. In what is certainly a reference to the Qajars, he bemoaned the "thick clouds of tyranny" that had "darkened the face of the earth, and enveloped its peoples."[71] He referred to the passage in his *Most Holy Book*, written nearly twenty years earlier, which prophesied that "a democracy of the people" would rule from Tehran, but regretted that as yet usurpers and tyrants had usurped the rights (*huqūq*) of the people. He singled out for opprobrium the Qajar prince, Mahmud Mirza Jalalu'd-Dawlih, the governor of Yazd, who had that spring been involved in the killing of seven prominent Baha'is.[72] He reaffirms that what Iran needs is a rule of law (*qanūn va usūl*). However, he does not think it can be forced on the shah, the Shi'ite clergy, and the great nobles but rather must be willingly accepted by them.

> With their knowledge a place should be fixed and therein honorable persons (*hadarāt*) would meet. There they should hold fast to the cord of consultation (*mashvirat*) and adopt and enforce that which is conducive to the security, prosperity, wealth, and tranquillity of the people. For were any measure other than this to be adopted, it could not but result in chaos and commotion.[73]

Echoing his tablet to Queen Victoria written nearly a generation earlier, he advocated that an Iranian parliament be called, like "the system of government which the British people have adopted in London."[74] He warned that without such government by consultation Iran would descend into chaos—a warning that took on particular urgency during the violent nationwide protests of the Tobacco Revolt.

Despite his hopes for Iran's regeneration and his disgust with Qajar tyranny, Baha'u'llah directed his followers to avoid conflict and contention and to eschew religious prejudice. He did not mean avoidance of violent protest during the Tobacco Revolt to signify acquiescence to tyranny or reaction, however. Baha'u'llah, convinced of the inevitability of constitutional and parliamentary government in Iran, wanted Baha'is to work for it peacefully, not with the old Babi scimitar. As for the point of dispute in the Tobacco Revolt, he wrote, "Special regard must be paid to agriculture. . . . Agriculture is highly developed in foreign lands, however in Persia it hath so far been grievously neglected. It is hoped that His Majesty the Shah— may God assist him by His grace—will turn his attention to this vital and important matter."[75] As of July 1891, a year and a half after Nasiru'd-Din

Shah granted the tobacco concession, Baha'u'llah maintained that the ruler had neglected to develop Iranian agriculture. The passage perhaps ironically implies that granting concessions to foreigners constitutes no agricultural policy at all but rather a neglect of this vital sector.

To place Baha'u'llah's thought in Iran's political spectrum of the time, it is instructive to compare the "Tablet of the World" to a petition from the "Liberal Movement" of reformist intellectuals in Iran protesting the tobacco concession early in 1892.[76] The petition decries Qajar officials as despotic and inhuman, just as did Baha'u'llah. It calls for the establishment of organic laws and the dismissal of the current ministers and demands the rule of Islamic law. It says the "reformers" do not wish to introduce European-style legal codes, satisfied that a true application of indigenous Islamic law would suffice. It calls upon the European powers to intervene diplomatically with the shah to temper his absolutism and pledges that the newly formed National League would, "in endeavoring to realise our sacred ideal . . . employ neither force nor rebellion."

Like Baha'u'llah, the reformers renounced violence as a means to their political ends. Still, one is struck that in many ways Baha'u'llah's program is more radical. The Baha'i prophet predicted and explicitly advocated representative government on the British model, as a solution to Iran's problems in general and to the Tobacco Revolt in particular, whereas the National League petitioners eschew European laws and institutions, wishing only to implement a rule of law according to the Islamic code. The mechanisms by which this code could curb absolutism in fact are left completely vague. Second, despite Baha'u'llah's own internationalism, he, unlike the National League, did not here seek the intervention of European powers in Iran's internal affairs. Instead, he advocated that the shah convene an indigenous parliament to negotiate an end to the conflict.

In view of these differences, if the supporters of such reformist petitions were progressive, then clearly Baha'u'llah was even more so. For instance, Mirza Malkum Khan had served in the 1860s and early 1870s with Mirza Husayn Khan Mushiru'd-Dawlih and was adviser to the latter in 1872 during the period of cabinet government. In 1873–1889 he served as Iran's ambassador to England. During all this time he went little beyond advocating mere administrative reforms and even seemed soft on British imperialism. In December of 1889 he lost his post as ambassador because of his involvement in a lottery scheme. In February 1890 he established a reformist journal, *Qanun* (Law), aimed at fostering the rule of law in Iran, and as a result he lost his government rank and salary. In December 1892 he finally came out clearly for elected parliamentary government in *Qanun*.[77] Historians of modern Iran have seen this call as something of a breakthrough. Yet Baha'u'llah had, of course, been making this argument openly since 1868, and in the context of the Tobacco Revolt he strongly reaffirmed it in the "Tablet of the World" a year and a half before that historic issue of *Qanun*. Abhorred by conservative nobles, and to the left of most reformist intellectuals, the Baha'is cast themselves as a sort of "loyal opposition," a force that would work within the Qajar system to achieve democracy without violence—and without corruption or undue foreign interference. Their millenarian belief in divine intervention in human affairs helped give them the patience for a moderate course.

The peaceful and evolutionary strategy toward the achievement of representative government advocated by Baha'u'llah lent itself, as would be expected, to a spectrum of interpretations among the tens of thousands of Baha'is living in Iran, far from their religion's headquarters in Palestine. Some Baha'is, disaffected with Qajar absolutism, came close to the radical camp in their attitude. Others, fearing the dangerous consequences should the charge of political dissidence be added to that of heresy, remained politically neutral.

The career of Abu'l-Hasan Mirza Shaykhu'r-Ra'is (c. 1848–1920), a Qajar prince and dissident, affords an example of the more activist interpretation of Baha'i ideals.[78] A grandson of Fath-'Ali Shah, Shaykhu'r-Ra'is was exposed to Babism by his mother, a convert to the new religion. After his father's death the family settled in Mashhad around 1862. Shaykhu'r-Ra'is studied in seminaries at Mashhad, then at Samarra' in the early 1880s, returning to Mashhad in 1883. He came into conflict with the provincial government in 1884 and had to flee, first to Quchan, then to Central Asia and Istanbul. He returned to Khurasan in 1888–1892, where he again came into conflict with the local power elite and suffered imprisonment. Indeed, he may have been incarcerated for most of the 1890–1892 period of the Tobacco Revolt. There is an indication in his poetry, however, that he saw the dramatic protests and riots of those years, which included on occasion the deliberate setting on fire of tobacco warehouses to spite the British Tobacco Corporation. He wrote,

> They mounted a blockade like smoke rings
>   When turmoil arose throughout Iran.
> The smoke of this apocalyptic commotion
>   Like manifest fumes overtook the world.[79]

The final verses are, "The fumes stood up in the midst and said, / '*A day when heaven shall bring a manifest smoke.*' " The last line quotes Qur'an 44:9, referring to the Judgment Day when God will castigate the people with this visible smoke for rejecting the prophets he sent to them. Shaykhu'r-Ra'is believed, as a Baha'i, that the Resurrection Day was a symbol for the revivification of religion through the coming of a new manifestation of God. Baha'u'llah was "a clear Messenger" who "already came to them, then they turned away from him." (Qur'an 44:13–14). These verses describe the revolt as the fulfillment of one of the Qur'an's prophecies about the end-time, thus endorsing Baha'u'llah's messianic station.

Shaykhu'r-Ra'is then returned to Istanbul. There, in 1892, he joined the pan-Islamist circle encouraged by Sultan Abdülhamid, which began with twelve eminent expatriate Iranians.[80] Its ranks included Shi'ites and also free-thinkers such as Sayyid Jamalu'd-Din "Afghani," and the ex-Azali Babi agitators Mirza Aqa Khan Kirmani and Shaykh Ahmad Ruhi. This circle wrote letters to the Shi'ite ulama in Iraq and Iran attempting to encourage Islamic unity against Europe through support for Sultan Abdülhamid.

In this period Shaykhu'r-Ra'is wrote a treatise on pan-Islam, *Ittihad-i Islam*, which was later published in India.[81] (I might point out parenthetically that Baha'i support for the unity of the Muslim world against European imperialism made perfect sense; Baha'i openness to certain Western political innovations derived from a desire to strengthen Asian societies, not from a willingness to be ruled by Westerners). Shaykhu'r-Ra'is opened a correspondence with Malkum Khan in which he employed the terminology of the latter's League of Humanity, a progressive secret society.[82] For reasons that remain obscure, Shaykhu'r-Ra'is left Istanbul and, after visiting 'Abdu'l-Baha in Akka, went to India. Shaykhu'r-Ra'is later returned to Iran and played a prominent role in the Constitutional Revolution in 1905–1908. He was imprisoned by Muhammad 'Ali Shah (r. 1906–1909) but was later released, and when the revolutionaries toppled that monarchy he served in parliament once again.

The more conservative side of the spectrum was taken by Baha'i merchants based in Bombay. A petition to the shah from the Bombay Baha'i community in early 1892 appeals for the release of unjustly arrested Baha'is and "contains expressions of sincere loyalty to the Shah, repudiates all suggestions that they have any connection with the disturbers of the public peace, and points to Sayyid Jamal-ud-Din and his followers as the fomenters of trouble and disaffection towards the Shah and his sovereignty."[83] A superficial reading of this letter, however, may give a more conservative impression than is warranted by Baha'i actions. These very Bombay Baha'is were at that moment engaged in printing Baha'i treatises calling for representative government and denouncing Qajar tyranny. The shah knew very well that the Baha'is stood for democracy, that they represented an "opposition," even if a cautious one, to absolutist monarchy. The Bombay community simply aimed at making the state understand that, unlike the Azali Babis and the political radicals, most Baha'is constituted a nonviolent loyal opposition.

The gradualist Baha'is, with their peace advocacy, then, held in common some ideals but differed on tactics with the radicals. The latter included political revolutionaries such as Sayyid Jamalu'd-Din and Aqa Khan Kirmani, who called for the violent overthrow of the shah, as well as outraged merchants and their followers, who staged street demonstrations in 1891, and some of the more nativist members of the Shi'ite clergy, who employed the mosque to begin demonstrations and bazaar strikes. Unlike the radicals, Baha'u'llah believed in the power of discourse to change human ideas and institutions. He took a dim view of several radical intellectuals who emerged as important during the Tobacco Revolt. One of these was Mirza Aqa Khan Kirmani (1854–1896). From a small land-holding family in Kirman, he was probably influenced by the unusual religious ideas of some relatives (Isma'ilis and Sufis). He studied at religious schools, then became a tax official in Kirman in 1881. He later served Zillu's-Sultan, the governor of Isfahan, for a while, and by 1886 he was in Istanbul. Having become an Azali Babi, he visited Cyprus and married a daughter of Subh-i Azal. In 1886–1891 he contributed to the expatriate Persian newspaper *Akhtar* in Istanbul. From 1891 he helped Mirza Malkum Khan with his London-based *Qanun* and was involved with the Ottoman pan-Islamist propaganda attempt. He eventually became an atheist, attacking all prophets, and developed a racist form of Iranian nationalism that rejected Islam and Arab culture as causes of Iranian decline. He also joined Malkum in advocating parliamentary democracy. When Nasiru'd-Din Shah was assassinated in 1896, suspicion fell on him and his circle, and he was extradited to Tabriz and executed. When Aqa Khan Kirmani came to Akka in the late 1880s to investigate the claims of Baha'is, Baha'u'llah dismissed him as a two-faced schemer.[84]

In the summer of 1891 Baha'u'llah also wrote against Sayyid Jamalu'd-Din Asadabadi "al-Afghani." After his exile from Egypt in 1879, Sayyid Jamalu'd-Din went to India, where he attacked the reformist Muslim Sir Sayyid Ahmad Khan for his "naturism," or capitulation to Western empiricism. In 1882 he proceeded to Paris, where he helped produce the journal *al-'Urwah al-Wuthqā*, which mixed anti-imperialist writings against

British encroachment on the Muslim world with a sort of romantic Muslim nationalism of an organicist nature. While in Paris he debated the prominent French scholar and theorist of racism, Ernest Renan, who argued that Islam as a Semitic religion was doomed to rigidity and torpor. Sayyid Jamalu'd-Din in reply revealed that he agreed that all religions were superstitious and intolerant and that Islam was responsible for extinguishing the light of science and philosophy in the Arab world. But he insisted that Muslims could overcome the legacy of their faith, just as Europeans had superseded reactionary Christianity. Sayyid Jamalu'd-Din then traveled in Iran and Russia. He spent December 1889 to July 1890 in Tehran, where he held clandestine meetings with local intellectuals and notables in hopes of spreading his reformist ideas and stirring resistance to a despotism he felt too complaisant toward European imperialism. From July 1890 to January 1891 he was forced to take refuge at a local shrine to avoid being expelled from the capital by the cautious shah, and he continued to give reformist speeches to audiences that gathered there. In January of 1891 the shah finally grew so annoyed that he violated the sanctuary and had Sayyid Jamalu'd-Din arrested and expelled to the Ottoman Empire. The reformer spent the last years of his life in Istanbul. He helped foment agitation against the Tobacco Monopoly in 1891–1892, then turned to working on pan-Islamic projects for Sultan 'Abdülhamid. At the end of his life he is said to have regretted having put too much faith in enlightened nobles and dictators rather than concentrating on grassroots activism among the ordinary folk.[85]

In Akka in the summer of 1891 Baha'u'llah included in his "Tablet of the World" a passage was perhaps written a bit earlier, before Sayyid Jamalu'd-Din fell from the shah's favor and was expelled from Iran. He said,

A thing hath recently happened which caused great astonishment. It is reported that a certain person [Sayyid Jamalu'd-Din] went to the seat of the imperial throne in Persia and succeeded in winning the good graces of some of the nobility by his behaviour. How pitiful indeed, how deplorable. . . . Certain dignitaries have allowed themselves to be treated as playthings in the hands of the foolish. The aforesaid person hath written such things concerning this people in the Egyptian press and in the Beirut *Encyclopedia* that the well-informed and the learned were astonished. He proceeded then to Paris where he published a newspaper entitled *Urwatu'l-Wuthqa* [The Firm Handle] and sent copies thereof to all parts of the world. He also sent a copy to the Prison of Akka, and by so doing he meant to show affection and to make amends for his past actions. In short, this Wronged One hath observed silence in regard to him.[86]

Baha'u'llah criticized Sayyid Jamalu'd-Din for his scapegoating of the Baha'is and his manipulative approach to politics.[87] Sayyid Jamalu'd-Din, after all, never put the achievement of democracy in the forefront of his program, considering it more important to win the ear of rulers and to persuade them to rule in an enlightened manner.

Of the three main political currents, the conservative typified by the Qajar ruling elite, the liberal reformism of the middle strata, and the radicalism of revolutionaries, the Baha'i stance most resembled that of the liberal reformers. Yet Baha'u'llah's open and constant insistence on British-style parliamentary democracy distinguished his community from both the Iranian liberals and from many revolutionaries during his lifetime. His refusal to condone violence and his commitment to a constitutional rule of law that would tame the Qajars without overthrowing them further distinguished him from the radicals. From the 1870s through the early 1890s Baha'i thought on representative government put this religion in the progressive camp, especially given the conservative reaction during this era both in Istanbul and in Tehran. Baha'u'llah's writings on politics, though clear about the need for representative government, allowed both an activist and a quietist reading among Baha'is back in Iran. Shaykhu'r-Ra'is represented the activist wing, whereas the Bombay merchants adopted a less confrontational style.

Many Iranians appeared ready, from the 1840s onward, to listen to a messianic leader who might turn the world upside down. Neither the sometimes militant Babis, nor their more peace-loving successors, the Baha'is, had any use for Qajar absolutism or for its base in the exploitation of ordinary folk. The Baha'is elaborated their ideals of governance in a detailed fashion, singling out British constitutional monarchy and the democracies of the Americas for praise. For them the advent of the world messiah signified the end of absolutism, of the tyranny of shah and mullah, and the coming of a new world where the lay public would exercise influence over political and religious affairs. The introduction of a rule of law, of an elected legislature, of constitutional limits on monarchy, of low taxes on the poor and increased state investment in their welfare, and of greater freedom for women, would have truly turned the society upside down. Baha'u'llah envisaged the use of typically liberal means for implementing his vision of representative government, of discourse and discussion (*bayān*). Baha'is would convince Iranians to become democratic through consultative practices in the local houses of justice and through spreading belief in the Baha'i scriptures and ideology. Baha'u'llah's plan for democracy and social welfare, during an era of semifeudal Qajar absolutism, had the advantage of being radical enough to appeal to disgruntled artisans and intellectuals while remaining liberal enough to attract merchants of large property. That is, Baha'u'llah's critique of the inequalities inherent in premodern absolutism appealed to some, while his utopian realist critique of aspects of modernity itself appealed to others.

Surprisingly, Baha'is in the period 1866–1892 had the same sort of links with dissident movements as did the Azali Babis. In their contacts with the Young Ottomans, in their advocacy of parliamentary democracy, in the relations of their intellectuals such as Shaykhu'r-Ra'is with Iranian dissidents in Istanbul the Baha'is appear to differ from the Azalis mainly in two ways. First, they had less antipathy toward the Qajars, though they still wanted them reduced to constitutional monarchs. Second, they sought peaceful ways to effect social change, whereas the Azalis were willing to encourage violent demonstrations in 1891–1892 and to advocate the assassination of Nasiru'd-Din Shah. Historians have tended, without warrant, to read the temporary policy of nonintervention in politics adopted by 'Abdu'l-Baha in 1908 (and intensified by his successor and grandson, Shoghi Effendi Rabbani from 1921 to 1957) back into the period 1866–1892. Baha'is read Baha'u'llah in several ways, both in a liberal fashion and in a more radical one, though all agreed on the desirability of representative government. In short, Shaykhu'r-Ra'is may not have been such an anomaly, as an activist Baha'i constitutionalist, as he has heretofore appeared. Nor was the later Baha'i turn to political neutrality unique. Most Young Ottomans, disillusioned after 1878, took little part in the 1908 Young Turk Revolution. The 'Urabi Revolution ended with a British takeover of Egypt, and 'Urabists like Muhammad 'Abduh later concluded that the Egyptians were not ready for democracy. The constitutionalists—mostly intellectuals, merchants, artisans, and peasants—had little chance of immediate success in a Middle East dominated by landlords and aristocrats supported by the European powers, though they articulated a long-term aspiration of Middle Eastern peoples.

The episode of Aqa Jamal speaks powerfully to issues in the new egalitarianism. In Usuli Shi'ism the laity were commanded to imitate blindly the rulings of trained jurisprudents. Burujirdi wanted to perpetuate such practices in the Baha'i religion, ensuring a high position for the learned. But the other members of the consultative assembly wanted an egalitarian sort of community government, run by laymen. The great clergyman, Aqa Jamal, was to have only one vote, making his counsels equal to those of Aqa Muhammad Karim, the seller of broadcloth.

The establishment of the consultative assemblies signaled the beginning of the end of the power of the Baha'i ulama. The latter often attempted to continue to make their living within the framework of Shi'ite religious institutions, but were quickly identified and exiled from the city by the Shi'ite clergy, forcing them to wander from town to town. This mobility made it difficult, in succeeding decades, for them to remain prominent on the consultative assemblies. The very social order of Baha'i ulama declined in the second generation, because young men from known Baha'i families could hardly go off to Shi'ite seminaries and most probably had no desire to do so, preferring the new professional schools such as the Polytechnic (*Dār al-Funūn*). The abolition of the Muslim practice of having weekly sermons and the placing of administrative and judicial power in the hands of the assemblies left the Baha'i learned with no recognized place in the community and discouraged congregations from giving preachers financial support. The assemblies came to be dominated by local notables and professionals and the religion became increasingly lay and anticlerical, even anti-intellectual. (Ironically, lay assembly members could prove even more fundamentalist and intolerant than conservative clergy, insofar as they lacked the intellectual subtlety that even a seminary education can bestow.) This evolution within the Baha'i community was paralleled to some extent in the Ottoman millets such as the Eastern Orthodox, Greek Catholics, and others, wherein the Tanzimat gradually gave more power to middle-class councils and less to the clerical hierarchy.

Historians have seen thinkers such as Akhundzadih, Malkum Khan, Yusuf Khan, Talibuf, Sayyid Jamalu'd-Din, and Aqa Khan Kirmani as intellectual forebears of the Constitutional Revolution of 1905–1911. Some of these figures laid little stress on democracy and others had a limited audience for their ideas in Iran during their lifetimes. On the other hand, that Baha'u'llah's writings circulated in manuscript and in some printed editions throughout Iran during his lifetime, and were read and memorized by tens of thousands of Baha'is, is beyond doubt. Given the evidence here presented, Mirza Husayn 'Ali Nuri Baha'u'llah must be added to this canon. As the founder of a new religion with tens of thousands of adherents, drawn from illiterate artisans and peasants as well as from merchants, intellectuals, and notables, Baha'u'llah attained a large audience in Iran. By studying both his writings and how they were understood by his audience, engaging in both a writerly and a readerly analysis, we can hope to gain insights into the social history of ideas in Iran rather than merely into the ideas of reformist officials and diplomats.

4 • Disciplining the State: Peace and International Collective Security

In April of 1890 the young British specialist in Iranian studies Edward G. Browne found himself a nervous guest of the Baha'is at the mansion of Bahji in Akka, Ottoman Syria. He had made his way there with a burning desire to meet Baha'u'llah but was unsure he would succeed. He had been delayed in Beirut while merely attempting to arrange permission to come see the Baha'is in Akka at all. Once he reached the city his Baha'i contact disappeared to Haifa for a while, and he had to get himself introduced to the community in more circuitous ways. Finally, he was put up at Baha'u'llah's own house. But was that as close as he would get to his goal? One morning he was mysteriously summoned to a chamber that lay behind a curtained anteroom, "along the upper end of which ran a low divan, while on the side opposite the door were placed two or three chairs." Slowly Browne's eyes became accustomed to the dim light, and he realized with surprise that someone was in the room, a bearded elderly figure sitting where the divan met the wall and wearing the tall fezlike hat, preferred by Muslim mystics, called a "crown" (*tāj*). The figure was, of course, Baha'u'llah, and Browne reported that his host spoke the following words:

> Praise be to God that thou hast attained! Thou hast come to see a prisoner in exile. . . . We desire but the good of the world and the happiness of the nations; yet they deem us a stirrer up of strife and sedition worthy of bondage and banishment. . . . That all nations should become one in faith and all men as brothers; that the bonds of affection and unity between the sons of men should be strengthened; that diversity of religion should cease, and

differences of race be annulled—what harm is there in this? . . . Yet so it shall be; these fruitless strifes, these ruinous wars shall pass away, and the "Most Great Peace" shall come. . . . Do not you in Europe need this also? Is not this that which Christ foretold? . . . Yet do we see your kings and rulers lavishing their treasures more freely on means for the destruction of the human. race than on that which would conduce to the happiness of mankind. . . . These strifes and this bloodshed and discord must cease, and all men be as one kindred and one family. . . . Let not a man glory in this, that he loves his country; let him rather glory in this, that he loves his kind.[1]

Browne was more sympathetic to the Babis and the Azalis than to the Baha'is on the whole, but this encounter with Baha'u'llah clearly made a profound impression on him. He wrote, "The face of him on whom I gazed I can never forget, though I cannot describe it. Those piercing eyes seemed to read one's very soul; power and authority sat on that ample brow."[2]

As Browne discovered, Baha'u'llah's social vision included a strong globalist perspective. With the goal in mind of achieving a manageable, ongoing international peace that would be interrupted by war as little as possible, he advocated a union of the nations, collective security, small standing armies, an end to religious strife and warfare, education for tolerance, a universal language, and disarmament. I am struck by how little interest Browne appears to have shown in the provenance of these remarkable ideas, which were not widely held in either the nineteenth-century Middle East or in Europe and the immediate context of which still remains obscure. Romantic nationalism and the positing of the nation as natural (i.e., racial), eternal, and sovereign were all key elements in modernity. The resulting evils of chauvinism, racism, and total war are a product of modernity no less than is science. Baha'u'llah's utopian realism led him to attempt to combat the evils of mass warfare (introduced by the conscripted Napoleonic armies) and the principle of unbridled national sovereignty that so often underlay the new, vaster scale of bloodshed. Here we move into the second part of this book, in which we examine more thoroughly key points in Baha'u'llah's critique of modernity and advocacy of a countermodernity (or perhaps we could call it a precocious postmodernity).

Background and context are less easy to establish here than in the instance of his ideas on politics and constitutionalism. Contemporary scholars have seen a similarity between some of Baha'u'llah's ideals regarding peace and the unity of religions and a few principles espoused at the Persian-speaking court of the Mughal Emperor Akbar. In his peace program Baha'u'llah was also responding to his contemporary cultural and political setting in the greater Mediterranean, just as his ideas on democracy have much in common with the ideals of the constitutional movement in Istanbul. Any serious thinking about peace in that part of the world during the nineteenth century had a general background, whether remote or immediate, in a tradition of European utopian and political writing. Contemporary international relations were also important. The even more specific political context of such thinking in the 1860s and after raises questions about the impact here of the gradual breakdown during that decade of the diplomatic "Crimean system" set up by the major powers after the Crimean War. Another key question concerns Baha'u'llah's response to the vast extension of European imperial rule in Africa and Asia during the second half of the nineteenth century.

The Abolition of Holy War

The first mention of war between states in Baha'u'llah's writings is a critique of the practices of medieval Muslim statecraft. Religious absolutism in the Middle East served to mark severe boundaries between Self and Other. Classical Muslim jurisprudence treated this boundary drawing under three rubrics. The first concerned the relationship of the Muslim state with non-Muslim neighbors, against whom many Muslim jurists called for unrelenting war. Jihad, or struggling for the sake of Islam, was commanded in the Qur'an in the Medina period, as the Prophet Muhammad came to rule an embryonic state under military pressure from his polytheist Meccan rivals (Qur'an 61:11). The military aspect of this struggle is stressed in 2:190–91, "And fight in the way of God with those who fight with you, but aggress not; God loves not the aggressors; and slay them wherever you come upon them, and expel them from where they expelled you; persecution is more grievous than slaying." Muslim jurists later affirmed that one means of waging this struggle was by the sword, and they said it could be fought against polytheists, apostates, rebels, deserters, and members of pre-Islamic religions such as Judaism and Christianity. In classical Twelver Shi'ite thought only the Prophet or the imam had the authority to authorize an offensive holy war. Many Shi'ites felt that after the Occultation of the Twelfth Imam no offensive holy war could be mounted until his supernatural return. Defensive holy war, as with the Iranian campaigns against Russian expansion in the early nineteenth century, was allowed by many Shi'ite jurists. Most Sunni thinkers continued throughout to allow offensive jihad to be fought. The jurists divided the world into the realm of peace (*dār as-salām*), wherein Muslims ruled, and the realm of war (*dār al-ḥarb*), wherein non-Muslims ruled, and viewed it as a duty of the Muslim rulers to reduce the latter to submission. Some late medieval jurisprudents did speak of an intermediate realm of peaceful accord (*dār aṣ-ṣulḥ*), wherein a Muslim state lived amiably with a non-Muslim ally, with Ethiopia often given as an example. Not all jurisprudents accepted this category. The Bab's legislation on jihad did not materially differ from that of Islam, though he appears never to have actually called the Babis to a holy war against the Qajars, despite his authority within Babism to do so.[3]

The second realm wherein identity was established by marking religious difference was within the Muslim state itself. Where Muslims ruled, non-Muslims were most often demarcated by law and status as subordinate. In classical Islamic jurisprudence non-Muslims living in Muslim lands were either members of protected minority groups (chiefly Jews and Christians, though some clerics accepted Zoroastrians in this category) or were polytheists; the latter were in theory liable to forced conversion or execution. The protected groups were called dhimmis, and they were forced to pay a special poll tax (*jizyah*) and were barred from serving in the army. Muslims were exempt from the poll tax and could pursue military careers. Most jurists held that dhimmis could practice their religion but not build new places of worship. In contrast, the ulama demanded that polytheists be given a choice between conversion to Islam or the sword, though a delay of some months was allowed for those polytheists who had taken refuge with a Muslim ruler from a mutual enemy.[4]

The third marker of difference was among various sects and branches of Islam. The Ottoman state that came to rule what is now Turkey and the Arab world from the sixteenth century treated Shi'ites harshly, forcibly exiling thousands of them from Anatolia to eastern Europe or persecuting them in the shrine cities near Baghdad. The Safavid dynasty that came to power in Iran in 1501, on the other hand, established Shi'ism, expropriating the land of Sunnis, burning Sunni mosques, and humiliating or even executing die-hard Sunnis. Religious absolutism in the Muslim world therefore entailed warfare with non-Muslim neighbors, subordination of and discrimination against non-Muslim subjects, and persecution of those Muslims perceived as heretics or dissidents. These policies are not on the whole required by the Qur'an but rather are simply features of medieval society in the Mediterranean world, and many can be seen in Christendom, as well, at least until the late eighteenth century. Nor were they universally implemented. Muslims, Christians, and Jews lived relatively amicably together at certain points in medieval Spain, for instance. And no

Muslim ruler of the Indian subcontinent seriously considered presenting the millions of polytheistic Hindus with a choice between conversion to Islam and death, however much some Muslim clerics might have called for this step.

Baha'u'llah's abolition of holy war was not unprecedented in Persian culture. Some Muslim thinkers had earlier dreamed utopian dreams of comprehensive harmony, as witnessed especially in the thought of Abu'l-Fadl 'Allami, the chronicler of the reign in India of Mughal emperor Akbar (r. 1542–1605). Swiss Islamicist Johann-Christoph Bürgel has, with good reason, called Akbar's experiment "sort of precursor to what Baha'u'llah intended with his idea of general peace."[5] Abu'l-Fadl speaks of the ideal of "universal peace" (ṣulḥ-i kull) as the goal of Akbar's policies. The Mughal government of the sixteenth century differed from some Islamic polities in making less of a distinction between Muslim and non-Muslim subjects. Even during the reigns of the great Mughals (1526–1707), it was ludicrous of the small elite of Muslim rulers to think about massacring their millions of Hindu subjects or about forcing them to all convert. Akbar in particular self-consciously rejected the framework of medieval Muslim jurisprudence. He recognized Hinduism as a legitimate religion, despite its polytheism and idol worship, and in 1579 he abolished the collection of the jizyah or poll tax. Hindu Rajputs served in the Mughal army, and Hindus were allowed to build new temples. These moves made all Akbar's subjects effectively equal under the law (an experiment not tried again in the lands of Islam until the Ottoman Imperial Rescript of 1856). A historian points out that Abu'l-Fadl celebrated Akbar's decrees:

> Abu al-Fazl clearly recognized the importance of ending the collection of the *jizyah*. He considers this action "the foundation of the arrangement of mankind." The *jizyah* was unnecessary in Akbar's time because members of all religions joined in his service as if they were of the same religion. Only misguided dissenters held back. Abu al-Fazl presents religious strife as a basic cause of human misfortune and upholds *sulh-i kull* [universal peace or conciliation] as a fundamental good. The treatment of adherents of all religions as equals forms a part of his conception of equal justice.[6]

It is often mistakenly thought that Akbar attempted to promulgate a new syncretic religion called "the divine faith" (*dīn-i ilāhī*). In fact the "divine faith" appears to have been something like a small Sufi order for close courtiers, focused upon the person of the emperor as spiritual guide and open to the wisdom of the various religions. The emperor had a house of worship built where members of the various faiths debated one another, including Muslims, Christians, Hindus, and Zoroastrians. But Akbar did not attempt to promulgate the divine faith as a religion to supplant Islam. Rather, the author quoted above argues that the idea of the emperor as guarantor of universal peace (ṣulḥ-i kull) supplanted Muslim state jurisprudence in Akbar's India, insofar as it required a virtual recognition of the legal equality of Muslims and non-Muslims in his realm and the abolition of disabilities on the latter such as the poll tax. Since Abu'l-Fadl 'Allami's writings about Akbar's policies were in Persian, and literate nineteenth-century Iranians had an extensive acquaintance with Indo-Persian history and thought, it is likely that Baha'i leaders knew this Mughal terminology. Akbar's policy of universal peace and religious ecumenism was reported in the influential seventeenth-century Indo-Persian work on comparative religions *School of Manners* (*Dabistan-i Madhahib*), and this book was much lithographed and widely available.[7]

Akbar's Mughal successors rolled back many of his innovations, reestablishing firm legal distinctions between Muslims and Hindus. But the early modern period, with its mingling of empires, forced other Muslim rulers to innovate in the area of relations between Muslim sects and between Muslims and non-Muslims. In Iran the Safavid state (1501–1722) was explicitly devoted to Shi'ism as a state religion. In the late 1600s and early 1700s Sunni tribespeople from Baluchistan and what is now northern Afghanistan revolted against Safavid rule, partially on religious grounds, and these tribal Sunni rebellions brought the Safavid state down in 1722. Nadir Shah (r. 1736–1747) in response attempted to promote a Sunni-Shi'i ecumenism, though the experiment was short-lived.[8] The succeeding Qajar dynasty (1785–1925) reestablished Twelver Shi'ism. In the mid-nineteenth century European powers put pressure on the Iranians and on the Ottomans to end or moderate disabilities laid on non-Muslims on account of their religions, and these Middle Eastern powers were themselves increasingly eager to gain the active loyalty of their non-Muslim subjects. In 1856 the Ottoman Sultan Abdülaziz issued an imperial rescript known as the Reform Decree (*Islahat fermanı*) recognizing Christians and Jews as full subjects with the same rights as Muslims. The decree abolished the poll tax.[9] The Iranian government did not go as far in establishing civil equality, but under pressure from the Zoroastrian community in Bombay Nasiru'd-Din Shah did revoke the poll tax on members of that religion. The Iranian state continued, however, to repress or discriminate against Babis and Baha'is.

Baha'u'llah's attack on religious exclusivity involved an abrogation of the premodern Muslim differentiation between believers and infidels and the establishment of a new model of religious universalism. Central to the former critique was his prohibition of holy war. As a youth in Tehran Baha'u'llah had read a biographical compendium about the life of the Prophet Muhammad, which included an account of the Muslim raid on the Jewish tribe, Banu Qurayzah, which had thrown in with the Meccan polytheists and attacked the Muslims. When the Muslims defeated the Banu Qurayzah and took them captive, the Prophet Muhammad gave the decision as to their treatment into the hands of the Aws clan, of which they had been clients and allies, who appointed Sa'd b. Mu'adh to judge them. For some reason Sa'd decided that the men should be put to the sword, their property divided, and the women and children taken as captives, a severe judgment that was carried out. Baha'u'llah wrote, "In my childhood, this wronged one read in a book by Mulla Baqir Majlisi about the raid on the Banu Qurayzah. From that moment I was distressed and full of sorrow, to the extent that my pen cannot express it—even though what happened was the decree of God, and its intent was only to foil oppressors."[10] By 1862, however, Baha'u'llah had decided to make a prophetic claim of his own, and was determined to ensure that such religious conflict and such severe behavior was abolished. He continues,

> But when the ocean of forgiveness and grace appeared, therefore in those days I beseeched God for that which was the cause of love, fellowship, and unity among all who are on earth. Then, on the second day of the month of my birth before the Dawning (of my mission) [Muharram 2, 1279/June 30, 1862?], all my mental states, my words and thoughts, were turned upside down, an inversion that bore the glad tidings of the Ascent. This transformation (*inqilāb*) was revealed and manifested for twelve days continuously and unremittingly. Afterward, the waves of the ocean of utterance appeared, and the effulgences of the light of harmony were radiant. Then the matter eventuated in a time of full revelation (*zuhūr*), when I attained to that which God rendered the source of joy to the worlds and the dawn of bestowal on all who dwell in the heavens and on the earth. After the Most High Pen (the Bab), we abrogated all that which was the cause of hardship and discomfort and strife by our decisive decree, and we revealed and implemented all that which was a source of concord and unity.[11]

If I am correct, Baha'u'llah is here speaking of a twelve-day, private mystical experience he had beginning on his birthday, Muharram 2, 1279/June 30, 1862, in the months before his formal prophetic declaration of April-May 1863—a mystical experience that was centered on a strong desire for peace and a feeling that the normal order of the world (warfare and strife) had been reversed (*munqalab*). As he indicates in this passage,

Baha'u'llah's first overt announcement of his commitment to concord between religions came at his Ridvan 1863 declaration. He pitched tents at the garden of Necip Pasha in Baghdad and for twelve days spoke to close disciples and family members, then to local friends and admirers, before setting out for Istanbul in accordance with the sultan's decree. The public twelve-day commemoration at this time appears to mirror the early twelve-day private mystical experience that had descended on him ten months earlier. A Persian letter of Baha'u'llah summarizes his message to close disciples and family members during Ridvan. "He 1) abrogated the Islamo-Babi law . . . of offensive "holy War" (jihad), advocating a pacifist attitude to the propagation of Babism; 2) asserted that no independent Messenger or Manifestation of God would appear (presumably after him) for at least a millennium (1,000 [presumably solar] years); and 3) claimed that through his declarative utterance creation had been renewed (or the like)."[12] Baha'u'llah's secretary, Mirza Aqa Jan "Khadimu'llah" Kashani, later explained that "peace for the sake of the entire world became manifest at the beginning of the Blessed Beauty's arrival in Ridvan."[13] One of the three teachings Baha'u'llah promulgated at Ridvan, then (in addition to his cosmos-renewing declaration and his insistence that no new messenger of God would come for a thousand years), was that the command to wage warfare (*hukm-i sayf*) had been abrogated in this religion.

Although before 1863 it would have been difficult to imagine a pacifist Babi, Baha'u'llah's new emphases very quickly spread among those in the community who felt a special attraction to him, especially after his public declaration of messianic status, probably in winter 1865–1866. Interestingly, these oral teachings appear to have taken root even before Baha'u'llah's first major written statement on peace—his circa autumn 1867 "Tablet to the Kings." In March 1867 the Baha'i community of Baghdad wrote a petition to the U.S. government through its consul in Beirut, seeking diplomatic support in pressuring the Iranian government to grant religious liberty to the Baha'is. This document, interestingly enough, conflates the Bab with Baha'u'llah, suggesting that the latter's claim to be the mystical "return" of the Bab was taken very seriously by these Babi-Baha'is. They estimate the number of Baha'is in Iran at that point to be forty thousand. Of Baha'u'llah and his teachings, they say:

> He saw that the people oppose, hate, and kill, abstain and [are] afraid to mix with each other. Nay, they consider each other unclean, though they are all human beings, having different and numerous religions, and that the people are like unto sheep without a shepherd. That learned and wise man wrote many works containing the rules of union, harmony, and love be-

tween human beings, and the way of abandoning the differences, untruthfulness, and vexations between them, that people may unite and agree on one way and walk straightforwardly in the straight and expedient way, and that no one should avert or religiously abstain from intercourse with another, of Jews, Christians, Mohammadans, and others.[14]

The petition and its enclosures were signed by numerous seals, including a free masonic one. It makes the point that all religions teach much the same ethical standards and a belief in a supreme being, and that therefore adherents really differ with one another only over essentials such as "the manner of worshipping" and on specific "regulations and customs." This document clearly points to a sea change in attitudes toward persons of other faiths visible in Baha'u'llah's followers among the Babis, and it is not incidental that the writer of the petition was himself a convert from Judaism. The abolition of holy war and of ritual pollution were already firmly ensconced among Baha'is at this early date.

Baha'u'llah's teaching of peace between religious communities became an often-repeated theme in his subsequent writings, and he laid stress on it for decades thereafter. In his 1891 "Tablet to the World," he wrote: "Strife and conflict befit the beasts of the wild. It was through the grace of God and with the aid of seemly words and praiseworthy deeds that the unsheathed swords of the Babi community were returned to their scabbards."[15] In his summation of his religious teachings at the end of his life, he once again forbade the taking of life and urged that religious competition be conducted through discourse, saying, "We have abolished the law to wage holy war against each other."[16] He went beyond prohibiting formal jihad to enjoining his followers against all forms of contention, struggle, and bloodshed with members of other religions. Religious faction fighting was so common in Iran that he had to deny explicitly to his own followers that any of his previous verses criticizing Shi'ite leaders for their persecution of Baha'is could be interpreted so as to justify Baha'is engaging in violence against them. He intended to efface religious hatred, and even, in the late 1880s, forbade Baha'is from speaking ill of other religions.[17] These directives have led to the relative paucity of polemic as a form of Baha'i literature.

In the passage quoted above from Baha'u'llah's secretary concerning Ridvan, the advent of peace is first and foremost connected with the abrogation of holy war rather than, as in Akbar's conception, being primarily based on the abolition of legal inequalities between Muslim and non-Muslim subjects of the realm. In later writings Baha'u'llah particularly stressed his religion's distinctiveness from Islam and Babism in this regard.

In a letter written in 1889 he links his abolition of holy war and the prohibition on interreligious contention to his permission granted Baha'is to associate with members of other religions, including Christians, to wear foreign clothes, and to read the holy books of other religious communities, including the Bible, all of which he says was previously forbidden (by both Islam and Babism). Instead, he says, in this revelation "liberty" (*hurriyat*) has been bestowed. He instructs that the Baha'i faith be spread with wisdom and articulate speech (*bayān*) rather than through violence or contention.[18] In the "Words of Paradise" (also 1889) he urges that children be schooled in religion so as to learn what is forbidden and what is commanded and the spiritual sanctions and rewards that uphold these values. He adds, "But this in such a measure that it may not injure the children by resulting in ignorant fanaticism (*ta'aṣṣub*) and bigotry [*hamiyyih-'i jāhiliyyih*, literally, 'pagan zealotry']."[19]

The theory of classical Muslim statecraft was driven by legal distinctions between Self and Other. It mattered whether a state was Islamic or not, and conflict with non-Muslim states was most often presumed by the Muslim jurists who wrote on such matters. In actuality, Muslims often allied themselves with non-Muslims, and Muslim states fought each other as fiercely as they fought non-Muslim neighbors. But the theory divided the world into the Muslim Realm of Peace and the non-Muslim Realm of War. One hastens to add that most sixteenth- and seventeenth-century European thinkers also assumed that there would and should be war between Christendom and the Ottomans. For the Muslim jurists, religious identity governed a social hierarchy, in which orthodox Muslims occupied the highest rank, followed by recognized people of the Book (Jews, Christians, and sometimes Zoroastrians), and then followed by illegitimate groups such as Muslim heretics and then polytheists. Baha'u'llah argued against making juridical distinctions between members of various religions, expecting, as we saw in chapter 1, that each individual should have the same civil rights guaranteed by the state. He abrogated the Islamic and Babi laws of holy war, erecting instead an expectation that even states with different religious ideologies should abide in peace with one another. His vision of world peace had other bases, as well, to which I will now turn.

French Peace Thought

If Baha'u'llah's abolition of holy war has parallels in early modern Mughal India, his advocacy of collective security has a context in early modern

European thought. The nineteenth-century intellectuals, journalists, and translators of Algiers, Cairo, Beirut, Istanbul, and Tehran were more likely to know French and French culture than any other European language or national tradition, so French works set the tone for globalist thinking. A brief review of some major Western authors and ideas will be useful in placing Baha'u'llah's own peace thought in general context. European ideas about peace grew out of the same early modern processes that gave rise to early modern and modern political theories more generally. The emergence of powerful nation-states, each with a claim to absolute sovereignty, coinciding with the use of artillery (from the late 1400s) and increasingly effective hand-held weapons, new forms of military technique and organization, and growing prosperity and sources of funding with the rise of mercantile capitalism, all contributed to the outbreak of increasingly bloody and destructive wars. The eighteenth century saw 68 major wars with four million killed, while in the nineteenth century the powers fought 207 wars, killing eight million. Deaths per war for an average major European power rose from 9,400 during the sixteenth century to nearly a quarter million in the twentieth.[20]

The need to mobilize capital for these increasingly costly wars, along with the spread of printing from the mid-fifteenth century, also helped create strong, centralized nation-states. The doctrine of national sovereignty, enunciated in the Treaties of Westphalia in the seventeenth century, implied that states were free to conquer one another whenever they felt strong enough to make the attempt, without intervention from any higher authority. The vast majority of political theorists agreed with Hobbes (d. 1679), who evinced great fear of civil war and bloodshed within states but was untroubled by war among them, on the grounds that war provides a positive economic impetus and so does not cause the same misery as civil anarchy: "Yet in all times Kings . . . because of their Independency, are in continuall jealousies and in the state and posture of Gladiators . . . but because they uphold thereby, the Industry of their Subjects; there does not follow from it, that misery, which accompanies the Liberty of particular men."[21]

Some thinkers espoused alternative views. In the wake of the decline of the Holy Roman Empire and the emergence of a system of competing nation-states, a number of peace plans were proposed that showed nostalgia for Europe's old imagined unity and aimed at some political goal (security for small states, predominance of the Bourbons or Habsburgs, a new Crusade, battling the Ottomans, etc.). We are interested here, however, only in peace plans for the sake of peace, since that is the nature of Baha'u'llah's proposals. Emeric Cruce published *Le nouveau cynée* (The New

Cyneas, referring to a character in *Plutarch's Lives*) in 1623–1624, which "was, in the records of modern history, the first proposal for an international organisation that was also a proposal for maintaining peace."[22] Crucé urged the establishment in Venice of a standing assembly of ambassadors from the world's major states (including not only the Europeans but also the Ottoman Empire, Safavid Iran, the Indian Mughal Empire, and Ethiopia, among others).[23] Although he recognized the sovereignty of each individual state, he thought they should work together to curb war by restraining any monarch from trying to conquer his or her neighbor. Crucé's work was not widely read, but some of his ideas may have influenced the duc de Sully, who urged a European union and the settlement of religious strife in Christendom as a means of expelling the Ottomans and establishing perpetual peace; Sully in his 1638 memoirs quite fraudulently fathered his "Grand Design" on French monarch Henry IV (r. 1589–1610). Although much more widely read, his plan was less universal and enlightened than Crucé's.[24] William Penn's 1693 *Essay Towards the Present and Future Peace of Europe* represented an early Quaker attempt to formulate a peaceful world order, and it followed in the Crucé-Sully line of thought, but it is difficult to identify any channel for its influence in the nineteenth-century southern Mediterranean.[25]

In the eighteenth century a few thinkers continued to disagree with Hobbes about the benefits of international warfare, often meeting derision or obscurity for having done so. Charles de Saint-Pierre (d. 1743), an abbé who purchased a position at the French court in 1692 in order to gain practical experience in government, published his *Projet de la Paix Perpetuelle* (Project of Perpetual Peace) in three volumes between 1713 and 1717).[26] Saint-Pierre felt Hobbes's conclusion had been incorrect, that war impoverishes rather than enriches nations and impedes commerce and manufacture, the true source of wealth. He therefore proposed that just as individuals within a nation need a central state to prevent a war of all against all so the community of nations required a higher central authority to prohibit international warfare. This international assembly would continue to allow national sovereignty in most areas but would legislate for the common good laws that superseded merely national ones, fix boundaries, and forbid the subsequent acquisition of territory from one state by another through violence. Under the principle of collective security aggressor nations could be punished by the assembly by having territory taken away from them, and subjects who supported illegitimate warfare against neighbors would be liable to punishment, as well. Individual member nations were to be allowed standing armies, but only six thousand conscripts each.[27] Saint-Pierre's vision had begun by including the Ottoman Empire (in a 1712 version), but on grounds of practicality and acceptability he moved toward a less truly international scheme.[28] His 1713 plan was to begin with pan-European and pan-Christian concerns, and he allowed Russia into the assembly along with twenty-three other European nation-states despite its Eastern Orthodoxy, on the grounds that the truth of doctrines would become clear over time, without any need for governmental intervention. He did, however, continue to envisage that eventually the association of nations would encompass the entire world. He advocated the study of all existing religions, on the grounds that beliefs only present in one faith cannot form a basis for human unity. Only doctrines taught by all the great religions, he thought, could reliably be considered revelations of "Universal Reason." The abbé read widely in the works of explorers and others on the ideas in the other religions, including John Chardin's *Voyages in Persia* about Safavid Iran, in order to gain a sense of what religious teachings might be universal (though he thought such creeds as Protestantism, Islam, and the religion of the ancient Greeks purely human inventions). Among the universal teachings, he thought, was the golden rule.[29] Like most previous such plans, Saint-Pierre's involved both a settlement of international conflict and an arrangement to deal with religious dissension (implicated in many sixteenth- and seventeenth-century wars). Unlike some previous writers, however, he did not advocate that a single religion be dictated by the state or international assembly.

Saint-Pierre's work on peace was widely read in the eighteenth and nineteenth centuries, and proved influential, but never entered the canon of modern political theory in the way that Hobbes, Locke, Rousseau, Voltaire and other thinkers did, who focused more upon the theory of the modern nation-state. Because Saint-Pierre's works have not for the most part been taught in school or college curricula, the ideas therein have not formed part of the standard knowledge expected of educated persons, though he has been rediscovered in each generation, with a good deal of surprise, by thinkers interested in globalism and its evolution. His project was reviewed, positively or negatively, by Leibniz, Rousseau, Voltaire, and Kant in the eighteenth century. Immanuel Kant, of course, produced his own essay on perpetual peace. In the nineteenth century Saint-Pierre was commented upon by Saint-Simon and many others. In the twentieth century he has been studied by a host of scholars interested in the theoretical background of the League of Nations and the United Nations and for his influence on Rousseau and Kant.[30]

Jean-Jacques Rousseau (1712–1778) wrote a widely influential summary of Saint-Pierre's *Projet* as well as a separate critique.[31] Some Rousseau scholars have increasingly seen the influence of Saint-Pierre and the concern with peace as more central to Rousseau than they had earlier acknowledged.[32] With Rousseau's summary of Saint-Pierre's *Projet*, we have now identified a text, rooted in the whole history of peace thought in Europe from Sully to Leibniz to Saint-Pierre, that Francophone Middle Eastern intellectuals were likely to encounter. Many important Middle Eastern modernist writers publishing in the 1850s and 1860s, including Rifaʻah at-Tahtawi in Cairo, Namık Kemal in Istanbul, and Malkum Khan in Tehran knew French and mentioned reading extensively in Rousseau.

The major peace thinking after Rousseau that struck chords in the Middle East was that of the Saint-Simonians. Although Saint-Simonianism and the Bahaʼi faith differ in many crucial regards, some of their ideals appear to overlap.[33] How much of the agreement between them is genuine, and how much merely superficial? Were there new problems or opportunities in the nineteenth-century global context, affecting both early nineteenth-century France and late nineteenth-century Iran, that help explain the similarities?

Henri de Saint-Simon (d. 1825) championed the American and French Revolutions, but wrote his most memorable essays under the Restoration monarchy. He founded toward the end of his life a new religion—the New Christianity. After his death in 1825, Prosper Enfantin gradually emerged as the leader of the movement, emphasizing the religious elements in Saint-Simon's thought, establishing a utopian commune in the midst of Paris, and proselytizing the young engineers of the Polytechnic as well as prominent banking and business families. Enfantin came to be called "father"; some thought him the return of Christ. He attempted to create a priesthood for the new religion and stressed ideas of central authority and hierarchy. He was tried and convicted in 1832 on charges of holding large political meetings and promoting public immorality. The movement, then forty thousand strong, was less vital thereafter.[34]

Saint-Simonianism sought social cooperation and rejected war, competition, and conflict. Saint-Simon proposed that England and France become allies, forming together with other European states the foundation for a political union of Europe, presided over by elected technocrats and businessmen. This international government would arbitrate conflicts but also oversee international public works projects. He wrote, "Europe would have the best possible organization, if each one of the nations which it encompasses were to be governed by a parliament, recognizing the supremacy of a general parliament set above all the national governments and invested with the power to judge their disputes."[35] His vision was limited to Western Europe, and he seems even to have approved of colonial projects as a way of uniting Europeans. He rejected the idea of the nations forming a pact that would impose collective security on member countries, proposed earlier by Saint-Pierre, as impractical.[36]

Saint-Simonians, in contrast to liberals, thought that one businessman driving another out of business and one state seeking to conquer another were useless diversions of humankind's energies from more productive and cooperative projects from which all would benefit. Their concentration on large public works projects helps explain their emphasis on the role of the state, since individual entrepreneurs were little attracted to long-term, low-yield investments such as the railroads. Saint-Simon and his followers saw early that big infrastructural improvements such as the building of a railroad network would have what economists later called "multiplier effects," reverberating through and greatly quickening the economy.

Although it sought to promote global cooperation, Saint-Simonianism does recognize the reality of class conflict. The classes at loggerheads in his system, however, are not the factory workers and the industrialists of Marxist dialectic but rather the productive and the unproductive. The unproductive classes included the landed nobility, absentee landlords, military men, the clergy, and all others who did not actively participate in the creation of wealth. Saint-Simonianism accepted a labor theory of value and thus posited that only through some sort of work (as opposed to mere inheritance of title or wealth) could value be added to the economy. Unlike the later Marxists, however, Saint-Simonians accepted that entrepreneurs, bankers, investors, and other members of the new bourgeoisie engaged in fruitful work. The future belonged to these producers (*industriels*), not to the sluggard (*oisif*) nobles, landlords, and generals who dominated Restoration society in France. Moreover, Saint-Simon sought to guarantee equal opportunity to talent in each generation, and so advocated the abolition of property inheritance. In the early 1830s, after Saint-Simon's death, a large number of Saint-Simonians took up the cause of the industrial working class, many of whom joined the movement.

Enfantin not only supported a better position for workers but also for women, and women played a major role in the movement.[37] Some Saint-Simonians believed a female Messiah would soon come, from the East, and this was one reason some went to Egypt; the major thrust of the movement was toward political economy. Michel Chevalier condemned the "feudal" practice of giving 300 million francs each year to the minister of war, whereas there was no minister of industry and the government was hostile toward the striking workers of Lyons. For only 100 million francs a railroad could be built across France that would put thousands to work. Chevalier advocated the binding of the entire Mediterranean, including Europe, North Africa, and Asia Minor, into a single system of rail and sea transportation, reducing nations to mere provinces and establishing industry, peace, and communication.[38] He says, "Definitive peace must be established through the association of the Orient and the West."[39] The problem is that the association is not envisaged as one of equals. The one blind spot in this vision is Western, and especially French, imperialism. The Saint-Simonians appear never to have doubted the superiority of the West, and Enfantin uncharacteristically accepted the violent French conquest of Algeria. In Europe Emperor Napoleon III, some prominent bankers and engineers, and intellectuals such as Victor Hugo and Heinrich Heine were influenced by Saint-Simonian thought. Later in their lives many Saint-Simonians entered peace groups and Masonic lodges and brought their ideas into those milieus.

Rousseau, who summarized Saint-Pierre's ideas, was in the canon of political theorists much read in the nineteenth-century Middle East by Western-educated reformers. The Saint-Simonians, because of their influence in French higher education and their activities (discussed below) in Egypt, Algeria, and Istanbul, had a demonstrable influence on Middle Eastern thinkers. It would be fruitless to search for a single conduit of knowledge about the later peace groups and their ideas into the Ottoman Empire. Nineteenth-century Middle Eastern political figures and intellectuals were keen observers of Europe, reading European books and newspapers, translating selections from both for the local press, and discussing developments at cultural evenings in their homes. The tradition of European peace thought was by the mid-nineteenth century a pan-Mediterranean one, and the network of intellectuals, statesmen, and expatriate Europeans in which Baha'u'llah moved was aware of the issues it raised.

Middle Eastern thinkers in the 1860s certainly debated the prospect that modernity might contain the preconditions for the advent of perpetual peace. Among the major advocates of this view was Münif Pasha. He had begun his career in the Translation Bureau, and had translated philosophical dialogues by Voltaire, Fontenelle, and Fénélon into Ottoman Turkish. In 1859, upon his return to Istanbul from a posting in the Ottoman Embassy in Berlin, he joined the French Freemasonry lodge that had just been founded in the capital. In 1861 he founded the Ottoman Scientific Society, a major venue for elite debates about modernity. In the mid-1860s Münif Pasha published an article in which he "defended the thesis that with the spread of science and education recourse to force in relations between states would eventually be abandoned."[40] He was vigorously opposed in this view by Namık Kemal, who feared European militarism and felt the need to keep the empire prepared to defend itself from attack. Münif's extensive grounding in modern European thought, and his involvement in French freemasonry (in which Saint-Simonian ideas circulated long after that movement had ceased to be a force in its own right), suggest that he can be situated in the intellectual tradition of peace thought just discussed. That major Ottoman intellectuals were vigorously debating the prospects for permanent peace while Baha'u'llah was exiled in Edirne provides a potentially important context for his own evolution from Babi militancy toward commitment to world unity.

Collective Security

The abolition of holy war would have had implications for international relations in premodern times, when religious ideologies functioned rather as political and nationalist ideologies do now. But Baha'u'llah did turn his attention from purely religious struggles to the issue of secular statecraft. His first statement on international relations between modern states comes in his "Tablet to the Kings," authored sometime in fall-winter 1867–1868. Therein Baha'u'llah apostrophizes the rulers of the earth, saying,

> Lay not aside the fear of God, O kings of the earth, and beware that ye transgress not the bounds which the Almighty hath fixed. Observe the injunctions laid upon you in His Book, and take good heed not to overstep their limits. Be vigilant, that ye may not do injustice to anyone, be it to the extent of a grain of mustard seed. Tread ye the path of justice, for this, verily, is the straight path.
>   Compose (*iṣlaḥū*) your differences, and reduce your armaments, that the burden of your expenditures may be lightened, and that your minds and hearts may be tranquillized. Heal the dissensions that divide you, and ye will no longer be in need of any armaments except what the protection of your cities and territories demandeth.[41]

He urges states to engage in proactive peace making of a sort that will allow them to have low military expenditures, to maintain something akin to militias for self-defense rather than armies for conquest. He complains bitterly, "We have learned that you are increasing your outlay every year, and are laying the burden thereof on your subjects. This, verily, is more than they can bear, and is a grievous injustice." He reaffirms that the poor are "a trust of God" in the midst of the rulers, and warns them against betraying that trust.[42] The "Tablet to the Kings" subordinates the issue of world peace to that of poverty. That is, one of the primary reasons given for the implementation of a peaceful world order is that this step will reduce military budgets and in turn allow lower rates of taxation on those least able to afford it. The corollary of this principle is the implication that martial, praetorian states create poverty and social injustice. The link Baha'u'llah establishes here, between militarism, overtaxation, and lack of government concern with improving the public welfare, would have been appreciated by the Saint-Simonians. So far (1867), there is no explicit mention of collective security as a mechanism for managing the peace, simply a call for disarmament, lower taxes, and a commitment to peaceful resolution of outstanding conflicts.

This call for peace comes as part Baha'u'llah's proclamation of his mission to the monarchs, in emulation of the prophet Muhammad (which early Muslim authorities in turn saw as echoing Jesus's sending his followers to the nations in Acts). It was believed that the Prophet addressed epistles to the Byzantine emperor, to the governor of Egypt, and to Chosroes of Sasanid Iran. The "Tablet to the Kings" is, in addition, very much in the tradition of the "Mirrors for Princes" literature, which goes back as a literary tradition to the *andarz* (advice) works of Sasanid Iran, and became extremely important in Perso-Islamic culture. Baha'u'llah's own call to the rulers to believe is coupled with a demand for the end of war as ordinary political practice. Diplomatic peace is the secular corollary of the abolition of holy war in the religious institution and one of the reasons for seeking a universal language to facilitate communication and avoid misunderstandings.

The political context of late 1867 was the imminent breakdown of the Crimean system established in 1856. The Crimean War of 1854–1856 had pitted the major powers against one another. The initial phase of the war concerned primarily what is now Romania, but in retaliation for Russian advances there Austria, England, and France joined the Ottomans in attacking Russia in the Crimean Peninsula, a formerly Muslim-ruled territory on the Black Sea that had been part of the Russian Empire for many decades. They thereby sought to force an end to Moscow's designs on the Balkans. Tsar Alexander II sullenly admitted defeat early in 1856. The subsequent Treaty of Paris guaranteed the territorial integrity of the Ottoman Empire and neutralized the Black Sea (forbidding both Russian and Ottoman naval operations there). In addition, the three European victors signed a second treaty thereafter, setting up a mechanism for observing Russian actions and providing that any subsequent attack on Ottoman lands would form a casus belli, or legitimate cause for the three allies to go to war again against Russia.[43] The Crimean system seems clearly to have been important for Baha'u'llah's own thinking about peace. Although he absented himself from Baghdad during the period 1854–1856, while the war was being fought, he returned in time to hear of the settlement and its terms. As a resident of the Ottoman Empire in close contact with Baghdad notables and with access to the Ottoman and other press, Baha'u'llah would naturally have learned of the collective security pact. He wrote, "When Russia and the Ottomans launched their conflicting claims, the French emperor arose to assist the Ottomans. After strife and conflict, killing and raiding, a number of monarchs intervened and a peace settlement (*muṣālaḥah*) was achieved."[44]

Baha'u'llah was pained by the carnage involved in that infamous war (which gave rise, through Florence Nightingale, to the modern profession of nursing) but recognized that the treaties concluding it contained important elements of collective security. Perhaps not coincidentally, the late 1850s saw a renewed interest in Saint-Pierre's conception of collective security on the part of writers such as Molinari.

The Crimean system was shaken periodically by wars and conflicts in Europe before its final demise in the vortex of the Franco-Prussian War of 1870–1871. In 1866 France had almost gone to war against the Ottoman Empire over the latter's Romanian principalities, which had elected a prince from outside the empire in contravention of international treaties and which looked set to make a bid for complete independence. In the end the Ottomans blinked and accepted the new prince as a vassal rather than sending troops to impose their own choice. Had they chosen the latter course, Napoleon III might easily have decided to send French troops to liberate Romania, initiating an Ottoman breakup in the Balkans and raising the specter of a free-for-all between Austria and Russia over the spoils.[45] Baha'u'llah, in Edirne, was very close to the scene of action in eastern Europe, and would have been sensible of the danger that the Crimean undertakings of collective security and Ottoman territorial integrity might soon collapse. Also in 1866, Austria and Prussia fought a war. In 1863 and again in 1866 just before the outbreak of the latter conflict, Napoleon III had proposed the convening of an international conference to settle all outstanding European conflicts (remember the influence upon this monarch of Saint-Simonian ideas). At the conclusion of the Austro-Prussian War Russia likewise called for a European congress to settle the issue of Germany. The proposals were stymied by British and other (Austrian, Prussian) opposition. British statesmen in particular were won over by the argument that the status quo was best maintained by observing treaties already signed, not by opening up all European wounds at once.[46]

The dangers to peace were also being trumpeted by the renewed peace movement in Europe. Secular peace groups had grown up from 1854, when the Crimean War began. In that year a Peace Society was established in England. A decade later the Reform League (founded 1864) and the International Working Men's Association (in its 1865 proclamation) condemned war as inimical to the interests of the working class. In 1858–1859, in France, Edmond Potonié-Pierre urged the resumption of the activist Peace congresses that had earlier been held and founded the League for Public Welfare, which in 1866 called for an international republic. In 1867 several new organizations were established on the continent: at Le Havre Ferdinand Santallier founded the Union de la Paix (Union of Peace) and at Paris Frederick Passy set up the Ligue International et Permanent de la Paix (International and Permanent League of Peace). A more radical, third group "was the International League of Peace and Liberty, set up, also in 1867, with yet another journal, *Les États Unis de l'Europe*, by a meeting of 'the friends of peace' in Geneva under the presidency of Garibaldi. Its guiding spirit was the veteran Saint-Simonian, Charles Lemonnier."[47] It argued for democracy rather than monarchy in all nations, the separation of religion and state, and the formation of a United States of Europe. The International League of Peace and Liberty held a conference in 1868, with thirteen countries represented, that called for the elimination of national standing armies and for the establishment of an international army that would enforce the peace.

As we have seen, Baha'u'llah urged the monarchs to adopt both consultative government and the pursuit of peace. In both instances, this general, ideal advice raises the question of how precisely such goals could be attained and what exact political mechanisms might achieve them. Baha'u'llah and the great Muslim political philosophers gave similar political advice, on the importance of consultation, reasonable levels of taxation, and justice. Baha'u'llah differed from the latter, however, in going on to specify modern institutional arrangements for the achievement of those aims, in accordance with his utopian realist approach. In the instance of consultative government, as of late 1868 he began championing the parliamentary system as practiced in Britain. In regard to peace he adopted the idea of collective security, proposed for so long by thinkers such as Crucé, Penn, Saint-Pierre, and (with reservations) Rousseau, which was echoed, however faintly, in the treaties ratified by the victors of the Crimean War.

In a text that derives from 1868, soon after his arrival in Akka, Baha'u'llah spoke in more detail about international relations. He stated that only peace (*sulḥ*) and unity could cure the malaise of the world. "Peace between monarchs," he wrote, "is and always will be the cause of repose for their subjects and the people of the realm."[48] A universal peace regime, he asserted, would allow each country to maintain a very small military and police force, purely for the purposes of self-defense and the maintenance of internal security. The vast reduction in war budgets would in turn allow very low taxes. After such a general peace is achieved, he wrote, should any king rise up in aggression against another, all the others must unitedly repulse him. He attributed the reluctance of the international community to institute such a system to the martial pride of some rulers, who presided over great military forces and sought worldly grandeur. He lamented that such leaders were being shortsighted, since true glory lies in internal character, not in outward pomp. The rulers should recognize this principle and establish the Most Great Peace. This passage, which elaborates upon the ideas laid out in the "Tablet to the Kings," is perhaps the first to enunciate clearly the principle of collective security as a mechanism for the attainment of peace. These principles are also affirmed in his "Tablet to Queen Victoria" (circa 1868–1869, in Akka). There, too, he expressed his hope that the world's rulers would establish peace and reconciliation (*aṣ-ṣulḥ*), so as to spare their subjects overtaxation for military expansion. But by this time he had concluded that the great powers had rejected the Most Great Peace (*aṣ-ṣulḥ al-akbar*) he offered them and could achieve only a lesser peace (*aṣ-ṣulḥ al-asghar*). He added, "Be united, O kings of the earth. . . . Should any one among you take up arms against another, rise ye all against him, for this is naught but manifest justice."[49] As in Saint-Pierre's system, the international settlement is envisaged as being obligatory upon constituent countries, not voluntary, and as having effective means of implementation. Baha'u'llah thus implicitly disagrees with critics of obligatory collective security such as Rousseau and Saint-Simon, the former having feared overcentralization and the latter having doubted that any great power could be induced to give up that degree of sovereignty. His conception of the Most Great Peace appears to have involved a widespread acceptance of him as the Manifestation of God by the reigning monarchs of his day, such that he could throw his prophetic authority behind the immediate end of secular and religious warfare. Having rejected his claims or at least not accepted them, the rulers could now only work toward a secular, lesser peace based on the harsh discipline of collective security.

Baha'u'llah's utterances on world unity and peace are issued in a prophetic and elliptical style. In 1875 'Abdu'l-Baha laid some of these principles out in expository prose, in his *The Secret of Divine Civilization*. Like Saint-Simon, he sees all humanity as a single "corporeal form." He urges respect for the highly educated and proposes judicial reform as well as mass education to promote sciences, industry, and the arts. He condemns the lack of public morality in Europe as well as European militarism and warfare. He advocates universal peace, based on a covenant that will bind the nations of the world into a union, fixing permanent borders, limiting the size of armaments, and enforcing collective security.[50]

The similarity of these ideas to Saint-Simonianism may be largely the result of utopian realist reformers responding in similar ways to similar challenges. But Baha'is may have been in dialogue with heirs of Saint-Simon. As I have shown above, Saint-Simonianism had a significant impact on the Middle East. Enfantin took a group of engineers to Egypt in 1833–1836 to advocate the building of a Suez canal, in hopes it would help unite the world. Instead, they ended up working for the Ottoman viceroy, Muhammad 'Ali Pasha, in building dams and establishing technical schools. Most in this group either died in or fled from the great Cairo plague of 1835. Some went to Istanbul, others settled in Palestine. Saint-Simonian engineers later became prominent in French Algeria and in the continued drive to build a Suez canal (a plan finally realized in 1869). One, Ismail Urbain, who was black, converted to Islam and worked out some ideas on the unity of religions.[51]

Saint-Simonian concepts were adopted by some Middle Eastern intellectuals, including the Egyptian reformist thinker Rifa'ah at-Tahtawi (1801–1873). At-Tahtawi studied in Paris 1825–1831, associated with the Saint-Simonians who came to Egypt in 1833, and integrated many Saint-Simonian ideas into his social thought. In his 1869 work on political economy he quotes a passage from an unnamed author that praises technological advances such as the Suez canal, the intercontinental railroad in the United States, and the possibility of a Panama canal as a means of fostering world unity and peace.[52] I think it certain that 'Abdu'l-Baha read at-Tahtawi's book, *Paths for Egyptian Minds in the Joys of Contemporary Arts*, because he adopts from him the unusual technical term "public benefits" (*al-manāfi' al-'umūmiyyah*)—a phrase rooted in Sunni Muslim legal thought—to denote key developments of modernity such as industry.[53] At-Tahtawi's Middle Eastern version of Saint-Simonianism therefore entered into the discourse of Baha'i and other reformers as well.

We might here recall that the Iranian pro-Western reformer Mirza Malkum Khan studied engineering and then political science in Paris in the 1840s. He developed "a keen interest in Freemasonry and contemporary political philosophy, especially in Saint Simon's school of social engineering and in Auguste Comte's controversial Religion of Humanity."[54] Malkum Khan's long career as an Iranian reformer, diplomat, and then journalist gave him an opportunity to propagate these ideas. Saint-Simonianism, influential in Egypt and Iran, also had supporters in Istanbul. Later I will come back to the similarities and differences between Saint-Simonianism and the Baha'i faith.

Baha'u'llah goes beyond his earlier call for a pact of collective security in his "Tablet of Maqsud," penned on December 31, 1881 (Safar 9, 1299).[55] In it he wrotes that the time had come for "the holding of a vast, an all-embracing assemblage of men." He continued, "The rulers and kings of the earth must needs attend it, and, participating in its deliberations, must consider such ways and means as will lay the foundations of the world's Great Peace amongst men." He urged his listeners to dedicate themselves "to the service of the entire human race." He advocated that great affairs be accomplished through consultation and compassion. Here he was calling for the sort of international peace congress that had been supported in vain by Napoleon III in the 1860s, such as would not be staged in actuality until the 1898 Hague peace conference called by Tsar Nicholas II (though this conference signally failed in its aim of inducing nations to agree to submit to international arbitration of disputes among them).

The "Tablet of Maqsud" exhibits an underlying interest in the pedagogy of peace, in the use of education to form world citizens. Baha'u'llah wrote,

> Man is the supreme Talisman. Lack of a proper education (*tarbiyat*) hath, however, deprived him of that which he doth inherently possess. Through a word proceeding out of the mouth of God he was called into being; by one word more he was guided to recognize the Source of his education; by yet another word his station and destiny were safeguarded. The Great Being saith: Regard man as a mine rich in gems of inestimable value. Education can, alone, cause it to reveal its treasures and enable mankind to benefit therefrom. If any man were to meditate on that which the Scriptures, sent down from the heaven of God's holy Will, have revealed, he would readily recognize that their purpose is that all men shall be regarded as one soul.[56]

Baha'i scripture has as one of its goals the education of human beings to a belief in world unity, but, in addition, Baha'u'llah says, other forms of pedagogy should be informed by the same object.[57] Moreover, this emphasis on the formation of world citizens shifts the responsibility for global reform from rulers, who had neglected to respond to the tablets to the kings, to ordinary persons. In the 1891 "Tablet to the World" Baha'u'llah characterizes his revelation as "the most effective instrument for the education of the whole human race."[58] Baha'u'llah wishes to see humankind educated to a higher ideal than nationalism, an ideal of love for the entire world.

Education is therefore seen as a means of actualizing the inherent potential in human beings for universal love and dedication to global rehabilitation. The revelation is itself a form of education (*tarbiyah*), and institutes of learning (*dār at-ta'līm*) must also teach these values. Baha'u'llah recognizes the dangers of religious education, however, and insists that it must produce broad-minded universalists rather than narrow fundamentalists if it is truly to achieve its goals. Education in the nineteenth century was most often an instrument for the indoctrination of children into a tribal set of allegiances, to church, ethnic group, and, increasingly, nation. Baha'u'llah wanted a countereducation that would open minds rather than closing them and would serve as a pedagogy of planetary inclusion rather than small-minded exclusion.

The international context for the urgent tone in the "Tablet of Maqsud" was the contest between Egyptian constitutionalists and the European powers during the 'Urabi Revolution in 1881–1882, an episode that Baha'u'llah comments on forcefully, as we shall see below. That is, an important element in Baha'u'llah's peace thought is anti-imperialism. In the four decades after the fall of France to Germany in 1871, European powers put most of their military energies into colonial wars of conquest against African and Asian peoples rather than into wars on European soil. This process had begun much before, of course. The initial European military expansion into Africa and Asia, led by the Portuguese in the sixteenth century, had mainly depended upon controlling the high seas and maintaining a few strategic garrison-colonies such as Hurmuz in the Persian Gulf, Goa on the western coast of India, and in the straits of Molucca off the coast of what is now Malaysia. From 1757 the British East India Company innovated in conquering Bengal, a large province of the Mughal Empire, and administering it directly, ushering in the age of land-based colonization. The British defeated the French in India and then went on gradually to conquer most of the subcontinent, taking Delhi in 1803 and the northern provinces of Sindh and the Punjab in the late 1840s.

The Europeans proceeded much more cautiously in the Middle East.

The British initially feared that if the Western Europeans conquered territories away from the Ottoman Empire, the latter would grow too weak to fend off the Russians in the east. For Russia to invade the Balkans and perhaps Asia Minor would put them astride one of the major trading routes from Europe to India, something the British wished to prevent. Therefore, British statesmen on the whole supported the integrity of the Ottoman dominions. The French under Bonaparte tried and failed to colonize Egypt and Akka (1798–1801) but were expelled by joint British and Ottoman forces. The Russians conquered territory away from Iran's northeast in 1811–1813 and again in 1826–1828. The French conquered Algeria in 1830, though it took decades of fierce fighting to subdue the country, after which the best lands went into the hands of French colonists and winegrowers and the local Muslim population was widely expropriated, living in poverty and cultural repression. The British attacked Iran at Bushihr in 1856 but did not hold territory. The Russians fought the Ottomans in 1877–1878, leading to an Ottoman loss of territory in the Balkans. The French took Tunisia in 1881.[59]

In 1881–1882 important segments of the population in the Ottoman vassal-state of khedivial Egypt agitated for and achieved a constitution and parliament, though they were opposed in this by their Ottoman-sanctioned ruler, Khedive Tawfiq, as well as by Sultan Abdülhamid in Istanbul and by the French and British governments.[60] Egypt was deeply in debt to Western European banks, investors, and governments, and some British and French politicians feared that a more democratic government might default on these loans, many of which were given out under terms that can only be characterized as usurious, with outrageous service fees. The struggle between the khedive and his European backers on the one hand and the constitutionalists on the other led the latter to make a revolution in the summer of 1882, in which they declared the khedive deposed. The revolution was joined by large numbers of military men (led by General Ahmad 'Urabi), the educated classes, urban artisans, and villagers. On June 11, 1882, a riot broke out in the port city of Alexandria in which perhaps fifty Europeans died and probably hundreds of Egyptians, which was interpreted by the European press as a "massacre" of Christians by Muslims (it could more accurately be characterized the other way around).[61] On July 11, 1882, the British navy bombarded Alexandria, beginning or provoking fires that destroyed the city and forced a mass exodus of its population to the interior. In August-September the British invaded the country, restored Khedive Tawfiq to his throne, arrested 'Urabi, the Muslim modernist Muhammad 'Abduh, and other constitutionalists, and imposed a "veiled protectorate" on the country that differed only in name from direct colonial rule. The official British sources attempted to suggest that they had saved Egypt from a military junta allied to Islamic fanaticism, but more impartial observers have characterized the British invasion as the quashing of a grassroots democratic movement by an imperial power in the service of the European bond market.[62]

Baha'u'llah in Akka was not far from the Egyptian events, which he followed intently. After the July 11, 1882, bombardment of Alexandria, he wrote a letter to Iran speaking of the complete breakdown of security there and instancing this event as proof of the ephemerality of wealth and opulence (as a port city for the export of cotton, Alexandria had been among the most flourishing urban centers along the Mediterranean). He mentions that the Baha'i families resident there had fled to the Holy Land and were safe, though empty-handed.[63] About eight months later, after the consolidation of British rule over Egypt, Baha'u'llah issued a strong denunciation of European imperialism. He complains,

> Today, in truth, the divine party (*hizb-i ilāhī*) is surrounded and all the others can be seen to besiege it, as you yourself have observed. They [the Europeans] have conquered the lands of Islam under various pretexts (*bi bahānih-hā-yi mukhtalifih*). A time will come when all will turn with self-effacing supplication to God, the Self-Subsisting, the All-High, and will be completely rapt and immersed in reflection. . . . That which has befallen and is befalling the community that is the object of divine forgiveness [*ummat-i marḥūmih*, i.e., the Muslims] is their own fault.[64]

This anti-imperial theme reemerges in several tablets penned in the 1880s, during which the European powers began their historic scramble for Africa. Baha'u'llah instructs the "forgiven" community to pray to God that the conflagration ignited by the European nonbelievers (*mushrikīn*) be extinguished, and has his secretary add, "The greed and avarice in the hearts of the unbelievers has ignited a blaze. They control a number of countries, and advance over a span of territory with the speed of lightning."[65] In a letter of 1888 to the Afnan clan, he makes it clear that he believes that the "people of monotheism" (i.e., the Muslims) are undergoing these tribulations at the hands of the Europeans because they have rejected God's Law as revealed by Baha'u'llah. "Blessed," he says, "are the souls who cling to the grandest legal code (*nāmūs-i akbar*) and the most great Law (*qānūn-i a'ẓam*)."[66]

As we saw in chapter 1, a consistent theme in Baha'u'llah's calls for a peace regime is his consternation over the expense and destructiveness of modern armaments. In 1889 he warned against the excesses of modern technology, and said, probably with reference to advances in artillery, that "an infernal engine hath been devised, and hath proved so cruel a weapon of destruction that its like none hath ever witnessed or heard."[67] He cautions that below the earth things exist "capable of changing the whole atmosphere of the earth and their contamination would prove lethal" and speaks of having seen, perhaps in a vision, that "lightning or a force similar to it is controlled by an operator and moveth at his command." The great increase in the destructiveness of modern warfare, which would become fully apparent in 1914, was among Baha'u'llah's chief concerns in his call for an end to the practice of war on the Clausewitzian model, as diplomacy by other means.

Baha'u'llah's proposal in the "Tablet of Maqsud" of an international peace conference to be attended by the world's major heads of state has a context in the Egyptian crisis and the unleashing of European imperialism. Peace involves not only the abolition of holy war among Middle Easterners, an institution that had threatened Europe in the medieval and early modern periods, but also a renunciation of conquest by the European colonial powers. Baha'u'llah radically questions the justifications given for the European advance (we can imagine them—the civilizing mission, the restoration of order, the safeguarding of European rights), dismissing them as mere pretexts for rapacious invasions. Collective security would function not only to prevent major wars in Europe but to end the white man's burden in Africa and Asia. But this peace regime could only benefit the Muslims facing the threat of colonization if they adopted it as an ideal and pressed for it, that is, only if they accepted this teaching of Baha'u'llah. In addition, both the Young Ottomans and the 'Urabists were convinced that only democratic societies could hope to escape imperial domination; parliamentary governance may also have been among the principles Baha'u'llah saw as necessary to stop the European war machine.[68] In a country with an absolute monarch, after all, the Europeans only had to subdue one man in order to gain vast influence over the entire society. Baha'u'llah saw his laws and social principles as promoters of peace but also its safeguard.

The medieval empires had, of course, fought wars. But premodern warfare was most often pursued by professional soldiers, and although civilians could suffer during the fighting, weapons of mass destruction did not yet exist. The rise of nineteenth-century nationalism led to the splitting of the world into relatively small polities based on a constructed notion of "nation" or ethnicity, cobbled together from linguistic similarities, religion, and other particularistic cultural forms. This divisive nationalism arose at the same time that military weaponry was growing increasingly sophisticated and destructive. Nationalist warfare is a key element of modernity that its champions most often neglect to mention, and it is an element forcefully rejected by Baha'u'llah.

The abolition of holy war and even of religious polemic, the acknowledgement of the authenticity and value of previous revelations, and a restriction of missionary activity solely to the spoken word, are all strategies aimed at achieving the twin goals of peace among various religious communities and their ultimate ingathering into a new universal faith. Like the Emperor Akbar and Abu'l-Fadl 'Allami, Baha'u'llah and 'Abdu'l-Baha speak of the results of these policies as *sulh*, or peace and reconciliation, using the phrases *as-sulh al-akbar* (Most Great Peace) and *sulh-i 'umumi* (universal peace). Even if Baha'u'llah and 'Abdu'l-Baha knew of the Indian precedent, however, they saw the fulfillment of the *sulh-i kull*, or universal peace, to be possible not by means of an emperor's decrees but through the revelation of a new religion promulgated by a prophet from God. The early Baha'i faith contained all the tolerance of Akbar's "divine faith" and "universal peace" but was not limited to a small circle of courtiers or to the government of a single empire. Indeed, 'Abdu'l-Baha's vision was so universal that he, in *A Traveller's Narrative*, implicitly incorporated into it the Enlightenment ideals of religious liberty and the Rights of Man as vehicles for the Most Great Peace among religious communities.

Nineteenth-century Baha'i peace thought also has some remarkable similarities with that of Saint-Pierre, Rousseau, and the Saint-Simonians, though differing in key respects. Most of the resemblance to Saint-Simonianism probably derives from the way in which these two traditions of thought faced similar problems and prospects. The industrial and scientific revolutions, the conflict of science and religion, mass wars, the arms race, the impact of democratic movements, and the felt need for social justice in the face of a growing gap between the wealthy and the poor all confronted any reformist movement of the time.

The parallels between the Saint-Simonians and the Baha'is are particularly striking. Both Saint-Simonianism and the nineteenth-century Baha'i faith were mass movements in the sense that they attracted a following in a wide range of social groups. The intellectual core of Saint-Simonianism lay among engineers graduated from the Polytechnique, but it also spread among banking and industrialist families as well as among factory workers. As for the Baha'is, Momen has estimated on the basis of a major biographical dictionary that three largest groups among them during the period 1866–1892, each with between a quarter and a fifth of the total, were merchants, skilled urban workers, and younger or less prominent members of the Muslim clergy. About 10 percent were in government service.[69] Momen does not attempt to calculate women's participation, but it was important and included major feminist thinkers such as 'Ismat Khanum Ta'irih (d. 1911). This union of merchants, skilled artisans, disgruntled ex-clergymen, some feminists, and a smaller number of bureaucrats included more of the "old" social classes than did the Saint-Simonians, but the social profile of both is similar insofar as these movements grouped social strata who thought of themselves as active producers of wealth or knowledge, oppressed by quasi-feudal nobles and high-ranking clergymen.

As for differences between the two movements, they are legion. Baha'u'l-lah's and 'Abdu'l-Baha's approval of parliamentary democracy was much more consistent and heartfelt than that of Saint-Simon. 'Abdu'l-Baha called for "the free exercise of the individual's rights, and the security of his person and property."[70] Baha'is did have a profound concern for the amelio-ration of the condition of the poor, and advocated government-initiated economic improvements and a graduated income tax, but it is not clear that they wanted the state to play the sort of overpowering economic role that it does in Saint-Simonianism. Although Baha'is approved of modern science and technology, they did not see it or its practitioners as quite the vanguard that Saint-Simon did, emphasizing organization and discourse over technocracy, and a world language over the railroad. The Baha'i vision of a world assembly is also more universal than that of Saint-Simon, includ-ing the Ottoman Empire, Iran, and other non-European powers as equals, and it was based on the principle of collective security, an idea advocated by Penn and Saint-Pierre but not embraced by Saint-Simon. Most impor-tant, they differed in their staying power. Saint-Simonianism, an artificial and at times cultlike religion, gradually died out by the end of the nine-teenth century. The Baha'i faith, as a prophetic religion, has had more suc-cess, though it remains relatively small nearly a century and a half after its founding. Still, it arose in the same world as, and addresses many concerns raised by, Saint-Simonians.

Baha'u'llah's peace thought is distinctive in the elements it draws to-gether, such as the abolition of holy war, the recognition of freedom of con-science and the civil equality of the members of all religions, the call for a world language, the linkage of peace and the succoring and empowerment of the poor (*fuqarā*) and the people, and the vision of a new architecture for international relations (peace conferences held at the level of heads of state, obligatory collective security, arms limitation, and the prohibition of colonialism and military aggression). The Baha'is' turn to quietism from the 1930s blunted their effectiveness as practical advocates of peace, but these ideals had their origins in politics. The contexts for the promulgation of these principles are various and complex, and many of these can only be suggested as broadly contributory to the construction of a nineteenth-century peace discourse. The ideas of Rousseau and the Saint-Simonians were part of the cultural heritage of the southern Mediterranean by the 1860s and 1870s. The contemporary political conjuncture was certainly important, including the erection and gradual breakdown of the Crimean system, the shock of the Franco-Prussian War, the sudden annexations of Tunis (1881) by the French and Egypt (1882) by the British, and the subsequent European conquests in Africa. The practical needs of world science and diplomacy argued for a universal language (discussed in chapter 5). These contexts must not be seen in isolation from Baha'u'llah's millenarian mission of creating a new religion and a new global civilization, a mission that involved reversals of tradition. Where religion had mandated war, it now mandated peace; where it had ordained a lesser status for nonbelievers, it now required equality; where it had persecuted the nonconformist, it now guaranteed freedom of belief; where it had sought to rule, it now left government to civil authorities; where it had viewed nonbelievers as the Other, it now promoted political union among the earth's diverse peoples. Baha'u'llah saw an international system in crisis and advocated a set of utopian realist mechanisms to resolve those problems. He thereby created the Middle East's first indigenous peace movement in the era of modernity, and one of the very few to become institutionalized over the long term.

5 • The Earth Is But One Country

Along with moves away from absolutism in the form of greater freedom of conscience and democracy, and disasters such as the industrialization of war, modernity has been characterized by the rationalization of identity in the form of the nation-state. As one historian has written, "The basic characteristic of the modern nation and everything connected with it is its modernity."[1] Nations are not natural, they are not ancient, and they have not been "awakened" in the nineteenth and twentieth centuries. Another theorist of nationalism bitingly observed, "It is nationalism which engenders nations, and not the other way around. . . . Nationalism is not what it seems, and above all it is not what it seems to itself."[2] The prerequisite for the emergence of the modern nation-state is the creation of national identity, or "imagined community," a community that calls into being a territorial state that in turn creates the nation.[3] The word *imagined* does not by any means suggest that the nation is merely imaginary, or only an epiphenomenon. Nations, once constructed, are quite real, and have vast real-world consequences. And, of course, this process requires not only the efforts of intellectuals and politicians but also those of workers and peasants, who must for reasons of their own forsake their initially more local conception of identity for a powerful cosmopolitan national movement.

The nation is a key component of modernity, which posits the nation-state as a free actor, unconstrained in its sovereignty with regard to other states, except insofar as military weakness curbs its ambitions (this is clear in the French Declaration of the Rights of Man, for instance). It is possible to have a revolutionary-democratic conception of nationhood that is not tied to ethnic identity, as was the case in late eighteenth-century France and the United States. But I shall be discussing primarily a particularistic form of the phenomenon. This sort of ethnic nationalism, which is linked in the minds of its proponents to race, religion, and language, did not really develop in Europe in earnest until the mid-nineteenth century, and it had immediate echoes among European-trained Middle Eastern intellectuals. Eric Hobsbawm has suggested that the mid-century shift to a conception of nation based on ethnicity came about, in part, as a result of the unification of Germany and Italy, the partition of Austria-Hungary, the Polish revolts, and the ethnically based movements among Balkan peoples for independence from the Ottoman Empire.[4]

Baha'u'llah had severe reservations about both elements in the term *nation-state.* In the last chapter we saw how he wished to discipline the individual state by constraining its aggressiveness through the authority of collective security and international conferences. But he was also keenly aware of the subjective element in the imagining of the nation, was concerned by the modern propensity to employ ethnicity, religion, and language as bases, not only for group identity and pride, but for exclusion and hatred as well.

Medieval sovereigns ruled not a single people or "nation" but a polyglot assemblage of communities.[5] Empires made war on one another, and these communities were called upon to support their sovereign in their capacity as vassals. But they did not fight an ethnic Other, only the army of an enemy monarch. Some of what we would now call Italians served the French, while others served the Austrians, and they might easily find themselves in opposing armies. Nor would they, before the nineteenth century, even have conceived themselves as speaking a single language, "Italian"; indeed, most spoke mutually unintelligible dialects, and at the time of unification only about 2.5 percent of the population knew standard literary Italian.[6] In the Middle East Turkic-speaking tribes were the backbone of the Iranian military in the Safavid Empire and thought nothing of fighting other Turkic speakers on behalf of a state that employed Persian as its primary bureaucratic language. Arabic speakers served the Turkish-dominated Ottoman state in its clashes with local elites in the Arab lands.

By mid-century theorists of nationalism were instancing a number of particularistic bases for national identity, beyond loyalty to a sovereign or simply subscribing to a set of ideals. One context for these theories was the widespread nineteenth-century European belief that peoples differed from one another biologically and that biology dictated intelligence and national character.[7] For such thinkers race was conceived as based on "blood" and consisting in a set of traits common to a group. Thus, some "races" were thought braver, or more intelligent, than others, and an attempt was made to rank them hierarchically according to the great chain of being. Some thinkers held to a theory of polygenesis, of a separate creation of each race.[8] In the nineteenth century historical linguistics was drafted into this taxonomical effort, so that race and language were seen as congruent. Racist thinkers such as Renan and Gobineau saw "Semites" as rigid, static, and fanatical, in contrast to the dynamic and intellectually agile Indo-Europeans. Thus began the infamous modern antisemitism that contributed a century later to the Holocaust of European Jewry, and that has been implicated, as well, in many colonialist outrages perpetrated by the French, Italians, and British in the Arab world (Hebrew and Arabic are both "Semitic" languages, and so Jews and Arabs were considered kindred "races"). This way of thinking reconfigured the Baron de Rothschild, a wealthy and refined European male banker, as of the "Semitic race" and therefore inferior to his fellow Frenchmen. French thinker Louis Agassiz went so far as to posit that Africans might represent an altogether different species from Europeans. Racism fed into the building nationalisms of nineteenth-century Europe, as well. Germany or Italy could only be built as modern countries by defining them *against* non-Germany and non-Italy. Ernst Moritz Arndt wrote in 1815 that "the fortunate Germans are an original people" because they "are not bastardized by alien peoples, they have not become mongrels."[9]

Most nationalist bases for group identity can now rather easily be shown to be problematic, but none as easily as "race." Recent findings by population geneticists suggest that the entire idea of race in the nineteenth-century sense is incorrect. There are vague "geographical races," in the sense that gene transfer is statistically somewhat more frequent within continents, and these racial groupings are marked by minor differences in outward appearance. But only 7 percent of human genetic diversity is accounted for by differences among these broad geographical "races," whereas 85 percent of total human genetic diversity is found *within* local populations. That is, humans across races are vastly more alike underneath than their superficial differences of outward appearance might suggest.[10] This relative homogeneity of human genetic inheritance is partially explained by continual interbreeding across groups, especially along their frontiers, such that over time genetic material circulates widely. Indeed, all human beings now living are probably descended from every childbearing person alive sixty generations ago. Gene pools exist, but they are mere statistical concentrations of genes, highly fluid and interpenetrable, and internally diverse. In short, "races" are more social construct than biological reality.

If race is easily deconstructed as a concept, cultural forms of ethnicity continue to have great purchase on the twentieth century fin-de-siècle mind. Anthony Smith has argued that modern nations do often have ethnic roots, in the sense that they base themselves on some preexisting social and cultural formation.[11] But in fact any long-term "ethnicity" such as he identifies in history (that of Armenians, Jews, Maronites on Mount Lebanon, Druze, Persians, etc.) can rather easily be shown to be so desultory, dispersed, and internally diverse that only an act of the modern national imagination could constitute it as a continuous and concrete "ethnicity" in the first place. Medieval China and Japan have the best claims on a strong premodern sense of cultural identity of the sort that came in the nineteenth century to underpin modern nationalism, but this probably affected only a quarter to a third of their populations, leaving the peasants relatively untouched. And it was achieved by a precocious use of "modern" tools such as printing, relatively high rates of literacy, a standardized governmental language, and an extensive bureaucracy.[12]

Languages have some correlation with ethnic descent, insofar as the family tends to transmit both, but the correlation is weak over the long term. Families, even entire tribes and peoples, sometimes give up one language and begin speaking another. Franks and Visigoths who invaded Gaul and Spain ended up adopting vernaculars descended from Latin. In the Middle East after the seventh-century C.E. Muslim conquests, North Africans, Syrians, and Mesopotamians began gradually giving up Berber, Coptic, and Aramaic in favor of Arabic. The Mongols who invaded Iran began speaking Persian, as did many of the Turkic-speaking tribespeople. On the other hand, Turkic-speaking pastoral nomads who invaded Asia Minor gradually displaced Greek from Anatolia. Many formerly Greek-speaking Eastern Orthodox Christian peasants became Turkish-speaking Muslims, especially through the proselytizing of mystics and Sufis. Nationalism assumes that each "people" has a natural "language," but very frequently in history groups have been bilingual or trilingual and have developed very sophisticated ways of intermingling languages and registers in their speech.[13] Moreover, individual languages themselves are not static and have no unchanging essence. They split into many dialects, some of which become separate languages and can no longer be mutually understood. Languages have changed over time (as witness the difference between Old English and modern English or between Zoroastrian Middle

Persian and Muslim New Persian). Peoples speaking any language have been diverse with regard to religion and other markers of identity, while peoples sharing a religion have usually spoken more than one language (as Shi'ites on the Iranian plateau include speakers of Persian, Azeri Turkish, and other regional languages and dialects).[14]

Modern nationalist politicians and intellectuals varied in their strategies. Some appealed to language or dialect similarities in instances where that seemed to offer the greatest chance of uniting disparate groups across a large territory, as in what became Germany and Italy. In other instances religion as a cultural marker offered greater chances of success. Serbian nationalism could not be pursued through language, since Serbs, Bosnian Muslims, and Croats all spoke much the same language. It was Eastern Orthodoxy that set the Serbs apart. Likewise, Zionism emphasized a religious and ethnic identity (though often more ethnic than religious until recently), insofar as the European Jews lacked both a compact territory and a common language (though Yiddish was widespread and Hebrew widely studied).

The older, absolutist hierarchies of religion were not always entirely transcended in modern nationalism, whose proponents were entirely capable of reworking them for nationalist purposes. This appropriation occurred most frequently in states where a particular ethnic and religious group was seen as the essential basis of the nation. Even in the twentieth century the state often favors a particular religion as part of the nationalist project. The Greek constitution prohibits proselytizing, in an attempt to preserve Eastern Orthodoxy, to which 95 percent of the population belongs. In practice, only Protestant evangelists and Muslim ulama are arrested under this law, whereas the Eastern Orthodox clergy freely preach. Indeed, the Orthodox church is given the prerogative of authorizing the opening of a house of worship, even by other denominations.[15] Even in countries where freedom of religion is well established, political frameworks can often favor the legitimation of a particular national religion. Sweden's official Lutheran Church for most of the twentieth century was supported out of monies collected for it by the state from citizens, though they could petition to be relieved of this burden. Post-Soviet Poland gave the authority to license television broadcasters to the Roman Catholic Church. Ireland's prohibition on abortion (and, for most of the twentieth century, on divorce) served as a subtle reinforcement of the majority Catholicism. A state bias toward Catholicism is apparent in some Latin American countries, such as Bolivia, where it is enshrined in the constitution as the "state religion" and where Catholic officials are given a special role in public ceremonial and in religious instruction in schools. Israeli laws disallow civil marriage and concede much other authority to the Orthodox Jewish rabbis, even over non-Orthodox Jews; a little-enforced, unduly vague 1977 law prohibits anyone from proselytizing Israelis by offering material inducements.[16] Many modern Muslim nation-states enforce an ethnic religion on certain segments of their populations. Even in comparatively liberal republican Egypt, Egyptian Muslims may not convert to other faiths, or change their identity papers to reflect such a conversion, and Christian Egyptians, Baha'is, and foreign missionaries have occasionally been jailed for proselytizing Muslims. The proselytizing by other faiths of Malay Muslims is forbidden in some of Malaysia's states and strongly discouraged in others. On the other hand, Malaysian citizens of Chinese Buddhist and Indian Hindu background are free to practice their religions and to convert to other faiths. The old absolutist law of the medieval Muslim jurisprudents prescribing death for apostasy from Islam is now the law of the land in Iran. Despite its rhetoric of pan-Islamic solidarity, the Khomeinist regime requires that certain high officers of state be Shi'ite Muslims, reinforcing the majority religious identity of Iranians. It actively discriminates against non-Muslims and has executed around two hundred Baha'is merely for their religious beliefs. In these instances the state has, either overtly or covertly, recognized a religious ethnicity as one key to the nation it wishes to create or sustain and has acted so as to preserve and privilege it. This strategy is not the predominant one among national movements worldwide, but it has been a significant phenomenon. One study of subnationalism in modern India suggests that such movements have the greatest chance of success where a group has both a different language (or set of closely related dialects) and a different religion from the majority.[17]

If there existed before modernity peoples, ethnicities, and polyglot empires, but few nations and no nation-states, then how exactly did modern nations come to be? The eastern European theorist Miroslav Hroch argued that the nation-state grew up in tandem with modern capitalism, and he posited three stages to the emergence of nationalism among the smaller European countries in the nineteenth century. The first was the rise of a group of intellectuals with an interest in local culture, who collect folklore and do linguistic studies, most often without any political agenda. In Hroch's second stage local intellectuals and politicians who seek greater autonomy or feel themselves blocked in their career advancement by metropolitan officials attempt to cobble together nativist symbols and to appeal to the middle classes, workers, and peasants to work together for self-rule.

In the third phase a separate state is achieved, which in turn imposes on the peoples within its territory a national identity.[18] Hroch's stages, if not universal, are at least widespread. The state accomplishes the task of creating a nation by setting up national school systems that impose a single linguistic standard and a cobbled-together "national" history, and by establishing conscript armies that throw young men from all over the country together and forge affective links between them. The nation-state is not, as an earlier generation of Marxists thought, created by the emergence of a regional market; rather, the nation-state itself creates a national market.

The centrality of the state to this process cannot be overestimated. It has been persuasively argued that the contemporary nations of formerly Soviet-ruled territories were in important respects fashioned by Soviet nationalities policy.[19] A consideration of the state leads us to a recognition of the violence and coercion inherent in nation making. The state must subdue and encompass the peasants, often with much bloodshed, or must reorganize them into estates or collectives, or must delegate such disciplining of their imaginations to big landlords and private property law. Gory peasant struggles against a local landed elite or against a colonial state have often figured largely in their accession to a nationalist consciousness. Through conscripting peasants into a national army and casting them against a foreign power, as well, the state employed massive violence to constitute them as a nation. Not only Baha'u'llah but also 'Abdu'l-Baha was keenly aware of the vast scale of modern warfare, complaining that "at the time of the Franco-Prussian War, in the year 1870 of the Christian era, it was reported that 600,000 men died, broken and beaten, on the field of battle. How many a home was torn out by its roots; how many a city . . . was toppled down by sunrise. How many a child was orphaned."[20]

In addition to state action, other institutions of civil society play a role in the creation of nations. It has been argued that print capitalism, the press, the novel, censuses, museums, and maps also helped many persons to begin to imagine a national community, though some historians have pointed out that these media affected mainly the consciousness of the literate middle classes and the rich.[21] The thesis, put forward in different forms by Marxists and by Ernest Gellner, that the shift from feudalism to capitalism (or as Gellner would have said, from agrarian to industrial society) is universally implicated in the growth of nationalism seems to me problematic.[22] Many individual societies where something that looks an awfully lot like nationalism emerged were largely agrarian at the time—for instance, the Balkans in the nineteenth century and the Arab lands in the teens of the twentieth century. In some early European instances large-scale economic changes and the emergence of industrial bourgeoisies and working classes may have had implications for the development of nationalism. Once the nation-state model was developed, however, ambitious groups anywhere could employ its techniques to attempt to shape a nation, even if their economy remained largely agrarian.

The fashioning of nations has the advantage of creating greater unity within national borders. But such a unity sometimes comes only at the awful price of genocide. This internal unity also has the disastrous effect of creating an Other, of opposing "French" to "Germans," "Germans" to "Jews," "Arabs" to "Turks." The world wars, the Holocaust, and countless nationalist conflicts, which have extirpated millions of human beings in the twentieth century, derived in large part from the modern invention of nationalism, with its attendant national markets and international competition, and the harnessing to it of powerful new technologies of destruction. On one level, nation-making has been part and parcel of the rationalizing Enlightenment project. On another, the operation of reason on ethnicity created a monster that overwhelmed reason in turn and unleashed irrational furies upon the earth.

Echoes of European nationalist thought reverberated loudly in the Ottoman Empire (and to a much lesser extent among Iranian intellectuals) in Baha'u'llah's lifetime. Middle Eastern proponents of regional patriotism pointed out that the Prophet Muhammad is said to have declared that love of one's birthplace (*watan*) is an element of faith. The word *watan* in its original medieval context simply means the village or town where one was born. Nineteenth-century Arab nationalists such as Butrus Bustani in Beirut had employed the saying of the Prophet for the purposes of modern nationalism, reinterpreting *watan*, or "birthplace," as "nation."[23]

The specifically racial argument for nationalism was a minority view in the nineteenth-century Middle East, but such voices could be heard. For instance, new forms of Persian chauvinism emerged among intellectuals under the impact of European racism. Akhundzadih and Mirza Aqa Khan Kirmani excoriated Islam as a foreign imposition and condemned the Arabs as a race of barbarians who permanently set back Iranian civilization.[24]

In contrast, Baha'u'llah argued that humankind was now entering a globalist age, in which all were called to a higher loyalty than either ethnic group or nation, a loyalty to the planet earth and to the generality of humankind. He appears to have developed this vision gradually over the 1860s, but the egalitarian humanism on which it is based has roots in some aspects of the Persian mystical tradition, especially in the medieval poet and mystic, Jalalu'd-Din Rumi (1207–1273). The connection between mysticism and universalism is clear in Baha'u'llah's 1858 book of spiritual aphorisms, *The Hidden Words*, wherein he depicts God as addressing human beings, saying,

> O Children of Men! Know ye not why We created you all from the same dust? That no one should exalt himself over the other. Ponder at all times in your hearts how ye were created. Since We have created you all from one same substance it is incumbent upon you to be even as one soul, to walk with the same feet, eat with the same mouth and dwell in the same land, that from your inmost being, by your deeds and actions, the signs of oneness and the essence of detachment may be made manifest.[25]

This emphasis on the biological unity and sameness of all human beings argues against any form of racism. The insistence on a common human origin appears elsewhere as well. The Parsee agent, Manakji Sahib, reported to Baha'u'llah that Zoroastrians and Hindus in India often believed that they had a separate origin from other peoples; for instance, common Hindus believed themselves descended from the god Brahma, and said that other peoples had other, nondivine origins, in one of the four elements, earth, air, water, or fire. Although the idea of polygenesis, that each race was a separate creation, "was a minority position in eighteenth-century Europe, it has probably been the most common explanation of race throughout human history."[26] Baha'u'llah denied these racial particularisms, insisting that all human beings were created of the same substance, by the same God, and were descended from a common ancestor (though, aware of Hindu texts that spoke of a world eons old, he traced this monogenesis or common ancestry back much farther than the biblical Adam).[27]

Baha'u'llah counsels that narrow loyalties be transcended and declares that "it is not his to boast who loveth his country, but it is his who loveth the world."[28] Elsewhere he urges, against nationalism,

> Address yourselves to the promotion of the well-being and tranquillity of the children of men. Bend your minds and wills to the education of the peoples and kindreds of the earth, that haply the dissensions that divide it may, through the power of the Most Great Name, be blotted out from its face, and all mankind become the upholders of one Order, and the inhabitants of one City. Illumine and hallow your hearts; let them not be profaned by the thorns of hate or the thistles of malice. Ye dwell in one world, and have been created through the operation of one Will. Blessed is he who mingleth with all men in a spirit of utmost kindliness and love.[29]

Nationalism is about the affirmation of a sameness among a group of people, but that affirmation is not possible without the simultaneous exclusion of others. It is, in short, the process of creating strangers, an alienation from humanity that Baha'u'llah opposed. He wrote, in 1881: "The Tabernacle of unity hath been raised; regard ye not one another as strangers. Ye are the fruits of one tree, and the leaves of one branch," adding, "The earth is but one country and mankind its citizens."[30]

Religious identity was a prime basis upon which intellectuals and politicians attempted to erect national communities in provinces of the Ottoman Empire. Because of their minority, second-class status, Ottoman Christians were among the first Europeans to be attracted to nationalist ideas. Thus, Greek merchants and intellectuals who studied in France began dreaming of a Greece independent of Ottoman rule early in the nineteenth century. By the 1820s mountaineers in what is now Greece had staged a war of independence, which the Ottoman sultan asked his vassal, Muhammad 'Ali of Egypt, to put down. The latter's son, Ibrahim Pasha, initially succeeded against irregular Greek forces, but in 1828 the European powers intervened on the side of the Greeks with their powerful navies. Lord Byron was the most famous martyr to the creation of a "Greek" nationality. Yet, as Hobsbawm notes, some of the best fighters against the Egyptian troops were Albanians.[31] One also should not forget the mixed nature of the population in the new Greek state (some "Greeks" were Muslims, others, Greek Orthodox; some spoke Ottoman Turkish, others spoke Albanian or a Slavic dialect).

The Ottoman willingness in 1856 to abolish the poll tax and make Christians equal derived in part from their desire to retain the loyalty of their Christian subjects, who then constituted a significant minority of the population. This move, however, had unexpected side effects in increasing the animosity of Muslims toward this minority, especially among artisans and others suffering because of the influx of cheap European manufactures. In 1860 these animosities flared up in a major Muslim-Christian riot in Damascus, following upon fierce fighting among the Druze and Christians in what is now Lebanon in 1858–1860. The veteran Tanzimat reformer Fuad Pasha was constrained to lead a commission to Damascus to investigate the anti-Christian riots there, and he had a number of Muslim notables and military men executed for not preventing it. These troubles contributed to the rise of a Maronite Christian political identity, an identity given some Ottoman encouragement by their establishment of an administrative district (*mutasarrifate*) of Mount Lebanon.[32]

In the second half of the nineteenth century and the early years of the twentieth the Ottomans gradually lost most of their Christian subjects to various forms of nationalism, usually with a religious tinge, including the Romanians and the Bulgarians. Baha'u'llah while in Baghdad would have been well informed of the religious strife around Mount Lebanon and in Damascus, a neighboring Ottoman province, and when he was exiled to Edirne his proximity to eastern Europe gave him insight into the restlessness of the Bulgarians and Romanians.

Among the grievances of the Christian peoples of the empire was a legacy of state discrimination against them and in favor of Muslims. Such religious discrimination was a feature of Mediterranean societies in general before the advent of modernity, as witness the treatment of Jews in Christian Europe. Muslim jurists often believed that non-Muslims were ritually impure, that they should not ride a donkey while Muslims walked, that they should not be allowed to build their houses as tall as those of Muslims, and that when their religious edifices fell into disrepair they should not be allowed to reconstruct them. Such medieval laws circumscribed the liberties of Muslims themselves, as well. An influential view in Muslim jurisprudence held that any Muslim who apostatized from Islam should be executed, and occasionally such executions were carried out. On the other hand, Lucette Valensi, in a still unpublished study, has shown that in actual practice hundreds of Muslims embraced Roman Catholicism between 1750 and 1850 in Egypt and Greater Syria, and they appear not to have been prevented from doing so.

The issue of civil equality among members of various religions is wrought up with the possibility for peace among them, as both Abu'l-Fadl 'Allami of Mughal India and the Ottoman Tanzimat men of 1856 saw, and here Baha'u'llah and 'Abdu'l-Baha concurred. Baha'u'llah in his *Most Holy Book* commanded Baha'is to associate in friendship with adherents of all religions, abolishing the concept (which was stressed in Shi'ite Islam) of the ritual impurity of nonbelievers, and he links this principle, as well, to his Ridvan 1863 declaration:

> God hath, likewise, as a bounty from His presence, abolished the concept of "uncleanness," whereby divers things annd peoples have been held to be impure. . . . Verily, all created things were immersed in the sea of purification when, on that first day of Ridvan, We shed upon the whole of creation the splendours of Our most excellent Names and Our most exalted Attributes. This, verily, is a token of My loving providence, which hath encompassed all the worlds. Consort ye then with the followers of all religions, and proclaim ye the Cause of your Lord.[33]

He adds elsewhere in this book, "Consort with all religions with amity and concord, that they may inhale from you the sweet fragrance of God."[34] Baha'u'llah effectively abrogated the Islamic ordinances of the poll tax and exclusion of nonbelievers from military service, since he never mentions any such provisions. In so doing he was agreeing with contemporary Ottoman legal practice, which had also jettisoned such laws. Baha'u'llah's commitment to parliamentary democracy reinforced the opportunities for members of various religions to enjoy civil equality. We saw in chapter 1 that absolute legal equality among citizens, regardless of religious adherence, was insisted upon by 'Abdu'l-Baha.

Baha'u'llah's pluralist theology, in which all the major religions are seen as in some sense true, also allowed him to deemphasize religious difference.[35] From his point of view, Judaism, Zoroastrianism, Hinduism, Christianity, and Islam were all different forms of the same underlying phenomenon, and recognizing their unity should remove any pretext for religious nationalism. In another letter to the Parsee agent in Tehran, Manakji Sahib, Baha'u'llah wrote:

> O contending peoples and kindreds of the earth! Set your faces towards unity, and let the radiance of its light shine upon you. Gather ye together, and for the sake of God resolve to root out whatever is the source of contention amongst you. Then will the effulgence of the world's great Luminary envelop the whole earth, and its inhabitants become the citizens of one city, and the occupants of one and the same throne. This wronged One hath, ever since the early days of His life, cherished none other desire but this, and will continue to entertain no wish except this wish. There can be no doubt whatever that the peoples of the world, of whatever race or religion, derive their inspiration from one heavenly Source, and are the subjects of one God. The difference between the ordinances under which they abide should be attributed to the varying requirements and exigencies of the age in which they were revealed. All of them, except a few which are the outcome of human perversity, were ordained of God, and are a reflection of His Will and Purpose. Arise and, armed with the power of faith, shatter to pieces the gods of your vain imaginings, the sowers of dissension amongst you. Cleave unto that which draweth you together and uniteth you.[36]

Here Baha'u'llah propounds what might be called "metareligion," a religion beyond religion that all adherents of concrete historical faiths should acknowledge sharing in common. For Baha'u'llah the purpose of religion is to aid in the acquisition of virtues, including the virtue of love for all one's human siblings, and all the apparatus of theology and canon law must have this as its aim, or it has failed. For any particular religion in any historical period to become a cause for hatred or the harming of others, then, constituted a profound betrayal of metareligion.

Baha'u'llah rejected, with regard to metaphysics, the Aristotelian principle of noncontradiction, though he appears to have accepted it in other fields, such as medicine. That is, Baha'u'llah did not believe all human discourse could be reduced to a set of rational propositions that could then be weighed against one another to determine which was right. Drawing on the legacy of Sufism, and especially the medieval Andalusian mystic, Muhyi'd-Din Ibnu'l-'Arabi, he adhered to a standpoint epistemology, believing that each human being in his or her life traversed a set of epistemological "stations" (*maqāmāt*).[37] Ibnu'l-'Arabi wrote, "The revealed religions are diverse only because of the diversity of the divine relationships. The divine relationships are diverse only because of the diversity of the states. The states are diverse only because of the diversity of the times."[38] For Baha'u'llah, as well, whether one thinks a metaphysical proposition true or not depends not only on the intrinsic truth-value of the proposition but upon which station one has reached in one's own perceptions. For him it is the difference in stations that explains why some persons in a religion see their prophet as an incarnation of God, whereas others emphasize his humanity. He thought both propositions could have a certain validity. Baha'u'llah's conception of culture was close to that of Wittgenstein, who spoke of discourses as "language-games," meaningful in themselves and not necessarily comparable.[39] Thus, Baha'u'llah's universalism makes a great deal of room for local knowledge and the idiosyncrasies of individuals.

These themes regarding unity in diversity also have at least a general background in the tradition of humane Persian mysticism. Rumi, who lived in Anatolian Konya at a time when it had substantial Jewish, Christian, and Muslim communities, argued that differences of religion and ethnic origin were unimportant:

> What is to be done, O Moslems? for I do not recognise
> myself.
> I am neither Christian, nor Jew, nor Gabr, nor Moslem.
> I am not of the East, nor of the West, nor of the land, nor
> of the sea;
> I am not of Nature's mint, nor of the circling heavens . . .
> I am not of India, nor of China, nor of Bulgaria, nor of
> Saqsin;
> I am not of the kingdom of Iraqain, nor of the country
> of Khurasan.

My place is the Placeless, my trace is the Traceless;
'Tis neither body nor soul, for I belong to the soul of
    the Beloved.
I have put duality away, I have seen that the two worlds
    are one;
One I seek, One I know, One I see, One I call.[40]

Baha'u'llah's conception of religious pluralism also bears some resemblance to Immanuel Kant's idea of "natural religion":

> There may certainly be different historical *confessions*, although these have nothing to do with religion itself but only with changes in the means used to further religion, and are thus the province of historical research. And there may be just as many religious *books* (the Zend-Avesta, the Vedas, the Koran, etc.). But there can only be *one religion* which is valid for all men and at all times. Thus the different confessions can scarcely be more than the vehicles of religion; these are fortuitous, and may vary with differences in time and place.[41]

The difference between Baha'u'llah's ideas on religious and national universalism and the earlier ones of Ibnu'l-'Arabi, Rumi, and Kant lies in his formulation of them as a basis for social and political organization, his expression of them not merely as an idiosyncratic philosophy for a mystical or rationalist elite but as the platform for a world religion that he hoped would encompass the planet's masses.

The religion beyond the religions constitutes the first—and general—basis for Baha'u'llah's attempt to dampen the fires of religious nationalism. But he had the more specific expectation that his own religion would compete so well in the global marketplace of ideas that the adherents of the various existing religions would in the long run prove willing to accept it as a uniting umbrella, within which their own former traditions were affirmed at the same time as new laws and values were added. The Baha'i faith is then, like Christianity and Islam, a missionary religion. In the 1869 "Tablet to Queen Victoria" Baha'u'llah points to his ideal of one universal religion for all of humankind as a key element in his peace thought. Apostrophizing the members of Parliament in England and elsewhere, Baha'u'llah wrote, "That which the Lord hath ordained as the sovereign remedy and mightiest instrument for the healing of all the world is the union of its peoples in one universal Cause (*amr wāḥid*), one common Faith (*sharī'ah waḥidah*)."[42] Literally, Baha'u'llah here advocates a single religious law for the entire world. Because of his belief in progressive revelation, he can call for a new universal religion to encompass the globe without declaring the falsity of the previous religions, which are historically contextualized as having been suited to the ages in which they developed. The Baha'i religion is therefore in his view only an essential restatement of the timeless truths embodied in past religions, along with a reformation of religious law and ideals so as to bring them into accord with the needs of a humanity verging on the creation of the first global civilization. The long-term goal of a single world religion, which acknowledges the truth and contributions of its predecessors, is to be achieved, however, solely through peaceful means. This is the significance of the opposition we have seen above between the "sword" of Islam and Babism and the "discourse" (bayān) of the Baha'i faith.

After race and religion linguistic differences formed among the more powerful bases for nationalist projects. By the 1860s Richard Böckh was attempting to show in his widely read essays that language was the only true marker of national identity, an argument with powerful appeal for the scattered concentrations of speakers of German dialects in central and eastern Europe.[43] His conviction was built in part on the work of two generations of folklorists, linguists, and philologists, who helped create the concept of a national language, which was in turn adopted by the new middle classes and propagandized to workers and peasants.[44] It should be remembered, however, that in the age before universal public schooling, widespread literacy and a vigorous private printing industry, languages were not standardized, and dialects were as little as 50 percent mutually comprehensible. This is still the case for various Quechua speakers of the Andean region, and the two major dialects of Kurdish are likewise quite different. Despite the pretensions of pan-Arabism, an educated Beiruti Arab could not necessarily understand very much of the "Arabic" of an illiterate Moroccan tribesman—still less so a century ago, before the transistor radio and the invention of modern standard Arabic for news broadcasts. There is a danger of outsiders' identification of groups as speaking a single language being taken for something real and concrete, for a strong ethnic identity. Peasants and tribespeople are likely to think of their identity more locally and to be little socialized to a national identity, even where a literate elite has managed to erect one for themselves.[45]

The story of how the Israelis successfully implemented a revived Hebrew as a national language is often remarked upon with wonder as an unusual achievement. It differs from other language projects of nation-building states, however, only in degree, not in kind. At the time of the French Revolution, only 50 percent of the French population spoke anything that could be called "French," and only 12 percent spoke standard

French. In nineteenth-century Iran only half the population spoke any form of Persian at home, and large numbers of Iranian subjects, especially non-Persian women, illiterate peasants, and tribespeople, knew little or no Persian, or just enough to barter in towns where it was the urban standard. Persian dialects themselves differed widely. That the French largely know a standard form of French, and most Iranians now know standard Persian, is for the most part an artifact of state policy. Anderson argues that print capital, the economic forces that had so much to gain from having a unified reading public, also played a key role in fixing and standardizing languages, and this may have been so in Europe.[46] In the Middle East, however, literacy rates were so low at the beginning of the twentieth century (as low as 7 percent in Egypt, and likely lower in Iran), and the capital involved in printing and journalism so tiny, that the activities of the print capitalists must be considered in tandem with a powerful set of state policies.

Baha'u'llah's utopian realist response to linguistic nationalism was to call for a world language. The issue of a universal language has as long a history in the Greater Mediterranean as does that of international peace. In the medieval period Arabic and Latin each served as the universal language for the literate classes of the realm of Islam and Christendom, respectively. Still, mystics such as the Catalan theologian Ramon Llull (1232–1315) and the Jewish Kabbalists saw the world as constituted by divine characters and words, and Llull and his followers dreamed of discovering the primeval, miraculous universal language that would help them make sense of the cosmos and in which its underlying realities could be communicated.[47] With the increased use of vernacular languages in Europe from the Renaissance onward, Latin's supremacy declined. This development, along with scientific advances requiring more linguistic precision, produced a European intellectual crisis and impelled many thinkers to call for or even attempt to work out a universal language, in which the literate throughout Europe could communicate about scientific and other manners. Initially, at least, several thinkers proposing a universal language were probably influenced by the earlier Llullist and kabbalistic projects but now turned them toward more practical purposes. Gottfried Leibniz (1646–1716) is remarkable in having proposed both a universal language scheme and a project for international peace (albeit one less ambitious than Saint-Pierre's), and several proponents of a universal language saw the promotion of peace and understanding as among their objectives. Among the bequests the movement left the modern world are the roots of symbolic logic and shorthand. Interest in the universal language project waned in the eighteenth century with the de facto rise of French as the universal language throughout Europe for diplomatic, commercial, scientific, and other purposes, a position it established in the Middle East as well in the following century. Of course, French reigned only among segments of the elite, falling well short of being truly universal (more especially if we look beyond the Greater Mediterranean). Still, several authors of articles in the *Encyclopédie* mentioned the need for a universal language, and some even proposed such projects. After the French Revolution of 1789 interest revived in an international language that might help clarify thinking, promote peaceful change toward republicanism, and form the basis for communication between the future republics of Europe.[48] In the nineteenth century the universal language movement continued, producing a number of new projects. Some impetus appears to have been given to such ideas by the invention of the telegraph in the 1840s and the subsequent use of Morse code internationally. The French thinker Sudre worked twenty-five years on a proposed universal language, and his project won the praise of Victor Hugo, Lamartine, Alexander von Humboldt, Napoleon III (who was said to understand it), and received a prize of ten thousand francs at the Universal Exposition in Paris in 1855 and a medal of honor at the London Exposition of 1862.[49] Among numerous other such projects was the Esperanto developed by Lazarus Zamenhof (1859–1917).

Problems of linguistic diversity plagued Iran and the Ottoman Empire, and Baha'u'llah was not alone in seeing the need for some sort of reform, which he did by the early 1860s. He was unusual, however, in rejecting the new project of recreating language for nationalist purposes and in urging instead an international language. Mirza Aqa Khan Kirmani mixed linguistic chauvinism with racism when he argued, in the late 1880s, that language "signifies the general and specific characteristics, behaviors, manners and forms of belief of a people," positing that a nation (*millat*) was a function of its language and that "the strength of the *millat* depends on the strength of the language."[50] For such modern thinkers language reform was a path to national strength, autonomy, and differentiation.

The first time Baha'u'llah broached the language issues was in the Ottoman capital in 1863. He was speaking with Kemal Pasha (1808–1888), who had been appointed minister of culture in 1861 after recent stints at the Ottoman embassies in Berlin and then Tehran (in the latter he had served as ambassador to Iran).[51] The pasha was typical of the new breed of government officials associated with the Tanzimat reforms and had learned a number of European languages as well as excellent Persian; he had been posted in Iran more than once dating back to the 1830s and was well-acquainted with that country. He had also authored a Persian grammar and textbook and made an anthology of the epic poetry of Firdawsi. Indeed, he gave copies of his Ottoman-Persian grammar to Baha'u'llah for the use of the women of his household in learning Ottoman. He boasted to Baha'u'llah that he had mastered ten or twelve tongues, enumerating them one by one. In reply Baha'u'llah questioned the value of having spent one's life learning over and over again how to say the same thing in a different way:[52]

> We observed: "You have wasted your life. It beseemeth you and the other officials of the Government to convene a gathering and choose one of the divers languages, and likewise one of the existing scripts, or else to create a new language and a new script to be taught children in schools throughout the world. They would, in this way, be acquiring only two languages, one their own native tongue, the other the language in which all the peoples of the world would converse. Were men to take fast hold on that which hath been mentioned, the whole earth would come to be regarded as one country, and the people would be relieved and freed from the necessity of acquiring and teaching different languages."[53]

He noted that Kemal Pasha delightedly agreed that this idea was salutary, and he urged the pasha to lay the matter before the Ottoman government. The minister, however, appears not to have followed up on the idea, and though he met several times with Baha'u'llah thereafter he never broached it again.[54]

The first frame for this encounter is the clever thrust and parry of the patronizing, linguistically gifted Ottoman minister of culture, veteran of European and Middle Eastern embassies, with someone he probably viewed as a leader of a backward millenarian movement based in a relatively isolated country like Qajar Iran. Kemal Pasha's enumeration of the languages in which he excelled elicited from Baha'u'llah a devastating reply that was both pragmatic and visionary. Rather than being awestruck by the advances of Paris, Berlin, and Istanbul, Baha'u'llah saw an immense waste of time and resources that could fairly easily be remedied through international cooperation in choosing a single auxiliary language. In this anecdote the pasha is reduced to playing the part of the unreflecting naïf, whereas it is Baha'u'llah who appears to have the more cosmopolitan vision.

The more general frame of the encounter, however, must have to do with questions of Ottoman and Mediterranean reform. Baha'u'llah's statements on these matters appear to be an answer to a question posed in his milieu. The rehabilitation of society and of the world, including script and language reform, were being debated by both Iranian and Ottoman intellectuals in this period. Mirza Malkum Khan, who knew Baha'u'llah in Baghdad briefly and who was in Istanbul during 1863, is one such thinker.

The most obvious Ottoman context for a discussion of language reform in this period is somewhat narrow. Many felt that the Arabic script made teaching of Turkish difficult and impeded literacy; the Albanian Muslims went over to a Latin script around 1860 in their province of the empire. Ottoman intellectuals such as Mehmet Münif Pasha from 1862 were heatedly debating the need for a reform of the Arabic alphabet (which was, owing to complex Turkish vowel harmonies, unsuited to that language, given the difficulty of representing vowels in it). Akhundzadih, the Persian translator for the tsarist government whom I discussed in chapter 3, became involved in this debate, meeting in July of 1863 with Fuad Pasha and Âli Pasha to promote his scheme for a reformed script. He also attended meetings that summer with the members of the Ottoman Scientific Society, including Münif Pasha, to further discuss the matter. This issue was later, in 1868, taken up with some fervor by Mirza Malkum Khan.[55] Thus, when Baha'u'llah was meeting with Ottoman officials in September-November of 1863 script reform was a lively issue—though not one that the Ottoman government in the end chose to pursue. The question of how Middle Eastern languages were to be represented, however, is only a small part of the issue Baha'u'llah was here addressing. Since we know that Münif Pasha was concerned not only with matters of national identity and the ease of teaching children but also with the preconditions for world peace, he may also have seen language and script reform as contributing to the latter.

The general Babi-Baha'i concern with a universal language and script may have some roots in Islamic esotericism, in the same Neopythagorean and Gnostic currents from the late Hellenistic world that so influenced Llull and the Kabbalists. Precisely this sort of esoteric cultural emphasis characterized Shaykhism, out of which the Babi and Baha'i faiths grew. Shaykh Ahmad al-Ahsa'i commented on the Most Great Name of God, as written in magical characters typical of Islamic talismans, and later Shaykhi leaders wrote on script reform.[56] It was thought that these talismanic notations had special characteristics and conformed to hidden realities in a way that conventional scripts did not. Muslim mystics asserted that ninety-nine names of God are known, but that the hundredth Most Great Name of God remained concealed, and they wrote it in a special script of squiggles and stars.

Although such esoteric concerns may have animated some of the other Babi-Baha'i thinkers with regard to this issue, Baha'u'llah's own stated concerns tend to be purely pragmatic. He stresses the value in scientific exchanges of a universal language and the contribution of an international auxiliary language to world peace.[57] In the wake of his fall 1863 conversation with Kemal Pasha, the idea of a world language and script became central to the new religion Baha'u'llah was gradually revealing. In his 1873 *Most Holy Book* he reiterates his teaching on the importance of a universal language, instructing members of parliaments (majālis) throughout the world to select one. "This will be the cause of unity, could ye but comprehend it, and the greatest instrument for promoting harmony and civilization."[58] In the Glad Tidings, probably written in the late 1870s or early 1880s, Baha'u'llah lays the responsibility for choosing a world language upon the sovereigns of the world or their ministers.[59] In late 1881, in the "Tablet of Maqsud," Baha'u'llah suggests that "it is incumbent upon all nations to appoint some men of understanding and erudition to convene a gathering and through joint consultation" choose a universal language.[60] In an undated tablet, probably written in the 1880s, Baha'u'llah points out that the *Most Holy Book* gives general responsibility for choosing an international language to the people of the world (represented by their parliaments and civic authorities [*ahl al-majālis wa al-mudun*]). Still, he says, specific responsibility lies with "the men of the houses of justice" (*rijāl-i buyūt-i 'adliyyih*), since they are in charge of implementing Baha'i law (the use of the plural here shows that Baha'u'llah is speaking of local houses of justice, what are now called local spiritual assemblies).[61] In the mid-1880s, when he wrote the Splendors, he charged the trustees of the Universal House of Justice with choosing the language.[62] Although this verse appears to contradict the phrasing of the *Most Holy Book*, it is in keeping with the distinction he made between the general responsibility of parliamentarians and the specific responsibility laid on Baha'i institutions to see that the law is implemented; thus, should the Universal House of Justice succeed in encouraging parliaments to fulfill their charge, it will have been involved in choosing the language. In 1889, in his "Words of Paradise," Baha'u'llah went further than the idea of an auxiliary language and envisaged a time when all human beings would speak only a single mother tongue. "We have formerly ordained," he wrote, "that people should converse in two languages, yet efforts must be made to reduce them to one, likewise the scripts of the world, that men's lives may not be dissipated and wasted in learning divers languages. Thus the whole earth would come to be regarded as one city and one land."[63]

The full context of Baha'u'llah's interest in a universal language remains unknown. The decline of Arabic as the literary standard of the Muslim world certainly provided part of the impetus, just as the decline of Latin had alarmed Leibniz. The Muslim world of the nineteenth century faced the same sort of linguistic balkanization as had Europe earlier. Whereas early Islamic chronicles were written in Arabic throughout the Islamic world, by the 1850s contemporary historical chronicles were written in Arabic in Cairo, in Ottoman Turkish in Istanbul, in Persian in Tehran, and in Urdu in Delhi. Arabic continued to be studied by the ulama, or clerical classes, but relatively few Iranian or Turkish ulama could converse fluently in classical Arabic, and even many works of theology and mysticism were written in Persian or Turkish. The new scientific knowledge was likewise being translated and summarized in the regional languages, and the more adventurous intellectuals desired to read such modern works in the original European tongues. This linguistic chaos is what led Kemal Pasha to try to master ten or eleven languages. In an Akka tablet Baha'u'llah observes that "most people, on account of the dispersion of the languages (*az tashattut-i lughāt*) of the inhabitants of the world, are deprived of social intercourse, friendship and the acquisition of knowledge and wisdom from one another."[64] He goes on later in the same tablet to say,

> Every community speaks its own language; the Turk, for example, in Turkish; the peoples of Iran, in Persian and the Arabs in Arabic. In addition, the people of Europe speak their own diverse languages (*bi alsinih-'i mukhtalifih-'i khūd*). Such multifarious languages are traditional among, and specific to, these aforementioned communities. Yet, a further language hath been decreed such that all the people of the world would converse therein.[65]

Baha'u'llah seems interested, later in this tablet, in promoting Arabic, as a supple classical language with a scientific and philosophical tradition and superior breadth (*basat* = lexical richness) to other languages. (In fact, Russian and English are among the two most vocabulary-rich languages in the world). His main concern here, however, is to compare Arabic with Persian, which he thought much less capacious. He states his appreciation for Arabic without mandating it, giving the choice to the peoples of the world (and thus once again demonstrating his faith in democracy). 'Abdu'l-Baha, whom Baha'u'llah appointed to interpret his writings, does not appear to have carried a similar brief for Arabic, arguing that the best course might be instead to create an artificial language that drew on several existing ones.[66]

The reasons Baha'u'llah gives for a world language include elimination of wasteful language study, the more efficient sharing of information and knowledge, and the creation of a world community. That is, linguistic unification could lead ultimately to the decline of linguistic nationalism and ethnic division. Linguistic nationalist ideas were beginning to be broached in the Middle East in Baha'u'llah's own lifetime, partially under the impact of the advent of large-scale printing (private and governmental), which requires a linguistically unified audience. Printing only began to be widespread in the Middle East in the nineteenth century, growing up with greater feelings of ethnic and regional nationalism that along with European colonialism would lead, after World War I, to the fragmentation of the Ottoman Empire. Baha'u'llah wished to combat this linguistic and ethnic fragmentation through his one-language policy, taking developments in the opposite direction, toward greater unity of humankind.

The nationalism of modernity consisted of an attempt by politicians and intellectuals to mobilize disparate populations into compact territorial units putatively based on race, religion, and language and under the control of a single state. Language, however, was shaped into a tool for national unification only after the state was already established. Races in the nineteenth-century sense of unadulterated descent groups never existed, and were for the most part posited on the basis of broad linguistic categories that were themselves shifting and inessential. Religion as a basis for ethnicity had the drawbacks that it almost always implied membership in a broad universal community, and religions were seldom without their own sectarian or linguistic cleavages. Where a common religion was employed to mobilize the population into a national identity, one often finds that prior state policy was heavily implicated in the creation of a core religious identity (as with Catholicism in seventeenth- and eighteenth-century France and Spain or the imposition of Shi'ite Islam on Iran by the Safavids).

Baha'u'llah rejected the nationalism so central to modernity on a number of grounds. As we saw in the last chapter, he repudiated the whole notion of absolute state sovereignty, wishing to replace it with a system of states constrained by international law and institutions. He saw the truth of the underlying biological and spiritual unity of humankind. He saw the inessentiality of linguistic differences and understood that the state could shape and unify linguistic practice. He asserted the underlying unity of the religions that some had attempted to make vehicles for nationalist separatism. When he said that the earth was a single country and humankind its citizens, he envisaged a future where the unstable and warring state system had been subordinated to a federation of nation-states jointly committed to preserving the peace. His own biography may have helped him to see the malleability of identity and underlying human unities. Born an Iranian, he became an Ottoman subject. Born a speaker of the Mazandarani dialect, he learned literary Persian and then spent much of his life in Arabic-speaking environments, becoming fluent in Arabic. He probably also knew Ottoman well. Born a Shi'ite Muslim, he became a Babi and then created a new religion. But nationalist intellectuals such as Aqa Khan Kirmani had similar experiences, and these appear only to have intensified their particularism. Baha'u'llah took a different, utopian realist tack, rejecting the entire idea of essential ethnicity and preferring to see human beings as one and the various elements of their ethnic identity as so many clothes that they could change and discard. If nationalist intellectuals were imagining compact territorial communities, Baha'u'llah imagined a global community. His conception of human unity was, in fact, so thoroughgoing that it even challenged one of the more central sets of values in Middle Eastern society, that is, gender differentiation and a strong form of patriarchy. Let us turn, now, to this key issue, both in modernity and in Baha'i thought.

6 • "Women Are as Men": Gender in the Making of the Baha'i Religion

The Baha'i religion came to be associated with the improvement of women's status in the Middle East, though by no means all its positions on gender issues can be characterized strictly speaking as "feminist" in the sense of requiring equality of the sexes in any particular sphere. Baha'i thinking about women was elaborated from diverse standpoints (the Prophet himself, Middle Eastern women and men, Western women and men, patricians and workers, artisans and peasants), and the standpoints of these various individuals and groups changed over time. How did it come to be that a millenarian offshoot of Shi'ite Islam should become identified in some important respects with women's emancipation? What internal challenges, what sets of dialogue and negotiation, and what external impetuses help account for this development? What role did women themselves play in fashioning the new religion? How did the attitude toward women and gender in the Baha'i faith change over time?

The Baha'i faith grew up at a time when new ideas were in the air concerning gender issues. New middle- and upper-class reformers, often with links to modern institutions such as reformed bureaucracies or modern commerce, focused on education, ending veiling and seclusion of women, and job training and opportunities. Many literate men justified these changes by appealing to the need for national revival, which required contributions from all citizens. The urban middle and upper classes were expanding rapidly, with the advent of agrarian capitalism and the growth of a strong import-export sector based in the cities, and their concerns about gender roles ultimately had an increasing impact. One factor affecting Iranian Muslim perceptions of gender roles was the travel accounts of Iranian sojourners in Europe, who often reported on the greater freedoms of Western women.[1] Another was the periodicals and writings of reformers. In Iran, an improvement of the status of women was often linked to social reform more generally. Because the Baha'i leaders lived in the Ottoman Empire and more especially in its Arab provinces, the movement was open to the influence of reformist thought not only in Iran but also in Istanbul, Cairo, and Beirut, not to mention Europe itself. The Iranian social and intellectual context remained important, however. Afsaneh Najmabadi has shown that as early as 1881 a book printed in Iran called for the education of girls alongside boys. In the late nineteenth century the militantly secularist thinker Mirza Aqa Khan Kirmani (1854–1896) pointed to the mother as the first educator of the child, even in the womb, and feared that the embryo imbibed character, including ignorance or learning, even at that time. He also argued against veiling and for women's education and employment in government, industry, and commerce.[2] How did the Baha'is respond to these social and intellectual challenges regarding the position of women?

The terms of much reformist discourse in the Middle East were set by European developments. Nineteenth-century modernity was caught up in a contradiction between universalist impulses and particularistic ones. The supposedly expansive ideals of the Enlightenment were in fact put forward with property-owning, adult white males in mind. Behind the façade of the universal lay a set of distinctions, of differences, that allowed a hierarchy to be erected, wherein rights were in fact unevenly distributed according to socially constructed categories. The striving for rights, for liberty and equality during the French Revolution, was framed as a search for "fraternity," which is to say that it excluded women as full citizens. Indeed, women were not even accorded the vote in most republics until the twentieth century. Moreover, colonial subjects, and even the European poor, were most often excluded from enjoyment of the Rights of Man, and the very existence of slavery negated the universality of such rights. Women, workers, and non-European peoples were juvenilized by the European male elite and seen as immature, as one means of excluding them from basic civil rights. In the nineteenth century what was called then "the woman movement," labor organizations, abolitionist movements, and anticolonial parties became major forces in society, demanding both Enlightenment rights from which they had initially been excluded and in some instances reconfiguring the whole notion of a "right."

In the West feminism emerged out of the nineteenth-century "woman movement," which had concentrated on charitable and benevolent service and civic reform, on gaining political rights for women similar to those enjoyed by men, and on emancipation from restricting social conventions. In the early twentieth-century United States three core elements in feminism emerged from the older woman movement, according to a leading historian of the movement. The first is opposition to gender or sexual hierarchy, that is, rejection of the privileges of men associated with patriarchy. This might be expressed as a commitment to gender equality, but equality only in the sense of equal rights and opportunities, not in the sense of sameness. The second is a conviction that women's position in society is socially constructed and a denial that women's subordinate status in patriarchal societies is dictated by unalterable divine decree or by biology. Finally, there is a recognition that women perceive themselves as a social grouping and not only a biological category.[3] Obviously, nineteenth-century Baha'i progressive activities more resembled the earlier set of programs called the woman movement, whereas in the opening decades of the twentieth century some Baha'is, especially in the West, developed a stance more closely approximating feminism.

Nineteenth-century modernists tended to see gender as a function of biology, and as a fixed category, just as they fixed racial and national categories, and positivism attributed to women certain "natural" characteristics that give them identities consistently different from those of men. This way of viewing sex constituted a change, in which biological differences between women and men were seen as essential and stark rather than as variations on a theme. It has been suggested that among the impetuses for the new Victorian conception of singular masculinity was the colonial experience itself, in which European males depicted themselves as virile in opposition to the effeminate colonized.[4] In contrast, the ancient Greek philosophers, Galen, and their medieval European and Middle Eastern successors had held to a one-body theory of sex, wherein women were simply inverted men, with their reproductive organs forming exact analogues to those of men. Some medieval thinkers held that one's sex was not a fixed and unchanging biological fate, that "inverted" women could turn inside out and become men. Indeed, some provisions of medieval patriarchy in Europe were aimed at ensuring that those born women stayed that way.[5] Both the medieval openness to sexual ambiguity and the modern idea of sexual fixity, put forward by male authors, assumed that the female term of the human sexual dyad was inferior.

Feminist theory offers us important conceptual tools in understanding the millenarian gender thinking of the Baha'is. Contemporary postmodernism has challenged the biological determinism associated with modernity, asserting instead that gender is to some degree a socially constructed category, and is moreover a category and a consciousness in flux, with an ever changing history. Other theorists have pointed out that it is necessary to attend both to the constructed nature of gender roles and to the specific experiences of the groups so constructed; that the roles are socially and psychologically built up does not mean they are any less real.[6] The rise of a new religion clearly allowed for the possibility of a new way of fashioning gender roles and of conceiving of women and men, more especially because the religion's genesis occurred at a time when the encounter with modernity was broaching these questions for Muslim society more generally.

Absolute equality between women and men in the sense of their performing the same roles in society would have meant nothing to the nineteenth-century Middle Eastern society Baha'u'llah was addressing. The urban, literate Islam of the old middle and upper classes had stressed gender segregation, the veiling of women, and, among the very wealthy, even secluding women in the house (as a sign of opulence). Male honor in the kinship group was based upon a man's ability to ensure the chastity of his sister, wife, and daughter, which led to many restrictions on women's interaction with unrelated men. As a result, urban women seldom entered the public or political spheres, though they did often own property, which they administered through male agents. To the extent that a sort of feminism grew up, it had primarily a middle- and upper-class social location and set of concerns. Peasant women, after all, worked in the fields, and most pastoral nomad women were less restricted, given the tribes' peripatetic style of life. In Middle Eastern common law, especially in the countryside, women often did not inherit, and even the more enlightened inheritance law of the Qur'an gave them only half the share their brothers received. By Islamic law a man could have as many as four wives and as many slave concubines as he could afford. In Shi'ite Iran men could also take temporary wives. The Qur'an allows a man to strike his wife in order to discipline her. Men could divorce women by fiat. A few women managed to become literate, and even learned, but most remained unlettered.[7] The liberal, middle-class attention to reform of women's position had a limited audience in the late nineteenth and early twentieth centuries. Neither peasants nor tribespeople, male or female, were likely to get much education or job training. In the period we are discussing pastoral nomads constituted on the order of 30 percent of Iranians, and peasants some 50 to 60 percent.

The new models of women's behavior arose from many sources. Accounts of Western women appeared in Middle Eastern periodicals and books, as did arguments for reform of women's position in Muslim societies. Some changes were brought about for practical reasons by middle- and upper-class Iranian families moving away from semifeudal styles of life to more "modern," often bourgeois ones. These changes, despite their relatively limited impact and scope, inspired great anxiety among Muslim conservatives, who frequently inscribed their resistance to modernity on the bodies of Muslim women. The reactionary leader of the Shaykhi school, Muhammad Karim Khan Kirmani (1810–1871), wrote:

> Can any Muslim allow the incompetent women to have the affairs in their hands so that they could go wherever they choose, sit with whomever they desire, leave the house whenever they wish? They [Europeans] have not yet gained control of Iran but they are already ordering our women not to cover themselves from men. Would any Muslim consent to women wearing makeup, sitting in the squares and at shops, and going to theaters? Can any Muslim consent to the independence and beautification of his wife and allow her to go to the bazaar and buy wine and drink it and get intoxicated . . . and sit with rogues and ruffians [*alwat va awbash*] and do whatever she chooses? God forbid! Would anyone consent to allowing freedom and losing charge of one's daughter, wife, slave and housekeeper?[8]

Despite heading a sectarian movement within Shi'ism, Karim Khan here voiced the majority view of the clerical class, and quite possibly the majority view of all Qajar men. These recognized that modernity contained within itself the potential for a profound challenge to then current norms of patriarchy, and in the mid-nineteenth century they were already beginning to develop an antimodernist critique of greater freedoms for women that identified these changes with foreign oppression, immorality, and male dishonor.

A theological grounding for positive Baha'i views of women was laid by Baha'u'llah's feminization of God in his mystical poetry. Medieval Islamic Sufism had developed a convention, worked out by 'Umar Ibnu'l-Farid, Ibnu'l-'Arabi, and others, of addressing God as the female beloved. Ibnu'l-'Arabi, who provided so many of the key technical terms in Baha'i theology, and whose works Baha'u'llah clearly knew well, held that a man's "witnessing of the Real [God] in the woman is the most complete and the most perfect."[9] Mainstream Islam, of course, had portrayed a highly patriarchal God. Baha'u'llah's openness to the mystical tradition that employed both genders to characterize the divine has the potential to set a different theological tone in his religion (though his followers, converts, have often simply retained the metaphysical patriarchalism of the traditions from which they converted). In his 1855 "Ode of the Dove," in his slightly later "Tablet of the Houri," and in many other works Baha'u'llah employed the symbolism of the unattainable and alluring maid of heaven to depict one aspect of the divine, sometimes employing erotic language and images.[10]

He actually called the "maid of heaven" in Arabic a "houri," a reference to the eternal virgins provided for the delight of saved men in the Qur'an's paradise. The term in the original is therefore heavy with erotic overtones. This houri is represented as a cosmic figure, her beauty bursting forth among the celestial suns, her breath trumpeting the judgment day, her perfume carried by the north wind. Yet although she is alluring and co-quettish, rejecting the human lover as having sacrificed too little to win her, she is also powerful and terrible, the conflagration at the midst of every fire, the wisdom underlying every law, the energy that causes the sun to revolve—at the appearance of whom Moses was struck unconscious.[11] Elsewhere he writes of the houri as pre-eternal and immaculate, striding across the horizon. He depicts a scene in which he gradually undresses her, first unveiling her curly black tresses and her face, listening to her song, which forms a commentary upon all knowledge, and then baring one of her breasts, such that "the firmament was illumined by the radiance of its light, contingent beings were made resplendent by its appearance and effulgence, and by its rays infinite numbers of suns dawned forth, as though they trekked through heavens that were without beginning or end."[12] As with the Song of Songs, Baha'u'llah here employs the beauty of the female form to symbolize the joy and ecstasy of union with the divine beloved. The houri is a sort of goddess figure (indeed, in the "Ode of the Dove," she is hyperbolically said to bestow godhood upon deities) and represents the feminine aspect of the divine. For an author to admit that the godhead has a feminine side, that it is not always and only male in its gendered symbolism, is no guarantee that he will go on to hold egalitari-an views on the position of women in society. But in this instance Ba-ha'u'llah's mystical theology of the creative feminine and the thrust of his reformist message do overlap.

Baha'u'llah envisaged a topsy-turvy world in which many ordinary sta-tuses were reversed. The honored, powerful, and wealthy Qajar nobles and Shi'ite clergymen had rejected his world-transforming message and there-fore had sunk to the lowest estate, whereas humble peasants of the perse-cuted Ahl-i Haqq sect who accepted the Baha'i faith were possessed of an exalted station. The first to apply this principle of reversal to gender issues had been Qurratu'l-'Ayn Tahirih, one of the nineteen disciples of the Bab.[13] She read and wrote Arabic theology, left her narrow-minded and domineering Shi'ite husband, wrote love poetry to God, emerged in Karbala as a major leader and preacher, and in Badasht in 1848 she threw off her veil. The Friday prayer leader of her home town, Qazvin, warned her father, "No glory remains in that house / From which the hens crow like cocks." She was not a feminist in the contemporary sense, but clearly she thought the Babi abolition of Islamic law opened up new spaces for women to play leading roles in public. Patriarchal authorities understood clearly that she was involved in a sort of gender politics. She was executed by the Iranian state in 1852. She was controversial even within the Babi community, but clearly Baha'u'llah was among those men who supported her.

Women were extremely important in the making of the Baha'i religion and existed in great numbers among Baha'u'llah's correspondents. An example is Shams-i Jahan Fitnih Qajar, a granddaughter of Fath-'Ali Shah who became a Babi and then a Baha'i. Her mother was from the district of Nur and was not a Qajar. Of a religious disposition, she had became intrigued by the news of the Bab's charismatic claims in the 1840s. Sayyid Muhammad "Fata'l-Malih" Gulpaygani, a sometime traveling companion of Tahirih, was earning his living in Tehran as a tutor to the wealthy around 1850, and he gained employment in Shams-i Jahan's household. There he won her adherence to the faith of the Bab, and encouraged her to meet Tahirih, then under house arrest at the home of Mahmud Khan Kalantar, the Tehran chief of police. Shams-i Jahan became an ardent Babi and having heard that Azal was the leader of the movement she determined, around 1858, to visit him in Baghdad. Like many other pilgrims, she found it impossible to see Azal, who was in hiding, and instead she sent her questions to Baha'u'llah. The answers were brought to her early the next morning by Mirza Aqa Jan Kashani, Baha'u'llah's amanuensis. He told her that the figure, "He whom God shall make manifest," promised by the Bab was Baha'u'llah. But he said that for the moment she must keep this secret to herself and reveal it to no one.[14] On her return journey she saw Kamalu'd-Din Niraqi in his hometown, and she said he was also aware of Baha'u'llah's station. She also met another Babi, Ibrahim "Mansur" Kashani, who had composed poetry in praise of Baha'u'llah. She wrote that she was therefore quite prepared when, seven years later (in 1282 A.H./ early 1866), Ahmad Yazdi arrived in Tehran with the news that Baha'u'llah had revealed himself as the promised one of the Bab.[15] Shams-i Jihan died in the late 1860s on her return from a visit to Baha'u'llah in Edirne, but some of her descendants, including a prominent prince, remained Baha'is.

During the crucial shift from middle Babism to the nascent Baha'i faith her influence among Babis in Tehran, especially women and nobles, may have been quite significant.

Another woman of great importance was Khadijah Begum, the widow of the Bab, who resided in Shiraz. Khadijih Begum received letters from Baha'u'llah, who was beginning in the late 1850s to put forth oblique signals that he was the promised one of the Bab, "He whom God shall make manifest." He carried on a lively correspondence with Khadijih Begum (and with many other prominent Babis). Khadijih Begum, in the meantime, convinced her thirteen-year-old nephew, Aqa Mirza Aqa Nuru'd-Din, to believe in the Bab. He in turn eventually won his mother, Zahra Begum, and his father, the great merchant Mirza Zaynu'l-'Abidin, over to Babism, in the opening years of the 1860s. The leader of this merchant clan was the maternal uncle ("Khal-i Akbar") of the Bab, Haji Sayyid Muhammad Shirazi, and his newly Babi relatives now urged him to investigate his martyred nephew's claims by going to speak with the Bab's mother as well as by going to see Azal and Baha'u'llah in Iraq. He did in fact undertake this journey, in 1862, and while in Baghdad Baha'u'llah responded to his written questions by penning in only three days a long theological and mystical treatise entitled *The Book of Certitude* (*Kitab-i Iqan*), often known at this time as the "Treatise for the Uncle." This book, which is characterized by a crisp, straightforward style of argumentation, persuaded Sayyid Muhammad Shirazi to become a Babi. He in turn brought many of his relatives into the faith. Gradually, a significant number of the Bab's relatives, most of them merchants, became Babis.[16]

Probably sometime between December 1865 and February 1866 Baha'u'llah's emissary, Muhammad "Nabil-i A'zam" Zarandi, came to Shiraz and met with the Afnan clan and other Babis there, announcing to them that Baha'u'llah was the promised one of the Bab and that Azal, widely thought to be the vicar of the Bab, was in fact a purveyor of satanic writings. This proclamation produced an uproar, and Haji Sayyid Muhammad Shirazi leapt to his feet, shouting, "What game is this?" Aqa Mirza Aqa Nuru'd-Din pointed out to him and to others that the Bab himself had at first been rejected and that it was after all Baha'u'llah whose *Book of Certitude* had brought them into the faith. They agreed to investigate the matter and Nabil left for Isfahan.[17]

Khadijih Begum came to hear Nabil from "behind a curtain," and reported that "as soon as I heard him say that the Blessed Beauty [Baha'u'llah] was 'He Whom God shall manifest', promised in the Bayan, I experienced the same feeling I had that night" when the Bab declared himself.[18] The Bab's widow was greatly respected and had wide contacts in the Babi community; she reports that "believers traveling to Shiraz always came to pay me a visit and I received them in the home of Mirza Aqa [Nuru'd-Din], my nephew."[19] Her embrace of Baha'u'llah's cause was therefore of great significance. Aqa Mirza Aqa Nuru'd-Din also quickly gave his allegiance to Baha'u'llah, agreeing with his beloved aunt, and he convinced several of his cousins to join him. Many of the Afnan clan became Baha'is, and, indeed, all the members of the clan resident in Shiraz did so.[20] The significance of Khadijah Begam's support for Baha'u'llah, given her charisma as the Bab's widow, cannot be emphasized enough.

Baha'u'llah only begins addressing women's status as a social issue in the 1870s. In his *Most Holy Book* he decrees that parents had the responsibility of seeing that both girls and boys were educated and that should they neglect this duty Baha'i institutions should step in to ensure its fulfillment. This was around the same time that Muslim reformists such as Rifaʿah at-Tahtawi (d. 1873) in Egypt and Mirza Taqi Khan Kashani in Iran were advocating women's education, as well.[21] The *Most Holy Book*, the laws of which are primarily drawn from the Bab's *Bayan*, do not, however, treat women and men exactly equally. In some instances this is a matter of pragmatism. In the nineteenth century Middle East it was not possible for every woman to go on pilgrimage, though some did make the journey with male relatives, and therefore pilgrimage is not made an absolute duty for women in the way that it is for men. Women are exempted from saying their obligatory prayers or fasting while menstruating and likewise do not fast when pregnant. Baha'u'llah retains the Bab's attempt to limit polygamy, allowing only two wives rather than the quranic four, but he states a strong preference for monogamy. Baha'u'llah had been married off by his family twice while still in Iran, to women of other Nuri notable clans of large property. While living in the Shiʿite Karkh quarter of Baghdad in the early 1860s his first wife, Asiyih Nuvvab Khanum, insisted on having a live-in maid. By the laws and customs of Shiʿite Islam of the time, Baha'u'llah was forced to take this maid in "temporary marriage" (*mutʿah*, *sighih*), since it was considered immoral for an unmarried woman to work and live in the household of an unrelated male. Later on, Baha'u'llah's first two wives and their children developed a vehement feud.[22] Baha'u'llah's eldest son and successor, 'Abdu'l-Baha, interpreted the preference for monogamy in the *Most Holy Book* as binding, thus requiring monogamy in subsequent Baha'i law. He was clearly influenced in this by the debate on women's emancipation provoked by reformers such as Mirza Aqa Khan Kirmani, Qasim Amin, and Muhammad 'Abduh as well as by the horror in which his many Western followers held polygamy. But it seems to me likely that his decision also reflected the bitter experiences he himself had with his mother's co-wife and her children. Although many men suffered through such conflicts in the extended family, few had 'Abdu'l-Baha's opportunity to set a binding precedent in the interpretation of religious law.

Following the Qur'an and the Bab's *Bayan*, Baha'u'llah prescribed inheritance shares. But he later more or less abrogated this schema by requiring all Baha'is to make their own wills and exempting them from following the divisions proposed in the *Most Holy Book*. Middle Eastern families were patrilineal and patrilocal, which is to say that descent and property obligations were reckoned in clans on the male side of the family, and that women came to live with their husbands, frequently in their fathers-in-law's houses. Women often married out of the area altogether and took their inherited property with them, which made it difficult to keep property together over time. In the inheritance schema Baha'u'llah presents, which is a slightly modified form of what is in the *Bayan*, he allots the family residence only to the male heirs, though where more than one residence was owned by the deceased the girls would get a share of the subsidiary homes. Women on the other hand were the sole inheritors of their mother's jewelry and effects. Since in the nineteenth century many Middle Eastern families invested heavily in women's jewelry, this wealth could be quite extensive. Sisters of the deceased get only a 6 percent share in the inheritance, whereas brothers receive a little over 8 percent. That patrilineality could be more of an issue than simple gender is demonstrated by the fact that where the deceased had children who died before he did, but who left children of their own, his grandchildren sired by his already dead son received greater shares than did his grandchildren given birth by an already dead daughter. The Bab's divisions clearly favored male heirs somewhat, and Baha'u'llah, who saw himself as an ethical teacher rather than primarily a legislator, seems to have felt constrained to follow the Bab in such matters, with slight alterations. The *Aqdas* inheritance laws do not, as a result, present a vision of complete equality, but of symbolic parity. Sons inherit the primary residence, daughters inherit their mother's jewelry. The unequal inheritance shares prescribed for women in the *Most Holy Book* show that Baha'u'llah did not, in the early 1870s, have a vision of women as equal with men socially, though his religion gave somewhat higher status and privileges to women than was common in Islamic law (and certainly in common law) as practiced in his day.

Baha'u'llah employed the word *rijāl*, or men, in the sense of "males" to refer to members of houses of justice. This usage appears to occur only once in the *Most Holy Book*. He apportions one-third of all fines to the "seat of justice," and then addresses its members as "O men (rijāl) of justice," urging them to safeguard their flock as a shepherd protects his sheep from wolves.[23] In *Questions and Answers* he says that two-thirds of found treasure shall revert to "the men (rijāl) of the house of justice," to be expended for the welfare of all people.[24] In supplements to the *Most Holy Book* he speaks of the "men of God's house of justice" being "charged with the affairs" of the Baha'i community (millat)[25] Elsewhere in the supplements he says, "We exhort the men of the House of Justice and command them to ensure the protection and safeguarding of men, women and children."[26] In addition to this duty, in the *Ishraqat*, or Splendors, Baha'u'llah makes it incumbent "upon the men of God's House of Justice" to work for the education of peoples and the upbuilding of nations.[27]

Later Baha'i tradition has it that Baha'u'llah spoke only of the members of the Universal House of Justice, the religion's international leadership, as "men," but that his diction allowed women to serve on local houses of justice. But it would be extremely difficult to see all these passages as referring solely to the men of the Universal House of Justice, the international body that is the ultimate religious authority for Baha'is. Rather, some of them would appear to do double duty, referring also to the men of the local house of justice. For instance, the duty of safeguarding the interests of men, women, and children, laid upon the men of the house of justice in the ninth leaf of the "Words of Paradise," seems no more especially apposite to the Universal House of Justice than to local houses of justice, and one must conclude that "House of Justice" in this instance is employed generically to mean the institution at all levels. It seems unlikely that one-third of fines collected from Baha'is in the city of, say, Kirman, are envisaged as being sent to the international House of Justice; rather, it seems more probable that Baha'u'llah was speaking of local fines going in part to a local house of justice. Likewise, the logistics of sending two-thirds of treasure found anywhere in the world to the international House of Justice for redistribution seem forbidding. Even the training and upbuilding of the nations, a charge laid upon the men of the house of justice in the Splendors, would seem to be a duty of both local houses of justice and of the international House of Justice. Further, Baha'u'llah demonstrably did refer to members of houses of justice other than the Universal House of Justice in this way. Thus, in a tablet on universal language, he speaks of the duty to promote it on the part of parliaments (*majālis*) and men of Baha'i houses of justice (*rijal-i buyut-i 'adliyyih*). The plural proves that he cannot be speaking here of the Universal House of Justice. "For the implementation of revealed commands, laws, and ordinances hath in the book been delegated to the men of the houses of justice."[28] If he was using the word *rijāl* in its ordinary sense, Baha'u'llah must be understood as having thought of the membership of houses of justice at all levels as male. There is, however, reason to think he may not have been using the word in its ordinary Arabic sense. I will return to this point below.

In the later nineteenth century women's issues began to come to the fore in the Middle East, and the incipient feminism of notable and middle-class women clearly had an impact on Baha'i culture. New thinking about women began being published first of all in Ottoman periodicals such as *Terakki* (Progress, begun in 1869). This early Ottoman writing on women's issues has not, however, yet been well-studied, though Istanbul was much more central to cultural movements throughout the Middle East than is usually now recognized.[29] Elite women themselves contributed articles (sometimes anonymously) to these magazines and played a powerful role in shaping a new discourse about women. As noted above, male reformers such as the Egyptian at-Tahtawi urged women's education and training for some sorts of work, though at-Tahtawi, who is said to have owned a concubine, was hardly a feminist. Another reformer, the Iranian Sayyid Jamal al-Din "al-Afghani" (d. 1897), gave a celebrated talk in Alexandria in spring of 1879, printed in the newspaper *Misr*, which we know was being read by the Baha'is in Akka. In it he said that the attainment of civilization was impossible as long as women were not educated and that "if the mothers are educated, know human rights, and what the precepts of honor and civilization require, there is no doubt that their children will adopt their characters and will acquire from them these virtues."[30] Also in Egypt Maryam Nimr, the wife of the publisher of the Masonic journal *al-Lata'if,* wrote many proto-feminist articles for it in the 1880s.[31] Ottoman and Arabic-language periodicals circulated in Iran, where the press was not as advanced before the 1890s. Women's periodicals, and the contributions of female journalists and correspondents, form a key background to the outbreak of a major cultural debate on the position of women. In Iran a debate broke out in the 1880s over a book entitled Disciplining Women (*Ta'dib an-niswan*), in which an elite male argued strongly for patriarchal values and the need for women to obey their husbands implicitly. Several replies were written by literate women, some of them at the royal court, and one was entitled Putting Men in Their Place (*Ta'dil ar-Rijal*), which had appeared by the late 1880s. The only refutation that has been published was written in 1894 by Bibi Khanum Astarabadi entitled The Vices of Men (*Ma'ayib ar-Rijal*).[32]

Bibi Khanum, an upper-class Shi'ite Iranian, responds to her opponent's denigration of women's mental abilities by saying that women do exist, of high social status, who, assisted by their rational souls, can reply to him. Not every man, she insists, is superior to every woman. Mother Mary, Fatimih the daughter of the Prophet, and Khadijah, his wife, were great women, whereas Pharaoh and Shimr (who slew the Prophet's grandson, Husayn) were men.[33] She defends those women whom he had criticized for refusing to marry elderly men or bearded clergymen, saying that especially women of the upper and merchant classes might not have anything in common with such men, and a common origin (*sinkhiyyat*) was a prerequisite for marriage.[34] Here, she is invoking a principle of Muslim societies, that a woman may not be forced to marry below her socially. For his statement that if a man commands his wife to jump into the fire she must obey, she labels him a confidence man and criminal of the sort one finds sitting in law courts and contrasts him unfavorably with European ideals.[35] When he advises women to be silent in view of the great harm harsh words can do, she suggests that no one replies to a polite statement such as "May I be your sacrifice" with insults and where women do speak out it is likely because of the man's misbehavior; women's anger, which he also criticizes, likewise derives from a loveless relationship.[36] In short, she gives him no quarter with regard to his criticisms of women. Bibi Khanum then goes on to discuss men's vices, pointing to their all-male parties for the purposes of drinking wine, gambling, and smoking hashish and opium.[37] She also criticizes the summary divorce of women by their husbands and the lies men tell their first wives when they take a second wife.[38] One must underline the highly classed nature of her thought about gender relations, for she uses her social location as a battering ram against gender discrimination. It is a commonplace among upper-class women of this period that allowing their denigration in turn dangerously allows lower-class males to claim superiority to members of the upper classes (who happen to be female). Still, her spirited defense of women and attack on the gender inequities of Qajar society is a fascinating window into the mind of an educated woman of the 1880s and 1890s, and we are no doubt hearing from her what many women of her social class thought at that time.

In this context of incipient cultural debate Baha'u'llah later in the Akka period appears to have moved toward a more egalitarian vision of gender relations. After all, two of his wives, Asiyih Khanum Nuvvab and Fatimih Khanum Mahd-i 'Ulya (a daughter of Mirza Buzurg Nuri's sister), were from a social class similar to that of Bibi Khanum Astarabadi. Baha'u'llah makes three sorts of statement about gender attributes and their distribution among the sexes. In the first he says that women are "as men," elevating them to honorary male status. He says, for instance, "Today the female believers (*awrāq-i sidrih*) must with complete sanctity and detachment show the path to the maidservants [women] of the world. Today, the maidservants of God are accounted as men (*imrūz imā'u'llah az rijāl mahsūb*)."[39] To other women, he wrote, "O maidservants, arise in a masculine way (*mardānih*) for the sake of God's Cause. A goodly number of women are today mentioned by God as men, whereas some men are reckoned as women."[40] This identification of some exemplary women as in some sense masculine was not a completely new idea in Islamic culture. The great medieval mystic Faridu'd-Din 'Attar, in explaining why he included the female mystic Rabi'ah in his biographical dictionary of exemplary Sufis, explained that she was truly a man, given her high spiritual attainments. He quotes the Prophet Muhammad that "God does not regard your outward forms." And occasionally even a Muslim clergyman would admit that some women could be jurisprudents on the grounds that they were possessed of "manhood" (*rajūliyyat*) in their characters.[41] Baha'u'llah's promotion of women believers to the status of honorary men, then, does not in and of itself imply a social and legal equality for women. Indeed, this way of speaking in Islamic culture somewhat keeps in place the unequal conceptual hierarchy wherein attributes usually associated with women are seen as inferior to attributes usually associated with males, while admitting that exemplary women can attain honorary male status. After all, 'Attar was hardly a feminist.

In the second sort of statement Baha'u'llah actually speaks of women and men being equivalent. He says that "the servants of God and His handmaidens are regarded on the same Plane."[42] He also writes, "Verily, in the eyes of Baha women are the same as men. All are God's creation, which He created in his image and likeness, that is, they are manifestations of His names and attributes."[43] Equating one gender to the other in essence does seem to imply the abolition of gender as a basis for status distinctions. In the third sort of statement, however, Baha'u'llah goes further and actually sees a role reversal between women and men, such that some women are not simply elevated to the status of a man but actually gain a superiority over most men. He wrote one correspondent, "O my leaf (*waraqati*), thank your Lord, for you have attained to the verses of God and his tablets, while the men were in doubt and quarreling."[44] Elsewhere he remarks that women had gained the honor of attaining mystical insight (*'irfān*) in great numbers, and that one believing woman is superior (*muqaddam*) to most other souls.[45] To another woman he wrote that whereas champions and powerful men had been deterred from embracing the Baha'i faith by fear of tyrants, she had bravely adopted the new religion. Here the ultimate symbol of masculinity, the muscle-bound champion wrestler or fighter (Ar. *baṭal*, Persian *pahlavān*) is devalued in favor of a fearless woman of faith.[46] Perhaps impressed by Qurratu'l-'Ayn Tahirih's earlier theophanic aura, Baha'u'llah even goes so far as to accept the possibility that God might send female prophets and manifestations of God, writing,

> Know thou moreover that in the Day of Revelation were He to pronounce one of the leaves [female believers] to be the manifestation of all His excellent titles, unto no one is given the right to utter why or wherefore, and should one do so he would be regarded as a unbeliever in God and be numbered with such as have repudiated His Truth.[47]

In his reconstruction of gender roles Baha'u'llah detaches masculinity and femininity (as conceived in premodern Muslim societies) from biology and sees them as qualities distributed among both genders. Again, his is not a unique perspective. A nineteenth-century Urdu manual of manners for Muslim women even begins the chapter on exemplary women's lives by recapitulating the life of the Prophet Muhammad, who is seen as a moral exemplar for both sexes and whose moral qualities are not solely "masculine."[48] In particular, Baha'u'llah depicts bravery in facing persecution as an attribute often associated with males that many women possess but large numbers of men lack. His conception of the positive, even potentially central role of women in the world religions (such that he would admit the possibility of a future female manifestation of God) contrasts sharply with one Islamic literary tradition that casts women as the tempters and villains of sacred history.[49]

It is difficult to know how exactly to interpret Baha'u'llah's statements on gender equality. It would be possible to read some of them as mildly reformist but as containing nothing that seriously challenged patriarchal norms. The Qur'an, too, established unequal laws for women and men, while affirming their spiritual equality. But other statements, in which Baha'u'llah praises Baha'i women for bravery superior to that of men or in which he admits the possibility of a female theophany, seem to have more serious implications for changes in gender roles. This ambiguity in diction mirrors the ambiguity in his laws, wherein girls and boys are both to be educated but daughters' share of any inheritance is less than that of sons (though still more than had been allotted to women in the Qur'an). The one legal issue on which Baha'u'llah's statements concerning gender equality does seem to bear directly is when he makes Baha'i women "men" (*rijāl*), since it acutely raises the question of whether he really did mean to exclude women from his houses of justice by addressing their members as "men." In any case, it should be remembered that most of the texts we have discussed probably come from the 1870s and 1880s and that equality feminism was not being argued for by any Middle Eastern intellectuals at that point. A closer approximation to a feminist sort of equality is only found in some remarks of his son, 'Abdu'l-Baha, much later on.

It is clear that Baha'u'llah carried on an extensive correspondence with female believers. Although he was hardly alone among Middle Eastern men in rethinking gender relations in the 1880s, it is remarkable that he did so through correspondence with hundreds of women themselves. Although Baha'i orthodoxy would insist that in these letters he revealed the truth to them, and so that the relationship was highly unequal, it seems clear that in other areas Baha'u'llah was influenced by his followers (he had not wanted to write a book of laws, for instance, but yielded to a flood of requests to do so), and there is no reason to reject out of hand the notion that his reformist ideas about women derived in part from an extensive interaction with them through correspondence.

Women Baha'is in Iran took on a key role in the establishment and development of the religion. The activities of Baha'i women leaders mentioned in their biographies include preaching the faith to others—presumably mainly to women in this gender-segregated society, though some wrote letters proclaiming the religion to Shi'ite clergymen! They are also said to have given classes to women and girls, ensuring that they became literate, conducted consultation, called committee meetings (*tashkīl-i jilsāt*), and cared for poor and imprisoned Baha'is.[50] The stories of the poor Baha'i women themselves, many of whom no doubt played important local roles in city quarters and villages, are now difficult to recover.

An example of a powerful woman leader in Tehran is Ummu'l-Awliya', the daughter of a high government official, Rahim Khan Farrash-Ghadab, the executioner who waited upon the shah in his royal antechamber. His daughter adopted the Baha'i faith when she married the wealthy merchant Haji Muhammad Rahim 'Attar, an adherent. Her conversion posed problems for her pious Shi'ite father, who was close to the very orthodox Nasiru'd-Din Shah. Even so, Rahim Khan lent his protection to Baha'is, at his daughter's behest. During the great famine of 1869–1872 about one in ten Iranians perished, and another one in ten left for other lands. In response the government put Rahim Khan in charge of emergency bakeries throughout Tehran. The 'Attars were thus able to provide famine relief to Baha'is, as well, even though they had been banned on grounds of unorthodoxy from receiving such help. During the famine Ummu'l-Awliya' and her family ate smaller portions, donating some of their stock to starving Baha'is. Khanum 'Attar's activism in ensuring Baha'is food came to the notice of Baha'u'llah, who thenceforward called her "the mother of the Friends" (Ummu'l-Awliya').[51]

The importance of the 'Attar women and men as focal points of the community and as hosts of Baha'i meetings is underlined by Mirza Haydar 'Ali Isfahani, who lived in Tehran for several years. He wrote,

> The only ones who were well off among the friends in Tihran were Aqa Muhammad Karim 'Attar and his brother, Haji Muhammad Rahim. These two believers and their sisters were all devoted to the Cause of God. Whenever the friends desired to have a sumptuous meal, they would send them a message, and the family would comply with their wishes and send Persian rice and roast meat. One night the brothers themselves attended such a banquet, and the delicious food was followed by fresh fruit.[52]

In the mid-1870s Muhammad Rahim 'Attar gained a reputation as a Baha'i and he was made to leave Tehran. In vain, Ummu'l-Awliya' gathered two hundred of her powerful relatives to stage a protest. He had to spend five years in Baghdad, and even when he returned his house was watched vigilantly by Shi'ite enemies and he had to seek refuge in his father-in-law's mansion until the uproar died down. In the early 1880s Rahim Khan received a posting abroad, and during his absence enemies of the Baha'is high in the government launched a mass arrest. In 1882 Kamran Mirza Na'ib us-Saltanih, the governor of Tehran, incarcerated and sentenced to death some fifty Baha'is, 'Attar among them.[53] Ummu'l-Awliya' organized the feeding of the prisoners in the meantime and also intervened with a leading Shi'ite mujtahid, arguing that they should be spared, but to no avail. When Rahim Khan returned to Tehran, his daughter Ummu'l-Awliya' had him intervene on behalf of his son-in-law, and the government released all these prominent Baha'is after nineteen months of harsh imprisonment.[54]

Fatimih Sultan Khanum was married to Haji Faraj, a nephew of Aminu's-Sultan, one of Iran's first ministers. She was the daughter of the military officer, Muharram Bey. She often tried to help arrested Baha'is and their families, using her high status as a woman of two prominent military families to approach Kamran Mirza and Nasiru'd-Din Shah with petitions for the release of her coreligionists, sometimes with great success. When Mulla 'Ali Jan Mazandarani was killed for being a Baha'i, she paid his burial expenses. When local Shi'ite toughs continued to bother Mazandarani's widow, the family brought in men from the palace to intimidate them into leaving her alone.[55]

Among early Baha'i feminists was 'Ismat Khanum Ta'irih. She was born into the household of the notable Mirza Isma'il Khan Ashtiyani Mustawfiy-i Nizam in 1861. Her mother, Hasinih Khanum Zahrih, wrote poetry and was extremely accomplished. 'Ismat Khanum's maternal grandfather, a physician and writer, had been the family doctor of the prince Husamu's-Saltanih. 'Ismat Khanum and her brother 'Isa were orphaned in 1868, when their father died. They were raised for a while by their grandfather and then for a while by their maternal uncle, Faraju'llah Khan, the Tehran building inspector general. He hired tutors for them and had them taught polite Persian letters and Arabic. 'Ismat as a girl impressed Nasiru'd-Din Shah once with her boldness. In 1877, at the age of sixteen, 'Ismat was given in marriage to Mihr 'Ali Khan, the deputy imperial bodyguard of the shah and a fierce persecutor of Baha'is who often brought them as prisoners to his own house.

When 'Ismat's maternal uncle, the Sufi Baha'i, Abu'l-Barakat, returned from India to Tehran, he preached the faith to his niece and she became a Baha'i. 'Ismat Khanum now began treating the Baha'i prisoners who were brought to her house with compassion. Her husband and brother, however, discovered her new adherence, and her attempts to help the Baha'is resulted in her being badly and repeatedly beaten by her husband. She remembered going outside in the snow to sit on the steps after being battered one winter evening and leaving the snow around her dyed red. She nevertheless persevered and taught her daughters the faith, as well as finally convincing her brother, 'Isa Khan, to join. In the mid-1880s her husband died, releasing her from her nearly decade-long captivity. 'Ismat's state stipend and family wealth allowed her to maintain an independent household thereafter. She threw herself into Baha'i and cultural activities, holding classes for Baha'i students in the capital. She wrote poetry under the pen name of Ta'irih (Bird). She was known as a free-thinker (ḥurrat al-afkār) and worked for women's emancipation (ḥurriyyat al-nisvān). She moved in the highest society of elite Qajar women, including that of princesses, serving as a storyteller and moral preacher and subtly spreading Baha'i ideas. She not only taught girls informally, incurring much criticism from conservatives, but at length managed to establish a girls' school. She also strove to introduce mixed-gender meetings into the Baha'i community. When the press became freer during the Constitutional Revolution, she published articles on women's emancipation. She died in 1911.[56]

Ta'irih's prominence in feminist journalism during the Constitutional Revolution underlines how much gender issues had come to the fore by the first decade and a half of 'Abdu'l-Baha's ministry (which began in 1892). In Iran itself the upheavals of the late nineteenth and early twentieth century opened up a number of social questions, including feminism and socialism. As Najmabadi has shown, the materialist thinkers Mirza Aqa Khan Kirmani and Shaykh Ahmad Ruhi (who had once been Babis) decried the veiling and seclusion of women, the failure to educate them, and their exclusion from employment in government and commerce. They took these positions in their manuscript, "Eight Heavens," which was written in exile in Istanbul around the time of the Tobacco Revolt (1890–1892). They predicted that "the world of humanity cannot reach for perfection unless women become equal and partners with men in all affairs and rights."[57] For these authors, as for most male reformers, however, the key reason for which women needed to be educated was to make them more adequate mothers and managers of the household, a theme that also appears in 'Abdu'l-Baha's thinking on women's issues.

Building on women's journalism of the late nineteenth century, the Egyptian judge Qasim Amin provoked further debate about women among Middle Eastern intellectuals in 1899–1901. He called for women to enter every field of endeavor, from higher education and science to the ranks of laborers. In his first book on the subject, secretly coauthored with reformers Muhammad 'Abduh and Ahmad Lutfi as-Sayyid, he presented proofs for his "feminist" position from the Qur'an and Islamic sources, but later turned to secular rationales.[58] His book was immediately translated into Persian.[59] 'Abdu'l-Baha, who had attended Muhammad 'Abduh's study classes in Beirut in the 1880s, and who followed the Cairo intellectual scene, certainly knew Qasim Amin's work and appealed to arguments put forward by the 'Abduh school in his disallowal of polygamy.

During the Iranian Constitutional Revolution of 1905–1911 women's groups, called *anjuman*s, grew up. On the same day that the constitution was signed by the shah, on December 30, 1906, the new parliament's own organ printed a petition by a woman alleging that "Iran had fallen behind the caravan of civilization because women were denied an education."[60] On the other hand, conservative Shi'ite clergymen opposed the opening of girls' schools, just as they opposed the civil parliament itself, as contrary to Islam.[61] The terms of all these debates clearly formed the context for 'Abdu'l-Baha's evolving positions on these issues. He wrote,

In this most great cycle and this century of the preexistent Monarch, human limitations have been lifted and the laws of the worlds of being have been abrogated and annulled. Masculinity and femininity do not depend upon beards, mustaches, athletic strength, and wielding maces. [Masculinity] depends on courage, power, knowledge, steadfastness, uprightness, passion and attraction. How many mistresses of the bridal chamber have been sent forth and how many men have been consigned to head scarves and meekness?[62]

'Abdu'l-Baha, like his father, saw gender as contingent and indeterminate, an acquired attribute rather than a function of mere biological fate.

Moreover, he was insistent that the Islamic subordination of women to men had been abrogated, writing to an Iranian woman:

O handmaiden of God: In past eras no female, however much she might come forward in rendering services or traverse the wilderness of the love of God, could be reckoned in the ranks of men. For "men are the managers of the affairs of women" [Qur'an 4:38] had been stipulated. Now, in this wondrous age, the work of women has advanced. These fetters have been thrown off. Anyone who steps forward will receive the reward . . . whether man or woman, whether male or female. O Lord, the mistress of the women's quarters has surpassed the males and triumphed over the amassed army, and raised the standards of superiority in the arena of [spiritual] ecstasy and joy.[63]

This image of the embattled Baha'i woman achieving a military conquest over men, and gaining superiority over them, is suffused with millenarian fervor. Here, in contrast to the earlier bestowal of masculine qualities upon women, we see the admission that some women had achieved superiority over most men and a decisive abrogation of the Qur'anic mandate to men to manage the affairs of women.

The spread of the Baha'i faith to the United States in the 1890s and the contact 'Abdu'l-Baha had with Western women who came to Akka on pilgrimage from 1899 introduced a new variable into the Baha'i position on women. Western Baha'i women such as Corinne True forcefully rejected the gender segregation implied in nineteenth-century Iranian Baha'i practices, wherein women had their own committees and leaders while pan-community authority rested with the all-male house of justice or local assembly. Although the first house of justice established in Chicago included women, it was reformed as an all-male body in 1901. Women were thrown off it, partially at the instance of Persian male teachers, apparently on the grounds that women menstruated and were therefore frequently ritually impure.

True appealed to 'Abdu'l-Baha, who initially also would not allow Western women to serve on the houses of justice. 'Abdu'l-Baha argued in a 1902 letter to True concerning the Chicago house of justice that Baha'u'llah's use of the word rijāl to refer to members of Baha'i houses of justice (apparently at all levels) excluded female membership on them.[64] Corinne True was not a woman to take "no" for an answer, and she continued to seek to overturn the decision. In 1909 True pressed the issue again and received a letter from 'Abdu'l-Baha that remains difficult to interpret with certainty. He said women could serve on "spiritual assemblies" and committees, but in this period a "spiritual assembly" was frequently the designation of the women's gatherings. He continued to exclude women from what he called the "general (*'umumi*) house of justice," by which he probably meant the Chicago governing body, though some have argued that he meant here to exclude women only from the (then nonexistent) Universal House of Justice.[65] The former interpretation was the one arrived at by the Chicago community, and so women continued to be barred from service on the "local spiritual assembly," or general house of justice. Since 'Abdu'l-Baha had earlier excluded women from the houses of justice on the grounds that their members were addressed by Baha'u'llah as "men," it is difficult to see on what grounds he should have, suddenly, in 1909, decided that this restriction applied only to the Universal House of Justice—since members of lesser houses of justice were also addressed by Baha'u'llah as "men," as we have seen. By 1912, during his visit to the United States, he had been convinced by the Baha'i suffragists to allow women to serve on local administrative bodies. Reversing himself on the issue, he decreed that women should be allowed to stand for election to the Chicago house of justice.[66] Confusingly, however, he wrote a letter a year later, in 1913, in which he said women would enter all fields except military service and service on "the house of justice," adding, "When the women attain to the ultimate degree of progress, then, according to the exigency of the time and place and their great capacity, they shall obtain extraordinary privileges."[67] Was this last phrase meant to hold out hope that women would eventually serve on all levels of house of justice? Later Baha'i tradition has held that he meant only to put women on local and national houses of justice and that they remain forever ineligible to serve on the Universal House of Justice (first elected in 1963), but the texts and their historical context regarding this issue remain unclear. (As a simple logical issue, if the reason for which women were excluded from houses of justice was, per the 1902 letter, that Baha'u'llah addressed their members as "men," or rijāl, then this form of address cannot be employed to explain why they could serve on local bodies but not on the Universal House of Justice). Later Baha'i leaders even misunderstood the 1902 letter concerning exclusion of women from the Chicago house of justice to refer solely to the Universal House of Justice, which, it seems to me, simply cannot be correct. It may be that this was an issue 'Abdu'l-Baha left to future generations to settle.

With regard to civil institutions 'Abdu'l-Baha promoted what was for its time a thoroughgoing feminism. Echoing a key theme in Middle Eastern writing on women's issues of the previous two or three decades, he said that "the education of woman is more necessary and important than that of man, for woman is the trainer of the child from its infancy."[68] During a talk on May 7, 1912, in Pittsburgh, he expressed the view that women should be educated to enter public life and that if they did so they would form a powerful lobby against war, since they would be reluctant to sacrifice on the battlefield the children that they had reared.[69] One should be careful to note that 'Abdu'l-Baha's vision of women as noncombatants and as playing a special role in child rearing did not derive from any essentialism of the "biology is fate" variety. He explicitly says that nature gives no evidence of the female of the species being in any way inferior and that were women to be trained as soldiers they would equal men even in the "accomplishment" of "slaughter."[70] Women do differ from men in some respects, in his view, but this is a function of the way they are educated and of the roles allotted them in society, not of some essential inborn pacifism.[71] In 1913, after extensive touring in the United States and Europe, 'Abdu'l-Baha wrote to one Western Baha'i woman, "In this Revelation of Baha'u'llah, the women go neck and neck with the men. In no movement will they be left behind. Their rights with men are equal in degree. They will enter all the administrative branches of politics. They will attain in such a degree as will be considered the very highest station of the world of humanity and will take part in all affairs."[72] Although he spoke in such almost utopian terms about the future, 'Abdu'l-Baha could be quite pragmatic about the need for Iranian Baha'is to appear to conform to Iranian mores with regard to women, and his letters on the subject of women to Iran are far more conservative than his pronouncements in the West.

Abdu'l-Baha's positions on many issues moved the religion closer to a feminist perspective than it had been in the nineteenth century. His advocacy of women's suffrage, his statement that the Qur'anic injunction that men manage women's affairs had been abrogated, his conviction that women should enter every sphere of public life—all these stances were remarkable in an Eastern religious leader of the time. Of course, some elements of patriarchy do remain in 'Abdu'l-Baha's vision, which sees a special role for women as mothers and homemakers, excludes women from combat and, depending upon how the surviving texts are read, may exclude women from service on the Universal House of Justice (this is certainly current Baha'i practice, and it is hard to see how it does not have the effect of putting the affairs of women back under the management of men). Yet 'Abdu'l-Baha actively encouraged women's entry into every other field of human endeavor on a basis of equality with men.

The evolution of Baha'i stances on women's issues and gender demonstrates the falsity of the proposition, put forward by a social historian of the Middle East over a generation ago, that with regard to women's position in society over the course of the nineteenth century "nothing changed." Rather, gender roles were clearly in significant flux among some elements of the population. Tahirih's determined exploration of new social spaces in which she could express herself as mystic poet, preacher, and religious leader, not only to women but to men as well, inevitably put into question practices such as veiling and seclusion. The expansion in the period 1850–1910 of cities and external trade, the growth of agrarian capitalism that made Iran a key exporter of tobacco, opium, and rice, in addition to silk, created newly wealthy families with new values. These often derived from such practical considerations as a better sense of double-entry bookkeeping, such that for them the old feudal practice of maintaining wholly separate and often duplicate male and female households seemed increasingly wasteful. These same families, of course, were also the most likely to be exposed to cosmopolitan ideas about new opportunities for educated women. Men educated after the modern style often wanted educated spouses with whom they could have conversations about culture.

Baha'i leaders' and adherents' views concerning women and gender paralleled that of Middle Eastern modernism more generally, despite some idiosyncracies. In the mid-nineteenth century the most vivid symbols of women as powerful occurred in Baha'u'llah's mystical works about the divine houri who brought God's inspiration and then revelation to him. If Allah is the male aspect of God, the houri is clearly the female aspect, and it is important that Baha'u'llah recognized the divine as having a feminine side. This depiction of women as coeval sites for the manifestation of the divine names and attributes continues as an important theme in Baha'u'llah's works into the Akka period.

His laws treat women more equally than was true of the Qur'an but nevertheless give them unequal inheritance shares, require a small dowry, excuse them from the duty of pilgrimage, and make other exemptions concerning ritual performances. Insofar as he later commanded all Baha'is to make their own wills and allowed them to ignore the inheritance divisions proposed in his *Most Holy Book,* the issue of unequal inheritance laws never became a central one for Baha'i women. Like other Middle Eastern reformers of the 1870s, he required that girls be educated along with boys. Many of Baha'u'llah's later writings on gender were produced in dialogue with women themselves, either through their reformist journalism or through extensive correspondence. His position in his religion as immaculate manifestation of God and his distant exile in Akka allowed him in his correspondence to breach the barriers of gender segregation and to interact with hundreds of women adherents in this way, evolving a new conception of gender roles as he did so. Baha'u'llah stressed the spiritual equality of women and men and the actual superiority of some women over some men with regard to issues of character. Baha'u'llah saw the attributes associated with specific genders in medieval Islam to be detached from biology and to be distributed among individuals without regard to sex. Thus, women could be braver than male champions, and more spiritual than ayatollahs, and were in fact considered to have the status of "men," or "male notables," in the Baha'i religion. This approach denies that gender is inexorably determined by sex as an essentialist category and rather admits of the constructed and transgendered nature of traits usually apportioned either to males or females. Writing in the 1870s and 1880s, his main themes in the amelioration of the condition of women and the expansion of their social roles had to do with educating them and encouraging them to play an active role in social service and religious good works.

Women played a key role in the formation and development of the Baha'i religion in Iran. Baha'u'llah gained invaluable support for his assertions of prophethood from eminent Babi women such as Khadijah Begam, the widow of the Bab, and from the princess Shams-i Jihan Fitnih. As a Baha'i community formed in the 1870s and 1880s, prominent notable women in Tehran took an active part in Baha'i famine relief and in succoring imprisoned and persecuted coreligionists. One irony that emerges from our discussion of these prominent early women believers is that they so often found themselves in a position to succor others, despite their own marginality in a patriarchal society. They could play this role for several reasons. First, in a society where clan and family counted for so much, and wherein its membership in the governmental, or *nawkar,* class bestowed so many benefits, even the women of the clan gained some prerogatives of access and ability to intercede with powerful men from allied or related clans who were also members of the same nawkar stratum. In any highly classed patriarchal society upper-class women have the anomalous position of deriving some perquisites from their status that contradict the supposedly low standing derived from their gender roles. This is a point that a contemporary of these debates, Bibi Khanum herself, made in her polemic against male chauvinism. Second, it is probably the case that women's heterodoxy was most often taken less seriously than that of males, allowing them to play a nonthreatening intercessory role.[73]

Many Baha'i women of the notable class appear to have joined the religion over the vehement objections of spouses or other close male relatives and yet to have prevailed in their beliefs. Indeed, in some instances women's conflicts with Shi'ite male relatives may have reinforced their desire for independence, which they in part expressed by adopting the new religion. By 1910 one sees in Ta'irih's Baha'i feminist journalism a wholly new vision of gender roles in Iranian society, with calls for the abolition of the veil, seclusion, and gender segregation. The Baha'i religion was only one arena in which this vast social and cultural contest over the shape of gender roles was fought out.

Leaders such as Baha'u'llah and 'Abdu'l-Baha, who were sympathetic to the ideal of human unity across gender boundaries, set a tone that allowed Ta'irih Khanum, Corinne True, and other strong women to have an important impact in moving the Baha'i community away from strict Middle Eastern and Islamic, as well as Edwardian American, norms of patriarchy. 'Abdu'l-Baha argued in his talks in the West that it is the experience, upbringing, and positionality of women in society that make them distinctive. That distinctiveness should not, in his view, deny them any opportunity or civil career open to males. He held that society has an interest in continuing to educate women as agents for peace. In gender as in race, ethnicity, and language the Baha'i religion configured humankind as one, arguing for a unity in diversity. Aspects of patriarchy remain embedded in Baha'i texts and practice, most notably the all-male Universal House of Justice, the designation of men as heads of the household, and dowry. Whereas these seem old-fashioned to postmoderns, a century ago they seemed to women like Corrine True as minor affairs compared to the generally progressive tone of the religion at that time. If unity and peace are the two pillars of Baha'i social thought, the place of women was considered by 'Abdu'l-Baha to be crucial to both, and in important respects he argued for a significantly feminized global civilization, concerned with peace making and nurturing rather than hierarchy and war.

Conclusion

The "procedural" liberal tradition of value-free individualism tended to portray the Middle East as a "unified system, one characterized by stationariness, lack of social change, the absence of modernization, the absence of a middle-class bourgeois culture, and the absence of civil society."[1] Anyone conversant with the enormous social and cultural changes that have occurred in Iran during the past two centuries, with the centrality of the nexus (the "bazaar class") of merchants, artisans, shopkeepers, and the religious, and with the lively debates there over the appropriate responses to modernity (which continue today), can only gape in astonishment at the first few of these propositions. The last two points are simply criticisms of any absolutist, royal-feudal order, in Europe (e.g., Prussia) or elsewhere. This examination of the response of tens of thousands of nineteenth-century Iranian millenarians to modernity has suggested that if one moves away from a concentration upon governmental and intellectual elites and looks at the margins of Middle Eastern society the region appears as a cauldron of dynamic change, and the values of democracy and civil society have meant a great deal more to more ordinary people and intellectuals than is usually recognized.

How can we get beyond the Orientalist essentialisms and dichotomies that have characterized much academic writing about the reception of modernity in the Middle East? Sociologist Bryan S. Turner has suggested four strategies. The first is to jettison all notions of "Islam" as a universal essence, admitting that there are many Islams, each complex and different. Second, the various Muslim traditions and groups must be seen "within a global context of interpenetration with the world-system." Third, social scientists must abandon an exclusive concern with particular nation-states in favor of a "global" social science, since only the perspective of the world can highlight the limitations of the Orientalist tradition. Fourth, "the anthropological gaze should be also directed toward the otherness of Western culture in order to dislodge the privileged position of dominant Western cultures."[2] Telling the unfamiliar story of the genesis of the Baha'i religion in Iran and the Ottoman Empire is one way of emphasizing the diversity of modernities and the multiplicity of Middle Easts. The community largely derived from, but broke with, Iranian Islam, and so considering it introduces an element of plurality into any discussion of Muslim reactions to modernity. To the objection that the Baha'is left Islam one can only reply that so did many liberals and Marxists leave Judaism and Christianity, yet liberalism and Marxism must surely be seen in some part as responses to modernity growing out of Judeo-Christian civilization. The Baha'i faith grew up in a rich intellectual atmosphere of the first serious encounter of Muslims with European thought since the Greek translation movement under Harun ur-Rashid. It is therefore not useful to discuss it only in relation to the Iranian tradition. Since the religion is a global phenomenon, and even in the nineteenth century had more than one national context, it lends itself to analysis within a global, or at least Greater Mediterranean, perspective. Its critiques of Western modernity provide an opportunity to examine critically the privileged position claimed by the dominant Western cultures.

What of modernity itself? How do the experiences of these Middle Eastern millenarians resonate with debates on whether modernity is liberating or disciplining in nature? The early Baha'i faith embraced almost Jeffersonian conceptions of freedom of religion and conscience, and of a separation of religion and state, as its response to those Muslims advocating an absolutist intertwining of religion and state, the granting of perquisites to orthodox Muslims, the relegation of Jews and Christians to the status of second-class subjects, and the persecution of Muslims considered heretical. In context this liberal response made the same sort of sense for adherents of the Babi-Baha'i movement as it had for the American Baptists, both of which had faced persecution from an Established Church. This separation of religion and state was seen as liberating, so that we witness here the critique of local knowledge traditions with reference to the new globalist norms of modernity.

At the same time, the early Baha'is roundly criticized the Jacobin version of the separation of religion and state, wherein the state is officially committed to deism or even atheism, and wherein it attempts to displace religion from its role in civil society. This explains Baha'u'llah's lament over the dying light of religion in every land, and 'Abdu'l-Baha's fierce condemnation of Voltaire and of the German kaiser's Kulturkampf against Roman Catholicism. The Baha'i utopian realist response to militant rationalism was a plea for balance, for freedom of religion not only from an Established Church but also from state coercion on behalf of instrumental rationality and civil-bureaucratic control. The same civil state that could form an instrument for liberating citizens from oppression by an Established Church, they recognized, could also act to repress religious freedoms on grounds of state interest. Modernity presents us not only with the image of Jefferson liberating dissenters such as Baptists and Quakers from the iron discipline imposed by Anglican and Congregationalist clergy and magistrates but with the spectacle of the French and German states (and later, of course, the Soviet state as well) attacking religious institutions. This Janus-faced aspect of modernity with regard to freedom of religion is usually not acknowledged by liberals but clearly was part of the Baha'i perception of the phenomenon.

The Baha'is were entirely comfortable in critiquing localist traditions of royal absolutism in the Ottoman Empire and Qajar Iran with reference to the international parliamentary ideals of modernity. They disparaged tyranny and depriving the people of their rights. They demanded a rule of law, codification of law, and due process. They announced that absolutism as a political system was foreordained for the trash heap of history, in view of the advent of Reason among all citizens. They saw these aspects of European modernity as potentially liberating in the context of the absolutist nineteenth-century Middle East. The radical and daring nature of this critique by prisoners of conscience is now hard to appreciate, given that Ottoman and Qajar tyranny so long ago faded from the scene. The Baha'is' only allies in speaking in this way were revolutionaries such as the Young Ottomans, the 'Urabists, the Young Turks, and the Iranian constitutionalists.

Yet Baha'u'llah and 'Abdu'l-Baha, for all their endorsement of parliamentary democracy, also saw what Michael J. Sandel called "procedural liberalism" as problematic. He maintains that the liberal tradition contains two subvariants, one that emphasizes the rights of individuals to do as they please, which he calls procedural liberalism, and another that aims at the development of citizens' character as part of a responsible group, which he calls "formative republicanism."[3] It is the second vision that comes closest to that of the Baha'i leaders. They decried the overwhelming of morality and ethical concerns by individual self-interest, political expediency, horse trading, and instrumental rationality. They denounced libertinism and the demand for freedom from all moral and religious restraint, for detaching individuals from their grounding in virtue (just as early American theorists called for a republic of virtue). Baha'u'llah expressed a preference for constitutional monarchy over simple republicanism (though he also praised the latter), insofar as even a figurehead monarchy could stand as a symbol of the divine and so resist the disenchantment of the world. The early Baha'is argued for popular sovereignty and a form of social democracy in which the state would be bound to ameliorate the condition of the poor and work against extreme stratification of wealth. Their ideal was not, in the end, the procedural liberalism of the bourgeoisie with its contentious, amoral politicians and its tilt toward ensuring the power and perquisites of capital. They sought something closer to Sandel's formative republicanism—a democratic constitutional regime dedicated to enabling citizens to attain individual self-realization in the mystical sense as well as a sense of social unity and community as group, though with the twist that they sought it on a global rather than merely national scale. The tradition of procedural liberalism has seldom acknowledged the ways in which its regime of rights can oppress as well as liberate. In the Middle East the advent of Western ideals of property rights often meant that for the first time peasants could be thrown off their land, which could be expropriated by banks, whereas traditional Middle Eastern custom and law had required that peasants retain their tenure in the land and be forgiven shortfalls owing to bad weather.

British and French social theorists put forward the liberal state as an agent of liberation but ignored the repressive and militaristic aspects of its colonialism (and, indeed, argued for the benevolence of that colonialism). The Baha'i denunciation of European militarism and expansionism highlights this disciplining project of the procedurally liberal state, which is often harder to perceive from the European metropole (except among the very poor, social deviants, and intellectuals). Baha'u'llah did not wholly reject the modern nation-state, but he was sickened by the mass slaughter that the industrialization of warfare had allowed, and he opposed the concept of absolute state sovereignty. Like Saint-Pierre, he felt that only a regime of compulsive, international collective security could curb the nation-state's expansionism, militarism, and colonialism. To Rousseau's and others' skepticism that the state could ever be induced to surrender so key an element of its sovereignty, Baha'u'llah implicitly replied that the material and human cost of industrialized warfare would ultimately grow too great to be borne, more especially by populations overtaxed to pay for it. The Treaty of Paris signed after the Crimean War had already enshrined the principle of collective security in international law with regard to protection of the

Ottoman Empire from Russian attack. Baha'u'llah wished to extend this principle and make it universal. In so doing he radically critiqued the entire foundation of the modern states system, which is grounded in absolute state sovereignty. Nationalists had argued that the nation-state would liberate peoples, such as the Italians, who had been oppressed by foreign empires or local petty princes, but the nation-state's propensity to engage in conflicts with neighbors, to attempt to expand and to grow dominant creates the most restrictive disciplining agent of all, the modern army and military-industrial complex.

While Baha'u'llah conceded the legitimacy of the state, provided it avoided aggression without and tyranny within, he considered nationalist chauvinism a great evil that threatened world peace. He insisted on the biological and spiritual unity of the human race, the transcendent unity of the religions, and the desirability of a universal language. In each instance it was his intention to forestall ethnic separatism and the violence that accompanied it. He imagined a global community, wherein the political loyalty of all human beings was owed to humankind as a whole. His own appreciation for Iran's past glory shows that he did not mean to abolish a sane and reasonable patriotic sentiment. But he did intend to extirpate nationalism and the construction of Self and Other on the basis of racial, religious, and linguistic markers of identity. National identity offered villagers and others the possibility of participating in much wider sorts of politics, but it could also become a straitjacket limiting the personality and encouraging paranoia about the Other.

Baha'u'llah challenged at least to some degree the norms of patriarchy inherent in both absolutism and the first wave of modernity, and 'Abdu'l-Baha gradually developed a vision of extensive women's participation in public and private life. They saw gender attributes as coexisting in both men and women, so that women could develop their masculine side and show forth the bravery of a champion, whereas men could develop their feminine side and become peace makers. 'Abdu'l-Baha explicitly abrogated the quranic statement that the affairs of women had been delegated to men. The distinctive identity and values of women as opposed to men, deriving from their positionality in society, were not denied. The emphasis on the need to educate women for the central roles of mother and housewife was common to the progressive wing of reformist thought in the Middle East in the early twentieth century. Both because of the movement's millenarian openness to radical change and because of its close contact with Western developments owing to the growth of an American Baha'i community, the Baha'i position as witnessed in 'Abdu'l-Baha's talks in the West and later letters probably moved closer to a "feminist" stance than was common among other Middle Eastern reform groups of the time. Women played key roles in the development of the Baha'i faith in Iran and were crucial to its establishment and spread in both Iran and the United States. Since the religion lacks a clergy and women are eligible for both elective and appointive office, there is no bar to women's full participation in the leadership of the local and national communities—though women remain barred from eligibility to serve on the international house of justice. Still, considering the nineteenth-century Middle Eastern background of the Baha'i faith, even this amount of women's participation in the religion's leadership is a remarkable development.

Millenarianism implied a willingness to see local culture radically changed and some local knowledge challenged in favor of more universalist or globalist norms, yet it also implied a utopian realist critique of oppressive aspects of modernism. One sociologist has spoken of modernity as an agent of both liberty and discipline at once, a formulation whereby he attempts to capture "the ambivalence of modernity in three major dimensions, namely the relations between individual liberty and community, between agency and structure, and between locally situated human lives and widely extended social rules."[4] The Middle Eastern millenarian experience of modernity that we have discussed appears to share this view of its ambiguity, and to reflect it in practice by employing modernity's liberating aspects to critique absolutism, and simultaneously by using forms of utopian realism to critique the disciplining aspects of modernity.

Among the Middle Eastern religious responses to modernity surveyed in the introduction above, where can we place the early Baha'is? Clearly, they were a millenarian movement. Baha'u'llah announced himself as not only the figure, "He whom God shall make manifest," prophesied by the Bab but as the messianic fulfillment of all the past major world religions. He saw himself as at once the culmination of the six-thousand-year-long Adamic cycle of prophecy and the inaugurator of a new age in world history, the major theme of which would be the gradual establishment of a global world civilization animated by his teachings. Early Baha'is believed that the advent of the end-time had turned the world upside down. Poor and humble workers were reconfigured as the backbone of the modern economy; women were reimagined as equal citizens full of manly courage and enterprise; voiceless subjects, shorn and led like sheep, were elevated to an electorate that would rule by reason in the place of emasculated monarchs; the sciences and modern philosophy were exalted over theology and the minutiae of religious law. Many Middle Easterners, of course, reached these same conclusions without adopting a millenarian view of the world, insofar as many of these reversals were implicit in modernity. Workers' movements, women's movements, democratic movements, and attempts to establish modern education and the sciences in the place of absolutist institutions have characterized the region broadly. Thus, in addition to the millenarian motif, early Baha'is were, like Egypt's Muhammad 'Abduh or the Ottoman Namık Kemal, modernists. Yet, the communitarian or "formative republican" liberal emphases of the religion—the concern for the poor of Istanbul's growing slums, the fear of unbridled individual self-interest, the location of ultimate values in divine revelation as embraced by a covenanted religious community—all give the Baha'is things in common with revivalists and fundamentalists (a convergence that accelerated throughout the twentieth century). It seems clear that attempting to categorize the response to modernity of any particular Middle Eastern religious group as conservatism, revivalism, millenarianism, modernist liberalism, or fundamentalism would be too limiting. Most actual movements have combined elements of each of these responses.

We need a further category, of utopian realism. It is the latter that appears to me to best characterize the early Baha'i response to modernity, even as we recognize the importance of other motifs to the movement. Touraine rightly says,

> We now have mixed feelings about all philosophies of progress. We rarely reject them, but we often find the Enlightenment as dazzling as it is illuminating. Above all, we are afraid of becoming purely social human beings who are completely dependent on a political power, as we know that power never coincides with the general will, which is more mythical than real. The return of the religious is, of course, often an antimodernist development; it is a reaction against secularization and an attempt to reconstruct a community by combining spiritual and temporal power, but it is also an attempt to reintroduce a non-social force in to social life, to reintroduce an ethics of conviction in to a world dominated by the ethics of responsibility, to adopt Weber's terminology. As at the beginning of the modern era, we are now witnessing a convergence between three great forces: rationalization, an appeal to human rights, and religious communitarianism. And who would be so bold as to claim to be certain that only the first defends modernity, that the second means no more than respect for the consumer and that the third is completely reactionary?[5]

Within the early Baha'i movement all three forces invoked by Touraine can be seen, of rationalization, an appeal to human rights, and religious communitarianism. His reluctance to hold these principles up as easy contrasts is therefore here vindicated.

The Baha'is' attempt to ground their critiques of both absolutism and of modernity in a religious revelation constitutes the religion as a field of contention between more liberal and more fundamentalist interpretations, though in the twentieth century the fundamentalist strands have become increasingly powerful. Christian and Muslim fundamentalists have attempted similar sorts of dual critiques of tradition and modernity. Fundamentalism in any contemporary religion constitutes an attempt "to secure political hegemony within the global political structure, while at the same time securing at the local level a degree of control over the life-world by attempting to exclude the pluralism of contemporary patterns of consumption."[6] The tensions in the world religions between the values of religious community and of secular modernity have remained unresolved and have been fought over throughout the past two centuries. They are at the end of the twentieth century again being powerfully broached. This phenomenon is especially salient on the political right, as with the Christian Coalition in the United States, the Islamic Revolution and the Khomeinist state in Iran, or the movement in India for *Hindutva,* or Hindu polity. To these problems of international and local control and of pluralism some contemporary leaders of the Baha'i faith have given answers increasingly similar to those of fundamentalists, stressing scriptural literalism, patriarchy, theocracy, censorship, intellectual intolerance, and denying key democratic values.[7] While the values of the nineteenth-century Baha'i movement, which were far more tolerant, continue to exist as a minority view, by the late 1990s a different set of emphases prevailed. The radical reorientation of the religion in the course of the twentieth century further underlines the fallacy of essentialism in speaking about Middle Eastern religious movements, which have often demonstrated startling changes over time.

The themes of the early Baha'i faith continue to be salient, if embattled, in the Middle East. A majority of Turks still desires a separation of religion and state. A majority of Turks and Pakistanis is committed to democracy (however dissatisfied, like all democrats, with its workings), and many more peoples in the region are clearly intrigued with its possibilities. Saad Eddin Ibrahim and others have courageously worked for human rights in the Arab world, establishing the first organization for that purpose. Although most countries in the region have turned away from socialism at the end of the twentieth century, concern with the welfare of the poor and with the values of community versus individual self-aggrandizement remain major themes in politics. Despite the resurgence of patriarchy among Muslim fundamentalists, women's movements and governmental commitments to women remain vigorous if embattled. Although nationalism has been rampant and destructive, discontent with it continues to be strong, as interest among intellectuals in wider loyalties such as pan-Arabism and pan-Islam demonstrates. In the Arab world a favorable view of the United Nations is even common, a legacy of its more evenhanded stance on the Arab-Israeli struggles than was characteristic of the West and of its valuable peace-keeping and refugee work in the area. The oil price revolution of the 1970s has left a legacy in the region of economic globalization, for ill or good, that no one would deny. None of these developments is without its own ambiguities, and Middle Easterners have continued to respond to the global impact and contradictions of modernity, either by accepting elements of modernity or experimenting with utopian realist ripostes to it. Ironically, it is other, progressive religious and political movements in the Middle East that are now the primary heirs of the main motifs of the early Baha'i faith.

Notes

Introduction

1. Touraine, *Critique of Modernity*, p. 1.
2. Hobsbawm, *The Age of Revolution*.
3. Jürgen Habermas, *The Structural Transformation of the Public Sphere*.
4. A good overview here is Michel Foucault, *The Foucault Reader*, ed. Paul Rabinow (New York: Pantheon, 1984).
5. Foucault, *Politics, Philosophy, Culture*, pp. 57–85.
6. Mitchell, *Not by Reason Alone*, p. 17.
7. Touraine, *Critique of Modernity*, p. 52.
8. Turner, *Theories of Modernity and Postmodernity*, p. 6.
9. Finke and Stark, *The Churching of America*; Stark and Iannaccone, "A Supply-Side Reinterpretation."
10. Touraine, *Critique of Modernity*, p. 19.
11. A vision of the potential of public reasoning for truly democratic process is presented by Habermas, *Communication and the Evolution of Society*; White, *The Recent Work of Jürgen Habermas*, pp. 25–47.
12. Touraine, *Critique of Modernity*, p. 52.
13. Giddens, *The Consequences of Modernity*, pp. 158–59.
14. Ibid., pp. 74–75.
15. Ibid., pp. 160–61.
16. Anderson, *Imagined Communities*.
17. Touraine, *Critique of Modernity*, pp. 222–23.
18. Said, *Orientalism* (New York: Vintage, 1979); Turner, *Orientalism, Modernism, and Globalism*; on the opposite side of the political spectrum from Said the argument for the antimodernism of Islam is made in Pipes, *In the Path of God*, though he allows for the possibility and argues the need for an Islamic modernism on the model of Reform Judaism.

19. Al-Asad, *Genealogies of Religion*; al-Azmeh, *Islams and Modernities*; Turner, *Orientalism, Postmodernism, and Globalism*; Zubaida, "Is There a Muslim Society?"

20. These points are made in an interesting way by Deal, "Postmodern and New Historicist Perspectives," especially pp. 6–7; see also the introduction to my *Comparing Muslim Societies.*

21. Deniz Kandiyoti, "Women, Islam, and the State," in Cole, *Comparing Muslim Societies*, pp. 237–60; see also her edited book, *Women, Islam, and the State.*

22. Lach, *Asia in the Making of Europe*; Said, *Culture and Imperialism.*

23. Berger, *Facing up to Modernity*; Berger, *The Heretical Imperative.*

24. Voll, *Islam.*

25. Exceptions include Algar, *Religion and State in Iran*; Keddie, *Scholars, Saints, and Sufis*; Qureshi, *Ulama in Politics*; Green, *The Tunisian Ulama*; Cole, *Roots of North Indian Shi'ism*; and Zilfi, *The Politics of Piety.*

26. For example, Hairi, *Shi'ism and Constitutionalism in Iran.*

27. Danziger, *Abd al-Qadir and the Algerians*; Metcalf, *Islamic Revival in British India*; Gammer, *Muslim Resistance to the Tsar.*

28. Amanat, *Resurrection and Renewal*; Smith, *The Babi and Baha'i Religions*; Holt, *The Mahdist State in the Sudan.*

29. Kerr, *Islamic Reform*; Binder, *Islamic Liberalism.*

30. Mitchell, *The Society of the Muslim Brothers*; Kepel, *Muslim Extremism in Egypt*; Cole and Keddie, *Shi'ism and Social Protest*; Munson, *Islam and Revolution in the Middle East*; Watt, *Islamic Fundamentalism and Modernity*; Choueri, *Islamic Fundamentalism*; Ferjani, *Islamisme, laïcité, et droits de l'homme*; for comparative observations as well as further analyses of Islamism see Marty, *Fundamentalisms Observed.*

31. Smith and Momen, "The Baha'i Faith, 1957–1988."

32. British Orientalist E. G. Browne concentrated his efforts upon the messianic precursor of the Baha'i faith, the early Babi religion of the 1840s and 1850s. In Orientalist fashion he tended to see the Baha'i movement as an inauthentic departure from the pristine purity of primitive Babism, as a cosmopolitan, Western-influenced reworking of Babi millenarianism, and as a betrayal of Iranian nationalism because of its emphasis on globalism. Since Iranian (and Babi) authenticity and Romantic nationalism were key commitments of Browne, he wrote little about the Baha'i faith per se. His translations and other writings include 'Abdu'l-Baha, *A Traveller's Narrative*; Hamadani, *Tarikh-i Jadid*; "Some Remarks on the Babi Texts"; "The Babis of Persia"; *Materials for the Study of the Babi Religion*; Momen, *Selections from the Writings of E. G. Browne.*

The Russian Orientalists Victor Rosen and Aleksandr Tumanskii were better informed about the Baha'i movement, but their writings on it languished in Russian Orientalist periodicals and had little influence: Rosen, "Manuscrits Babys"; Baha'u'llah, *Kitab-e Akdas*, ed. Tumanskii; for other works by Tumanskii see Momen, *The Babi and Baha'i Religions*, pp. 42–43.

More recent writing on the Babi and Baha'i movements includes Amanat, *Resurrection and Renewal*; Balyuzi, *The Bab*; Balyuzi, *Baha'u'llah*; Bausani, *Persia Religiosa*; Bayat, *Mysticism and Dissent*; Buck, *Symbol and Secret*; Michael M. J. Fischer, "Social Change and the Mirrors of Tradition: Baha'is of Yazd," in Fischer and Abedi, *Debating*

Muslims, pp. 222–50; MacEoin, *The Sources for Early Babi Doctrine*; MacEoin, *Rituals in Babism and Baha'ism*; MacEoin has also published numerous valuable journal articles and encyclopedia entries, noted in MacEoin's own bibliographies; Momen, *The Babi and Baha'i Religions*; Smith, *The Babi and Baha'i Religions*; Towfigh, *Schopfung und Offenbarung*; Walbridge, *Sacred Acts*. Stephen Lambden's working papers on Baha'u'llah's writings in his photocopied *Baha'i Studies Bulletin* and Todd Lawson's journal articles on Babi hermeneutics are also worth mentioning, though I have surveyed only published books here. Chapters on aspects of the Baha'i movement written by academics based in the West appeared throughout the 1980s and 1990s in the book series Studies in Babi and Baha'i History/Religions, published by Anthony Lee's Kalimat Press in Los Angeles. The rise of academic Baha'i scholarship has caused tension in the community, whose present-day leadership tends to be fundamentalist and antiliberal in orientation, and this has led to pressure on a number of prominent academics to resign or dissociate themselves from the movement.

1. Religious Liberty and Separation of Religion and State

1. McLoughlin, *Soul Liberty*; Jefferson, *Public and Private Papers*, pp. 20–22; Eisenach, *Two Worlds of Liberalism*, pp. 80–81. One is aware, of course, that in the eighteenth century *citizen* most often referred to free male citizen, but this tradition of rights discourse was later expanded.

2. In Curtis, *The Great Political Theories*, 2:403–4; for a modernist Catholic view of this pope and this issue see John Courtney Murray, *Religious Liberty: Catholic Struggles with Pluralism*, ed. J. Leon Hooper (Louisville, Ky.: Westminster/John Knox Press, 1993), pp. 49–125. Murray was disciplined by the Church for his views.

3. Shaykh Fadl Allah Nuri, "Book of Admonition to the Heedless," in Arjomand, *Authority and Political Culture in Shi'ism*, pp. 354–70; Bayat, *Iran's First Revolution*, p. 186.

4. Butterfield, *Historical Development*, pp. 15–16.

5. Locke, "A Letter Concerning Toleration," *Political Writings of John Locke*, p. 431.

6. Ibid., pp. 424–26; Eisenach, *Two Worlds of Liberalism*, pp. 80–81.

7. Al-Asad, *Genealogies of Religion*, pp. 239–68.

8. Lapidus, "The Separation of State and Religion"; see also Zubaida, *Islam*; and Keddie, "Islam, Politics, and Revolt: Some Unorthodox Considerations," in her *Iran and the Muslim World*, pp. 220–32.

9. Essential surveys of this subject include Bausani, *Persia Religiosa*; Corbin, *En islam iranien*; Momen, *An Introduction to Shi'i Islam*; and Arjomand, *The Shadow of God*.

10. On these developments see my journal articles: "Rival Empires"; "Shi'i Clerics in Iraq and Iran"; "Ideology, Ethics, and Philosophical Discourse"; and "The World as Text."

11. See Cole and Momen, "Mafia, Mob, and Shi'ism in Iraq"; for the political economy of the shrine cities see my " 'Indian Money.' "

12. Arjomand, *The Shadow of God*, p. 176.

13. Ibid., pp. 223–27.

14. Cole, *Roots of North Indian Shi'ism*, p. 247.

15. Amanat, *Resurrection and Renewal,* pp. 109–294, treats the emergence of the Babi movement in 1844.

16. Zarandi, *The Dawn-Breakers,* pp. 102–20; Anon., *Kitab-i Nuqtat al-Kaf,* pp. 239–40; 'Abdu'l-Baha, *Maqalih-'i Shakhs-i Sayyah,* 1:72–78, 2:56–62; for a short list of major converts to Babism at Baha'u'llah's hand in his ancestral village of Takur, see 'Abdu'l-Baha, "Safar-i Jamal-i Mubarak bih Mazandaran," in Ishraq-Khavari, *Ma'idih-'i Asmani,* 2:414.

17. Anon., *Kitab-i Nuqtat al-Kaf,* pp. 145–54, 240–41; Hamadani, *Tarikh-i Jadid,* pp. 43–44, 281–83; for Baha'u'llah's role see Zarandi, *The Dawn-Breakers,* pp. 278–300, 459–61, 584–85; Amanat, *Resurrection and Renewal,* pp. 324–28.

18. Anon., *Kitab-i Nuqtat al-Kaf,* pp. 242–43; Zarandi, *The Dawn-Breakers,* pp. 368–77, 461–62, 583–84; Hamadani, *Tarikh-i Jadid,* pp. 64–65.

19. 'Abdu'l-Baha, in Ishraq-Khavari, *Rahiq-i Makhtum,* 2:1149.

20. "Traduction d'un article du Journal Officiel de Téhéran [*Ruznamih-'i Vaqa'i'-i Ittifaqiyyih*] relatif à l'attentat commis sur la personne du Roi," trans. J. B. Nicolas, in Lavalette/Ministre des Affaires Étrangères, Thérapia, October 25, 1852. English translation quoted in Momen, *The Babi and Baha'i Religions,* p. 139.

21. Zarandi, *The Dawn-Breakers,* p. 433; Baha'u'llah, *La'ali al-Hikmah,* 3:15–16, 18; 'Abdu'l-Baha, *A Traveller's Narrative,* 1:79–80, 2:62–63. For Baha'u'llah's denial that the Bab ever appointed Azal anything like an "imam," or *vasi,* see Baha'u'llah, "Lawh-i Siraj," in Ishraq-Khavari, *Ma'idih-'i Asmani,* 7:40; also cited by MacEoin, "Divisions and Authority Claims," 94.

22. Abadih-'i, "Tarikh-i Aqa Mirza Qabil," pp. 66–67; Zarandi, *The Dawn-Breakers,* pp. 595–602; Sipihr, *Nasikh,* 3:172–76; Fasa'i, *History of Persia,* pp. 302–4; Sheil/Malmsbury, correspondence 1852, FO 60/171, in Momen, *The Babi and Baha'i Religions,* pp. 128–46; MacEoin, "Divisions and Authority Claims," pp. 106–7; Balyuzi, *Baha'u'llah,* p. 90.

23. PRO, FO 60/173, Sheil/Malmesbury, no. 143, 2 Oct. 1852, in Momen, *Babi and Baha'i Religions,* p. 146; 'Abdu'l-Baha, "Safar-i Jamal-i Mubarak," 2:414; Malik-Khusravi, *Iqlim-i Nur,* pp. 61–65.

24. Baha'u'llah, *Lawh-i Mubarak Khitab,* pp. 15–16; Baha'u'llah, *Epistle to the Son of the Wolf,* pp. 21–22; Kazemzadeh and Kazemzadeh, "Baha'u'llah's Prison Sentence."

25. Abadih-'i, "Tarikh-i Aqa Mirza Qabil," pp. 67–68; Sipihr, *Nasikh,* 3:176–77.

26. I am grateful to Abbas Amanat for this point. These attitudes can be seen in the narratives related in Nasru'llah Pourjavady and Peter Lamborn Wilson, *Kings of Love: The Poetry and History of the Ni'matu'llahi Sufi Order* (Tehran: Imperial Iranian Academy of Philosophy, 1978); see especially p. 117.

27. Mazandarani, "Tarikh-i Zuhur al-Haqq," 4:297; quote translated in Rabbani, *God Passes By,* p. 162. The text of this 1863 letter to the Ottoman state is not extant, but Mazandarani alleges that it was incorporated into the c. 1867 "Surih-'i Muluk," or "Tablet to the Kings."

28. Mazandarani, "Tarikh-i Zuhur al-Haqq," 4:297.

29. Baha'u'llah, *Kitab-i Iqan,* pp. 80–81; Baha'u'llah, *The Kitab-i-Iqan: The Book of Certitude* (hereafter, *The Book of Certitude*), pp. 106–7.

30. Baha'u'llah, *Kitab-i Iqan,* p. 96; *The Book of Certitude,* p. 125.

1. Religious Liberty • *203*

31. Salmani, "Sharh-i Hal," p. 15; Salmani, *My Memories of Baha'u'llah*, pp. 39–41.

32. Gobineau, *Correspondence*, pp. 288–89; also translated in Momen, *Babi and Baha'i Religions*, p. 187.

33. Davison, *Reform in the Ottoman Empire*, esp. chapters 2, 3, 4, and 7; and Berkes, *The Development of Secularism in Turkey*, chapters 5 and 6.

34. Devereux, *The First Ottoman Constitutional Period*, p. 23.

35. Baha'u'llah, "Surat al-Muluk," *Alvah-i Nazilih*, pp. 17–21, 34–35, 38, 41.

36. Arjomand, *The Shadow of God*, pp. 89–95.

37. Ibid., pp. 95–96.

38. Baha'u'llah, "Lawh-i Sultan," *Alvah-i Nazilih*, p. 166.

39. Ibid.; my translation.

40. Mitchell, *Not by Reason Alone*, p. 17.

41. Baha'u'llah, "Lawh-i Sultan," p. 158.

42. Ibid., p. 178; my provisional translation.

43. Baha'u'llah, *Iqtidarat*, p. 324, my translation. Compare that of Shoghi Effendi in Baha'u'llah, *Gleanings*, p. 241; the term *irtikab* has connotations of committing a crime, whereas Shoghi Effendi's rendering implies that even legal political criticism is being forbidden here, which is manifestly not Baha'u'llah's intention, given his own quite radical demands for parliamentary democracy.

44. Baha'u'llah, *Iqtidarat*, p. 261; my translation.

45. Baha'u'llah, "Ishraqat," *Majmu'ih-'i az Alvah-i Jamal-i Aqdas*, p. 75; the translation given in *Tablets of Baha'u'llah*, p. 128, is inaccurate and misleading, giving "affairs of the people" for *umūr-i millat* or the "affairs of the (religious) community." A *millat* in the nineteenth-century Ottoman empire was an organized religious community. The word could also be used in Persian to mean "nation," but that would make no sense here. It always in any case referred to a bounded community, and not to "people" in a universal way.

46. Baha'u'llah, "Lawh-i Dunya," *Majmu'ih-'i az Alvah-i Jamal-i Aqdas*, p. 135; Baha'u'llah, *Tablets of Baha'u'llah*, p. 93.

47. Baha'u'llah, *Epistle to the Son of the Wolf*, pp. 89–91; Baha'u'llah, *Lawh-i Mubarak khitab bih Shaykh*, pp. 60–61.

48. Baha'u'llah, "Kitab-i 'Ahd," *Majmu'ih-'i az Alvah-i Jamal-i Aqdas*, p. 135; trans. *Tablets of Baha'u'llah*, pp. 220–21.

49. Bayat, *Mysticism and Dissent*, p. 130.

50. 'Abdu'l-Baha, *Maqalih-'i Shakhs-i Sayyah*, 1:193; 2:158.

51. Draper, *A History of the Intellectual Development*, 2:226–28; proof of 'Abdu'l-Baha's familiarity with Draper's book is in 'Abdu'l-Baha, *Risalih-'i Madaniyyih*, p. 110; 'Abdu'l-Baha, *The Secret of Divine Civilization*, pp. 92–93.

52. 'Abdu'l-Baha, *Maqalih-'i Shakhs-i Sayyah*, 1:194–95; 2:158–59.

53. Ibid., 1:196; 2:160.

54. Locke, "A Letter Concerning Toleration," p. 428.

55. 'Abdu'l-Baha, *Maqalih-'i Shakhs-i Sayyah*, 1:197–98; 2:160–61.

56. Ibid., 1:199–201; 2:161–63.

57. D. Sutherland, *The Regulations of the Bengal Code* (Calcutta, n.d.). Regulation 3 of 1793, quoted in Powell, *Muslims and Missionaries*, pp. 79–80.

58. Carson, "Missionaries, Bureaucrats"; Powell, *Muslims and Missionaries*, pp. 80–81, and passim.

59. Mukherjee, *Awadh in Revolt;* Cole, *Roots of North Indian Shi'ism*, chapter 10.

60. Quoted in Powell, *Muslims and Missionaries*, p. 283, note 59.

61. Powell, *Muslims and Missionaries*, p. 284.

62. Draper, *A History of the Intellectual Development*, 1:349–438, 2:1–150.

63. Stark and Iannaccone, "A Supply-Side Reinterpretation."

64. Nuri, "Book of Admonition to the Heedless," pp. 356–57.

65. 'Abdu'l-Baha, *Maqalih-'i Shakhs-i Sayyah*, 1:200–6; 2:162–66.

66. 'Abdu'l-Baha, in Ishraq-Khavari, *Ma'idih-'i Asmani*, 5:177–78.

67. 'Abdu'l-Baha, *Promulgation of Universal Peace*, p. 197.

68. Ibid., p. 390.

69. Rabbani, *World Order of Baha'u'llah*, p. 66. I am grateful to Sen McGlinn for drawing my attention to this passage. Fundamentalist Baha'i leaders argue, however, that this stricture of Shoghi Effendi's was intended to stand only for the time being. Other statements by Shoghi Effendi, especially though not exclusively in unpublished "pilgrim's notes," have a more theocratic tone, so that many contemporary Baha'is have a theocratic orientation, and this is especially strong in the religion's top leadership. Within Baha'i law such pilgrim's notes do not have real authority, though there are some written texts from Shoghi Effendi with a similar undercurrent. We have seen both Baha'u'llah and 'Abdu'l-Baha reject theocracy, though as Middle Easterners they would have drawn the line between religion and state rather differently than do most contemporary Westerners. From the outside there appears to be an irresolvable contradiction between the vision of a permanent separation in some key regards between religion and state upheld by Baha'u'llah and 'Abdu'l-Baha and the dedication to a far-future takeover of secular governments by Baha'i institutions, which has become the orthodoxy of many fundamentalist current Baha'i leaders.

70. Locke, "A Letter Concerning Toleration," p. 395.

71. Mitchell, *Not by Reason Alone*, p. 77.

72. Smith, *German Nationalism*, pp. 38–42.

73. Smith, *German Nationalism*, p. 37, quoting Heinrich von Treitschke and Heinrich von Sybel.

74. Baha'u'llah, *La'ali al-Hikmah*, 3:376–77; Baha'u'llah, *Gleanings*, p. 200.

75. 'Abdu'l-Baha, *Risalih-'i Madaniyyih*, pp. 84–89; 'Abdu'l-Baha, *The Secret of Divine Civilization*, pp. 72 ff.

76. Ibid., pp. 73–74; ibid., pp. 62–63.

77. Baha'u'llah, "Lawh-i Hikmat," in *Majmu'ih-'i Matbu'ih*, pp. 37–53; Baha'u'llah, *Tablets of Baha'u'llah*, pp. 137–52.

78. Baha'u'llah, "Lawh-i Mubarak dar javab," in Ishraq-Khavari, *Ma'idih-'i Asmani*, 7:148–73.

79. Baha'u'llah, *La'ali al-Hikmah*, 3:376.

80. Baha'u'llah, "Lawh-i Maqsud," *Majmu'ih-'i az Alvah-i Jamal-i Aqdas*, p. 103; Baha'u'llah, *Tablets of Baha'u'llah*, p. 168.

81. Baha'u'llah, *Muntakhabati az Athar*, p. 220; Baha'u'llah, *Gleanings*, pp. 342–43.

82. 'Abdu'l-Baha, *Risalih-'i Madaniyyih*, p. 32–41; *The Secret of Divine Civilization*, pp. 25–33.

83. See, e.g., 'Abdu'l-Baha, *Majmu'ih-'i Khitabat*, 2:136–37; 'Abdu'l-Baha, *Promulgation*, pp. 175–76.

2. Baha'u'llah and Ottoman Constitutionalism

1. For working-class constitutionalism in England, see Thompson, *The Making of the English Working Class*; and Stedman Jones, *Languages of Class*; see also Eley, "Nations, Publics, and Political Cultures."

2. Giddens, *The Consequences of Modernity*.

3. Christopher Hill, "John Mason and the End of the World," in Hill, *Puritanism and Revolution*, pp. 311–23, and the same author's *Antichrist in Seventeenth-Century England*; Hill, *The World Turned Upside Down*; Capp, *The Fifth Monarchy Men*; Hatch, *The Sacred Cause of Liberty*; Garrett, *A Respectable Folly*.

4. For this theme see Smith, "Millenarianism in the Babi and Baha'i Religions." Smith does not, as I intend to, link Baha'i millenarianism with social reform motifs.

5. Buck, "A Unique Eschatological Interface."

6. Keddie, "Religion and Irreligion"; Adamiyyat, *Andishihha-yi Mirza Aqa Khan Kirmani*; Bayat, *Mysticism and Dissent*, esp. pp. 157–61; Bayat, *Iran's First Revolution*, pp. 53–75.

7. Browne, "Babiism," in *Selections from the Writings of E. G. Browne*, p. 425.

8. Goldziher, *Introduction to Islamic Theology and Law*, pp. 251–52. Some of Goldziher's evidence for this assertion comes from 'Abdu'l-Baha's stances in the period 1908–1909, which I think it anachronistic to conflate with Baha'u'llah's writings of the 1860s and 1870s.

9. The policy of nonintervention in politics adopted by Baha'i leaders beginning in 1908 has also impeded our understanding of the earlier period. Like the seventeenth-century English religious dissidents, the Baha'is' relationship with the revolution itself, once it came, was complex. 'Abdu'l-Baha called some of the early reforms, dated by internal evidence to 1906, "the basic foundation of the Most Great Civilization." See 'Abdu'l-Baha, *Majmu'ih-'i Mubarakih*, pp. 89–90. Upon the granting of the constitution, he had Mason Remey organize the American Baha'is to send telegrams of congratulations to the Iranian government. Richard Hollinger, personal communication, September 5, 1995. In letters to Yunis Khan Afrukhtih, also dated by internal evidence to 1906 or 1907, 'Abdu'l-Baha insisted that it was an absolute duty for Baha'is to campaign for the election of some of their coreligionists to the parliament (*majlis-i milli*; I have photocopies of five of these letters from a collection in private hands). After supporting the moderate constitutionalists in 1905–1907, 'Abdu'l-Baha in 1908 declared his community's neutrality for the remainder of the conflict, for several reasons. In 1907 Baha'is were excluded from membership in parliament, as heretics, giving them little stake in it, and convincing them that it was turning into a tool of Shi'ite theocracy. 'Abdu'l-Baha, a peace advocate, foresaw civil war and foreign intervention should the revolution continue, and could abide neither prospect. Some Baha'is continued to fight for the revolution, and, in any case, the neutrality of the community differed from the actively pro-royalist stance of the majority of Shi'ite

clergymen and their followers. Even during the countercoup of Muhammad 'Ali Shah in 1908, 'Abdu'l-Baha continued, in private correspondence with the shah, to insist forthrightly that he must yield to constitutional monarchy, which was the "exigency of the times." Pilgrim notes of Marie Wilson et al., Peter Coyne Papers, National Baha'i Archives, Wilmette, Ill.; I am grateful to Richard Hollinger for this citation). 'Abdu'l-Baha remained convinced that his father, Baha'u'llah, had prophesied the revolution and constitution. Thompson, *The Diary of Juliet Thompson*, pp. 100–3. All this is a bit moot here, since I am concerned in this chapter primarily with the development of Baha'i ideas on democracy in the period up to Baha'u'llah's death in 1892.

10. Salmani, *Sharh-i Hal*, p. 15; Salmani, *My Memories of Baha'u'llah*, pp. 39–41.

11. Baha'u'llah, "Surat Allah," in *Athar-i Qalam-i A'la*, 4:16–23; this passage on p. 23; Cole, "Redating the Surah of God," p. 11.

12. Shoghi Effendi Rabbani dated the "Surat al-Muluk," or "Tablet to the Kings," as after the Most Great Separation between Baha'u'llah and Azal, presumably referring to the latter's failure to appear for the divine contest in the Selimiyye Mosque in September, 1867; see Ishraq-Khavari, *Ganj-i Shayigan*, pp. 90–96.

13. Baha'u'llah, "Surat al-Muluk," *Alvah-i Nazilih*, pp. 3–70, esp. p. 17–21.

14. Ibid., p. 235.

15. For the political and economic characteristics of this period in world history, see Hobsbawm, *The Age of Capital.*

16. Baha'u'llah, "Surat al-Muluk," p. 236.

17. Davison, " 'Ali Pasha."

18. Baha'u'llah, "Surat al-Muluk," pp. 35–37; Baha'u'llah, *Proclamation of Baha'u'llah*, pp. 47–54.

19. I am grateful to John Walbridge for this suggestion.

20. Kayka'us b. Iskandar b. Qabus, *Qabusnamih*, p. 227. Franklin Lewis initially set me to looking at such literature for this principle.

21. Tavakoli-Targhi, "Athar-i Agahi az Inqilab," p. 419.

22. Seyitdanlioğlu, *Tanzimat Devrinde Meclis-i Vala*; Findley, *Bureaucratic Reform in the Ottoman Empire*, pp. 175–76.

23. Persian translation from the Ottoman given in Faydi, *La'ali-yi Dirakhshan*, p. 501.

24. "Hurşid Paşa, Mehmed," *Türk Ansiklopedisi*, 33 vols. (Ankara: Milli Egitim Basimevi, 1946–1984), 19:390.

25. Ashchi, "Tarikh-i Vaqa'i'-i Baghdad," fol. 27a.

26. Ibid., fol. 36a.

27. Baha'u'llah, "Lawh ar-Ra'is," in *Majmu'ih-'i Matbu'ih*, pp. 88–89; Rabbani, *The Promised Day Is Come*, p. 62.

28. Baha'u'llah, "Lawh-i Ra'is," *Majmu'ih-'i Matbu'ih*, pp. 113–14; my translation.

29. Davison, "Fu'ad Pasha."

30. Baha'u'llah, "Lawh-i Fu'ad," in Rosen, "Manuscrits Babys," 6:231–32; this passage translated by Rabbani, *The Promised Day Is Come*, p. 63. For a fuller discussion of this work see Cole, "Baha'u'llah's 'Tablet of Fu'ad.' " Shoghi Effendi Rabbani's book is the major modern theological discussion of Baha'u'llah's "Tablets to the Rulers." Baha'u'llah's spirited letters to Âli Pasha of 1868, the Arabic "Lawh ar-Ra'is"

("Tablet to the Premier") and the Persian "Lawh-i Ra'is" are in Baha'u'llah, *Alvah-i Nazilih Khitab bi Muluk*, pp. 203–51, see esp. p. 233.

31. Baha'u'llah, *Kitab al-Mubin* (Bombay, n.p., 1308/1890–91), p. 196.

32. Mardin, *Young Ottoman Thought*, p. 224.

33. Baha'u'llah/Mulla 'Ali Bajistani, Jumada II 12, 1293/ June 6, 1876, in Ishraq-Khavari, *Ma'idih-'i Asmani*, 7:254–55.

34. Baha'u'llah, *Kitab-i Mubin*, pp. 223, 256, 294, 299–300.

35. Balyuzi, *Baha'u'llah*, pp. 277–85.

36. Baha'u'llah, *Kitab al-Mubin*, p. 341.

37. Baha'u'llah's letters to the monarchs were published by Victor Rosen in the *Collections scientifiques de l'institut des langues orientales du Ministère des Affaires Etrangères*, 6:141–233. I shall cite the more accessible edition published by the Baha'i Publishing Trust in Tehran. The only extended academic discussion of these texts in English is that of Browne, but these articles were preliminary and contain many errors, and may therefore not be relied upon: see Browne, "The Babis of Persia," and Browne, "Some Remarks."

38. Quoted in Sec. to Baha'u'llah/Afnans, Rabi' I 11, 1298/February 11, 1881, in Baha'u'llah, *Athar-i Qalam-i A'la*, 7:129.

39. Baha'u'llah, "Lawh-i Salman," *Majmu'ih-'i Matbu'ih*, pp. 125–26; my translation. Compare the translation of this passage in Rabbani, *The Promised Day Is Come*, p. 72, which rather strangely renders *'aql* as "wisdom." Since this word is the precise technical equivalent in Islamic philosophy of *nous*, or intellect, and differs radically in its connotations from *sophia* (Ar. *ḥikmah*), or wisdom, I am at a loss to explain this translation choice. The original, however, does show a certain confluence of Baha'u'llah's thought with Enlightenment ideals, such that the advent of Reason among the citizenry obviates the need for kingship, and it may be that that confluence offended the Romantic and antimodernist sentiments of Baha'is in the 1920s and 1930s.

40. Baha'u'llah, quoted in Rabbani, *God Passes By*, p. 230.

41. Ridvani, "Qadimtarin zikr-i dimukrasi," 257–63, 367–70; Farman-Farmayan, "The Forces of Modernization"; Cole, "Invisible Occidentalism."

42. An insider's account of the Young Ottoman movement is Ebüzziya Tevfik, *Yeni Osmanlılar*; the most detailed modern English academic treatment is still Mardin, *The Genesis of Young Ottoman Thought*; Ali Suavi's demand for an elected legislature is in "Istanbuldan tahrirat," *Muhbir*, October 26, 1867, cited in Mardin, *The Genesis of Young Ottoman Thought*, pp. 46–47.

43. Seyitdanlioğlu, *Tanzimat Devrinde Meclis-i Vala*, p. 61.

44. Lewis, "Madjlis al-Shura."

45. Bakhash, *Iran*, pp. 44–45; Pistor-Hatam, *Iran und die Reformbewegung*.

46. For Malkum and the Young Ottomans, see Ebüzziya Tevfik, *Yeni Osmanlılar*, 2:18; for Malkum and Baha'u'llah in Baghdad, see Balyuzi, *Baha'u'llah*, pp. 151–52 (citing Muhammad Nabil-i A'zam Zarandi, *Matali' al-anwar*, MS); on Malkum in general, see Algar, *Mirza Malkum Khan*, esp. p. 89, for his article in *Hürriyet*.

47. Baha'u'llah, "Lawh Malikah Wikturiya," *Alvah-i Nazilih*, p. 131; Baha'u'llah, *Proclamation of Baha'u'llah*, p. 33.

48. "Lawh Malikah Wikturiya," p. 133; Baha'u'llah, *Proclamation of Baha'u'llah*,

p. 34. The translation unaccountably adds the phrase "the representatives of the people," which is lacking in the Arabic, where something closer to actual popular sovereignty seems increasingly envisaged by Baha'u'llah. For the issue of slavery in the Ottoman Empire see Toledano, *The Ottoman Slave Trade*; for slavery in Iran see Issawi, *The Economic History of Iran*, pp. 127–28.

49. For *jumhūr*, see Ayalon, *Language and Change*, pp. 100–9; Steingass, *A Comprehensive Persian-English Dictionary*, S.V. *jumhūr*. The democratic connotations of the term are revealed by its semantic field: "a high heap of sand; a large gathering of people; the populace; a community; all; universal." The upper and lower houses of parliament are also called *majma'* (gathering) in Akhundzadih, *Maktubat*, p. 13–14. These fictional letters of "Kamalu'd-Dawlah" and "Jalalu'd-Dawlih" were written in the mid-1860s, and they circulated in manuscript.

50. Baha'u'llah, "Lawh-i Napuli'un-i Sivvum," *Alvah-i Nazilih*, pp. 102–3; Baha'u'llah, *Proclamation of Baha'u'llah*, p. 33.

51. 'Abdu'l-Baha, *Some Answered Questions*, pp. 32–33; Rabbani, *The Promised Day Is Come*, pp. 51–52.

52. Baha'u'llah, "Khitab bi Qaysar-i Alman," from *al-Kitab al-Aqdas*, pp. 95–96; Baha'u'llah, *Proclamation of Baha'u'llah*, p. 39.

53. Baha'u'llah, *al-Kitab al-Aqdas*, in *Alvah-i Nazilih*, p. ; Baha'u'llah, *The Kitab-i-Aqdas*, pp. 52–53.

54. Baha'u'llah, *al-Kitab al-Aqdas*, p. 98; my literal translation, necessary for this technical discussion.

55. Smith, *Napoleon III*, pp. 90 ff.; Eyck, *Bismarck and the German Empire*, pp. 198 ff.

56. Baha'u'llah, "Khitab bi ru'asa-yi jumhur-i Amriqa," in *al-Kitab al-Aqdas*, in *Alvah-i nazilih*, p. 258; Baha'u'llah, *Proclamation of Baha'u'llah*, p. 63.

57. Baha'u'llah, "Lawh-i Padshah-i Rus," in *Alvah-i Nazilih*, p. 122; Baha'u'llah, *Proclamation of Baha'u'llah*, p. 27.

58. Baha'u'llah, *Al-Kitab al-Aqdas*, pp. 178–79; my inelegant, literal translation, necessary for this technical discussion.

59. Ayalon, *Language and Change*, pp. 89–91.

60. Bernard Lewis, *The Emergence of Modern Turkey*, p. 66, quoting the memorandum of Ahmed Atif Effendi, 1798, reprinted in the chronicle of Ahmed Cevdet Pasha. See for this issue Zolondek, "The French Revolution"; and Nikki R. Keddie, "The French Revolution in the Middle East," in *Iran and the Muslim World*, chapter 14.

61. Tavakoli-Targhi, "Athar-i Agahi az Inqilab," pp. 411–39.

62. Baha'u'llah, *al-Kitab al-Aqdas*, p. 122; Baha'u'llah, *Gleanings*, pp. 335–36.

63. Namık Kemal in Ebüzziya Tevfik, *Nümûne-yi edebiyat-i Osmaniye*, pp. 370–71.

64. Ayalon, *Language and Change*, p. 53.

65. Baha'u'llah/Afnans, Ramadan 24, 1305/June 5, 1888, in Baha'u'llah, *Athar-i Qalam-i A'la*, 7:101.

66. Baha'u'llah, letter of 1889, *Iqtidarat*, pp. 28–29.

67. 'Abdu'l-Baha, *Risalih-'i madaniyyih*, p. 19; my translation, for technical purposes.

68. Ebüzziya Tevfik, *Yeni Osmanlılar*, 3:64. My thanks to James Stewart Robinson

for his help in interpreting this passage, which the editor had unfortunately translated into modern Turkish.

69. Namık Kemal, *Hususi Mektuplar*, 1:240–41, 450, 454.

70. For the loss of Namık Kemal's correspondence with 'Abdu'l-Baha, see Nazif, *Nasiru'd-Din*, pp. 52–53. The possibility exists that the Baha'i leader's letters are still to be found somewhere in Namık Kemal's private papers.

71. Bereketzade Ismail Hakki Effendi, *Yad-i mazi*, pp. 105–21.

72. Balyuzi, *Baha'u'llah*, pp. 378–79; Balyuzi fixes the meeting between Midhat Pasha and 'Abdu'l-Baha in Beirut sometime in 1879.

73. Hanioğlu, *Bir Siyasal*; I am grateful to the author himself for drawing these facts to my attention. For the beginnings of the Young Turk movement see Lewis, *The Emergence of Modern Turkey*, pp. 196–201.

74. Some of the colorful details in this sketch are from Davison, "Midhat Pasha."

75. See Devereux, *The First Ottoman Constitutional Period*; Shaw and Shaw, *Reform, Revolution, and Republic*, pp. 105–86; Lewis, *The Emergence of Modern Turkey*, chapter 5; Berkes, *The Development of Secularism in Turkey*, chapters 7–8; Mardin, *The Genesis of Young Ottoman Thought*; Findley, *Bureaucratic Reform in the Ottoman Empire*, pp. 222–28; Hasan Kayali, "Elections and the Electoral Process," esp. 266–71.

76. *Al-Jawa'ib*, no. 848 (1877), in Sulh, *Ahmad Faris ash-Shidyaq*, pp. 218–19.

77. Pistor-Hatam, *Iran und die Reformbewegung*, pp. 185–214, drawing on issues of *Akhtar* published in 1877.

78. Undated ('Akka period) letter of Baha'u'llah, in Baha'u'llah, *La'ali al-Hikmah*, 3:97; my translation.

79. Baha'u'llah/Mulla 'Ali Bajistani, Jumada II 12, 1293/June 6, 1876, in Ishraq-Khavari, *Ma'idih-'i Asmani*, 7:254–55.

80. Baha'u'llah, quoted in Faydi, *Khitabat-i Qalam*, pp. 40–41.

81. Baha'u'llah, *Majmu'ih-'i Alvah-i Mubarakih*, p. 8. The earliest dated letters in this facsimile MS are from 1297 A.H./1879–1880, but this undated letter occurs very early in the collection and could be from a year or two before, when the Ottoman constitutional system was still intact. Even in 1879 it would be possible to argue that the parliament had been only temporarily prorogued by the sultan because of the crisis caused by the Russo-Ottoman war of 1877–1878, and many constitutionalists at that time retained hopes it would be reinstated.

82. Baha'u'llah/Ibn-i Asdaq, n.d., quoted in Faydi, *Khitabat-i Qalam*, pp. 69–70. My translation.

83. Baha'u'llah, *Iqtidarat*, p. 167.

84. Baha'u'llah, "Bisharat," *Majmu'ih-'i az Alvah-i Jamal-i Aqdas*, p. 15; Baha'u'llah, *Tablets of Baha'u'llah Revealed*, p. 28.

85. Ahmad Faris ash-Shidyaq, "Fi nisba al-fitna ila al-faransiyyin," *al-Jawa'ib*, October 26, 1870, repr. in ash-Shidyaq, *Kanz ar-ragha'ib*, 2:78.

86. Afshar and Mahdavi, *Majmu'ih-'i asnad*, plate 62 (p. 133 of facsimiles); my translation. The letter is signed "al-Da'i al-Babi al-Masjun fi 'Akka, 'Abbas" ("the Babi publicist imprisoned in Akka, 'Abbas"). It is not dated, but *Misr* was published 1877–1879. For Sayyid Jamalu'd-Din, see Keddie, *Sayyid Jamalu'd-Din*.

87. Ishaq, *Ad-Durar*, pp. 55–57; the article appeared originally in *Misr* in the

spring of 1878; for this period in Egypt see Cole, *Colonialism and Revolution in the Middle East.*

88. Baha'u'llah, letter of Shawwal 9, 1296/September 26, 1879, in *Athar-i Qalam-i A'la,* 7:246.

89. Sec. to Baha'u'llah/Afnans, Dhu'l-Hijjah 9, 1295/December 4, 1878, *Athar-i Qalam-i A'la,* 6:311–12.

3. "Ere Long Will the Reins of Power Fall Into the Hands of the People": Reform in Iran

1. In English see Afary, *The Iranian Constitutional Revolution;* Bayat, *Iran's First Revolution;* Martin, *Islam and Modernism;* McDaniel, *The Shuster Mission;* also still valuable is Browne, *The Persian Revolution.*

2. See, e.g., Adamiyyat, *Fikr-i azadi;* Adamiyyat, *Andishihha-yi taraqqi;* Adamiyyat, *Fikr-i dimukrasi;* Adamiyyat, *Idi'uluzhi;* Adamiyyat and Natiq, *Afkar-i ijtima'i;* Hairi, *Shi'ism and Constitutionalism in Iran.* For the Baha'is see Momen, "The Baha'i Influence"; and Buck, "Baha'u'llah as 'World Reformer.' "

3. It has been argued that even most modern intellectuals were quietists in this period: Atael, "The Iranian Graduates."

4. On Qajar society, see Lambton, *Qajar Iran;* Bakhash, *Iran;* Bosworth and Hillenbrand, *Qajar Iran;* and Keddie, *Roots of Revolution,* pp. 24–62.

5. Akhundzadih, *Maktubat;* Bayat, *Mysticism and Dissent;* Kia, "Mirza Fath Ali Akhundzade"; Sanjabi, "Rereading the Enlightenment"; Cole, "Marking Boundaries, Marking Time."

6. Mirza Fattah Garmrudi, "Shabnamih," quoted in Tavakoli-Targhi, "Women of the West Imagined," p. 112.

7. See Nashat, *The Beginnings of Reform;* Bakhash, *Iran,* chapter 2; Karny, "Mirza Husein Khan and His Attempts at Reform"; Kazemzadeh, *Russia and Britain in Persia,* esp. pp. 100–47.

8. Bayat, *Mysticism and Dissent,* pp. 165–66.

9. Isfahani, "Tarjumih-'i Ahval-i Mirza Abu'l-Fada'il," pp. 143–50; Faydi, *La'ali-yi Dirakhshan,* pp. 120–21.

10. Samandar, *Tarikh-i Samandar,* p. 199. Samandar placed this conversation in 1291/1874–75, but says that at the time Mirza Husayn Khan was the "first person in Iran" (*shakhs-i avval-i Iran*), which makes it sound as if he was still the prime minister. I suspect that Samandar may have misremembered the date and that this conversation took place in 1872 or early 1873.

11. Baha'u'llah/Mihdi, circa 1880, quoted in Faydi, *Khitabat-i Qalam,* p. 106.

12. *Asrar al-ghaybiyyah li asbab al-madaniyyah* was first printed in Bombay at the Hasani Zivar Press by al-Hajj Muhammad Husayn al-Hakim al-Baha'i in Rabi' I 1299/January-February 1882, according to the frontispiece reprinted in Rosen, *Collections scientifiques,* 6:253. I have used the fourth printing: 'Abdu'l-Baha, *Risalih-'i Madaniyyih;* a translation is 'Abdu'l-Baha, *The Secret of Divine Civilization.* A modern Iranian sociologist's useful reading of this book is Sa'idi, *Risalih-'i Madaniyyih.*

13. Baha'u'llah, quoted in Faydi, *Hayat-i Hadrat-i 'Abdu'l-Baha,* pp. 42–43.

14. 'Abdu'l-Baha', *Risalih-'i Madaniyyih*, pp. 2–7; 'Abdu'l-Baha', *The Secret of Divine Civilization*, pp. 1–6.

15. Ibid., pp. 8–16; ibid., pp. 7–12.

16. See Akhundzadih, *Maktubat*, pp. 16–21.

17. 'Abdu'l-Baha', *Risalih-'i Madaniyyih*, pp. 18–19, 119–20; 'Abdu'l-Baha', *The Secret of Divine Civilization*, pp. 14–15, 101–2.

18. 'Abdu'l-Baha', *Risalih-'i Madaniyyih*, pp. 22–24; 'Abdu'l-Baha', *The Secret of Divine Civilization*, pp. 17–19.

19. Sa'idi, *Risalih-'i Madaniyyih*, pp. 47–48.

20. Akhundzadih, *Maktubat*, p. 52–56.

21. 'Abdu'l-Baha', *Risalih-'i Madaniyyih*, pp. 30–31; my translation, modified from Gail, in 'Abdu'l-Baha', *The Secret of Divine Civilization*, p. 24.

22. 'Abdu'l-Baha', *Risalih-'i Madaniyyih*, p. 118; 'Abdu'l-Baha', *The Secret of Divine Civilization*, p. 100.

23. Baha'u'llah, *al-Kitab al-aqdas*, p. 98.

24. 'Abdu'l-Baha', *Risalih-'i Madaniyyih*, pp. 44–45; 'Abdu'l-Baha', *The Secret of Divine Civilization*, p. 37.

25. 'Abdu'l-Baha, *The Secret of Divine Civilization*, pp. 24–25.

26. 'Abdu'l-Baha', *Risalih-'i Madaniyyih*, pp. 124–30; 'Abdu'l-Baha', *The Secret of Divine Civilization*, pp. 105–10.

27. 'Abdu'l-Baha', *Risalih-'i Madaniyyih*, p. 136; 'Abdu'l-Baha', *The Secret of Divine Civilization*, p. 115.

28. Sa'idi, *Risalih-'i Madaniyyih*, pp. 38–40, 44–46, 64 ff. Sa'idi treats 'Abdu'l-Baha's critique of modernity under five headings: 1) he rejects the Enlightenment marginalization of religion; 2) he rejects the cult of reason; 3) he rejects extreme individualism; 4) he rejects complete liberty; and 5) he rejects the differentiation of various spheres of life (religion, the economy, politics, the family) inherent in modernity. It seems to me, however, that this discussion is insufficiently nuanced, since most Enlightenment thinkers never put forth such extreme propositions in the first place, and that the last point is simply incorrect, representing a later conservative Baha'i misreading of the text.

29. For English-language writing about these Iranian reformers, see Bayat, *Mysticism and Dissent*, chapter 5; Bakhash, *Iran*, pp. 29–42; Parsinejad, *Mirza Fath 'Ali Khundzadeh*.

30. Bakhash, *Iran*, pp. 35–41. The 1287 A.H. lithograph of this book in Tabriz is noticed in Yarshater, *Fihrist-i Kitab*, 2:3453. *Yik Kalimih* was reprinted in Tehran in 1305 A.H./1887.

31. Mustasharu'd-Dawlih, *Yik Kalimih*, pp. 16–17.

32. Ibid., pp. 20–22.

33. Majdu'l-Mulk, *Risalih-'i Majdiyyih*, pp. 33–37, 67, 70–71, 90.

34. His membership in the *Faramushkhanih*, or freemason lodge, of Mirza Malkum Khan is pointed out by Amini in ibid., pp. 30–32; and by Algar, *Mirza Malkum Khan*, p. 49. For Majdu'l-Mulk's biography see Bamdad, *Rijal*, 3:286–89.

35. Mirza Husayn Khan Dabiru'l-Mulk, "Risalih-'i siyasi," printed in Adamiyyat and Natiq, *Afkar-i ijtima'i*, pp. 420–21.

36. Ibid., pp. 422–48.

37. Qazvini, *Qanun-i Qazvini*.

38. Bruce/Church Mission Society, November 19, 1874, in Momen, *Babi and Baha'i Religions*, p. 244; see also Momen, "Early Relations," pp. 49–82.

39. Browne, *Materials for the Study of the Babi Religion*, p. 190.

40. Isfahani, "Tarjumih-'i Ahval-i Mirza Abu'l-Fadl," pp. 50–52; Mihrabkhani, *Sharh-i Ahval*, pp. 44–45; for the thought of this figure, see Gulpaygani, *Miracles and Metaphors*; and Gulpaygani, *Letters and Essays*.

41. For the Hamidian reaction see Berkes, *Secularism*, pp. 252–88; Lewis, *Emergence*, pp. 175–209; and Shaw and Shaw, *History of the Ottoman Empire*, pp. 172–272 (the latter stress continuities with the Tanzimat period but do not deny Abdülhamid's turn to despotism).

42. See Bakhash, *Iran*, pp. 146–86, 261–93.

43. Farahani, *A Shi'ite Pilgrimage to Mecca*, pp. 133–38; quote on p. 135.

44. I'timadu's-Saltanih, *Khalsih, Mashhur bih Khvabnamih*, pp. 9, 45–48. This work was written in 1893. See for further discussion of it, Alavi, "Critical Writings on the Renewal of Iran," pp. 243–60; and Cole, "Marking Boundaries, Marking Time."

45. For Ottoman censorship see Shaw and Shaw, *History of the Ottoman Empire*, pp. 251–52; and Küdret, *Abdülhamid devrinde Sansür*; for Iran, see Bakhash, *Iran*, pp. 146–86, 361–93; and Ahmad Karimi-Hakkak, "Censorship," *EIr*.

46. Browne, "The Babis of Persia," p. 944.

47. Baha'u'llah, *al-Kitab al-Aqdas*, p. 30; Baha'u'llah, *The Kitab-i-Aqdas*, p. 29.

48. Shaw and Shaw, *History of the Ottoman Empire*, 2:124.

49. Ibid., 2:125–28.

50. Ruhu'llah Mihrabkhvani, "Mahafil-i shawr dar 'ahd-i Jamal-i Aqdas-i Abha," *Payam-i Baha'i*, nos. 28 and 29 (1982), pp. 9–11 and pp. 8–9; based Isfahani, "Yad-Dashtha." I am grateful to the author for sharing with me a photocopy of this MS. See also Samandar, *Tarikh-i Samandar*, pp. 203–5.

51. Maneck, "The Conversion of Religious Minorities."

52. Mihrabkhvani, "Mahafil," 28:10–11, 29:8.

53. Quote from Sec. to Baha'u'llah/Afnans, Rabi' I 4, 1301/January 3, 1884, in Baha'u'llah, *Athar-i Qalam-i A'la*, 6:118; cf. Sec. to Baha'u'llah/Afnans, Muharram 4, 1301/November 6, 1883, in Baha'u'llah, *Athar-i Qalam—i A'la*, 6:112.

54. Undated letter of Baha'u'llah to anonymous recipient, probably of late 1880s, in Baha'u'llah, *Athar-i Qalam-i A'la*, 7:288.

55. Baha'u'llah, quoted in Universal House of Justice, ed., *The Compilation of Compilations*, 2 vols. (Sidney: Baha'i Publications Australia, 1991), 1:504, cf. 1:515. I am grateful to Seena Fazel for this citation.

56. Baha'u'llah, *Athar-i Qalam-i A'la*, 7:236–37.

57. Baha'u'llah, *Majmu'ih-'i Alvah-i Mubarakih*, p. 196.

58. Baha'u'llah, *Athar-i Qalam-i A'la*, 6:283.

59. Baha'u'llah in Ishraq-Khavari, *Payam-i Malakut*, p. 231. As will be discussed in a later chapter, in contemporary practice women serve on local and national spiritual assemblies (or houses of justice), but not on the world body, the Universal House of Justice, based in Haifa.

60. Baha'u'llah/Ismu'llah al-Mahdi, n.d. (c. 1880–1882), *Athar-i Qalam-i A'la*, 7:275.

61. Baha'i, "Tarikh-i Dawda'-i Tihran."

62. Momen, "The Baha'i Community of Ashkhabad," pp. 287–88.

63. 'Abdu'l-Baha, *Tablets of 'Abdu'l-Baha 'Abbas*, 1:7; for the early American Baha'i community see Stockman, *The Baha'i Faith in America*; and Hollinger, "Ibrahim George Kheiralla."

64. Baha'u'llah, "Ishraqat," *Majmu'ih-'i az Alvah-i Jamal-i Aqdas*, pp. 75–76; Baha'u'llah, *Tablets of Baha'u'llah*, pp. 128–29.

65. Bernard Lewis, *The Political Language of Islam* (Chicago: University of Chicago Press, 1988).

66. The following works in Baha'u'llah, *Majmu'ih-'i az Alvah-i Jamal-i Aqdas*: "Bisharat," pp. 14–15; Baha'u'llah, *Tablets of Baha'u'llah*, pp. 26–27; "Lawh-i Dunya," p. 50; Baha'u'llah, *Tablets of Baha'u'llah*, p. 89; "Ishraqat," pp. 74–77; Baha'u'llah, *Tablets of Baha'u'llah*, pp. 127, 129–34.

67. Bamdad, *Sharh-i Hal-i Rijal*, 3:405; I'timadu's-Saltanih, *Ruznamih*, p. 584 old/514 new, entry for Dhu'l-Hijjah 14, 1304/September 3, 1887.

68. Baha'u'llah, "Kalimat-i firdawsiyyih," in *Majmu'ih-'i az Alvah-i Jamal-i Aqdas*, pp. 35–36; Baha'u'llah, *Tablets of Baha'u'llah*, p. 65.

69. See Keddie, *Religion and Rebellion in Iran*; Lambton, "The Tobacco Regie"; and Adamiyyat, *Shurish bar imtiyaznamih*.

70. See Issawi, *Economic History of Iran*.

71. Baha'u'llah, "Lawh-i Dunya," p. 47; Baha'u'llah, *Tablets of Baha'u'llah*, p. 84.

72. Ibid., pp. 47–48; ibid., p. 85; for the persecution at Yazd in May of 1891, see the diplomatic reports in Momen, *Babi and Baha'i Religions*, pp. 301–5, which confirm the role of Mahmud Mirza.

73. Baha'u'llah, "Lawh-i Dunya," pp. 52–53; my translation, modified from Taherzadeh, Baha'u'llah, *Tablets of Baha'u'llah*, pp. 92–93; cf. Sa'idi, *Risalih-'i Madaniyyih*, p. 20, where he also points to this passage's implications for the establishment of democracy in Iran.

74. Baha'u'llah, "Lawh-i Dunya," p. 53; Baha'u'llah, *Tablets of Baha'u'llah*, p. 93.

75. Ibid., pp. 50–51; ibid., p. 90.

76. "A Petition from Iranian Reformers to the Foreign Representatives in Tehran in Early 1892," quoted from "The Liberal Movement in Persia," *Manchester Guardian*, April 20, 1892, appendix 5 of Keddie, *Religion and Rebellion in Iran*, pp. 152–54.

77. Mirza Malkum Khan, in *Qanun*, no. 35, quoted in Algar, *Mirza Malkum Khan*, p. 237.

78. Sulaymani, *Masabih-i hidayat*, 7:419–47; Safa'i, *Rahbaran-i mashrutih*, 1:561–91 (though this author commits many errors and does not accept the overwhelming evidence that Shaykhu'r-Ra'is was secretly a Baha'i); Sa'idi Sirjani, *Vaqa'i'-i Ittifaqiyyih*, see index under Shaykhu'r-Ra'is; Momen, *Babi and Baha'i Religions*, pp. 363–64; Balyuzi, *Eminent Baha'is*, pp. 142–55; Afary, *The Iranian Constitutional Revolution*, pp. 47–48; Kia, "Pan-Islamism"; and Cole, "Autobiography and Silence."

79. Mazandarani, "Tarikh-i Zuhur al-Haqq," 6:39.

80. See Afzalu'l-Mulk Kirmani, "Biography of Mirza Aqa Khan Kirmani," appendix to Keddie, "Religion and Irreligion"; and Abu'l-Hasan Mirza Shaykhu'r-Ra'is, "Mudhakkarat ra'ji'ih bi ittihad-i Islam ba Jinab-i Cevdet Pasa," in his *Muntakhab-i nafis,* pp. 117–23.

81. Shaykhu'r-Ra'is, *Ittihad-i Islam.*

82. Shaykhu'r-Ra'is/Malkum Khan, Safar 20, 1312/August 23, 1894, Supplément Persan, 1991, fol. 90b, Bibliothèque Nationale; also cited in Algar, *Mirza Malkum Khan,* pp. 225–26.

83. First Minister Aminu's-Sultan's summary, reported in F.O. 539/56, Lascelles/Salisbury, no. 124 (35), Feb. 16, 1892, and quoted in Keddie, *Religion and Rebellion in Iran,* pp. 108; a similar line, urging Baha'i noninvolvement in the Tobacco Revolt, was taken late in 1892 upon his succession to the leadership of the Baha'i community by 'Abdu'l-Baha, *Risalih-'i siyasiyyih.* He was especially worried about the prominence in the revolt of the Shi'ite ulama, enemies of the Baha'is.

84. 'Abdu'l-Baha, in Ishraq-Khavari, *Ma'idih-'i Asmani,* 5:17–18; see also Balyuzi, *Baha'u'llah,* chapter 40, esp. p. 385. For Kirmani see Adamiyyat, *Andishihha-yi Mirza Aqa Khan Kirmani;* and Bayat, *Mysticism and Dissent.*

85. For Sayyid Jamalu'd-Din in this period, see Keddie, *Sayyid Jamalu'd-Din "al-Afghani,"* pp. 283–388.

86. Baha'u'llah, "Lawh-i Dunya," pp. 54–55; Baha'u'llah, *Tablets of Baha'u'llah,* pp. 94–95.

87. The criticisms of Sayyid Jamalu'd-Din are repeated and amplified in a letter from Baha'u'llah to Ibn-i Asdaq, excerpted in Ishraq-Khavari, *Ma'idih-'i Asmani,* 4:120–21.

4. Disciplining the State: Peace and International Collective Security

1. Browne, "Introduction," in 'Abdu'l-Baha, *A Traveller's Narrative,* 2:xl.

2. Browne, *A Traveller's Narrative,* 2:xxxix–xl.

3. MacEoin, "The Babi Concept of Holy War."

4. Khadduri, *War and Peace in the Law of Islam;* Lambton, *State and Government in Medieval Islam;* Calder, "The Structures of Authority," pp. 147–51; Lambton, "A Nineteenth-Century View of *Jihad*"; Cole, *Roots of North Indian Shi'ism,* chapters 9 and 10.

5. Bürgel, "The Baha'i Attitude Towards Peace," p. 21.

6. Streusand, *The Formation of the Mughal Empire,* p. 137.

7. Shea and Troyer, *Oriental Literature; The Dabistan, or School of Manners,* pp. 365–70; cf. Rizvi, *Religious and Intellectual History,* p. 414.

8. Algar, "Shi'ism and Iran in the Eighteenth Century"; and Lambton, "The Tribal Resurgence."

9. Davison, *Reform in the Ottoman Empire;* Lewis, *The Emergence of Modern Turkey,* pp. 115–18.

10. Baha'u'llah in Ishraq-Khavari, *Ma'idih-'i Asmani,* 7:136.

11. Ibid. My interpretation, that this passage refers to a twelve-day mystical experience beginning Muharram 2 (Baha'u'llah's birthday) 1279/June 30, 1862, although new, has some things to recommend it. First, we know Baha'u'llah did make his an-

nouncement of his station in late April 1863, and that many of his writings in the months before that time have ecstatic and messianic overtones pointing to the imminent declaration; therefore, it makes sense that this was a decision he had come to some months beforehand. In addition, 1279 was the year 19 after the Bab's declaration of 1260/1844, and some Babi speculation centered on that year; Baha'u'llah may well have been expecting something to happen. Finally, as we shall see, concern with the abolition of holy war and the advent of peace formed a crucial aspect of the Ridvan declaration of April-May, 1863.

12. Stephen Lambden, "Some Notes on Baha'u'llah's Gradually Evolving Claims," p. 82, citing the Iran National Baha'i Archives Private Printing, 44:225.

13. Baha'u'llah/Afnans, Rabi' I 11, 1298/February 12, 1880, in *Athar-i Qalam-i A'la,* 7:134

14. Yerom Shoster/I. Augustus J. Wilson, U.S. Consul General, Beirut, Dhu'l-Qa'dah 10, 1283/March 16, 1867, Arabic letter and consular translation enclosed with Wilson/Hon. W. H. Seward, secretary of state, July 22, 1867, United States National Archives, State Department, Record Group 59, T 367, Roll 5; digitally reprinted in Stauffer, "Petitions," available on the World Wide Web at http://h-net2.msu.edu/~bahai/trans.htm.

15."Tablet of the World," *Tablets of Baha'u'llah,* p. 85; Baha'u'llah, *Majmu'ih-'i az Alvah-i Jamal-i Aqdas,* p. 47.

16. Baha'u'llah, *Epistle to the Son of the Wolf,* p. 25.

17. Baha'u'llah/Zaynu'l-'Abidin, 1306/1888 or 1889, *Athar-i Qalam-i A'la,* 6:303–4.

18. Baha'u'llah, letter of c. 1889, *Iqtidarat,* pp. 28–29.

19. Baha'u'llah, "Kalimat-i Firdawsiyyah 8," *Tablets of Baha'u'llah,* p. 68; Baha'u'llah, *Majmu'ih-'i az Alvah-i Jamal-i Aqdas,* p. 37.

20. Tilly, *Coercion, Capital, and European States,* pp. 67–74.

21. Hobbes, *Leviathan,* p. 65.

22. Hinsley, *Power and the Pursuit of Peace,* p. 20.

23. Pierre Louis-Lucas, *Un plan de paix générale;* Crucé, *The New Cyneas.*

24. Hinsley, *Power and the Pursuit of Peace,* pp. 33–29.

25. Penn, *An Essay Toward the Present.*

26. Saint-Pierre, *Projet pour rendre.*

27. Perkins, *The Moral and Political Philosophy,* pp. 58–62, 137.

28. Hinsley, *Power and the Pursuit of Peace,* p. 34.

29. Perkins, *The Moral and Political Philosophy,* pp. 64–66.

30. Ibid., p. 136.

31. These are published in Rousseau's collected works; a recent and contextualized retranslation is in Roosevelt, *Reading Rousseau,* pp. 199–229.

32. For Rousseau's perhaps self-serving account of how he became involved with the Saint-Pierre project, see Rousseau, *The Confessions,* p. 393 (book 9, 1756); cf. pp. 379–80; for important reassessments of the place of the peace issue and Saint-Pierre's thought in Rousseau's oeuvre, see Perkins, *The Moral and Political Philosophy,* chapter 8; and Roosevelt, *Reading Rousseau.*

33. In Cairo in 1977–1978 I noticed the similarity while was writing my M.A.

thesis on the Egyptian reformer Rifaʿah at-Tahtawi, who was close to the Saint-Simonians. I later discovered Rojas, "The Saint-Simonians," which makes some interesting comparative observations.

34. Manuel, *The New World of Saint-Simon;* Carlisle, *The Proffered Crown.*

35. Saint-Simon, *The Political Thought of Saint-Simon,* p. 88.

36. Manuel, *The New World of Saint-Simon.*

37. Moses and Rabine, *Feminism, Socialism, and French Romanticism.*

38. Carlisle, *The Proffered Crown,* pp. 200–6.

39. Michel Chevalier, *Système de la Mediterranée,* quoted in Regnier, "Le mythe oriental des saint-simoniens," p. 46, n. 26.

40. Mardin, *Genesis of Young Ottoman Thought,* p. 244.

41. Bahaʾuʾllah, "Surat al-Muluk," *Alvah-i nazilih,* pp. 7–8; Bahaʾuʾllah, *Gleanings,* pp. 250–51.

42. Bahaʾuʾllah, *Gleanings,* pp. 250–51.

43. Mosse, *The Rise and Fall of the Crimean System.*

44. Bahaʾuʾllah, "Lawh-i Istintaq," quoted in Faydi, *Khitabat-i Qalam-i Aʿla,* p. 25. My provisional translation.

45. Mosse, *The Rise and Fall of the Crimean System,* pp. 131–57.

46. Hinsley, *Power and the Pursuit of Peace,* pp. 242–43.

47. Ibid., pp. 119–24, quote on p. 120.

48. Quoted in Sec. to Bahaʾuʾllah/Afnans, Rabiʿ I 11, 1298/February 11, 1881, *Athar-i Qalam-i Aʿla,* 7:128; the following points come from pp. 128–29.

49. Bahaʾuʾllah, "Lawh Malikah Wikturiya," in *Majmuʿih-ʾi Alvah,* p. 138; Bahaʾuʾllah, "Tablet to Queen Victoria," excerpt in *Gleanings,* p. 253; the people and sovereigns of the world are commanded to work toward the Most Great Peace in the "Splendors" (*Ishraqat*) of the late 1870s or the 1880s: Bahaʾuʾllah, "Ishraqat 2," *Tablets of Bahaʾuʾllah,* p. 126; *Majmuʿih-ʾi az Alvah-i Jamal-i Aqdas,* pp. 73–74.

50. ʿAbduʾl-Baha, *The Secret of Divine Civilization,* pp. 39, 64–65.

51. For these developments see the essays in Morsy, *Les Saint-Simoniens et l'orient;* and Hanna, "The Saint-Simonians"; and ʿIsa, *San Simun.*

52. Rifaʿah at-Tahtawi, *Kitab Manahij al-Albab al-Misriyyah fi Mabahij al-Adab al-ʿAsriyyah,* in *al-Aʿmal al-Kamilah,* 1:337–39.

53. E.g., ʿAbduʾl-Baha, *Risalih-ʾi Madaniyyih,* p. 18; cf. Cole, "Rifaʿa al-Tahtawi."

54. Abrahamian, *Iran Between Two Revolutions,* p. 65.

55. Some MSS of this tablet apparently have colophons giving the date of its composition: see Ishraq-Khavari, *Ganj-i Shayigan,* p. 213.

56. Bahaʾuʾllah, "Lawh-i Maqsud," *Tablets of Bahaʾuʾllah,* p. 162.

57. My attention was drawn to the issue of education's importance in the formation of world citizens by Roosevelt, *Reading Rousseau,* pp. 123–74.

58. Bahaʾuʾllah, "Lawh-i Dunya," *Tablets of Bahaʾuʾllah,* pp. 87–88; Bahaʾuʾllah, *Majmuʿih-ʾi az Alvah-i Jamal-i Aqdas,* p. 49.

59. Hobsbawm, *The Age of Empire;* Kiernan, *The Lords of Human Kind;* Porter, *The Lion's Share;* Shannon, *The Crises of Imperialism.*

60. Schölch, *Egypt for the Egyptians!;* Cole, *Colonialism and Revolution.*

61. Cole, "Of Crowds and Empires."

62. Schölch, "The 'Men on the Spot.' "

63. Baha'u'llah, letter of Shawwal 12, 1299/August 27, 1882, *Majmu'ih-'i Alvah-i Mubarakih*, p. 131.

64. Baha'u'llah/Nabil ibn Nabil, Jumada I 23, 1300/April 1, 1883, ibid., pp. 192–93.

65. Baha'u'llah/Nabil ibn Nabil, Shawwal 24, 1302/August 7, 1885, ibid., p. 261.

66. Baha'u'llah/Afnans, Ramadan 24, 1305/June 5, 1888, *Athar-i Qalam-i A'la*, 7:98.

67. This and subsequent quotations from "Kalimat-i Firdawsiyyah," or *Words of Paradise, Tablets of Baha'u'llah*, p. 69; *Majmu'ih-'i az Alvah-i Jamal-i Aqdas*, p. 38.

68. Note the parallelism between Baha'u'llah's language in the letter of Ramadan 24, 1304/June 5, 1888 cited in note 64 above, about the need for Muslims to accept Baha'i law (*Tūbā barā-yi nufūsī kih bi nāmūs-i akbar va qānūn-i a'zam tamassuk justih and*), "Blessed are the souls who have clung to the greatest code and the most great law," and the undated letter in *Majmu'ih az Alvah-i Jamal-i Aqdas*, p. 8, where he says, *"Dar har ḥāl ḥukm-i shūrā nāzil va bāyad bi ān tamassuk just"* (In any case, the command of parliamentary governance has been revealed and must be clung to).

69. Moojan Momen, "Iran," *Encyclopaedia of the Baha'i Faith*, forthcoming.

70. 'Abdu'l-Baha, *Secret of Divine Civilization*, p. 115.

5. The Earth Is But One Country

1. Hobsbawm, *Nations and Nationalism*, p. 14.

2. Gellner, *Nations and Nationalism*, pp. 55–56.

3. Anderson, *Imagined Communities*.

4. Hobsbawm, *Nations and Nationalism*, p. 23.

5. Gellner, *Nations and Nationalism*, pp. 8–18.

6. Hobsbawm, *Nations and Nationalism*

7. Gould, *The Mismeasure of Man*.

8. Curtin, *The Image of Africa*, chapter 2.

9. Greenfield, *Nationalism*, p. 368.

10. Griffiths, *An Introduction to Genetic Analysis*, pp. 745–46.

11. Smith, *The Ethnic Origins of Nations*.

12. I am grateful to my colleagues Paul Forage and Victor Lieberman for this qualification.

13. Gumperz, *Discourse Strategies*.

14. For a critique of naturalist approaches to Iranian nationalism, see Vaziri, *Iran as an Imagined Nation*.

15. U.S. Department of State, "Greece Human Rights Practices 1993," January, 1994, downloaded from the World Wide Web from http://cyfer.esusda.gov:70/00/ace/hot.topic.links/hrcr/greece.txt. Reports on the privileging of state religions can be found at this address for other countries by simply substituting the name of the country for "greece" in this address, though countries with long names must be truncated to the first eight letters.

16. Ibid., "Israel/Occupied Territories Human Rights Report, 1993," January 1994.

17. Brass, *Language, Religion, and Politics*.

18. Hroch, *Social Preconditions.*

19. Suny, *The Revenge of the Past.*

20. 'Abdu'l-Baha, *Secret of Divine Civilization,* p. 62; 'Abdu'l-Baha, *Risalih-'i Madaniyyih,* p. 73.

21. Anderson, *Imagined Communities.*

22. Gellner, *Nations and Nationalism,* pp. 8–52; see also his reply to Hroch in *Encounters with Nationalism* (Oxford: Blackwell, 1994), pp. 182–200.

23. Hourani, *Arabic Thought in the Liberal Age,* pp. 110–1.

24. Akhundzadih, *Maktubat;* Cole, "Marking Boundaries, Marking Time"; Bayat, "Mirza Aqa Khan Kirmani; Tavakoli-Tarkhi, "Refashioning Iran," p. 83.

25. Baha'u'llah, *Majmu'ih-'i Matbu'ih,* p. 31; Baha'u'llah, *The Hidden Words of Baha'u'llah,* p. 20.

26. Curtin, *The Image of Africa,* p. 41.

27. Baha'u'llah, "Lawh-i Mubarak dar Javab-i 'Aridih-'i Jinab-i Abu'l-Fada'il-i Gulpaygani . . . dar barih-'i Lawh-i Manakji," in Ishraq-Khavari, ed., *Ma'idih-'i Asmani,* 7:168.

28. Baha'u'llah, "Lawh-i Dunya," *Tablets of Baha'u'llah,* pp. 87–88; Baha'u'llah, *Majmu'ih-'i az Alvah-i Jamal-i Aqdas,* p. 69.

29. Baha'u'llah, *Gleanings,* 333–34.

30. Baha'u'llah, "Lawh-i Maqsud," *Tablets of Baha'u'llah,* 164, 167; Baha'u'llah, *Majmu'ih-'i az Alvah-i Jamal-i Aqdas,* pp. 97–98, 101.

31. Hobsbawm, *Nations and Nationalism,* p. 65.

32. Fawaz, *An Occasion for War;* for a general argument against the notion that Lebanese national identity is any older than the twentieth century, see Salibi, *House of Many Mansions.*

33. Baha'u'llah, *The Kitab-i-Aqdas,* p. 47 (K75).

34. Ibid., p. 72 (K144).

35. Cole, " 'I Am All the Prophets,' " pp. 447–76.

36. Baha'u'llah, *Gleanings,* p. 217; Baha'u'llah, *Majmu'ih-'i Misr,* pp. 284–85.

37. Chittick, *Imaginal Worlds,* pp. 137–60; Fananapazir, "A Tablet."

38. Chittick, *Imaginal Worlds,* p. 157.

39. Wittgenstein, *Philosophical Investigations;* Wittgenstein, *Culture and Value;* a canny presentation of the implications of Wittgenstein for critical theory is Brill, *Wittgenstein and Critical Theory.* For an application of Wittgensteinian thought to problems of the diversity of religions, see Hick, *Problems of Religious Pluralism,* and the same author's *An Interpretation of Religion.*

40. Rumi, *Selected Poems,* pp. 125, 127; quoted and discussed in Iqbal, *The Life and Work,* p. 136.

41. Asad, *Genealogies,* p. 42, quoting Kant, *Kant,* p. 114.

42. Baha'u'llah, "Lawh Malikah Wikturiya," *Alvah Nazilih,* p. 135; Baha'u'llah, *Gleanings,* p. 255.

43. Hobsbawm, *Nations and Nationalism,* p. 22.

44. Anderson, *Imagined Communities,* chapter 5.

45. Many of these points, though with different examples, are made in Hobsbawm, *Nations and Nationalism,* pp. 51–63.

46. Anderson, *Imagined Communities*, pp. 42–46.
47. Eco, *La Recherche*, pp. 41–91, 141–68.
48. Knowlson, *Universal Language Schemes*; Eco, *Langue parfaite*, pp. 241–341.
49. Eco, *La Recherche*, p. 347.
50. Tavakoli-Targhi, "Refashioning Iran," pp. 91–92, quote on p. 92.
51. S.V. "Kemal Paşa, Es-Seyyid Ahmed Kemal Paşa," *Türk Ansiklopedisi*, 21:474; Mazandarani, "Tarikh-i Zuhur al-Haqq," 4:291.
52. Quoted in Sec. to Baha'u'llah/Afnans, Rabi' I 11, 1298/February 11, 1881, *Athar-i Qalam-i A'la*, 7:121 (quoting a tablet originally written in 1868 or so, soon after Baha'u'llah's arrival at 'Akka).
53. Baha'u'llah, *Epistle to the Son of the Wolf*, pp. 136–37.
54. Quoted in Sec. to Baha'u'llah/Afnans, Rabi' I 11, 1298/February 11, 1881, *Athar-i Qalam-i A'la*, 7:121.
55. Algar, *Mirza Malkum Khan*, pp. 82–97.
56. Cole, "The World as Text"; al-Ahsa'i, *Jawami' al-kalim*, 2:103; Kirmani, *Risalih dar Ikhtira'-i khatt*.
57. Esoteric concerns with script are, however, not completely lacking in Baha'u'llah's oeuvre. He wrote a gloss on Shaykh Ahmad's interpretation of the Most Great Name, and the symbol employed by Baha'is on their finger rings has similar talismanic roots. As the messianic fulfillment of Muslim chiliastic hopes, Baha'u'llah claimed to be the Most Great Name on his way to Istanbul. That he believed the Name to be written best in talismanic script may give a clue to one source of his concern with a universal language and script. See Baha'u'llah, *Majmu'ih-'i Matbu'ih*, pp. 67–87; Lambden, "At the Shore of the Black Sea"; cf. MacEoin, "Nineteenth-Century Babi Talismans."
58. Baha'u'llah, *al-Kitab al-Aqdas*, p. 185–86; Baha'u'llah, *The Kitab-i-Aqdas*, p. 88.
59. Baha'u'llah, "Bisharat," *Tablets of Baha'u'llah*, p. 22.
60. Baha'u'llah, "Lawh-i Maqsud," ibid., p. 166; Baha'u'llah, *Majmu'ih-'i az Alvah-i Jamal-i Aqdas*, p. 99.
61. Baha'u'llah, "Qad nazzalna fi Kitab al-Aqdas," in Ishraq-Khavari, *Ganj-i Shayigan*, pp. 210–13, translation in Froughi and Lambden, "A Tablet of Baha'u'llah," this passage on p. 28.
62. Baha'u'llah, "Ishraqat 6," in *Tablets of Baha'u'llah*, p. 127; Baha'u'llah, *Majumu'ih-'i az Alvah-i Jamal-i Aqdas*, pp. 74–75.
63. Baha'u'llah, "Kalimat-i Firdawsiyyih," ibid., p. 68; ibid., pp. 37–38.
64. Baha'u'llah, "Qad Nazzalna," p. 211; Baha'u'llah, in Froughi and Lambden, "A Tablet of Baha'u'llah," p. 28.
65. Ibid., p. 212; ibid., p. 29.
66. 'Abdu'l-Baha, *'Abdu'l-Baha in London*, p. 94.

6. "Women Are as Men": Gender in the Making of the Baha'i Religion
1. Tavakoli-Targhi, "Women of the West Imagined."
2. Najmabadi, "Crafting an Educated Housewife."
3. Cott, *The Grounding of Modern Feminism*, pp. 4–22.
4. Nandy, *The Intimate Enemy*; cf. Metcalf, *Perfecting Women*, p. 11.

5. Thomas Laquer, *Making Sex: Body and Gender from the Greeks to Freud* (Cambridge, Mass.: Harvard University Press, 1990).

6. Scott, *Gender and the Politics of History*; Lauretis, "Upping the Anti"; Alcoff, "Cultural Feminism."

7. For general background see Beck and Keddie, *Women in the Muslim World*; and Sayyid-Marsot, *Society and the Sexes in Medieval Islam*; a useful overview of women in Shi'ite Islam is Yeganeh and Keddie, "Sexuality and Shi'i Social Protest"; for the nineteenth century, see Mahdavi, "Women and Ideas in Qajar Iran"; and Afsaneh Najmabadi's important forthcoming book, "Female Suns and Male Lions: The Gendered Tropes of Iranian Modernity." The best social history of women has been written about Egypt: Tucker, *Women in Nineteenth-Century Egypt*; and Sayyid-Marsot, *Women and Men*.

8. Quoted in Tavakoli-Targhi, "Women of the West Imagined," p. 110; the most extended discussion of Karim Khan's thought is Bayat, *Mysticism and Dissent*, pp. 63–86.

9. Murata, *The Tao of Islam*, p. 192; this entire book is excellent in covering the subject of gendered images in Sufism. It builds on the earlier insights concerning the "creative feminine" in Sufism of Corbin, *Creative Imagination*, pp. 157–75.

10. 'Umar ibn 'Ali Ibnu'l-Farid (A.D. 1181–1235) was an Egyptian mystic who spent some twenty years in the Hijaz. For his classic "Nazm as-Suluk," see Arberry, *The Mystical Poems of Ibn al-Farid*; and Arberry, *The Poem of the Way*; for Ibnu'l-Farid's thought, see Nicholson, *Studies in Islamic Mysticism*; Hilmi, *Ibnu'l-Farid*; Boullata, "Verbal Arabesque and Mystical Union"; and Homerin, *From Arab Poet to Muslim Saint*; for Ibn al-'Arabi in this regard see Ibn al-'Arabi, *The Tarjuman al-Ashwaq*; for Baha'u'llah's works in this genre see Cole, "Baha'u'llah and the Naqshbandi Sufis"; and John Walbridge, "Erotic Imagery in the Allegorical Writings of Baha'u'llah," MS.

11. Baha'u'llah, "Qasidih-'i Varqa'iyyih," *Athar-i Qalam-i A'la*, 3:196–215.

12. Baha'u'llah, "Lawh al-Huriyyah," *Athar-i Qalam-i A'la*, 4:379–91.

13. The best overview of Tahirih's life is Amanat, *Resurrection and Renewal*, chapter 7; for a nuanced, feminist reading of her life and poetry, see Milani, *Veils and Words*, pp. 77–99; for Tahirih's meaning in the Baha'i religion, see Maneck, "Women and the Baha'i Faith," pp. 211–17, and her "Tahirih." We all await the forthcoming definitive study and translation of her poetry by Amin Banani.

14. Bayda'i, *Tadhkirih-'i shu'ara*, 3:185–87; cf. p. 172. Shams-i Jahan's memoirs survive in the form of an autobiographical poem, which Bayda'i printed and of which he gave a prose summary.

15. Ibid., 3:173–74.

16. Habibu'llah, "Tarikh-i Amri-yi Shiraz," pp. 153–68; Mazandarani, "Tarikh-i Zuhur al-Haqq," 6:856; a biography in English of Aqa Mirza Aqa Nur al-Din is Balyuzi, *Eminent Baha'is*, pp. 216–36.

17. Habibu'llah, "Tarikh-i Amri-yi Shiraz," pp. 169–74; Mazandarani, "Tarikh-i Zuhur al-Haqq," 6:857.

18. Khadijih Begum, quoted in Balyuzi, *Khadijih Begum*, pp. 30–31.

19. Ibid., p. 31.

20. Habibu'llah, "Tarikh-i Amri-yi Shiraz," p. 177; Mazandarani, "Tarikh-i Zuhur al-Haqq," 6:857.

21. Tahtawi, *Kitab Manahij al-Albab al-Misriyyah fi Mabahij al-Adab al-'Asriyyah*, in *al-A'mal al-Kamilah*, 1:282 and his book, *al-Murshid al-Amin li'l-Banat wa al-Banin* (The Sure Guide for Girls and Boys), included in this series of collected works; for Kashani, see Najmabadi, "Crafting an Educated Housewife."

22. Details of Baha'u'llah's marriages and children can be found in Malik-Khusravi, *Iqlim-i Nur.*

23. Baha'u'llah, *The Kitab-i-Aqdas*, p. 38.

24. Ibid., p. 137, no. 101.

25. Baha'u'llah, *Majmu'ih-'i az Alvah*, pp. 75–76; Baha'u'llah, *Tablets of Baha'u'llah*, p. 128.

26. Ibid., p. 38; ibid., pp. 69–70.

27. Ibid., p. 73; ibid., p. 125.

28. Ishraq-Khavari, *Ganj-i Shayigan*, pp. 210–11.

29. A useful bibliography for Ottoman-language periodicals related to women is Toska, *Istanbul Kütüphanelerindeki*; for substantive remarks see Deniz Kandiyoti's chapter on Turkish women in her edited book, *Women, Islam and the State.*

30. "Hakim al-Sharq," *Misr*, May 24, 1879, cited and partially translated in Keddie, *Sayyid Jamal al-Din "Al-Afghani,"* pp. 110–11.

31. Baron, *The Women's Awakening in Egypt*, p. 4; Cannon, "Nineteenth-Century Arabic Writings."

32. Javadi, Mar'ashi, and Shikarlu, *Ruyaru'i-yi Zan*; Bibi Khanum Astarabadi, *Ma'ayib ar-Rijal*, constitutes pp. 97–199. Another edition of the latter work is Najmabadi, *Ma'ayib ar-Rijal*, to which the author has prefixed a useful English introduction. A protofeminist perspective from a younger contemporary is apparent in Taj al-Saltana, *Crowning Anguish*; for this author see Najmabadi, "A Different Voice."

33. Astarabadi, *Ma'ayib ar-Rijal*, pp. 114–15.

34. Ibid., pp. 116–17.

35. Ibid., pp. 119–21.

36. Ibid., pp. 123–28.

37. Ibid., pp. 145–78.

38. Ibid., pp. 181–83.

39. Baha'u'llah, in Ishraq-Khavari, *Payam-i Malakut*, p. 231.

40. Ibid. p. 232.

41. Faridu'd-Din 'Attar, *Kitab Tadhkirat al-Awliya'*, ed. R. A. Nicholson, 2 vols. (Leyden: E.J. Brill, 1905–1907), 1:59; Farid u'd-Din 'Attar, *Muslim Saints and Mystics* (London: Routledge and Kegan Paul, 1966), p. 40; I am grateful to Afsaneh Najmabadi for this citation.

42. Baha'u'llah, quoted in *The Compilation of Compilations*, 2:358.

43. Baha'u'llah, in Yazdani, *Maqam va Huquq-i Zan*, p. 12: "Inna an-nisa'a 'inda 'l-Baha'i hukmuhunna hukmu 'r-rijal."

44. Baha'u'llah, *Athar-i Qalam-i A'la*, 6:281.

45. Ibid., 6:280.

46. Baha'u'llah, *La'ali al-Hikmah*, 3:349.

47. Baha'u'llah, *Majmu'ih-'i az Alvah*, p. 115; Baha'u'llah, *Tablets of Baha'u'llah*, p. 185.

48. Metcalf, *Perfecting Women* pp. 11, 253–58.
49. Malti-Douglas, *Woman's Body, Woman's World*, chapter 3.
50. E.g., Arbab, *Akhtaran-i Taban*, 1:121–26, 136, 146, 148–51, 286.
51. For this famine see Okazakis, "The Great Persian Famine."
52. Isfahani, *Stories from the Delight of Hearts*, p. 81.
53. Gulpaygani, *Letters and Essays*, pp. 81–82.
54. Mazandarani, "Tarikh-i Zuhur al-Haqq," 6:406–11; Baha'i, "Tarikh-i Dawda'-i Tihran, 1300," Uncatalogued Persian MS, 61 foll., National Baha'i Archives, Wilmette, Illinois; United Kingdom, Public Record Office, Foreign Office 60/453, Thomson/Earl Granville, Tehran, no. 33, March 17, 1883; Thomson/Earl Granville, Tehran, no. 62, May 15, 1882, reprinted in Momen, *The Babi and Baha'i Religions*, pp. 292–95.
55. Mazandarani, "Tarikh-i Zuhur al-Haqq," 6:444–50.
56. Mazandarani, "Tarikh-i Zuhur al-Haqq," 6:457–62; and Arbab, *Akhtaran-i Taban*, 1:284–91. For Ta'irih's feminist journalism in *Iran-i Naw*, see Afary, *The Iranian Constitutional Revolution*, pp. 197–99. According to Richard Hollinger, who has seen the original text of Charles Mason Remey's travel diary, this is the figure whom Remey met on his trip to Tehran in 1908 and whom he describes as working to get Baha'i women to unveil and to eschew gender segregation at Baha'i meetings: Remey, *Observations of a Baha'i Traveller*, pp. 106–9.
57. Najmabadi, "Crafting an Educated Housewife."
58. Cole, "Feminism, Class, and Islam."
59. Najmabadi, "Crafting an Educated Housewife."
60. Afary, "On the Origins of Feminism," quote on p. 69; see also her *Iranian Constitutional Revolution*, chapter 7; Najmabadi, "Zanha-yi Millat," and the same author's " 'Is Our Name Remembered?'"
61. Najmabadi, "Crafting an Educated Housewife."
62. Yazdani, *Maqam va Huquq-i Zan*, pp. 13–14.
63. 'Abdu'l-Baha, in Ishraq-Khavari, *Ma'idih-yi Asmani*, 9:7.
64. Stockman, *The Baha'i Faith in America*, 2:75.
65. Ibid., 2:323. Stockman gives the interpretation whereby 'Abdu'l-Baha in 1909 adopted a new position excluding women only from the Universal House of Justice but does not discuss alternative possibilities nor analyze the Persian text.
66. 'Abdu'l-Baha decisively intervened to allow women to serve on the Chicago assembly; see "Chicago News Notes." I am grateful to Richard Hollinger for this citation.
67. Letter of 'Abdu'l-Baha, dated August 28, 1913, in 'Abdu'l-Baha, *Paris Talks*, p. 183.
68. Ibid., p. 7.
69. 'Abdu'l-Baha, *Promulgation of Universal Peace*, p. 108.
70. Ibid., p. 75.
71. Cf. Alcoff, "Cultural Feminism"; and Lauretis, "Upping the Anti."
72. 'Abdu'l-Baha, *Paris Talks*, p. 182.
73. These remarks come out of discussions with Afsaneh Najmabadi, though I am responsible for the final formulation here.

Conclusion
1. Turner, *Orientalism, Postmodernism, and Globalism,* p. 5.
2. Ibid., p. 104.
3. Michael J. Sandel, *Democracy's Discontent* (Cambridge: Harvard University Press, 1996).
4. Wagner, *The Sociology of Modernity,* p. xii.
5. Touraine, *Critique of Modernity,* p. 59.
6. Turner, *Orientalism, Postmodernism, and Globalism,* p. 78.
7. Very little academic attention has been given to the Baha'i faith in the period after about 1925, which, as I have underlined, often has very different emphases than those of the early Baha'i faith. For Iran, see Michael M. J. Fischer, "Social Change and the Mirrors of Tradition: Baha'is of Yazd," in Fischer and Abedi, *Debating Muslims,* pp. 222–50; Smith, *The Babi and Baha'i Religions,* pp. 115–99; Smith and Momen, "The Baha'i Faith, 1957–1988. " For global and U.S. developments, see Association for Baha'i Studies, *The Vision of Shoghi Effendi;* Bramson-Lerche, "Some Aspects of the Development"; Morrison, *To Move the World;* Armstrong-Ingram, *Music, Devotions;* Hollinger, *Community Histories;* Stockman, "The Baha'i Faith"; McMullen, "The Atlanta Baha'i Community"; and Russell, "Spiritual Vertigo."

For issues in fundamentalism versus academic scholarship, see MacEoin, "Baha'i Fundamentalism"; MacEoin, "Afnan, Hatcher, and an Old Bone"; MacEoin, "The Crisis in Babi and Baha'i Studies" (this was in part a dialogue with Juan Cole, who now withdraws most of what he said then); see also a book MacEoin wrote under his nom de plume, Daniel Easterman, *New Jerusalems,* pp. 184–94, and passim.

Select Bibliography

Arabic, Persian, Turkish

Manuscripts

Abadih-'i, Aqa Mirza Qabil. "Tarikh-i Abadih va Tavabi'." Photocopy of MS in author's hands.

— "Tarikh-i Aqa Mirza Qabil-i Abadih-'i." Photocopy of MS in author's hands.

Afnan, Habibu'llah. "Tarikh-i Amri-yi Shiraz." Photocopy of MS in Afnan Library, London.

'Amidu'l-Atibba', Mirza Yahya. "Tarikh-i Rasht." Photocopy of MS from Afnan Library, London.

Anon. "Majmu'ih-'i Tavarikh-i Nur." Photocopy of MS from Afnan Library, London.

— "Tarikh-i Hamadan va Rasht." Photocopy of MS from Afnan Libary, London, BWC No. 3112.

— "Tarikh-i Isfahan." Photocopy of MS from Afnan Library, London.

— "Vuqu'at-i Tarikhiyyih . . . bar Ahibba-yi ilahi dar Abadih." Photocopy of MS from Afnan Library, London.

Ashchi, Aqa Husayn. "Tarikh-i Vaqa'i'-i Baghdad va Islambul va Edirne va 'Akka." Photocopy of MS in author's hands. Available on the World Wide Web in facsimile at http://h-net2.msu.edu/~bahai/bharab.htm Aqa Husayn.

Bab, Sayyid 'Ali Muhammad Shirazi. "Four Letters." CUL. Browne Or. MS F. 28 (7).

— "Miscellaneous Letters." Cambridge University Library. Browne Coll. F. 21 (9).

— "Persian and Arabic Pieces, Epistles and Prayers." Cambridge University Library. Browne Coll. F 23 (9).

— "Ar-Risalah adh-Dhahabiyyah." Photocopy of MS in Baha'i World Centre, Haifa.

— "As-Sahifah bayn al-Haramayn." CUL. Browne Or. MS F. 7 (9).

— "as-Sahifah ar-Ridawiyyah." CUL. Browne Or. MS F. 28 (6).

— "Tafsir Surat al-Baqarah." Reproduced in Todd Lawson, "The Qur'an Commentary of Sayyid 'Ali Muhammad Shirazi, the Bab (1819–1850)." Ph.D. diss., McGill University, 1987.

— "Tafsir Surat at-Tawhid." Photocopy of MS in Baha'i World Centre, Haifa.

— "Tafsir Surat 'Wa'l-'Asr.' " CUL. Browne Or. MS F 9 (6).

Baha'i, 'Ali Asghar. "Tarikh-i Dawda'-i Tihran, 1300 A.H." Photocopy of MS in National Baha'i Archives, Wilmette, Illinois.

Baha'u'llah, Mirza Husayn 'Ali Nuri. "Alvah." British Library MS Or. 11095. "Discourses ascribed to Baha'u'llah in the hand of Riza Shirazi said to have been copied in Adrianople." Actually Akka-period tablets.

— "Alvah." BL MS Or. 11096. Tablets of Baha'u'llah in the hand of Riza Shirazi.

— "Alvah." BL MS Or. 11097. Tablets of Baha'u'llah in the hand of Riza Shirazi.

— "Al-Kitab al-Aqdas va Su'al va Javab." BL MS Or. 2820.

— "Kitab-i Iqan." BL MS Or. 3116. Foll. 78–127. Followed by Seven Valleys and then by general short letters to Baha'is.

— "Tracts and Letters." BL MS Or. 3114. Foll. 96; bought 1886.

Barfarushi, Muhammad 'Ali "Quddus." "Abhar al-Quddusiyyah." BL MS Or. 5110. fols. 36.

Dahaji, Sayyid Mihdi. "Risalah." CUL. Browne Or. MS F. 57 (9).

Da'ud, Yuhanna. A Collection of 92 letters and reports from Baha'is of the East. Persian and Arabic. BL MS Or. 8118.

— A collection of 161 letters, mostly in manuscript, comprising copies of epistles by 'Abdu'l-Baha and original letters from distinguished Baha'i teachers. BL MS Or. 8895.

Gulpaygani, Mirza Abu'l-Fadl. "Istidlaliyyih." CUL. Browne Or. MS F. 27 (9), 1. Proofs written for the Jews.

Hamadani, Mirza Husayn. "Tarikh-i Jadid." Persian MS, Cama Oriental Library, Bombay. Very faint Indian photocopy. Inaccurately listed as missing in Denis MacEoin, *The Sources for Early Babi Doctrine and History: A Survey*, p. 215. Leiden: E. J. Brill, 1992.

Isfahani, Mirza Asadu'llah. "Yad-Dashtha." Photocopy of an MS in the library of Mr. Ruhu'llah Mihrabkhani, treating the history of the Tehran local assembly from 1879.

Ishraq-Khavari, 'Abdu'l-Hamid. "Muhadarat dar Barih-'i Kitab-i Mustatab-i Aqdas." Photocopy of handwritten MS dated 126 B.E./1975.

Malkum Khan Papers. Bibliothèque Nationale, Paris. Supplément Persan.

Mazandarani, Asadu'llah Fadil. "Tarikh-i Zuhur al-Haqq." Volume 4. Photocopy of MS in author's hands.

— "Tarikh-i Zuhur al-Haqq." Vol. 6. Photocopy of MS in author's hands.

Mihrabkhani, Ruhu'llah. "Qissih-'i 'ishq-i Mirza Muhammad 'Ali Zunuzi." Photocopy of MS in author's hands.

Niraqi. "Tadhkirat al-Ghafilin." CUL. Browne Or. MS F. 63 (10).

Nuri, Khanum-i Buzurg " 'Ammih." "Tanbih an-Na'imin." CUL. Browne Or. MS F. 60 (8).

Nuri, Mirza Aslam. "Qasidih-'i Alfiyyih." CUL. Browne Or. MS F. 27 (9), 2. Explains Babi terminology.

"Qahir," Rajab 'Ali. "Kitab." CUL. Browne Or. MS F. 24 (9).

Rashti, Sayyid Kazim. "Al-Lawami' al-Hikmiyyah." Cairo. Dar al-Kutub. Arabic MS Hikmah wa Falsafah 626.

— "Risalah fi Ajwibat as-Sa'il al-Khafidah." Cairo. Dar al-Kutub. Arabic MS 'Aqa'id an-Nihal al-Islamiyyah. Tawhid Shi'ah 80.

— "Risalat." School of Oriental and African Studies, London. Arabic Manuscript Collection. MS 277. Between 1233 and 1259.

Rida, A[qa] Sayyid Muhammad. "Sharh-i Vaqa'i'-i Qal'ih" [Tabarsi]. Photocopy of MS from Afnan Library, London.

Shirazi, Lutf 'Ali Mirza. Untitled MS. CUL. Browne Or. MS F. 28 (3). Account of the uprising of Mazandaran.

Usku'i, Mirza Haydar 'Ali. "Tarikh-i Amri-yi Adhirbayjan." Photocopy of MS from Afnan Library, London.

Zavarih-'i, Sayyid Muhammad Husayn. "Majlis-i Shahadat-i Qa'im-i Khurasani." CUL. Browne Or. MS F. 28 (2). Account of the martyrdom of Mulla Husayn.

— "Vaqa'i'-i Mimiyyih." CUL. Browne Or. MS F. 28 (1).

Printed Archival Materials

Adamiyyat, Faridun, and Huma Natiq. *Afkar-i ijtima'i va siyasi va iqtisadi dar asar-i muntashir nashudih-'i dawrih-'i Qajar.* Tehran: Agah, 1356 s/1977–78.

Afshar, Iraj, and Asghar Mahdavi, eds. *Majmu'ih-'i asnad va madarik-i chap nashudih dar barih-'i Sayyid Jamalu'd-Din Mashhur bi Afghani.* Tehran: Tehran University Press, 1963.

Ahsa'i, Shaykh Ahmad. "Al-Kashkul." 2 vols. MSS Alif-9 and Alif-10, Kerman Shaykhi Library. Wiesbaden: Harassowitz, 1983. On microfilm at Harlan Hatcher Library, University of Michigan.

— "Rasa'il al-Marhum Shaykh Ahmad al-Ahsa'i." V. 1:3. Kerman Shaykhi Library. Wiesbaden: Harassowitz, 1983.

— "Risalat Mukhtasar al-Haydariyyah." V. 1:2. Kerman Shaykhi Library. Wiesbaden: Harrasowitz, 1983.

Anon. "Nivishtijat va Athar-i Ashab-i Avvaliyyih-i Amr-i A'la." Iran National Baha'i Archives Private Printing 80 (b).

Baha'u'llah. "Su'al va Javab." Iran National Baha'i Archives Private Printing No. 63.

Banna, Ustad 'Ali Akbar. "Tarikh-i 'Ishqabad." INBA PP 94.

Isfahani, Mirza Haydar 'Ali. "Tarjumih-'i Ahval-i Mirza Abu'l-Fada'il." Iran National Baha'i Archives Private Printing No. 20. Tehran: National Spiritual Assembly of the Baha'is of Iran, 1976.

Kilas-i Mutali'ih va Sukhanvari. "Fihrist-i Kutub-i Amri." INBA PP 70.

Rashti, Sayyid Kazim. "Dalil al-Mutahayyirin." Arabic MS dated 1258, Kirman Shaykhi Library. Wiesbaden: Harrasowitz, 1983. On microfilm at Harlan Hatcher Library, University of Michigan.

— "Sitt Rasa'il." MS in 2 vols. Kirman Shaykhi Library. Wiesbaden: Harrasowitz, 1983. Ba'-3, ba'-4.

Yazdi, Aqa Muhammad 'Ilaqih-Band. "Tarikh-i Mashrutiyyat." INBA PP No. 2.

Published Works
'Abdu'l-Baha. *Alvah-i Vasaya.* Karachi: Sterling Garden Road, 1960.
— *Majmu'ih-'i Alvah-i Mubarakih bi-Iftikhar-i Baha'iyan-i Parsi.* Tehran: Mu'assasih-'i Milli-yi Matbu'at-i Amri, 133 B.E./1977.
— *Majmu'ih-'i Khitabat-i Hadrat-i 'Abdu'l-Baha fi Urubba wa Amrika.* 3 vols. in one. Hofheim-Langenhain: Baha'i-Verlag, 1984. Reprint of Egyptian editions of 1921 and 1943, and of Tehran edition of 1970.
— *Majmu'ih-'i Mubarakih.* Ed. 'Ali Akbar Milani. Tehran, 1326/1908. This volume contains many letters relating to the Constitutional Revolution, and one can trace therein 'Abdu'l-Baha's initial enthusiasm for and gradual disaffection with it.
— *Makatib-i 'Abdu'l-Baha.* Vols. 1–8. Cairo and Tehran, 1910–1977.
— *Maqalih-'i Shakhsi Sayyah.* Ed. and trans. E. G. Browne. 2 vols. Cambridge: Cambridge University Press, 1891.
— *Muntakhabati az Makatib-i Hadrat-i 'Abdu'l-Baha.* 2 vols. Wilmette and Haifa, 1979–1984.
— *An-Nur al-Abha fi Mufawadat 'Abdi'l-Baha.* New Delhi: Baha'i Publishing Trust, 1983.
— *Ar-Risalah al-Madaniyyah as-Sadirah fi sanat 1292.* Cairo: Matba'ah Kurdistan al-'Ilmiyyah, 1329/1911. Photocopy of the Egyptian 1911 edition. Repr. as *Risalih-i Madaniyyih.* Hofheim-Langenhain: Baha'i-Verlag, 1984.
— *Risalih-'i Siyasiyyih.* Tehran: Muhammad Labib, 1325/1907. Based on the 1893 Bombay edition. Digital repr., Lansing, Mi.: H-Bahai, 1997. Available on the World Wide Web at http://h-net2.msu.edu/~bahai/areprint/abtext.htm.
Adamiyyat, Faridun. *Amir Kabir va Iran.* Tehran: Kharazmi, 1969.
— *Andishihha-yi Mirza Aqa Khan Kirmani.* Tehran: Tahuri, 1970.
— *Andishihha-yi taraqqi va hukumat-i qanun-i 'asr-i Sipah Salar.* Tehran: Kharazmi, 1352 s./1973–74.
— *Fikr-i azadi va muqaddimih-'i nahzat-i mashrutiyyat-i Iran.* Tehran, n.p., 1340 s./1961–62.
— *Fikr-i dimukrasi-yi ijtima'i dar nahzat-i mashrutiyyat.* Tehran: Chap-i Zar, 1975.
— *Idi'uluzhi-yi nahzat-i mashrutiyyat-i Iran.* Tehran: Payam, 2535/1976.
— *Shurish bar imtiyaznamih-'i rizhi: Tahlil-i siyasi.* Tehran: Payam, 1981.
Afrukhtih, Yunis. *Khatirat-i Nuh Salih.* Los Angeles: Kalimat, 1983.
Ahsa'i, 'Abdu'llah. *Sharh-i Halat-i . . . Shaykh Ahmad b. Zaynu'd-Din al-Ahsa'i.* Persian trans. in Bombay: Haji Muhammad Hasan Sahib, 1310.
Ahsa'i, Shaykh Ahmad. *Hayat an-Nafs.* 2d printing. Persian trans. and intro. by Sayyid Kazim Rashti. Kirman: Sa'adat, n.d. [197?].
— *Jawami' al-Kalim.* 2 vols. Tabriz: Muhammad Taqi Nakhjavani, 1273–76.
— *Sharh al-Masha'ir.* Tabriz, 1278.
— *Sharh Kitab al-Hikmah al-'Arshiyyah.* Tabriz, 1278.
— *Sharh az-Ziyarah al-Jami'ah al-Kabirah.* 3d printing. Tehran: Matba'at al-Islam, 1390.
— *Sirat ash-Shaykh Ahmad al-Ahsa'i.* Ed. Husayn 'Ali Mahfuz. Baghdad: Matba'at al-Ma'arif, 1957.

Akhundzadih, Fath-'Ali. *Maktubat.* Ed. M. Subhdam. Germany: Intisharat-i Mard-i Imruz, 1985

Anon. *Kitab-i Nuqtat al-Kaf.* Ed. E. G. Browne. Leiden and London: E. J. Brill and Luzac, 1910.

Arbab, Furugh. *Akhtaran-i Taban.* Vol. 1. Tehran: Mu'assasih-'i Milli-yi Matbu'at-i Amri, 128 B.E./1972.

—— *Akhtaran-i Taban.* Vol. 2. New Delhi: Mir'at Publications, 1990.

Ardikani, Sadri Navabzadih. *Matalibi dar barih-'i tarikh-i Nabil-i Zarandi.* Mutali'ih-'i Ma'arif-i Baha'i no. 18. Tehran: Mu'assasih-'i Milli-yi Matbu'at-i Amri, 134 B.E./1978.

Arjumand, Mihdi. *Gulshan-i Haqayiq.* Los Angeles: Kalimat, 1982.

Avarih, 'Abdu'l-Husayn. *al-Kawakib ad-Durriyyih.* Vol. 1. Trans. from Persian into Arabic by Ahmad Fa'iq Rushd. Cairo: al-Matba'ah al-'Arabiyyah, 1924.

—— *al-Kawakib ad-Durriyyih.* Vol. 2. Persian. Cairo: Matba'at as-Sa'adah, 1914.

'Azizi, Rida. *Jinab-i Mustatab-i Haji Mirza Aqasi.* Tehran: Tabish, n.d.

Bab, Sayyid 'Ali Muhammad Shirazi. *Al-Bayan al-'Arabi.* In 'Abdu'r-Razzaq al-Hasani, *al-Babiyyun wa al-Baha'iyyun fi hadirihim wa madikim.* Sidon: Matba'at al-'Irfan, 1962.

—— *Bayan-i Farsi.* Tehran, n.d.

—— *Dala'il-i Sab'ih.* Tehran, n.d.

—— *Majmu'ih az Athar-i Nuqtih-'i Ula va Subh-i Azal.* Tehran: n.d.

—— *Muntakhabati az Athar-i Hadrat-i Nuqtih-'i Ula.* Wilmette, Ill.: Baha'i Publishing Trust, 1978.

—— *Sahifih-'i 'Adliyyih.* Tehran, n.d.

Baha'u'llah, Mirza Husayn 'Ali Nuri. *Abwab al-Malakut.* Beirut: Dar al-Badi', 1975.

—— *Alvah-i Nazilih Khitab bi-Muluk va Ru'asa-yi Ard.* Tehran: Mu'assasih-'i Milli-yi Matbu'at-i Amri, 126 B.E./1970.

—— *Alvah.* New Delhi: n.p. Facsimile of manuscript in hand of Zaynu'l-Muqarrabin dated A.H. 1311/1893–1894.

—— *Aqdas-i Buzurg va chand Lawh-i Digar.* Bombay: Matba'at an-Nasiri, 1314/1896–1897.

—— *Athar-i Qalam-i A'la.* 7 vols. Bombay, n.p., and Tehran: Mu'assasih-'i Milli-yi Matbu'at-i Amri, 1890–1978.

—— *Darya-yi Danish.* Tehran: Mu'assasih-'i Milli-yi Matbu'at-i Amri, 133 B.E./1977.

—— *Ishraqat va chand Lawh-i Digar.* Tehran, n.d.

—— *Iqtidarat va chand Lawh-i Digar.* Tehran, n.d. Facsimile of a Mishkin Qalam manuscript calligraphed in A.H. 1310/1892–1893.

—— *Al-Kitab al-Aqdas va alvah.* N.p., n.d.

—— *Kitab-e Aqdas.* Ed. Alexander Tumanskii. *Zapiskie Imperatorskoy Academii Nauk S. Petersburg.* Ser. 8. 3, 6 (1899).

—— *Kitab-i Badi' dar As'ilih-'i Qadi.* Tehran, 1940.

—— *Kitab-i Iqan.* Hofheim-Langenhain: Baha'i-Verlag, 1980. Facsimile of 1934 Egyptian edition.

—— *La'ali al-Hikmah.* Ed. Vahid Behmardi. 3 vols. Rio de Janeiro: Editora Baha'i-Brasil, 1986–1991.

— *Lawh-i Mubarak Khitab bih Shaykh Muhammad Taqi Mujtahid-i Isfahani Ma'ruf bih Najafi.* Hofheim-Langenhain: Baha'i-Verlag, 1982.

— *Al-Majmu' al-awwal min Rasa'il ash-Shaykh al-Babi Baha'u'llah.* Ed. Baron Victor Rosen. St. Petersburg: Matba'at Dar al-'Ulum, 1908.

— *Majmu'ih-'i Alvah-i Mubarakih.* Tehran: Mu'assasih-'i Milli-yi Matbu'at-i Amri, 132 B.E./1976. Photo offset of a manuscript in the hand of 'Ali Ashraf Lahijani " 'Andalib," A.H. 1304/1886–1887.

— *Majmu'ih-'i az Alvah-i Jamal-i Aqdas-i Abha kih ba'd az Kitab-i Aqdas Nazil Shudih.* Hofheim-Langenhain: Baha'i-Verlag, 1980.

— *Majmu'ih-'i Matbu'ih-'i Alvah-i Mubarakih.* Wilmette, Ill.: Baha'i Publishing Trust, 1978. Facsimile of the 1920 Egyptian edn.

— *Munajat.* Rio de Janeiro: Editora Baha'i-Brasil, 1981. The Arabic originals of *Prayers and Mediations.*

— *Muntakhabati az Athar-i Hadrat-i Baha'u'llah.* Hofheim-Langenhain: Baha'i-Verlag, 1984.

— *Nafahat al-Uns.* Rio de Janeiro: Editora Baha'i-Brasil, 1982. Facsimile of a small manuscript in the hand of Zaynu'l-Muqarrabin, calligraphed in 'Akka in 1304.

— *Surat al-Muluk.* Karachi: Mashhur Offset, n.d.

Baha'u'llah et al. *Ad'iyyih-'i Hadrat-i Mahbub.* Hofheim-Langenhain: Baha'i-Verlag, 1980. Facsimile of the Egyptian A.H. 1339/1920–1921 edition.

——— *Bisharat an-Nur.* 3 vols. in one. Hofheim-Langenhain: Baha'i-Verlag, 1983. Originally published in Tehran, 121, 130, 134 B.E./1965, 1974, 1978.

Bamdad, Mihdi. *Sharh-i Hal-i Rijal-Iran: dar qarn-i 12 va 13 va 14 Hijri.* 6 vols. Tehran: Kitabfurushi-yi Zuvvar, 1968–1975.

Bayda'i, Ni'matu'llah Dhuka'i. *Tadhkirih-'i Shu'ara-yi Qarn-i Avval-i Baha'i.* 4 vols. Tehran: Mu'assasih-'i Milli-yi Matbu'at-i Amri, 121–129 B.E./1965–1973.

Bereketzade Ismail Hakki Effendi. *Yad-i Mazi.* Istanbul: Tevsi-i Tibaat, 1332/1913–1914.

Dara Shikuh. *Muntakhab-i Athar.* Ed. S. M. Riza Jalali Na'ini. Tehran: Taban, 1958.

Dara Shikuh, trans. *Sirr-i Akbar (Upanishad).* Ed. Tara Chand and S. M. Riza Jalali Na'ini. Tehran: Kitabkhanih-'i Tahuri, 1978.

Davudi, 'Ali Murad. *Falsafih va 'Irfan.* Ed. Vahid Rafati. 3 vols. Los Angeles: Kalimat; Dundas, Ontario: Persian Institute for Baha'i Studies, 1987–1994.

Ebüzziya Tevfik. *Yeni Osmanlılar Tarihi.* Ed. Ziyad Ebüzziya. 3 vols. Istanbul: Kitab Yayınları, 1974.

Ebüzziya Tevfik, ed. *Nümûne-yi edebiyat-i Osmaniye.* Istanbul: Matbaa-yi Ebüzziya, A.H. 1308/1891.

Farid, Badi'u'llah. *Maqalih-'i dar mu'arrafi-yi Kitab-i Mustatab-i Aqdas.* 2d ed. Wilmette, Ill.: Persian-American Affairs Office, National Spiritual Assembly of Baha'is of the United States, 150 B.E./1994.

Faydi, Muhammad 'Ali. *Hadrat-i Baha'u'llah.* Hofheim-Langenhain: Baha'i-Verlag, 1994.

— *Hadrat-i Nuqtih-'i Ula.* Hofheim-Langenhain: Baha'i-Verlag, 1987.

— *Hayat-i Hadrat-i 'Abdu'l-Baha.* Tehran: Mu'assasih-'i Milli-yi Matbu'at-i Amri, 128 B.E./1971.

— *Khandan-i Afnan.* Tehran: Mu'assasih-'i Milli-yi Matbu'at-i Amri, 127 B.E./1972.

— *Khitabat-i Qalam-i A'la dar Sha'n-i Nuzul-i Alvah-i Muluk va Salatin.* N.p, 1336 s.

— *La'ali-yi Dirakhshan.* Shiraz: n.p, 1967.

— *Nayriz-i Mushkbiz.* Tehran: Mu'assasih-'i Milli-yi Matbu'at-i Amri, 129/1973.

Furutan, 'Ali Akbar, ed. *Dastanha'i az hayat-i 'unsuri-yi Jamal-i Aqdas-i Abha.* Tehran: Mu'assasih-'i Milli-yi Matbu'at-i Amri, 134 B.E./1978.

Gulpaygani, Mirza Abu'l-Fadl. *Burhan-i Lami'ih.* With English translation. Chicago: Press of Bahai News Service, 1912.

— *Ad-Durar al-Bahiyyah.* Cairo, 1900.

— *Kitab al-Fara'id.* Cairo, 1898.

— *Mukhtarat min Mu'allafat Abi al-Fada'il.* Brussels: Maison d'Editions Baha'ies, 1980.

— *Rasa'il va Raqa'im.* Ed. Ruhu'llah Mihrabkhani. Tehran: Mu'assasih-'i Milli-yi Matbu'at-i Amri, 134 B.E./1978.

— *Risalih-'i Sharh-i Ayat-i Muvarrakhih.* n.p., n.d.

— *Sharh-i Shajarih-namih-'i Mubarakih.* Bombay: Matba'-i Mustafa'i, A.H. 1321/1903.

Gulpaygani, Mirza Abu'l-Fadl, and Sayyid Mihdi Gulpaygani. *Kashf al-Ghita.* Tashkent, 1919.

Hanioğlu, M. Şükrü. *Bir Siyasal Düşünür olarak Doktor Abdullah Cevdet ve Dönemi.* Istanbul: Ucdal Neşriyat, 1981.

Hasani, 'Abdu'r-Razzaq, al-. *Al-Babiyyun wa al-Baha'iyyun fi hadirihim wa madihim.* Sidon: Matba'at al-'Irfan, 1962.

Hilmi, Mustafa. *Ibnu'l-Farid wa'l-hubb al-ilahi.* Cairo: Dar al-Ma'arif, 1971.

Ibrahimi, Abu'l-Qasim. *Fihrist-i Kutub-i Shaykh-i Ajal-i Awhad-i Marhum Shaykh Ahmad al-Ahsa'i.* 2 vols. Kirman: Sa'adat, n.d.

'Isa, Tal'at. *San Simun.* Cairo: Dar al-Ma'arif, 1959.

Isfahani, Mirza Haydar 'Ali. *Bihjat as-Sudur.* Bombay: Deccan Printing, 1914.

Isfandiyar, Kay-Khusrau. *Dabistan-i Madhahib.* Ed. Rahim Ridazadih Malik. 2 vols. Tehran: Kitabkhanih-'i Tahuri, 1983.

Ishaq, Adib. *Ad-Durar.* Ed. Jirjis Mikha'il. Alexandria, 1886.

Ishraq-Khavari, 'Abdu'l-Hamid. *Ganj-i Shayigan.* Tehran: Mu'assasih-'i Milli-yi Matbu'at-i Amri, 124 B.E./1968.

— *Muhadarat.* 2 vols. in one. Hofheim-Langenhain: Baha'i-Verlag, 1987.

— *Nurayn-i Nayyirayn.* Tehran: Mu'assasih-'i Milli-yi Matbu'at-i Amri, 123 B.E./1967.

— *Qamus-i Iqan.* 4 vols. Tehran: Mu'assasih-'i Milli-yi Matbu'at-i Amri, 128 B.E./1972.

— *Taqvim-i Tarikh-i Amr.* Tehran: Mu'assasih-'i Milli-yi Matbu'at-i Amri, 126 B.E./1970.

Ishraq-Khavari, 'Abdu'l-Hamid, ed. *Ayyam-i Tis'ih.* 5th ed. Tehran: Mu'assasih-'i Milli-yi Matbu'at-i Amri, 129/1973.

— *Ganjinih-'i Hudud va Ahkam.* New Delhi: Baha'i Publishing Trust, 1980. Facsimile of Tehran 128 B.E./1972 edition.

— *Ma'idih-'i Asmani.* 9 vols. Tehran: Mu'assasih-'i Milli-yi Matbu'at-i Amri, 129/ 1973; 9 vols. in three parts. New Delhi: Indian Publishing Trust, 1984–85. Only parts 2, 3 have appeared.

— *Payam-i Malakut.* Tehran: Mu'assasih-'i Milli-yi Matbu'at-i Amri, 130 B.E./1974.

— *Rahiq-i Makhtum.* 2 vols. Tehran: Mu'assasih-'i Milli-yi Matbu'at-i Amri, 103 B.E./1947.

— *Risalih-'i Tasbih va Tahlil.* New Delhi: Baha'i Publishing Trust, 1982.

I'timadu's-Saltanih, Muhammad Hasan Khan. *Khalsih, Mashhur bih Khvabnamih.* Ed. Mahmud Katira'i. Tehran: Tahuri, 1970.

— *Ruznamih-'i Khatirat.* Ed. I. Afshar. Tehran: 1350 s./1971.

Javadi, Hasan, Manizhih Mar'ashi, and Simi Shikarlu, eds. *Ruyaru'i-yi Zan va Mard dar 'Asr-i Qajar: Du Risalih-'i "Ta'dib an-Niswan" va "Ma'ayib ar-Rijal."* Washington, D.C.: Jahan Book, 1992.

Kayka'us b. Iskandar b. Qabus, *Qabusnamih.* Ed. Ghulam-Husayn Yusufi. Tehran: Nigah-i Tarjumih va Nashr-i Kitab, 1967.

Kemal, Namik. *Hususi Mektuplar.* Ed. Fevziye Abdullah Tansel. 4 vols. Ankara: Turk Tarih Kurumu Basimevi, 1967–1986.

Kirmani, Mirza Aqa Khan. *Namih-ha-yi Tab'id.* Ed. Huma Natiq and Muhammad Firuz. Cologne: Chap-i Ufuq, 1986.

Kirmani, Muhammad Khan. *Risalih dar Ikhtira'-i Khatt-i Jadid.* Kirman: Chapkhanih-'i Sa'adat, n.d. Originally written in A.H. 1296/1878.

Kitab al-Muqaddas. London: Richard Watts, 1831.

Küdret, Cevdet. *Abdülhamid devrinde Sansür.* Istanbul: Milliyet Yayınları, 1977.

Majdu'l-Mulk, Muhammad Khan. *Risalih-'i Majdiyyih [Bist Sal Ba'd az Amir-i Kabir].* Ed. 'Ali Amini and Fadlu'llah Gurgani. Tehran, n.p, 1985.

Malamiri, Muhammad Tahir. *Khatirat-i Malamiri.* Hofheim-Langenhain: Baha'i-Verlag, 1992.

— *Tarikh-i Shuhada-yi Yazd.* Karachi: MMMP, 135 B.E./1979 facsimile of the A.H. 1347/1928–1929 edition.

Malik-Khusravi, Muhammad 'Ali. *Iqlim-i Nur.* Tehran: Mu'assasih-'i Milli-yi Matbu'at-i Amri, 118 B.E./1962.

— *Tarikh-i Shuhada-yi Amr.* 3 vols. Tehran: Mu'assasih-'i Milli-yi Matbu'at-i Amri, 130 B.E./1974.

Mazandarani, Asadu'llah Fadil. *Asrar al-Athar.* 5 vols. Tehran: Mu'assasih-'i Milli-yi Matbu'at-i Amri, 124 B.E./1968.

— *Tarikh-i Zuhur al-Haqq.* Vol. 3. Tehran, 1941 or 1942. Biographical material on Babi movement.

— *Tarikh-i Zuhur al-Haqq.* Volume 8 in 2 parts. Tehran: Mu'assasih-'i Milli-yi Matbu'at-i Amri, 131–32 B.E./1975–76.

Mazandarani, Asadu'llah Fadil, ed. *Amr va Khalq.* 4 vols. in two. Hofheim-Langenhain: Baha'i-Verlag, 1985. Repr. of Tehran edition of 1954–74.

Mihrabkhani, Ruhu'llah. "Mahafil-i shawr dar 'ahd-i Jamal-i Aqdas-i Abha." *Payam-i Baha'i,* February 28, 1982, pp. 9–11; March 29, 1982, pp. 8–9.

— *Sharh-i Ahval-i Jinab-i Mirza Abu'l-Fada'il-i Gulpaygani.* Tehran: Mu'assasih-'i Milli-yi Matbu'at-i Amri, 131 b.e./1975.

— *Zindigani-yi Mirza Abu'l-Fadl Gulpaygani*. Hofheim-Langenhain: Baha'i-Verlag, 1988. A completely revised version of the previous biography.

Mu'ayyad, Habib. *Khatirat-i Habib*. Vols. 1–2. Tehran: Mu'assasih-'i Milli-yi Matbu'at-i Amri, 118–129 b.e./1962–1973.

Mudarris-Chahardihi, Murtada. *Shaykh Ahmad al-Ahsa'i*. Tehran: 'Ali Akbar 'Ilmi, 1324 s./1945.

— *Shaykhigari, Babigari*. Tehran: Furughi, 1966.

Mudir-Masiha'i, Ruh'u'llah, ed. *Mahbub-i 'Alam*. Toronto: National Spiritual Assembly of the Baha'is of Canada/*'Andalib*, 1993.

Mustasharu'd-Dawlih, Yusuf Khan Mirza. *Yik Kalimih*. Ed. Sadiq Sajjadi. Tehran: Nashr-i Tarikh-i Iran, 1985.

Na'im, Muhammad. *Ahsan at-Taqwim ya Gulzar-i Na'im*. New Delhi: Baha'i Publishing Trust, n.d.

Najmabadi, Afsaneh, ed. *Ma'ayib ar-Rijal: dar pasukh bih Ta'dib an-Nisvan*. Chicago: Midland, 1992.

Nazif, Suleyman. *Nasiru'd-Din Şah ve Babilar*. Istanbul, 1923.

Nuqaba'i, Husam. *Tahirih*. N.p. 1983.

Nur, 'Izzatu'llah. *Khatirat-i Muhajiri az Isfahan dar Zaman-i Shahadat-i Sultan ash-Shuhada' va Mahbub ash-Shuhada'*. Tehran: Mu'assasih-'i Milli-yi Matbu'at-i Amri, 128 b.e./1972.

Qa'ini, Aqa Muhammad Nabil-i Akbar. *Qasidih-'i Ta'iyyih*. Tehran: Mu'assasih-'i Milli-yi Matbu'at-i Amri, n.d. Composed c. 1857. Evidence for early partisanship for Baha'u'llah.

Qazvini, Muhammad Shafi'. *Qanun-i Qazvini*. Ed. Iraj Afshar. Tehran: Talayih, 1991.

Rabbani, Shawqi Afandi [Shoghi Effendi]. *Lawh-i Qarn-i Ahibba-'i Sharq*. Tehran: Mu'assasih-'i Milli-yi Matbu'at-i Amri, 123 b.e./1967.

— *Tawqi'at-i Mubarakih-'i Hadrat-i Vali-yi Amru'llah Khitab bih Ahibba-yi Sharq*. Hofheim-Langenhain: Baha'i-Verlag, 1992. Includes letters dated 88, 89, 101, 105, 108, 110, 111, 112 b.e./1932, 1933, 1945, 1949, 1952, 1954, 1955, 1956.

Rashti, Sayyid Kazim. *Dalil al-Mutahayyirin*. Kirman: Sa'adat, n.d.

— *Majma'-i Rasa'il-i Farsi*. Kirman: Sa'adat, n.d.

Ridvani, Isma'il. "Qadimtarin zikr-i dimukrasi dar nivishtih-ha-yi farsi." *Rahnama-yi kitab* 5 (1341/1962–63):257–63, 367–70.

Rosen, Victor, ed. "Manuscrits Persans." *Collections Scientifiques de l'institut des Langues Orientales du Ministère des Affaires Etrangères 3 (1886): 1–51*.

— *"Manuscrits Babys."* Collections Scientifiques 6 (1891): 143–255.

Ruhani-Nayrizi, Muhammad Shafi'. *Lama'at al-Anvar: Sharh-i Vaqa'i'-i Nayriz-i Shu-rangiz*. 2 vols. Tehran: Mu'assasih-'i Milli-yi Matbu'at-i Amri, 130 b.e./1974.

Sa'adat-Nuri, Husayn. *Haji Mirza Aqasi*. Tehran: Vahid, 1978.

Safa'i, Ibrahim. *Rahbaran-i mashrutih*. 2 vols. Tehran: Javidan-i 'Ilmi, 1984 [1966].

Sa'idi, Nadir. *Risalih-'i Madaniyyih: Mas'alih-'i Tajaddud dar Khavar-Miyanih*. Dundas, Ont.: Institute for Baha'i Studies in Persian, 1993.

Sa'idi Sirjani, 'Ali Akbar. *Vaqa'i'-i Ittifaqiyyih*. Tehran: Nashr-i Naw, 1982.

Salmani, Muhammad 'Ali. *Sharh-i Hal-i Ustad Muhammad 'Ali Salmani*. Lansing,

Mi.: H-Bahai, 1997. Available on the World Wide Web at http://h-net2.msu.edu/ ~bahai/bharab. htm Ustad.

Samandar, Kazim. *Tarikh-i Samandar va Mulhaqat.* Tehran: Mu'assasih-'i Milli-yi Matbu'at-i Amri, 131 B.E./1975.

Seyitdanliolu, Mehmet. *Tanzimat Devrinde Meclis-i Vala (1838–1868).* Ankara: Türk Tarih Kurumu Basimevi, 1994.

Sharif, Ridavi. *Tadhkirat al-Awliya' fi Sharh Ahwal . . . Muhammad Karim Khan Kirmani.* Bombay, A.H. 1313/1895–1896.

Shaykhu'r-Ra'is, Abu'l-Hasan Mirza. *Guzidih-'i az Surudih-ha-yi Shaykhu'r-Ra'is Qajar.* Ed. Mir Jalalu'd-Din Kazzari. Tehran: Nashr-i Markaz, 1990.

—— *Ittihad-i Islam.* Ed. Sadiq Sajjadi. Tehran: Nashr-i Tarikh-i Iran, 1984. Based on Bombay 1894 edition.

—— *Muntakhab-i Nafis.* Tehran, 1960. Based on Bombay 1896 edition.

—— *Badayi' as-Samar va Vaqayi' as-Safar.* Tehran: Intisharat-i Vahid, 1352 s./1973–1974.

Shidyaq, Ahmad Faris. *Kanz ar-ragha'ib fi muntakhabat al-Jawa'ib.* 7 vols. Istanbul, Matba'at al-Jawa'ib, 1871–1880.

Sipihr, Muhammad Taqi Lisan al-Mulk. *Nasikh at-Tavarikh.* Ed. Jahangir Qa'im-Maqam. 3 vols. in one. Tehran: Amir Kabir, 1958.

Sulaymani, 'Azizu'llah. *Masabih-i Hidayat.* Vols. 1–9. Tehran: Mu'assasih-'i Milli-yi Matbu'at-i Amri, 104–132 B.E./1970–1977.

—— *Rashahat-i Hikmat.* 3 vols. Tehran: Mu'assasih-'i Milli-yi Matbu'at-i Amri, 126–133 B.E./1970–1977.

Sulh, 'Imad. *Ahmad Faris ash-Shidyaq: atharuhu wa asruh.* 2d rev. ed. Beirut: Sharikat al-Matbu'at li at-Tawzi' wa an-Nashr, 1978.

Tahtawi, Rifa'ah at-. *al-A'mal al-Kamilah.* Ed. Muhammad al-'Imarah. 5 vols. Beirut: Arab Foundation for Study and Publication, 1973–81.

Tavakoli-Targhi, Mohamad. "Athar-i Agahi az Inqilab-i Firansih dar Shakl-Giri-yi Angarih-'i Mashrutiyyat dar Iran." *Iran-Namih* 8, 3 (Summer 1990): 411–39.

Toska, Zehra, et al. *Istanbul Kütüphanelerindeki eski harfli türkçe kadın dergileri bibliyografyasi.* Istanbul: Metis Yayınları, 1992.

Türk Ansiklopedisi. 33 vols. Ankara: Milli Egitim Basimevi, 1946–84.

Yarshater, Ehsan, ed. *Fihrist-i Kitabha-yi Chapi-yi Farsi.* 2 vols. Tehran: Bangah-i Tarjumih va Nashr-i Kitab, 1973.

Yazdani, Ahmad. *Maqam va Huquq-i Zan dar Diyanat-i Baha'i.* Tehran: Lajnih-'i Milli-i Nashr-i Athar-i Amri, 107 B.E./1951.

Zarandi, Muhammad 'Ali "Nabil." *Mathnavi dar Tarikh-i Amr-i Baha'i.* Cairo: al-Matba'ah al-'Izziyyah, 1924.

Zarqani, Mirza Mahmud. *Kitab-i Bada'i' al-Athar.* 2 vols. Hofheim-Langenhain: Baha'i- Verlag, 1982. Repr. of Bombay edition of 1914–21.

Translations and Works in European Languages

'Abdu'l-Baha. *'Abdu'l-Baha in London.* London: Baha'i Publishing Trust, 1982 [1912].

—— *Paris Talks.* London: Baha'i Publishing Trust, 1969.

— *Promulgation of Universal Peace.* Wilmette, Ill.: Baha'i Publishing Trust, 1982.

— *The Secret of Divine Civilization.* Trans. Marzieh Gail. 2d ed. Wilmette, Ill.: Baha'i Publishing Trust, 1970.

— *Some Answered Questions.* Trans. Laura Clifford Barney. Rev. ed. Wilmette, Ill.: Baha'i Publishing Trust, 1981.

— *Tablets of 'Abdu'l-Baha 'Abbas.* 3 vols. Chicago: Baha'i Publishing Society, 1909–16.

— *A Traveller's Narrative.* Trans. E. G. Browne. 2 vols. Cambridge: Cambridge University Press, 1891.

Abrahamian, Ervand. *Iran Between Two Revolutions.* Princeton: Princeton University Press, 1982.

Adlé, C., and B. Hourcade, eds. *Tehéran: Capitale Bicentenaire.* Paris and Tehran: Institut Francais de Recherche en Iran, 1992.

Afary, Janet. *The Iranian Constitutional Revolution, 1906–1911: Grassroots Democracy, Social Democracy, and the Origins of Feminism.* New York: Columbia University Press, 1996.

— "On the Origins of Feminism in Early Twentieth-Century Iran." *Journal of Women's History* 1, 2 (Fall 1989): 65–87.

Akiner, Shirin, ed. *Cultural Change and Continuity in Central Asia.* London: Kegan Paul International, 1991.

Alavi, Bozorg. "Critical Writings on the Renewal of Iran." In Edumund Bosworth and Carole Hillenbrand, eds. *Qajar Iran.* Edinburgh: Edinburgh University Press, 1983.

Alcoff, Linda. "Cultural Feminism Versus Post-Structuralism: The Identity Crisis in Feminist Theory." *Signs: Journal of Wormen in Culture and Society* 13, 3 (1988): 405–36.

Algar, Hamid. *Mirza Malkum Khan.* Berkeley and Los Angeles: University of California Press, 1973.

— *Religion and State in Iran, 1785–1906: The Role of the Ulama in the Qajar Period.* Berkeley and Los Angeles: University of California Press, 1969.

— "Shi'ism and Iran in the Eighteenth Century." In Thomas Naff and Roger Owen, eds., *Studies in Eighteenth Century Islamic History,* pp. 288–302. Carbondale: Southern Illinois University Press, 1977.

Amanat, Abbas. *Resurrection and Renewal: The Making of the Babi Movement in Iran, 1844–1850.* Ithaca: Cornell University Press, 1989.

Anderson, Benedict. *Imagined Communities.* 2d rev. ed. London: Verso, 1991.

Arberry, A. J., ed. and trans. *The Mystical Poems of Ibn al-Farid.* London: E. Walker, 1952.

—, ed. and trans. *The Poem of the Way.* London: E. Walker, 1952.

Arjomand, Said Amir. *The Shadow of God and the Hidden Imam.* Chicago: University of Chicago Press, 1984.

Arjomand, Said Amir, ed. *Authority and Political Culture in Shi'ism.* Albany: State University of New York Press, 1988.

Armstrong-Ingram, R. Jackson. *Studies in Babi and Baha'i History: Music, Devotions, and Mashriqu'l-Adhkar.* Vol. 4. Los Angeles: Kalimat, 1987.

Asad, Talal al-. *Genealogies of Religion.* Baltimore: Johns Hopkins University Press, 1993.

Association for Baha'i Studies, ed. *The Vision of Shoghi Effendi.* Ottawa: Baha'i Studies, 1993.

Atael, Farhad. "The Iranian Graduates of the European Universities and the Constitutional Revolution of 1906." Paper presented at the twenty-third annual Middle East Studies Association of North America conference, Toronto, November 15–18, 1989.

Avery, Peter, Gavin Hambly, and Charles Melville, eds. *Cambridge History of Iran.* Vol. 7. Cambridge: Cambridge University Press, 1991.

Ayalon, Ami. *Language and Change in the Arab Middle East: The Evolution of Modern Political Discourse.* Oxford: Oxford University Press, 1987.

Azmeh, Aziz al-. *Islams and Modernities.* London: Verso, 1993.

Bab, Sayyid 'Ali Muhammad Shirazi. *Selections from the Writings of the Bab.* Trans. Habib Taherzadeh. Haifa: Baha'i World Centre, 1976.

Baer, Gabriel. *Studies in the Social History of Modern Egypt.* Chicago: University of Chicago Press, 1969.

Baha'u'llah, Mirza Husayn 'Ali Nuri. Epistle to the Son of the Wolf. Trans. Shoghi Effendi. Wilmette, Ill.: Baha'i Publishing Trust, 1971.

— *Gleanings from the Writings of Baha'u'llah.* Trans. Shoghi Effendi Rabbani. Wilmette, Ill.: Baha'i Publishing Trust, 1976 [1939].

— *The Hidden Words of Baha'u'llah.* Trans. Shoghi Effendi Rabbani. Wilmette, Ill.: Baha'i Publishing Trust, 1979.

— *The Kitab-i-Aqdas: The Most Holy Book.* Haifa: Baha'i World Centre, 1992.

— *The Kitab-i-Iqan: The Book of Certitude.* Trans. Shoghi Effendi Rabbani. 3d ed. Wilmette, Ill.: Baha'i Publishing Trust, 1970.

— *Prayers and Meditations.* Trans. Shoghi Effendi Rabbani. Wilmette, Ill.: Baha'i Publishing Trust, 1971 [1938].

— *Proclamation of Baha'u'llah.* Haifa: Baha'i World Centre, 1967.

— *The Seven Valleys and the Four Valleys.* Trans. Ali Kuli Khan and Marzieh Gail. Wilmette, Ill.: Baha'i Publishing Trust, 1971.

— *A Synopsis and Codification of the Kitab-i-Aqdas, the Most Holy Book of Baha'u'llah.* Haifa: Baha'i World Centre, 1973.

— *Tablets of Baha'u'llah Revealed After the Kitab-i Aqdas.* Trans. Habib Taherzadeh et al. Wilmette, Ill.: Baha'i Publishing Trust, 1988.

— "Tablet to Manackji Sahib." *Star of the West* 1, 1 (March 21, 1910): 5–9

Bakhash, Shaul. *Iran: Monarchy, Bureaucracy, and Reform Under the Qajars, 1858–1896.* London: Ithaca, 1978.

Balyuzi, Hasan M. *The Bab: The Herald of the Day of Days.* Oxford: George Ronald, 1973.

— *Baha'u'llah, the King of Glory.* Oxford: George Ronald, 1980.

— *Eminent Baha'is in the Time of Baha'u'llah.* Oxford: George Ronald, 1985.

— *Khadijih Begum: The Wife of the Bab.* Oxford: George Ronald, 1981.

Baron, Beth. *The Women's Awakening in Egypt.* New Haven: Yale University Press, 1994.

Bausani, Alessandro. *Persia Religiosa.* Milan: Saggiatore, 1958.

— "Religion Under the Mongols." *The Cambridge History of Iran.* Vol. 5: *The Saljuq and Mongol Periods.* Cambridge: University Press, 1968.

Bayat, Mangol. *Iran's First Revolution: Shi'ism and the Constitutional Revolution of 1905–1909.* Oxford: Oxford University Press, 1991.
— "Mirza Aqa Khan Kirmani: A Nineteenth-Century Persian Nationalist. In Elie Kedourie and Sylvia Haim, eds., *Toward a Modern Iran*, pp. 64–95. London: Frank Cass, 1980.
— *Mysticism and Dissent: Socioreligious Thought in Qajar Iran.* Syracuse: Syracuse University Press, 1982.
Beck, Lois, and Nikki Keddie. *Women in the Muslim World.* Cambridge: Harvard University Press, 1976.
Berger, Peter. *Facing Up to Modernity: Excursions in Society, Politics, and Religion.* New York: Basic, 1977.
— *The Heretical Imperative: Contemporary Possibilities of Religious Affirmation.* Garden City, N.Y.: Anchor, 1979.
Berkes, Niyazi. *The Development of Secularism in Turkey.* Montreal: McGill University Press, 1964.
Binder, Leonard. *Islamic Liberalism: A Critique of Development Theory.* Chicago: University of Chicago Press, 1988.
Bosworth, Edmund, and Carole Hillenbrand, eds. *Qajar Iran: Political, Social and Cultural Change.* Edinburgh: Edinburgh University Press, 1983.
Boullata, Issa I. "Verbal Arabesque and Mystical Union: A Study of Ibn al-Farid's al-Ta'iyya al-Kubra." *Arab Studies Quarterly* 3 (Spring 1981): 152–69.
Bramson-Lerche, Loni. "Some Aspects of the Development of the Baha'i Administrative Order in America, 1922–1936." In Moojan Momen, ed., *Studies in Babi and Baha'i History*, pp. 255–300. Los Angeles: Kalimat, 1982.
Brass, Paul R. *Language, Religion, and Politics in North India.* London: Cambridge University Press, 1974.
Brill, Susan B. *Wittgenstein and Critical Theory: Beyond Postmodernism and Toward Descriptive Investigations.* Athens: Ohio University Press, 1985.
Browne, E. G. *The Persian Revolution of 1905–1909.* Cambridge: Cambridge University Press, 1910.
— *Selections from the Writings of E. G. Browne on the Babi and Baha'i Religions.* Ed. Moojan Momen. Oxford: George Ronald, 1987.
— "Some Remarks on the Babi Texts Edited by Baron Victor Rosen." *Journal of the Royal Asiatic Society* 24 (1892): 283–318.
— "The Babis of Persia." *Journal of the Royal Asiatic Society* 21 (1889): 953–72.
Browne, E. G., ed. *Materials for the Study of the Babi Religion.* Cambridge: Cambridge University Press, 1918.
Browne, E. G., and R. A. Nicholson. *A Descriptive Catalogue of the Oriental MSS. Belonging to the Late E. G. Browne.* Cambridge: Cambridge University Press, 1932.
Buck, Christopher. "Baha'u'llah as 'World Reformer.'" *Journal of Baha'i Studies* 3, 2 (December 1990-March 1991): 23–70.
— *Studies in the Babi and Baha'i Religions: Symbol and Secret—Qur'an Commentary in Baha'u'llah's Kitab-i-Iqan.* Vol. 7. Los Angeles: Kalimat, 1995.
— "A Unique Eschatological Interface, Baha'u'llah and Cross-Cultural Messianism."

In Peter Smith, ed., *Studies in Babi and Baha'i History: In Iran,* 3:157–79. Los Angeles: Kalimat, 1986.

Bürgel, Johann Christoph. "The Baha'i Attitude Toward Peace." In Heshmet Moayyad, ed., *The Baha'i Faith and Islam.* Ottawa: Association for Baha'i Studies, 1990.

Butterfield, Herbert. *Historical Development of the Principle of Toleration in British Life.* London: Epworth, 1957.

Calder, Norman. "The Structures of Authority in Imami Shi'i Jurisprudence." Ph.D. thesis, School of Oriental and African Studies, University of London, 1980.

Calhoun, Craig, ed. *Habermas and the Public Sphere.* Cambridge: MIT Press, 1992.

Cannon, Byron. "Nineteenth-Century Arabic Writings on Women and Society: The Interim Role of the Masonic Press in Cairo—(al-Lata'if, 1885–1895)." *International Journal of Middle East Studies* 17 (1985): 463–84.

Capp, B. S. *The Fifth Monarchy Men: A Study in Seventeenth-Century English Millenarianism.* London: Faber, 1972.

Carlisle, Robert B. *The Proffered Crown: Saint-Simonianism and the Doctrine of Hope.* Baltimore: Johns Hopkins University, 1987.

Carson, Penelope. "Missionaries, Bureaucrats, and the People of India, 1793–1833." In Nancy G. Cassels, ed., *Orientalism, Evangelicalism, and the Military Cantonment in Early Nineteenth-Century India,* pp. 125–55. Queenston, Ont.: Edwin Mellen, 1991.

Cassels, Nancy G., ed. *Orientalism, Evangelicalism, and the Military Cantonment in Early Nineteenth-Century India.* Queenston, Ont.: Edwin Mellen, 1991.

"Chicago News Notes." *Star of the West* 3, 9 (August 20, 1912): 16.

Chittick, William. *Imaginal Worlds: Ibn al-'Arabi and the Problem of Religious Diversity.* Albany: State University of New York Press, 1994.

Choueri, Youssef M. *Islamic Fundamentalism.* London: Pinter, 1990.

Cole, Juan R. I. "Autobiography and Silence: The Early Career of Shaykhu'r-Ra'is Qajar." In Johann-Christoph Bürgel, ed., "Der Iran um 19 Jahrhundert und die Enstehung der Baha'i-Religion," forthcoming.

— "Baha'u'llah and the Naqshbandi Sufis in Iraq, 1854–1856." In Juan R. I. Cole and Moojan Momen, eds., *Studies in Babi and Baha'i History: From Iran East and West,* 2:1–28. Los Angeles: Kalimat, 1984.

— "Baha'u'llah's 'Surah of the Companions.'" *Baha'i Studies Bulletin* 5, 3/6, 1 (June 1991): 4–74.

— "Baha'ullah's 'Tablet of Fu'ad' (*Lawh-i Fu'ad*): Text, Translation, Commentary." *Translations of Shaykhi, Babi, and Baha'i Texts,* no. 5 (July 1997). Available on the World Wide Web at http://h-net2.msu.edu/~bahai/trans.htm.

— *Colonialism and Revolution in the Middle East: Social and Cultural Origins of Egypt's 'Urabi Movement.* Princeton: Princeton University Press, 1993.

— "The Concept of Manifestation in the Baha'i Writings." *Baha'i Studies* 9 (1982): 1–38.

— "Feminism, Class, and Islam in Turn-of-the-Century Egypt." *International Journal of Middle East Studies* 13 (1981): 387–407.

— " 'I Am All the Prophets': The Poetics of Pluralism in Baha'i Texts." *Poetics Today* 14, 3 (Fall 1993): 447–76.

— "Ideology, Ethics, and Philosophical Discourse in Eighteenth Century Iran." *Iranian Studies* 22, 1 (1989): 7–34.

— "Imami Jurisprudence and the Role of the Ulama." In Nikkie R. Keddie, ed., *Religion and Politics in Iran*, pp. 33–46. New Haven: Yale University Press, 1983.

— " 'Indian Money' and the Shi'i Shrine Cities of Iraq, 1786–1850." *Middle Eastern Studies* 22, 4 (1986): 461–80.

— "Invisible Occidentalism: Eighteenth-Century Indo-Persian Constructions of the West." *Iranian Studies* 25, 3–4 (1992): 3–16.

— "Iranian Millenarianism and Democratic Thought in the Nineteenth Century." *International Journal of Middle East Studies* 24 (1992): 1–26.

— "Marking Boundaries, Marking Time: The Iranian Past and the Construction of the Self by Qajar Thinkers." *Iranian Studies* 29, 1–2 (Winter/Spring 1996): 35–56.

— "Of Crowds and Empires: Afro-Asian Riots and European Expansion, 1857–1882." *Comparative Studies in Society and History* 31, 1 (1989): 106–33.

— "Redating the Surah of God (*Surat Allah*): An Edirne Tablet of 1866?" *Baha'i Studies Bulletin* 6, 4/7, 2 (October 1992): 3–16.

— "Religious Dissidence and Urban Leadership: The Baha'is in Qajar Shiraz and Tehran," forthcoming.

— "Rifa'a al-Tahtawi and the Revival of Practical Philosophy." *Muslim World* 70, 1 (1980): 29–46.

— "Rival Empires of Trade and Imami Shi'ism in Eastern Arabia 1300–1800." *International Journal of Middle East Studies* 19, 2 (1987): 177–204.

— *Roots of North Indian Shi'ism in Iran and Iraq: Religion and State in Awadh, 1722–1859.* Berkeley and Los Angeles: University of California Press, 1988.

— "Shi'i Clerics in Iraq and Iran, 1722–1780: The Akhbari-Usuli Controversy Reconsidered." *Iranian Studies* 18, 1 (1985): 3–34.

— "The World as Text: Cosmologies of Shaykh Ahmad al-Ahsa'i." *Studia Islamica* 80 (1994): 145–63.

Cole, Juan R. I., ed., *Comparing Muslim Societies.* Ann Arbor: University of Michigan Press, 1992.

Cole, Juan R. I., and Moojan Momen. "Mafia, Mob, and Shi'ism in Iraq: The Rebellion of Ottoman Karbala, 1824–1843." *Past and Present* 112 (August 1986): 112–43.

Cole, Juan R. I., and Moojan Momen, eds. *Studies in Babi and Baha'i History: From Iran East and West.* Vol. 2. Los Angeles: Kalimat, 1984.

Cole, Juan R. I., and Nikki Keddie, eds. *Shi'ism and Social Protest.* New Haven: Yale University Press, 1986.

Collins, William P. *Bibliography of English-Language Works on the Babi and Baha'i Faiths.* Oxford: George Ronald, 1990.

Corbin, Henry. *Creative Imagination in the Sufism of Ibn 'Arabi.* Princeton: Princeton University Press, 1969.

— *En islam iranien.* 4 vols. Paris: Gallimard, 1971–72.

Cott, Nancy F. *The Grounding of Modern Feminism.* New Haven: Yale University Press, 1987.

Crucé, Eméric. *The New Cyneas.* Philadelphia: Allen, Lane and Scott, 1909.

Curtin, Philip. *The Image of Africa: British Ideas and Action, 1780–1850*. Madison: University of Wisconsin Press, 1964.

Curtis, Michael, ed. *The Great Political Theories*. 2 vols. New York, 1981.

Danziger, Raphael. *Abd al-Qadir and the Algerians*. New York: Holmes and Meier, 1977.

Davison, Roderic. "'Ali Pasha, Muhammad Amin." *Encyclopaedia of Islam*. 2d ed. Leiden: E. J. Brill, 1954– .

— "Fu'ad Pasha." *Encyclopaedia of Islam*. 2d ed. Leiden: E. J. Brill, 1954– .

— "Midhat Pasha." *Encyclopaedia of Islam*. 2d ed. Leiden: E. J. Brill, 1954– .

— *Reform in the Ottoman Empire, 1856–1876*. Princeton: Princeton University Press, 1963.

Deal, William E. "Postmodern and New Historicist Perspectives in Recent Western Scholarship on Japanese Religion." In Eldon Jay Epp, ed., *Critical Review of Books in Religion 1993*, pp. 1–39. Atlanta: Scholars, 1994.

Devereux, Robert. *The First Ottoman Constitutional Period: A Study of the Midhat Constitution and Parliament*. Baltimore: Johns Hopkins University Press, 1963.

Draper, John William. *A History of the Intellectual Development of Europe*. 2 vols. 2d rev. ed. London: George Bell, 1875 [1863].

Eco, Umberto. *La Recherche de la langue parfaite*. Trans. Jean-Paul Manganaro. Paris: Seuil, 1994

Easterman, Daniel, *see* MacEoin, Denis

Eisenach, Eldon J. *Two Worlds of Liberalism: Religion and Politics in Hobbes, Locke, and Mill*. Chicago: University of Chicago Press, 1981.

Eley, Geoff. "Nations, Publics, and Political Cultures: Placing Habermas in the Nineteenth Century." In Craig Calhoun, ed., *Habermas and the Public Sphere*. Cambridge: MIT Press, 1992.

Encyclopaedia Iranica. Boston: Routledge and Kegan Paul; Costa Mesa, Ca.: Mazda, 1984– .

Encyclopaedia of Islam. 1st ed. Leiden: E. J. Brill, 1908–36. 2d ed. Leiden: E. J. Brill, 1954– .

Eyck, Erich. *Bismarck and the German Empire*. New York: Norton, 1964.

Fananapazir, Khazeh. "A Tablet of Mirza Husayn 'Ali Baha'u'llah to Jamal-i Burujirdi." *Baha'i Studies Bulletin* 5 (Jan. 1991): 4–12.

Farahani, Mirza Mohammad Hosayn. *A Shi'ite Pilgrimage to Mecca, 1885–1886*. Ed. and trans. Hafez Farmayan and Elton L. Daniel. Austin: University of Texas Press, 1990.

Farman-Farmayan, Hafez. "The Forces of Modernization in Nineteenth-Century Iran." In W. Polk and R. Chambers, eds., *The Beginnings of Modernization in the Middle East*, pp. 119–51. Chicago: University of Chicago Press, 1968.

Fasa'i, Hasan. *History of Persia under Qajar Rule* [*Farsnamih-'i Nasiri*]. Trans. H. Busse. New York, 1972.

Fawaz, Leila Tarazi. *An Occasion for War: Civil Conflict in Lebanon and Damascus in 1860*. Berkely and Los Angeles: University of California Press, 1994.

Ferjani, Mohamed-Chérif. *Islamisme, laicité, et droits de l'homme*. Paris: L'Harmattan, 1991.

Findley, Carter V. *Bureaucratic Reform in the Ottoman Empire: The Sublime Porte, 1789–1922.* Princeton: Princeton University Press, 1980.

Finke, Roger, and Rodney Stark. *The Churching of America, 1776–1990: Winners and Losers in Our Religious Economy.* New Brunswick, N.J.: Rutgers University Press, 1992.

Fischer, Michael M. J. *Iran: From Religious Dispute to Revolution.* Cambridge: Harvard University Press, 1980.

Fischer, Michael M. J., and Mehdi Abedi, eds. *Debating Muslims: Cultural Dialogues in Postmodernity and Tradition.* Madison: University of Wisconsin Press, 1990.

Foucault, Michel. *Politics, Philosophy, Culture: Interviews and Other Writings.* Ed. Lawrence D. Kritzman. London: Routledge, 1988.

Froughi, Farzin, and Lambden, Stephen, "A Tablet of Baha'u'llah Commenting on That Verse of the Most Holy Book (Kitab-i-Aqdas) About the Need for an International Language." *Baha'i Studies Bulletin* 4, 3–4 (April 1990), 28–49.

Gammer, Moshe. *Muslim Resistance to the Tsar.* London: Frank Cass, 1994.

Garrett, Clarke. *A Respectable Folly: Millenarians and the French Revolution in France and England.* Baltimore: Johns Hopkins University Press, 1975.

Gellner, Ernest. *Nations and Nationalism.* Ithaca: Cornell University Press, 1983.

Giddens, Anthony. *The Consequences of Modernity.* Stanford: Stanford University Press, 1990.

Gobineau, C. S. de, ed. *Correspondence entre le Comte de Gobineau et le Comte de Prokesch-Osten (1854–76).* Paris, 1933.

Goldziher, Ignaz. *Introduction to Islamic Theology and Law.* Trans. Andras and Ruth Hamori. Princeton: Princeton University Press, 1981.

Gould, Stephen J. *The Mismeasure of Man.* New York: Norton, 1981.

Green, Arnold H. *The Tunisian Ulama, 1873–1915.* Leiden: E. J. Brill, 1978.

Greenfield, Liah. *Nationalism: Five Roads to Modernity.* Cambridge: Harvard University Press, 1992.

Griffiths, Anthony J. F., et al. *An Introduction to Genetic Analysis.* New York: W. H. Freeman, 1993.

Gulpaygani, Mirza Abu'l-Fadl. *Letters and Essays, 1886–1913.* Trans. Juan R. I. Cole. Los Angeles: Kalimat, 1985.

— *Miracles and Metaphors.* Trans. Juan R. I. Cole. Los Angeles: Kalimat, 1982.

Gumperz, John J. *Discourse Strategies.* Cambridge: Cambridge University Press, 1982.

Habermas, Jürgen. *Communication and the Evolution of Society.* Trans. T. McCarthy. Boston: Beacon, 1979.

— *The Structural Transformation of the Public Sphere: An Inquiry Into a Category of Bourgeois Society.* Trans. Thomas Burger, with Frederick Laurence. Cambridge: MIT Press, 1993.

———. *The Philosophical Discourse of Modernity.* Cambridge: MIT Press, 1987.

Hairi, Abdul-Hadi. *Shi'ism and Constitutionalism in Iran.* Leiden: E. J. Brill, 1977.

Hamadani, Mirza Huseyn. *Tarikh-i Jadid: The New History of Mirza 'Ali Muhammad, the Bab.* Trans. E. G. Browne. Cambridge: Cambridge University Press, 1893; repr. Amsterdam: Philo Press, 1975.

Hanna, Sami A. "The Saint-Simonians and the Application of State Socialism in

Egypt." In S. A. Hanna, ed., *Medieval and Middle Eastern Studies in Honor of Aziz Suryal Atiya.* Leiden: E. J. Brill, 1972.

Hasrat, Bikram Jit. *Dara Shikuh, Life and Works.* 2d ed. New Delhi: Munshiram Manoharlal, 1982 [1943].

Hatch, Nathan O. *The Sacred Cause of Liberty: Republican Thought and the Millennium in Revolutionary New England.* New Haven: Yale University Press, 1977.

Hick, John. *An Interpretation of Religion.* New Haven: Yale University Press, 1989.

— *Problems of Religious Pluralism.* London: Macmillan, 1985.

Hill, Christopher. *Antichrist in Seventeenth-Century England.* London: Oxford University Press, 1971.

— *Puritanism and Revolution.* Penguin: Harmondsworth, 1986 [1958].

— *The World Turned Upside Down: Radical Ideas During the English Revolution.* London: Temple Smith, 1972.

Hinsley, F. H. *Power and the Pursuit of Peace.* Cambridge: Cambridge University Press, 1963.

Hirsch, Marianne, and Evelyn Fox Keller, eds. *Conflicts in Feminism.* London: Routledge, 1990.

Hobbes, Thomas. *Leviathan.* Amherst, N.Y.: Prometheus, 1988.

Hobsbawm, Eric. *The Age of Capital: 1848–1875.* New York: New American Library, 1979.

— *The Age of Empire, 1875–1914.* London: Weidenfeld and Nicholson, 1987.

— *The Age of Revolution.* London: Weidenfeld and Nicholson, 1962.

— *Nations and Nationalism Since 1780: Program, Myth, Reality.* Cambridge: Cambridge University Press, 1990.

Hollinger, Richard. "Ibrahim George Kheiralla and the Baha'i Faith in America." In Juan R. I. Cole and Moojan Momen, eds., *Studies in Babi and Baha'i History: From Iran East and West,* 2:95–133. Los Angeles: Kalimat, 1984.

Hollinger, Richard, ed., *Studies in the Babi and Baha'i Religions: Community Histories.* Vol. 6. Los Angeles: Kalimat, 1992.

Holt, P. M. *The Mahdist State in the Sudan.* Oxford: Clarendon, 1958.

Homerin, Th. Emil. *From Arab Poet to Muslim Saint: Ibn al-Farid, His Verse and His Shrine.* Columbia: University of South Carolina Press, 1994.

Hourani, Albert. *Arabic Thought in the Liberal Age.* Cambridge: Cambridge University Press, 1986.

Hroch, Miroslav. *Social Preconditions of National Revival in Europe.* Trans. Ben Fowkes. Cambridge: Cambridge University Press, 1985.

Ibn al-'Arabi, Muhyi'd-Din. *The Tarjuman al-Ashwaq: A Collection of Mystical Odes.* Ed. and trans. Reynold A. Nicholson. London: Royal Asiatic Society, 1911.

Iqbal, Afzal. *The Life and Work of Jalalu'd-Din Rumi.* Islamabad: Pakistan National Council of the Arts, 1991.

Isfahani, Haydar 'Ali. *Stories from the Delight of Hearts.* Ed. and trans. A. Q. Faizi. Los Angeles: Kalimat, 1980.

Issawi, Charles, ed. *The Economic History of Iran, 1800–1914.* Chicago: University of Chicago Press, 1971.

Jefferson, Thomas. *Public and Private Papers.* New York: Vintage, 1990.

Kandiyoti, Deniz. *Women, Islam, and the State*. Philadelphia: Temple University Press, 1991.

Kant, Immanuel. *Kant: Political Writings*. Ed. H. Reiss. Cambridge: Cambridge University Press, 1991.

Karimi-Hakkak, Ahmad. "Censorship." S.V. *Encyclopaedia Iranica*. Boston: Routledge and Kegan Paul; Costa Mesa, Ca.: Mazda, 1984– .

Karny, Azriel. "Mirza Husein Khan and his Attempts at Reform in Iran, 1872–73." Ph.D. diss., University of California, Los Angeles, 1973.

Katz, Jonathan. "Shaykh Ahmad's Dream: A Nineteenth-Century Eschatological Vision." *Studia Islamica* 88 (1994): 157–80.

Kayali, Hasan. "Elections and the Electoral Process in the Ottoman Empire, 1876–1919." *International Journal of Middle East Studies* 27 (1995): 265–86.

Kazemzadeh, Firuz. *Russia and Britain in Persia, 1864–1914*. New Haven: Yale University Press, 1968.

Kazemzadeh, Kazem, and Firuz Kazemzadeh. "Baha'u'llah's Prison Sentence: The Official Account." *World Order* 13 (Winter 1978–79): 11–13.

Keddie, Nikki R. *Iran and the Muslim World: Resistance and Revolution*. New York: New York University Press, 1995.

— "Religion and Irreligion in Early Iranian Nationalism." *Comparative Studies in Society and History* 4 (1962): 265–95.

— *Religion and Rebellion in Iran: The Tobacco Protest of 1891–1892*. London, 1966.

— *Roots of Revolution: An Interpretive History of Modern Iran*. With a section by Yann Richard. New Haven: Yale University Press, 1981.

— *Sayyid Jamalu'd-Din "al-Afghani": A Political Biography*. Berkeley and Los Angeles: University of California Press, 1972.

Keddie, Nikki R., ed. *Scholars, Saints, and Sufis*. Berkeley and Los Angeles: University of California Press, 1972.

Keppel, Gilles. *Muslim Extremism in Egypt*. Berkeley and Los Angeles: University of California Press, 1985.

Kerr, Malcolm H. *Islamic Reform: The Political and Legal Theories of Muhammad 'Abduh and Rashid Rida*. Berkeley and Los Angeles: University of California Press, 1966.

Khadduri, Majid. *War and Peace in the Law of Islam*. Baltimore: Johns Hopkins University Press, 1955.

Kia, Mehrdad. "Mirza Fath Ali Akhundzade and the Call for Modernization of the Islamic World." *Middle Eastern Studies* 31, 3 (July 1995): 422–48.

— "Pan-Islamism in Late Nineteenth-Century Iran." *Middle Eastern Studies*. 32, 1 (January 1996): 30–52.

Kiernan, Victor. *The Lords of Human Kind*. London: Weidenfeld and Nicholson, 1969.

Knowlson, James. *Universal Language Schemes in England and France, 1600–1800*. Toronto: University of Toronto Press, 1975.

Lach, Donald F. *Asia in the Making of Europe*. 3 vols. Chicago: University of Chicago Press, 1965–1993.

Lambden, Stephen. "At the Shore of the Black Sea: The Lawh-i Hawdaj/Samsun of

Mirza Husayn 'Ali Baha'u'llah." *Baha'i Studies Bulletin*, 3, 4 (December 1985): 84–97

— "An Early Poem of Mirza Husayn 'Ali Baha'u'llah: The Sprinkling of the Cloud of Unknowing (*Rashh-i 'Ama*)." *Baha'i Studies Bulletin*, 3, 2 (Sept. 1984): 4–114.

— "Some Notes on Baha'u'llah's Gradually Evolving Claims of the Adrianople/Edirne Period." *Baha'i Studies Bulletin* 5, 3–6, 1 (June, 1991).

— "A Tablet of Baha'u'llah to Georg David Hardegg: The "Lawh-i Hirtiq." *Baha'i Studies Bulletin* 2, 1 (June 1983): 32–62.

— "A Tablet of Mirza Husayn 'Ali Baha'u'llah of the Early Iraq Period: The Tablet of All Food." *Baha'i Studies Bulletin* 3, 1 (June 1984): 4–67.

Lambton, Ann K. S. "A Nineteenth-Century View of *Jihad.*" *Studia Islamica* 32 (1970): 179–92.

— *Qajar Iran.* Austin: University of Texas Press, 1987.

— *State and Government in Medieval Islam: An Introduction to the Study of Islamic Political Theory—The Jurists.* Oxford: Oxford University Press, 1981.

— "The Tobacco Regie: Prelude to Revolution." *Studia Islamica* 22 (1965):119–57, 23 (1965): 71–90.

— "The Tribal Resurgence and the Decline of the Bureaucracy in the Eighteenth Century." In Thomas Naff and Roger Owen, eds., *Studies in Eighteenth-Century Islamic History*, pp. 109–29. Carbondale: Southern Illinois University Press, 1977.

Lapidus, Ira M. "The Separation of State and Religion in the Development of Early Islamic Society." *International Journal of Middle East Studies* 6 (1975): 363–85.

Laquer, Thomas. *Making Sex: Body and Gender from the Greeks to Freud.* Cambridge: Harvard University Press, 1990.

Lauretis, Teresa de. "Upping the Anti (sic) in Feminist Theory." In Marianne Hirsch and Evelyn Fox Keller, eds., *Conflicts in Feminism*, pp. 255–70. London: Routledge, 1990.

Lawson, B. Todd. "The Crucifixion of Jesus in the Qur'an and Qur'anic Commentary: A Historical Survey." *Bulletin of Henry Martyn Institute of Islamic Studies* 10, 2 (April-June 1991): 34–62, 10, 3 (July-September 1991): 6–40.

— "Interpretation as Revelation: The Qur'an Commentary of Sayyid 'Ali Muhammad Shirazi, the Bab (1819–1850)." In Andrew Rippin, ed., *Approaches to the History of the Interpretation of the Qur'an*, pp. 223–56. Oxford: Oxford University Press, 1988.

— "The Qur'an Commentary of Sayyid 'Ali Muhammad, the Bab." 2 vols. Ph.D. dissertation, Institute of Islamic Studies, McGill University, 1987.

Lewis, Bernard. *The Emergence of Modern Turkey.* 2d ed. Oxford: Oxford University Press, 1968.

— "Madjlis al-Shura." *Encyclopaedia of Islam.* 2d ed. Leiden: E. J. Brill, 1954– .

Locke, John. *Political Writings of John Locke.* Ed. David Wootton. New York: Mentor, 1993.

Lorentz, John H. "Iran's Greatest Reformer of the Nineteenth Century: An Analysis of Amir Kabir's Reforms." *Iranian Studies* 4 (1971): 85–103.

— " 'Modernization and Political Change in Nineteenth-Century Iran: The Role of Amir Kabir." Ph.D. diss., Princeton University, 1974.

Louis-Lucas, Pierre. *Un plan de paix générale et de liberté de commerce au XVIIe siècle: le nouveau Cynée d'Eméric Crucé (1623)*. Paris: Recueil Sirey, 1919.

McDaniel, R. A. *The Shuster Mission and the Persian Constitutional Revolution*. Minneapolis: Bibliotheca Islamica, 1974.

MacEoin, Denis. "Afnan, Hatcher, and an Old Bone." *Religion* 16 (1986): 195.

— "The Babi Concept of Holy War." *Religion* 12 (1982): 93–129.

— "Baha'i Fundamentalism in the Academic Study of the Babi Movement." *Religion* 16 (1986): 57–84.

— "The Crisis in Babi and Baha'i Studies: Part of a Wider Crisis in Academic Freedom?" *British Society for Middle Eastern Studies* 17, 1 (1990): 55–61.

— "Divisions and Authority Claims in Babism (1850–1866)." *Studia Iranica* 18, 1 (1989): 93–129.

— "Hierarchy, Authority and Eschatology in Early Babi Thought." In Peter Smith, ed., *Studies in Babi and Baha'i History: In Iran*, 3:95–155. Los Angeles: Kalimat, 1986.

— [Writing as Daniel Easterman.] *New Jerusalems: Reflections on Islam, Fundamentalism, and the Rushdie Affair*. London: Grafton, 1992.

— "Nineteenth-Century Babi Talismans." *Studia Iranica* 14, 1 (1985): 77–98.

— "Problems of Scholarship in a Baha'i Context." *Baha'i Studies Bulletin* 1, 3 (December 1982): 44–68.

— *Rituals in Babism and Baha'ism*. London and Cambridge: British Academic/I. B. Tauris and Centre for Middle Eastern Studies, University of Cambridge, 1994.

— *The Sources for Early Babi Doctrine and History: A Survey*. Leiden: E. J. Brill, 1992.

McLoughlin, William G. *Soul Liberty: The Baptists' Struggle in New England, 1630–1833*. Hanover, N.H.: University Press of New England, 1991.

McMullen, Mike. "The Atlanta Baha'i Community and Race Unity: 1909–50." *World Order* 26 (Summer 1995): 27–43.

Mahdavi, Shirin. "Women and Ideas in Qajar Iran." *Asian and African Studies* 19 (1985): 187–97.

Malti-Douglas, Fedwa. *Woman's Body, Woman's World: Gender and Discourse in Arabo-Islamic Writing*. Princeton: Princeton University Press, 1991.

Maneck, Susan Stiles. "The Conversion of Religious Minorities to the Baha'i Faith in Iran: Some Preliminary Considerations." *Journal of Baha'i Studies* 3, 3 (1991): 39–54.

— "Early Zoroastrian Conversions to the Baha'i Faith in Yazd, Iran." In Juan R. I. Cole and Moojan Momen, eds., *Studies in Babi and Baha'i History: From Iran East and West*, 2:70–74. Los Angeles: Kalimat, 1984.

— "Tahirih: A Religious Paradigm of Womanhood." *Journal of Baha'i Studies* 2, 2 (1989): 35–48.

— "Women and the Baha'i Faith." In Arvind Sharma, ed., *Religion and Women*, pp. 211–17. Albany: State University of New York Press, 1994.

Manuel, Frank. *The New World of Saint-Simon*. Cambridge: Harvard University Press, 1962.

Mardin, Şerif. *The Genesis of Young Ottoman Thought*. Princeton: Princeton University Press, 1962.

Martin, Vanessa. *Islam and Modernism: The Iranian Revolution of 1906.* London: Tauris, 1989.

Marty, Martin E. et al., eds. *Fundamentalisms Observed,* 4 vols. Chicago: University of Chicago Press, 1991–94.

Metcalf, Barbara Daly. *Islamic Revival in British India.* Princeton: Princeton University Press, 1982.

Metcalf, Barbara Daly, ed. and trans. *Perfecting Women: Maulana Ashraf ʿAli Thanawi's Bihishti Zewar.* Berkeley and Los Angeles: University of California Press, 1990.

Milani, Farzaneh. *Veils and Words: The Emerging Voices of Iranian Women Writers.* Syracuse: Syracuse University Press, 1992.

Mitchell, Joshua. *Not by Reason Alone: Religion, History, and Identity in Early Modern Political Thought.* Chicago: University of Chicago Press, 1993.

Mitchell, Richard P. *The Society of the Muslim Brothers.* Oxford: Oxford University Press, 1969.

Moayyad, Heshmet, ed. *The Baha'i Faith and Islam.* Ottawa: Baha'i Studies, 1990.

Moghadam, Valentine, ed. *Identity Politics and Women: Cultural Reassertions and Feminisms in International Perspective.* Boulder: Westview, 1994.

Momen, Moojan. "The Baha'i Community of Ashkhabad: Its Social Basis and Importance in Baha'i History." In Shirin Akiner, ed., *Cultural Change and Continuity in Central Asia,* pp. 278–305. London: Kegan Paul International, 1991.

— "The Baha'i Influence on the Reform Movements of the Islamic World in the 1860s and 1870s." *Baha'i Studies Bulletin* 3, 2 (1983): 47–65.

— "Early Relations Between Christian Misionaries and the Babi and Baha'i Communities." In Moojan Momen, ed., *Studies in Babi and Baha'i History.* Vol. 1. Los Angeles: Kalimat, 1982.

— *Hinduism and the Baha'i Faith.* Oxford: George Ronald, 1990.

— *An Introduction to Shi'i Islam.* New Haven: Yale University Press, 1985.

— "Iran." *Encyclopaedia of the Baha'i Faith.* Wilmette, Ill.: Baha'i Publishing Trust, forthcoming.

— "Relativism: A Basis for Baha'i Metaphysics" In Moojan Momen, ed., *Studies in the Babi and Baha'i Religions: Studies in Honor of the Late Hasan Balyuzi.* Vol. 5. Los Angeles: Kalimat, 1988.

Momen, Moojan, ed. *The Babi and Baha'i Religions, 1844–1944: Some Contemporary Western Accounts.* Oxford: George Ronald, 1981.

—— *Studies in Babi and Baha'i History.* Vol. 1. Los Angeles: Kalimat, 1982.

Morrison, Gayle. *To Move the World: Louis G. Gregory and the Advancement of Racial Unity in America.* Wilmette, Ill.: Baha'i Publishing Trust, 1982.

Morsy, Megali, ed. *Les Saint-Simoniens et l'orient: vers la modernité.* Paris: Edisud, 1989.

Moses, Claire Goldberg, and Leslie Wahl Rabine. *Feminism, Socialism, and French Romanticism.* Bloomington: Indiana University Press, 1993.

Mosse, W. E. *The Rise and Fall of the Crimean System, 1855–71.* London: Macmillan, 1963.

Mukherjee, Rudrangshu. *Awadh in Revolt, 1857–1858: A Study of Popular Resistance.* Delhi: Oxford University Press, 1984.

Munson, Henry. *Islamic Revolution in the Middle East.* New Haven: Yale University Press, 1988.

Murata, Sachiko. *The Tao of Islam.* Albany: State University of New York Press, 1992.

Murray, John Courtney. *Religious Liberty: Catholic Struggles with Pluralism.* Ed. J. Leon Hooper. Louisville, Ky.: Westminster/John Knox, 1993.

Naff, Thomas, and Roger Owen, eds. *Studies in Eighteenth-Century Islamic History.* Carbondale: Southern Illinois University Press, 1977.

Najmabadi, Afsaneh. "A Different Voice: Taj os-Saltaneh's Autobiography." In Afsaneh Najmabadi, ed., *Women Autobiographies in Contemporary Iran.* Cambridge: Harvard University Press, 1991.

———. "Crafting an Educated Housewife in Iran." In Lila Abu-Lughod, ed., "Remaking Women: Feminism and Modernity in the Middle East." Forthcoming.

— " 'Is Our Name Remembered?' Writing the History of Iranian Constitutionalism as if Women and Gender Mattered." *Iranian Studies* 29, 1–2 (Winter/Spring 1996): 85–109.

— "Zanha-yi Millat: Women or Wives of the Nation?" *Iranian Studies* 26, 1–2 (Winter/Spring 1993): 51–71.

Nandy, Ashis. *The Intimate Enemy: Loss and Recovery of Self Under Colonialism.* Delhi: Oxford University Press, 1983.

Nashat, Guity. *The Beginnings of Reform in Modern Iran.* Champaign-Urbana: University of Illinois Press, 1981.

Nicholson, R. A. *Studies in Islamic Mysticism.* Cambridge at the University Press, 1921; repr. Richmond, Surrey: Curzon, 1994.

Nizam-Mafi, Mansoureh Ettehadieh. "The Emergence of Tehran as the Cultural Center of Iran." In C. Adle and B. Hourcade, eds., *Tehéran: Capitale Bicentenaire.* Paris and Tehran: Institut Francais de Recherche en Iran, 1992.

Okazakis, S. "The Great Persian Famine of 1870–71." *Bulletin of the School of Oriental and African Studies* 49 (1986): 183–92.

Parsinejad, Iraj. *Mirza Fath 'Ali Khundzadeh: A Literary Critic.* Piedmont, Ca.: Jahan Book, 1990.

Pearson, O. "Islamic Reform and Revival in Nineteenth Century India: The Tariqah-i Muhammadiyyah." Ph.D. diss., Duke University, 1979.

Penn, William. *An Essay Toward the Present and Future Peace of Europe.* New York: Carnegie Endowment for International Peace, 1943.

Perkins, Merle L. *The Moral and Political Philosophy of the Abbé de Saint-Pierre.* Geneva: Librairie E. Droz, 1959.

Pipes, Daniel. *In the Path of God: Islam and Political Power.* New York: Basic, 1983.

Pistor-Hatam, Anja. *Iran und die Reformbewegung im Osmanischen Reich: Persische Staatsmänner, Reisende und Oppositionelle unter dem Einfluss der Tanzimat.* Berlin: Klaus Schwarz Verlag, 1992.

Porter, Bernard. *The Lion's Share: A Short History of British Imperialism, 1850–1983.* 2d ed. London: Longman, 1984.

Powell, Avril A. *Muslims and Missionaries in Pre-Mutiny India.* London: Curzon, 1993.

Qureshi, Ishtiaq Husain. *Ulama in Politics.* Karachi: Ma'aref, 1972.

Rabbani, Shoghi Effendi, *The Promised Day Is Come*. Preface by Firuz Kazemzadeh. Wilmette, Ill.: Baha'i Publishing Trust, 1967 [1941].

— *God Passes By*. Wilmette, Ill.: Baha'i Publishing Trust, 1970.

— *World Order of Baha'u'llah*. Wilmette, Ill.: Baha'i Publishing Trust, 1969.

Rawlinson, Henry Creswicke. "Notes on a March from Zohab . . . Through the province of Kurdistan to Kermanshah, in the Year 1836." *Journal of the Royal Geographical Society* 9 (1839): 26–116.

Razavi, Shahriar. "The Tablet of the Seven Questions (*Lawh-i Haft Pursish*) of Baha'u'llah: An Introduction and Provisional Translation." With appendix by Stephen Lambden. *Baha'i Studies Bulletin* 7, 3–4 (June 1993): 47–68.

Regnier, Philippe. "Le mythe oriental des saint-simoniens." In Megali Morsy, ed., *Les Saint-Simoniens et l'orient: vers la modernité*. Paris: Edisud, 1989.

Remey, Charles Mason. *Observations of a Baha'i Traveller, 1908*. Washington, D.C.: J. D. Milans, 1914.

Rizvi, Saiyid Athar 'Abbas. *Religious and Intellectual History of the Muslims in Akbar's Reign*. Delhi: Munshiram Manoharlal, 1975.

Rojas, Billy. "The Saint-Simonians." *World Order* 3, 4 *(1968): 29–37.*

Roosevelt, Grace. *Reading Rousseau in the Nuclear Age*. Philadelphia: Temple University Press, 1990.

Rosen, Baron Victor, ed. *Collections Scientifiques de l'Institut des Langues Orientales du Ministère des Affaires Étrangères. Manuscrits Arabes,* 1:179–212. St. Petersburg, 1877.

— *Collections Scientifiques de l'Institut des Langues Orientales du Ministère des Affaires Étrangères. Manuscrits Persans,* 3:1–51. St. Petersburg, 1886.

— *Collections Scientifiques de l'Institut des Langues Orientales du Ministère des Affaires Étrangères. Manuscrits Arabes,* 6:141–244. St. Petersburg, 1891.

Rousseau, Jean-Jacques. *The Confessions*. Trans. J. M. Cohen. Harmondsworth: Penguin, 1953.

Royce, William Ronald. "Mir Ma'sum Ali Shah and the Ni'mat Allahi Revival 1776–77 to 1796–97." Ph.D. diss., Princeton University, 1979.

— "The Shirazi Provincial Elite: Status Maintenance and Change." In M. Bonine and N. Keddie, eds., *Modern Iran: The Dialectics of Continuity and Change*. Albany: State University of New York Press, 1981.

Rumi, Jalalu'd-Din. *Selected Poems from the Divani Shamsi Tabriz*. Ed. and trans. R. A. Nicholson. Cambridge: Cambridge University Press, 1952.

Russell, Jane J. "Spiritual Virtigo at the Edge of Gender Equality." *World Order* 27 (Fall 1995): 41–56.

Said, Edward. *Culture and Imperialism*. New York: Knopf, 1993.

— *Orientalism*. New York: Vintage, 1979.

Saint-Pierre, Charles Iréné Castel de. *Projet pour rendre la paix perpétuelle en Europe*. Paris: Garnier, 1981.

Saint-Simon, Claude-Henri de. *The Political Thought of Saint-Simon*. Ed. Ghita Ionescu. Oxford: Oxford University Press, 1976.

Salibi, Kamal. *House of Many Mansions*. Berkeley and Los Angeles: University of California Press, 1988.

Salmani, Muhammad-'Ali. *My Memories of Baha'u'llah.* Trans. Marzieh Gail. Los Angeles: Kalimat, 1982.

Sanjabi, Maryam. "Rereading the Enlightenment: Akhundzada and his Voltaire." *Iranian Studies* 28, 1–2 (Winter/Spring 1995): 39–60.

Sayyid Marsot, Afaf Lutfi al-. *Women and Men in Eighteenth- and Nineteenth-Century Egypt.* Austin: University of Texas Press, 1995.

Sayyid Marsot, Afaf Lutfi al-, ed. *Society and the Sexes in Medieval Islam.* Malibu: Undena, 1979.

Schölch, Alexander. *Egypt for the Egyptians! The Socio-Political Crisis in Egypt, 1878–1882.* London: Ithaca, 1981.

—— "The 'Men on the Spot' and the English Occupation of Egypt in 1882." *Historical Journal* 19, 2 (1976): 773–85.

Scott, Joan Wallach. *Gender and the Politics of History.* New York: Columbia University Press, 1988.

Shannon, Richard. *The Crises of Imperialism, 1865–1914.* London: Hart-Davis, MacGibbon, 1974.

Shaw, Stanford J., and Ezel Kural Shaw, *History of the Ottoman Empire and Modern Turkey.* Volume 2: *Reform, Revolution, and Republic.* Cambridge: Cambridge University Press, 1985.

Shea, David, and Anthony Troyer, trans. *Oriental Literature; The Dabistan, or School of Manners: The Religious Beliefs, Observances, Philosophic Opinions, and Social Customs of the Nations of the East.* Washington and London: M. Walter Dunne, 1901.

Sherry, Patrick. *Religion, Truth and Language-Games.* New York: Harper and Row, 1977.

Shoghi Effendi, *see* Rabbani, Shoghi Effendi

Smith, Anthony. *The Ethnic Origins of Nations.* London: Blackwell, 1987.

Smith, Helmut Walser. *German Nationalism and Religious Conflict: Culture, Ideology, Politics, 1870–1914.* Princeton: Princeton University Press, 1995.

Smith, Peter. *The Babi and Baha'i Religions: From Messianic Shi'ism to a World Religion.* Cambridge: Cambridge University Press, 1987.

—— "Millenarianism in the Babi and Baha'i Religions." In Roy Wallis, ed., *Millennialism and Charisma,* pp. 231–83. Belfast: Queens University Press, 1982.

—— "A Note on Babi and Baha'i Numbers in Iran." *Iranian Studies* 15 (1984): 295–301.

Smith, Peter, and Moojan Momen. "The Baha'i Faith, 1957–1988: A Survey of Contemporary Developments." *Religion* 19 (1989): 63–91.

Smith, Peter, ed. *Studies in Babi and Baha'i History: In Iran.* Vol. 3. Los Angeles: Kalimat, 1986.

Smith, W. H. C. *Napoleon III.* London: Wayland, 1972.

Stark, Rodney, and Laurence R. Iannaccone. "A Supply-Side Reinterpretation of the 'Secularization' of Europe." *Journal for the Scientific Study of Religion* 33 (September 1994): 230–52.

Stauffer, Robert B., ed. "Petition of March 1867 to the U.S. Government, by Baha'is of Baghdad: Text and Consular Translation." *Translations of Shaykhi, Babi, and Baha'i Texts,* no. 3 (July 1997). Available on the World Wide Web at http://h-net2.msu.edu/~bahai/trans.htm.

Stedman Jones, Gareth. *Languages of Class: Studies in English Working Class History, 1832–1982.* Cambridge: Cambridge University Press, 1983.

Steingass, F. *A Comprehensive Persian-English Dictionary.* Beirut, 1975 [1892].

Stiles, Susan. *see* Maneck, Susan Stiles

Stockman, Robert. *The Baha'i Faith in America. Vol. 1: Origins, 1892–1900.* Wilmette, Ill.: Baha'i Publishing Trust, 1985.

—— *The Baha'i Faith in America.* Vol. 2. Oxford: George Ronald, 1995.

—— "The Baha'i Faith in America: One Hundred Years," *World Order* 25 (Spring 1994): 9–23.

Streusand, Douglas E. *The Formation of the Mughal Empire.* Delhi: Oxford University Press, 1989.

Studies in Babi and Baha'i History. Vol. 1. Ed. Moojan Momen. Los Angeles: Kalimat, 1982.

Studies in Babi and Baha'i History: From Iran East and West. Vol. 2. Ed. Juan R. I. Cole. Los Angeles: Kalimat, 1984.

Studies in Babi and Baha'i History: In Iran. Vol. 3. Ed. Peter Smith. Los Angeles: Kalimat, 1986.

Studies in Babi and Baha'i History: Music, Devotions, and Mashriqu'l-Adhkar. Vol. 4. R. Jackson Armstrong-Ingram. Los Angeles: Kalimat, 1987.

Studies in Babi and Baha'i Religions: Studies in Honor of the Late Hasan M. Balyuzi. Vol. 5. Ed. Moojan Momen. Los Angeles: Kalimat, 1988.

Studies in Babi and Baha'i Religions: Community Histories. Vol. 6. Ed. Richard Hollinger. Los Angeles: Kalimat, 1992.

Studies in Babi and Baha'i Religions: Symbol and Secret—Qur'an Commentary in Baha'u'llah Kitab-i-Iqan. Vol. 7. Christopher Buck. Los Angeles: Kalimat, 1995.

Studies in Babi and Baha'i Religions: New Perspectives on a Baha'i Theology. Vol. 8. Ed. Jack McLean. Los Angeles: Kalimat, 1997.

Suny, Ron. *The Revenge of the Past: Nationalism, Revolution, and the Collapse of the Soviet Union.* Stanford: Stanford University Press, 1993.

Taherzadeh, Habib. *The Revelation of Baha'u'llah.* 4 vols. Oxford: George Ronald, 1974–87.

Taj al-Saltana. *Crowning Anguish: Memoirs of a Persian Princess from the Harem to Modernity.* Ed. Abbas Amanat, trans. Anna Vanzan and Amin Neshati. Washington, D.C.: Mage, 1993.

Tavakoli-Targhi, Mohamad. "Refashioning Iran: Language and Culture During the Constitutional Revolution," *Iranian Studies* 23 (1990): 77–101.

—— "Women of the West Imagined: The *Farangi* Other and the Emergence of the Woman Question in Iran." In Valentine Moghadam, ed., *Identity Politics and Women: Cultural Reassertions and Feminisms in International Perspective*, pp. 98–120. Boulder: Westview, 1994.

Thompson, Edward P. *The Making of the English Working Class.* New York: Vintage, 1966.

Thompson, Juliet. *The Diary of Juliet Thompson.* Los Angeles: Kalimat, 1983.

Tilly, Charles. *Coercion, Capital, and European States, AD 990–1992.* Oxford: Blackwell, 1992.

Toledano, Ehud. *The Ottoman Slave Trade and Its Suppression*. Princeton: Princeton University Press, 1982.

Touraine, Alain. *Critique of Modernity*. Trans. David Macey. Oxford, Blackwell, 1995.

Towfigh, Nicola. *Schopfung und Offenbarung aus der Sicht der Baha'i-Religion*. Hildesheim: G. Olms, 1989.

Tucker, Judith. *Women in Nineteenth-Century Egypt*. Cambridge: Cambridge University Press, 1984.

Turner, Bryan S. *Orientalism, Postmodernism, and Globalism*. London: Routledge, 1994.

Turner, Bryan S., ed. *Theories of Modernity and Postmodernity*. London: Sage, 1990.

Vaziri, Mostafa. *Iran as an Imagined Nation: The Construction of National Identity*. New York: Paragon House, 1993.

Voll, John O. *Islam: Continuity and Change in the Modern World*. Boulder: Westview, 1982.

Wagner, Peter. *The Sociology of Modernity: Liberty and Discipline*. London: Routledge, 1994.

Walbridge, John. *Sacred Acts, Sacred Space, Sacred Time*. Oxford: George Ronald, 1996.

— *The Science of Mystic Lights*. Cambridge: Center for Middle Eastern Studies/Harvard University Press, 1992.

Wallis, Roy, ed. *Millennialism and Charisma*. Belfast: Queen's University Press, 1982.

Watt, W. Montgomery. *Islamic Fundamentalism and Modernity*. London: Routledge, 1988.

Weber, Max. *Economy and Society*. Ed. G. Roth and C. Wittich. 2 vols. Berkeley: University of California Press, 1978.

White, Stephen K. *The Recent Work of Jürgen Habermas: Reason, Justice, and Modernity*. Cambridge: Cambridge University Press, 1994.

Wittgenstein, Ludwig. *Culture and Value*. Trans. Peter Winch. Chicago: University of Chicago Press, 1984.

— *Philosophical Investigations*. Trans. G. E. M. Anscombe. New York: Macmillan, 1968.

Yeganeh, Nahid and Nikki R. Keddie. "Sexuality and Shi'i Social Protest in Iran," in Juan R. I. Cole and Nikki R. Keddie, eds., *Shi'ism and Social Protest*, pp. 108–36. New Haven: Yale University Press, 1986.

Zarandi, Muhammad. *The Dawn-Breakers: Nabil's Narrative of the Early Days of the Baha'i Revelation*. Ed. and trans. Shoghi Effendi Rabbani. Wilmette, Ill.: Baha'i Publishing Trust, 1970 [1932].

Zilfi, Madeleine. *The Politics of Piety*. Minneapolis: Bibliotheca Islamica, 1988.

Zolondek, Leon. "The French Revolution in Arabic Literature of the Nineteenth Century." *Muslim World* 57 (1967): 202–11.

Zubaida, Sami. "Is There a Muslim Society? Ernest Gellner's Sociology of Islam." *Economy and Society* 24, 2 (May 1995): 151–88.

— *Islam: The People and the State*. London: Routledge, 1989.

Index

'Abduh, Muhammad, 13–14, 107, 133, 171, 181

Abdülaziz, Sultan, 30, 32, 54, 55, 56, 57, 58, 60, 64–65, 70–71, 72, 74, 76, 89

'Abdu'l-Baha 'Abbas Nuri: Achaemenids' religious policy favored by, over that of Safavids, 39; artificial universal language favored by, 159; Baha'i institutions' right to curb expression of individual belief and conscience denied by, 42–43; British strength contrasted with Iranian weakness by, 40–41; class stratification decried by, 84–85; correspondence of, with Sayyid Jamalu'd-Din al-Afghani, 74, 209; democracy within religious organizations advocated by, 43; early American Baha'i communities instructed to hold elections according to U.S. norms by, 95; educational reform called for by, 85; equality for members of all religions advocated by, 36; free exercise of individual's rights advocated by, 85; freedom of conscience and speech advocated by, 36–42, 68; freedom of conscience linked to scientific progress by, 42; influence of Islamic reformist thought about women on, 181; liberty advocated by, 68, 83–84; Midhat Pasha met in Beirut by, 70; monogamy favored by, 171–72; Namık Kemal, relations of with, 69; parliamentary democracy advocated by, 83–84; peace thought of, 130; persecution of Babis decried by, 36; politics, intervention in, of, 205–6; reformist trends in Iran of mid-1870s responded to by, 81–91; relations of Nuri Bey and Hakki Effendi to, 69; science and technology approved by, if used ethically, 46; *Secret of Divine Civilization* authored by, 81–91; security of person, property, dignity, and good name for individuals advocated by, 85; sedition decried by, 38; visited by Shaykhu'r-Ra'is, 103; warfare condemned by, 145; women's position according to, 182–85, 193–94

Abdülhamid II, 71, 75–76, 89, 90, 103, 105

Mosul, 93

Mughals, 22, 40

Muhammad 'Ali Pasha (Egypt), 130, 148

Muhammad 'Ali Shah, 103, 205–6

Muhammad al-Mahdi, 21

Muhammad Shah, 27, 98

Muhammad, 21, 146, 176

Muharram Bey, 179

Muhbir, 61

Multiculturalism, 7

Münif Pasha, Mehmet, 124–25, 157

Murad Pasha, 69, 71

Mushiru'd-Dawlih, Mirza Husayn Khan Sipahsalar, 81, 86, 90, 101, 210

Mustafa Fazil Pasha, 61

Mustasharu'd-Dawlih, Mirza Yusuf Khan, 86–87, 89, 90

Mu'taminu's-Saltanih, Muhammad Rida, 97

Mutiny, Indian, *see* Great Rebellion

Nabil-i A'zam, *see* Zarandi, Muhammad

Nadir Shah, 23, 114

Najafi, Aqa Shaykh Muhammad Taqi, 99

Najmabadi, Afsaneh, 164, 181, 222

Napoleon Bonaparte, 6, 52

Napoleon III, 60, 63–64, 76, 124, 127, 131, 155

Nasiru'd-Din Shah, 28, 32–34, 46, 72, 74, 75, 81, 87, 89–90, 99, 100, 101, 104, 105, 179

National League, 101–2

Nationalism, 6, 7, 8, 11, 12, 85, 139–61, 193

Nayriz, 27

Necip Pasha, 28, 116

Nedim Pasha, Mahmud, 70

Neocolonialism, 9

Neoplatonism, 45, 82, 85

Ni'matu'llahis, 30, 202

Nicholas II, Tsar, 131

Nimr, Maryam, 174

Nizamu'l-Mulk, 32, 33

Nur, 28

Nuri Bey, 69

Nuri, 'Abbas Effendi " 'Abdu'l-Baha," *see* 'Abdu'l-Baha

Nuri, Aqa Khan I'timadu'd-Dawlih, 46

Nuri, Mirza 'Abbas "Buzurg," 27, 175

Nuri, Mirza Husayn 'Ali "Baha'u'llah": absolute monarchy's demise predicted by, 60–61; affairs of Baha'i community (*millat*) given into the charge of the house of justice by, 95–97; agricultural development urged on Iran by, 100–1; American republics praised by, 65; Arabic favored by, as world language, 159; assassination attempt on, at orders of Mirza Yahya, 29; asserts he is return of Christ, 63; Babi religion adopted by, 27; Badasht conference of Babis partially financed by, 27; Baha'i faith founded by, 27; Baha'i houses of justice or consultative assemblies created by, 91–97; *Book of Certitude*, authored by, 170; brother of, upbraided by Mushiru'd-Dawlih for denying their relationship, 81; civil state's legitimacy accepted by, 33–36, 54–55; death sentence on, passed by Muhammad Shah, 27; democratic revolution in Iran predicted by, 65; destructiveness of modern warfare decried by, 135; equality of the subjects under the monarch advocated by, 33–34, 47; exiled to Akka, 29, 56–57; exiled to Baghdad, 28; exiled to Edirne, 28–29; holy war (jihad) abolished by, 115–17; houses of justice commanded to function according to the norms of parliamentary democracy by, 91–97; imprisoned in Siyah-Chal dungeon, 28; Iran condemned by, for neglecting to adopt parliamentary democracy, 72; Kaiser Wilhelm I condemned by, 64; liberty as moral license condemned by, 66; liberty bestowed on followers by,

Rüşdü Pasha, Mehmed Mütercim, 70
Russia, 10, 24, 52, 60, 65, 80, 81, 95,
126–27
Russo-Ottoman War of 1877–1878,
75–76

Sadik Effendi, Sariyerli Hoca, 58–59,
68
Safavids, 18, 22, 23, 25, 39, 114, 121,
140
Saiedi, Nader, 211
Saint-Pierre, Charles de, 120–22, 127
Saint-Simon, Claude Henri de Rouvroy,
Comte de, 77, 122–23
Saint-Simonianism, 86, 122–24,
130–31, 136–37
Saint-Simonians, 84, 89, 122–24, 126,
130, 131
Salman, Shaykh, 60
Samarra', 99, 102
Sandel, Michael J., 191
Santallier, Havre Ferdinand, 128
Sasanians, 32, 33
Saudi Arabia, 8, 10
Science, 42, 44, 45, 46
Secret of Divine Civilization, 45, 81–91,
130, 145, 211
Secularization, 2, 10, 44–47
Sedan, 64
Şemsi Bey, 30
Separation of powers, 84
Separation of Religion and State, 21,
34–35, 38, 44, 54–55, 60
Serbia, 71, 75
Shah-Bahram, 51
Shamil, 13
Shams-i Jahan Fitnih Qajar, 169–70,
186
Shaykh Tabarsi, 27, 52
Shaykhism, 23, 39, 74, 82, 157
Shaykhu'r-Ra'is, Abu'l-Hasan Mirza
Qajar, 102–3, 106, 107
Shemiran, 28
Shi'ites: buffeted by change in the nine-
teenth century, 25; clergy among,

support hierarchical view of society,
88; disestablished by Afghans in the
eighteenth century, 23; doubted
legitimacy of civil government in
absence of Imam, 32, 34; holy war
seen as illegitimate in absence of
Imam by, 111–12; imams followed
by, 21; imposed Shi'ism on Iran, 22,
114; in India, 23, 25; kingship recognized by, 25; obedience (taqlid) of
laity to clergy in, 92; persecuted by
Ottomans, 112; privileged with
regard to high office in Khomeinist
Iran, 144; Qajar state supports, 23,
39; reposed all authority in infallible
Imam, 35
Shidyaq, Ahmad Faris ash-, 71, 74
Shiraz, 26, 67, 93, 94, 98, 170–71
Shirazi, Mirza Hasan, 99
Shirazi, Mirza Salih, 55
Shirazi, Sayyid 'Ali Muhammad "Bab:"
arrested in Shiraz, 1846, 26; declares
self "Bab" in 1844, 26; did not call
for holy war or jihad, 112; escapes to
Isfahan in 1846, 26; executed by the
Iranian government in 1850, 27;
execution of, condemned by
Baha'u'llah, 98; imprisoned in 1847,
26; predicts successor, 26; Shi'ite
clergy try him in Tabriz in 1848,
26–27; women and men not treated
equally in laws of, 171
Shirazi, Haji Sayyid Muhammad,
170–71
Siyah-Chal, 28
Siyasat, 95–97
Slavery, 63, 208
Smith, Anthony, 142
Socialism, 75, 84, 196
Spain, 45
Spiritual Board of Counsel
(Ashkhabad), 95
"Splendors," (Ishraqat), 35, 95, 158
St. Jean d'Acre, see Akka
State Consultation Council, 56